Multicultural Spanish Dictionary

Multicultural Spanish Dictionary

How Everyday Spanish Differs from Country to Country

Second Revised Edition

Morry Sofer
General Editor

Agustín Martínez
Spanish Editor

Schreiber Publishing
Rockville, Maryland

Multicultural Spanish Dictionary
Edited by Agustín Martínez

Published by:

Schreiber Publishing
Post Office Box 858
Savage, MD 20763 USA
www.schreiberlanguage.com

Library of Congress Cataloging-in-Publication Data

Multicultural Spanish dictionary : how everyday Spanish differs from country to country / Morry Sofer, general editor ; Agustín Martínez, Spanish editor. -- 2nd rev. ed.
   p. cm.
  ISBN 978-0-88400-317-5 (pbk.)

  1. Spanish language--Dictionaries--English. 2. English language--Dictionaries--Spanish.
3. Spanish language—Provincialisms—Latin America—Dictionaries. I. Sofer, Morry. II. Martínez, Agustín, 1967- Multicultural Spanish dictionary.

PC4640.M26 2006
463'.21—dc22

2006013957

Printed in the United States of America

TABLE OF CONTENTS

ACKNOWLEDGEMENTS

The publisher wishes to acknowledge the diligent work of the editors and contributors of this ground-breaking volume. The idea for this kind of innovative Spanish dictionary was born during annual conferences of the American Translators Association, to which most of the contributors belong. It grew out of the practical experience of Spanish translators who have been confronting the daily realities of having to find the right Spanish word for such common things as a flat tire or a bow tie. When called upon to participate in this effort, they all came forward and plunged into this exploratory task with great enthusiasm. Their contributions are greatly appreciated. Their names appear on the next page.

The same holds true with regard to this Second Revised Edition. My coworker, Diego Gutiérrez, volunteered to trim the entries from his native Colombia. Also, noting the absence of Paraguay, Lic. Oscar Manuel Pavía Benítez, a distinguished Paraguayan jurist and linguist, volunteered terms from his country, which Yamandú Sánchez, another Paraguayan, completed. The one country remaining was Nicaragua, which Lic. Margarita Cruz, a Nicaraguan linguist, graciously added to the mix. Finally, Alison Smith lent her editing and proofing skills in reviewing the final version. My sincerest thanks to all of them.

Mordecai Schreiber, Publisher

LIST OF CONTRIBUTORS

Ana María Berger, *Guatemala*

Teresa María Campero, *Bolivia*

Nefertiti Casado-Hagan,
Dominican Republic

Milagros Cobos, *Spain*

Lic. Margarita Cruz, *Nicaragua*

Enid González, *Puerto Rico*

Diego Gutiérrez, *Colombia*

Andrés Harnecker, *Costa Rica*

Ana Kalnay, *Argentina*

Ana Victoria Krizán, *Ecuador*

Agustín Martínez, *Cuba*

Anamaris Martínez, *Panama*

Arne Myne, *Costa Rica*

Lidia Nazak, *Uruguay*

Ruth Olson, *Venezuela*

Katia Panhans, *Mexico*

Lic. Oscar Manuel Pavía Benítez, *Paraguay*

Guadalupe Reynolds, *Peru*

Sandra M. Rivera de Aquino, *Puerto Rico*

Teresa Román, *Chile*

Yamandú Sánchez, *Paraguay*

Carolina Valencia, *Colombia*

Introduction
to the Second Edition

When this book first appeared in 1999, it enjoyed instant success. It went into several printings and elicited many comments from users near and far. It was quite clear that there was a great need for such a specialized reference. This has been particularly true in the United States, where the Spanish-speaking population has grown rapidly in the past thirty years, becoming the largest ethnic and linguistic minority. Millions of Hispanics interact daily throughout the U.S. with people who share their native language yet not all of their native words. It soon became clear that a new revised edition was needed, and after several years of research the Second Revised Edition was completed.

It should be pointed out that there have been more than a few misunderstandings about the nature of this book, and of the ways to use it. For this reason we add the following section on how to use this dictionary. More information about this dictionary can be found in the Introduction.

How to Use this Dictionary

This dictionary is different from other Spanish dictionaries in that it only provides words that are not the same in every Spanish-speaking country. The Spanish word for apple is *manzana*, used everywhere where Spanish is spoken, hence it is not included. Grapefruit, on the other hand, is called *toronja* in some countries, and *pomelo in* other countries, hence it is included.

What is also important to keep in mind is that there is a far greater mobility today than ever before, whereby many Latin Americans have moved to Spain in recent years, while others move from Central to South America and so on. All of this impacts on Spanish usage, and many linguistic distinctions have been blurred. Consequently, none of the Spanish terms in this book are cast in stone. All the contributors to this book brought the terms of their respective native countries, but keep in mind that some of those terms are not static. They do tend to change.

Do not use this dictionary as a substitute for the standard Spanish dictionary, but rather as a specialized source when confronted with variations or uncertainties of the use of common everyday words that differ from country to country. If you travel to a particular Spanish-speaking country, you may find this a very useful source for the common words of that country.

Introduction

What kind of Spanish do you speak?

This may seem to be an odd question, since Spanish is Spanish is Spanish. Not so. When you go to the grocery store in Uruguay, you go to the *almacén*. In Peru you go to the *bodega*. In Uruguay the *bodega* is a wine cellar. In fact, if you travel to a dozen different Latin American countries, you will find a dozen different names for "grocery store."

There are scores of Spanish-English dictionaries to choose from, but none of them takes cognizance of the variety of everyday Spanish words as used throughout Latin America and in Spain. In fact, if you compare the word "grocery" in a number of widely used Spanish-English dictionaries, you will find that there is little consistency among them as to which Spanish term they list first, and none of them lists them all.

This is where *The Multicultural Spanish Dictionary* comes in. It is not meant to replace the standard Spanish-English dictionaries, but rather to pick up where they leave off. As such, it has many uses. It can serve native speakers of Spanish who are interested in finding out how certain words vary in other parts of the Hispanic world. It can also serve non-native speakers who have dealings with or travel to one or more Spanish-speaking country and need to know how a particular word is rendered in each country. In short, anyone who works with the Spanish language needs to add this book to his or her reference shelf.

Since this small volume is breaking new ground, it is far from being an exhaustive work. The editors have chosen the most common areas of everyday life and have attempted to cover the most commonly used words in each area. To facilitate the use of this book, words are accessible in three ways:

PART I: ENGLISH - SPANISH: words which vary in one or more Spanish speaking countries (e.g., "apple," is not included in this section, since everyone calls it *manzana*; "grapefruit" is included, since most call it *toronja*, yet in Argentina, Chile, Spain, and Uruguay it is called *pomelo*). Each English word is matched with what appears to be the most widely used Spanish equivalent and followed by variations according to country (a key to country abbreviations is provided at the bottom of each page).

PART II: SPANISH - ENGLISH: words which vary in one or more Spanish-speaking countries. Here the most commonly used Spanish word is followed by Pri., for "Primary Term," while variations are given with the country indicator.

PART III: SUBJECT AREAS: This English-into-Spanish section include all the common words in that particular category. Words which vary are bolded.

Each Spanish-speaking country included in this book is represented by a native speaker of the language of that country. One must keep in mind, however, that even within a country—particularly large countries like Mexico or Argentina—there may be more than one way of rendering a common word. In a big city, "grocery store" may be *supermercado*, the free rendition of the American English word "supermarket," while in a smaller town one still goes to the corner grocery, which retains the old name. Language can never be reduced to one absolute term, especially in our fast-changing world. No matter how thoroughly researched, a dictionary is always a working guide rather than a definitive and immutable source. With this in mind, one can put this book to good use without expecting it to always provide the final word.

At a conference on the Spanish language held in Mexico in the late 1990s, scholars, writers, linguists, and even heads of state (including the King of Spain) discussed the nature and direction of the Spanish language. Is Spain still the standard-bearer of Spanish? Has Latin America, or one particular Latin American country, such as

Mexico, taken the lead? Is there a standard Spanish language? These questions sparked much debate but little agreement.

It is important to note that, three years after this book was first published, the official dictionary of the Royal Academy of the Spanish Language finally agreed to include words from Latin America and other parts of the Spanish-speaking world, as well as English words commonly used in Spanish (mostly in technical fields).

The Varieties of Spanish

There are several reasons for the great variety of common Spanish words. Historically, Spanish originated in the Iberian Peninsula, at the southwestern tip of Europe. It descended directly from the Latin spoken by the Romans who invaded the peninsula around 200 B.C. Three other Latin-based languages which emerged on the peninsula are Portuguese, Catalan, and Galician. In the eighth century, Spain was invaded by the Moors from nearby North Africa, who brought with them their Arabic culture and language. For nearly eight centuries they ruled the peninsula and left their mark on the Spanish language. Many Spanish words, particularly those beginning with *al*, Arabic for "the," are derived from Arabic. These include *almohada* (pillow), *albañil* (mason), and *albaricoque* (apricot). Other linguistic influences in the peninsula predate Latin. For example, the Basque language of northern Spain produced the word *izquierda* (left), derived from the Basque *ezkerra*.

But perhaps the greatest cultural impact on Spanish came after Spain colonized the New World. During the ensuing four centuries, Spanish spread from California in North America to Tierra del Fuego at the southern tip of South America, making Spanish one of the most widely spoken languages in the world. In the New World, the Spanish language was exposed to many indigenous languages and cultural influences. This had an enormous impact on European Spanish, creating in effect multiple varieties of the mother tongue. In Mexico, the Aztec language and culture provided Mexican Spanish with names of flora and fauna and with place names. In Peru, Ecuador, and Bolivia, the Quechua language of the Incas intermingled with Spanish and produced everyday words like *adobe* (sun-baked brick), and *choclo* (corn). In Caribbean countries like Cuba, African slaves gave Spanish words like *marimba* (an African xylophone). Many of Puerto Rico's place names date back to the Taino Indians. In Argentina and Uruguay, significant immigration from Italy greatly influenced the local Spanish, creating an accent which is a mixture of Spanish and Italian, and adding such greetings as *chau* to the local speech.

Another major influence on Spanish is American English. Its impact is felt in the areas of Latin America closest to the United States, such as northern Mexico and Puerto Rico, to a lesser extent in Central America, and much less in South America. In Guatemala, for example, "to park (a car)" is *parquear,* while Argentinians still say *estacionar.* In South America "soccer ball" is *pelota*, whereas in Puerto Rico it is *bola.*

One may wonder why there are so many ways of saying "trunk (of car)" and "flat tire" throughout Latin America. One possible explanation is the following: Unlike the United States, which established a unified economy early on and developed a uniform technical terminology in areas such as the automotive industry, each country or region within a country in Latin America operated within its own local economic and social structure and was compelled to develop its own technical words. Thus, when the first cars arrived in Uruguay with a trunk on the back resembling a large box, Uruguayans called it a *baúl* (storage trunk), a name which has stuck to this day, while in other Latin American countries the word for "car trunk" is of a more recent origin.

In some cases, politics has created a difference in terminology. Just take the Argentinian and Chilean coast guards, which have not always been on good terms. In maritime Spanish, what Chile called *boya* (buoy) Argentina at one point called *baliza* (beacon), and vice versa, just to make sure that their buoys and beacons along the coast were not mixed up.

To quote our Colombian contributor, "Irrational as life itself, Spanish is not cast in stone. It is a constant process of dynamic expressions of people from town and country." Clearly, Spanish speakers worldwide cherish their freedom of expression, and the day when they all will start calling things by the same name is not near.

PART I: ENGLISH—SPANISH

A

abdomen (n) abdomen
  Chi. guata
  Col., Dom.R., Nic. vientre
  Par. barriga, panza
  Per., Ur. barriga
Adam's apple (n phr) manzana de
  Adán
  Arg. nuez de Adán
  Col. coto
  Cub. nuez
  Nic. manzana
  Spa. nuez de la garganta
addicted (adj) adicto
  Col. narcómano
  Nic. drogadicto, drogo (colloq.)
addiction (n) dependencia
  Col., Cos.R., Dom.R., Mex., Nic.,
  Pan., Pue.R. adicción
adult (n) adulto
  Col. mayor de edad
  Nic. roco (colloq), vetarro (colloq),
  viejo
aerobics (n) aerobismo
  Col., Mex. aerobics
  Dom.R., ElS., Gua., Nic. Pan.,
  Pue.R., Uru. aeróbicos
  Spa. aerobic
air conditioning (n phr) aire
  acondicionado
  Cos.R. airecondicionado
airfare (n) precio del pasaje
  Arg., Ecu. tarifa
  Col. tarifa aérea
  Mex. tarifa de vuelo
  Spa. precio del billete de avión
  Venz. precio del boleto

airline (n) aerolínea
  Col., Dom.R., Nic. línea aérea
airplane (n) avión
  Col. aeronave
alcoholic beverage (n phr) bebida
  alcohólica
  Chi., Nic. trago
alley (n) callejón
  Per. pasaje
aluminum foil (n phr) papel de
  aluminio
  Chi., Col., Nic., Pan. papel
  aluminio
  Cos.R., ElS., Gua., Pan., Per.
  lámina de aluminio
amateur (n) amateur
  Col., Mex., Nic., Venz.
  aficionado
  Chi. amador
  Cub. no profesional
  Per. novato
anchovy (n) anchoa
  Chi. anchoveta
  Cos.R., Dom.R., Pue.R.,
  boquerón
  Per. anchoveta, boquerón
antiperspirant (n) desodorante
  Gua., Mex., Pue.R.
  antiperspirante
apartment (n) apartamento
  Arg., Bol., Chi., Mex.
  departamento
  Spa. piso
apartment building (n phr) edificio
  de apartamentos
  Arg., Bol., Mex. edificio de

departamentos
Chi., Col. edificio
Dom.R. torre de
apartamentos
Spa. edificio de pisos
Uru. propiedad horizontal
appetizer (n) aperitivo
Arg., Dom.R., Uru. entrada
Col. antojitos
Cos.R. bocas
Ecu. entrada, primer plato
Nic. bocas, boquitas
Pan. abreboca
Per. bocaditos
Venz. entremés
apricot (n) albaricoque
Arg., Chi., Uru. damasco
Mex. chabacano
armchair (n) silla de brazos
Arg., Chi., Nic., Spa., Uru.
sillón
Dom.R. butaca, sillón
Mex. silla con coderas
Pue.R. butaca
armpit (n) axila

Col., Dom.R. zobaco
Nic., Pan. sobaco
arrival (n) llegada
Chi. desembarque
artichoke (n) alcachofa
Arg., Uru. alcaucil
athlete (n) atleta
Nic., Pan. deportista
attaché case (n) maletín
Arg. portafolios
Mex. portafolio
automatic transmission (n phr)
transmisión automática
Spa. cambio automático
avocado (n) aguacate
Arg., Bol., Chi., Per., Uru. palta
awful (adj) horrible
Arg., Chi., Nic. espantoso
Col. espantoso, horrendo,
horroroso
Dom.R. terrible
awl (n) lezna
Bol., Nic., Spa., Venz. punzón
Col. lezana, punzón, tezna
Mex. berbiquí

B

baby (n) bebé
    Arg., Uru. beba, bebe
    Chi. guagua
babysit (v) hacer de niñero/a
    Arg., Uru. cuidar a un/a beba/
    bebe/chico/chica/nene/nena
    Chi., Col., Ecu., Nic., Per.,
    Pue.R., Venz. cuidar niños
    Mex. cuidar a un bebé/niño/a
babysitter (n) guardián
    Arg. babysitter, niñera
    Bol., Col., Dom.R., Ecu., Gua.,
    Pan., Spa., Uru. niñero/a
    Chi. niñera, nodriza
    Mex. nana, niñero/a
    Nic. niñera, china
    Par. niñero/a, criada
    Per. cuidadora de niños
    Venz. cuidador de niños,
    niñero/a
back (soccer) (n) defensa
    Spa. defensor
backstroke (swimming) (n) estilo
    espalda
    Cub. al revés
    Mex., Nic. dorso
bagel (n) rosca de pan
    Bol., Col., Pue.R. bagel
    Nic. rosca
baggage (n) equipaje
    Col., Cos.R., Nic. maletas
    Par. maletas, valijas
bags (under eyes) (n) ojeras
    Chi. chasquillas
    Dom.R. bolsas
baguette (n) baguette

Bol., Chi., Col., Dom.R.,
    Nic.,Venz. pan francés
    Pan. pan flauta, pan francés
    Par. pan flauta
    Spa. barra de pan
bake (v) hornear
    Spa. cocinar en el horno
bakery (n) panadería
    Chi., Col. pastelería
    Pue.R. repostería
balcony (n) balcón
    Chi. terraza
    Col. balconcillo
ball (soccer) (n) pelota de fútbol
    Col. balón
    Pue.R. bola de balompié
    Spa. balón
banana (n) plátano
    Arg., Par., Uru. banana
    Col., Cos.R., Nic. banano
    Dom.R., Pan., Pue.R. guineo
    Ecu. banano, guineo
    Venz. cambur
bangs (hair) (n) flequillo
    Col. capul, fleco
    Cos.R., Nic. pava
    Cub., Ecu., Per. cerquillo
    Dom.R., Venz. pollina
    Mex. fleco
    Pan. gallusa
banjo (n) banjo
    Spa. banyo
banned film (n phr) película
    prohibida
    Col., Dom.R. película
    censurada

---

*ABBREVIATIONS: Arg.=Argentina Bol.=Bolivia Chi.=Chile Col.=Colombia Cos.R.=Costa Rica
Cub.=Cuba Dom.R.=Dominican Republic Ecu.=Ecuador ElS.=El Salvador Gua.=Guatemala
Hon.=Honduras Mex.=Mexico Nic.=Nicaragua Pan.=Panama Par.=Paraguay Per.=Peru
Pri.=Primary Term Pue.R.=Puerto Rico Spa.=Spain Uru.=Uruguay Venz.=Venezuela*

bar (music) (n) compás
  Col. barra (entre compases)
bar (n) bar
  Col. taberna
  Mex., Nic., Pan. cantina
barber (n) barbero
  Arg., Ecu., Mex., Par., Per.
  peluquero
barracks (n) cuartel
  Pan. barracas
  Pue.R. barraca
barrette (n) broche para el pelo
  Arg., Bol., Col., Pue.R. hebilla
  Chi. traba
  Dom.R., Pan., Per., Spa.
  gancho para el pelo
  Nic. gancho de pelo
  Venz. ganchito de pelo
bartender (n) barman
  Col., Ecu., ElS., Gua., Hon.,
  Mex., Pan., Par., Pue.R.
  cantinero
  Dom.R. bartender
  Nic. bartender, cantinero
basket (basketball) (n) cesta
  Arg., Mex., Nic., Pan., Per.,
  Uru. canasta
  Bol. cesto
  Col. caneca
  Dom.R., Pue.R. canasto
basketball (n) baloncesto
  Arg., Per., Uru. basketbol
  Mex., Pan., Par. basketball
  Nic. basket
bass (stereo) (n) graves
  Col., Nic., Par. bajo
bass (voice) (n) bajo
  Col. contrabajo
  Nic. voz de bajo
batch (n) hornada
  Chi. horneada
  Col. tanda
  Cos.R. lote

Nic. lote, montón
Par. hornalla
bathing suit (n phr) traje de baño
  Arg. maya
  Col., Ecu., Pan. vestido de
  baño
  Cub. trusa
  Par. malla
  Spa. bañador
bathrobe (n) bata de baño
  Bol. batón
  Nic. salida de baño
  Par. bata
  Spa. albornoz
bathroom (n) cuarto de baño
  Bol., Chi., Cos.R., Ecu., Nic.,
  Par., Spa., Uru., Venz. baño
bean sprouts (n phr) germinados de
  soja
  Arg., Uru. brotes de soja
  ElS., Gua. retoños de soya
  Nic., Pan. frijol nacido
  Par. brotes de soje
  Pue.R. habichuelas de soya
beans (n) porotos
  Col. fríjoles
  Cub., Gua., Mex., Nic.,
  Pan. frijoles
  Dom.R., Pue. R. habichuelas
  Ecu. Frejoles
  Spa. alubias
  Venz. caraotas
beans, black (n phr) frijoles
  Arg., Par., Uru. porotos
  negros
  Col., Cub., ElS., Gua., Hon.,
  Mex., Nic., Pan. frijoles
  negros
  Pue.R. habichuelas negras
  Spa. alubias negras
  Venz. caraotas negras
beans, broad (n phr) habas
  Arg., Uru. chauchas

ABBREVIATIONS: Arg.=Argentina Bol.=Bolivia Chi.=Chile Col.=Colombia Cos.R.=Costa Rica
Cub.=Cuba Dom.R.=Dominican Republic Ecu.=Ecuador ElS.=El Salvador Gua.=Guatemala
Hon.=Honduras Mex.=Mexico Nic.=Nicaragua Pan.=Panama Par.=Paraguay Per.=Peru
Pri.=Primary Term Pue.R.=Puerto Rico Spa.=Spain Uru.=Uruguay Venz.=Venezuela

Dom.R. guandules
beans, green (n phr) habichuelas
   Arg., Uru. chauchas
   Dom.R., Ecu., Per., Venz.
   vainitas
   ElS., Gua., Hon., Mex. ejotes
   Nic. frijolitos verdes
   Par. arvejas
   Pue.R. habichuelas verdes
   Spa. judías verdes
beans, kidney (n phr) habichuelas
   Col. frijoles rojos
   Cub., Nic. frijoles colorados
   Dom.R. habichuelas rojas
   Spa. alubias rojas
beans, lima (n phr) frijoles de media
   luna
   Cub. habas limas
   Nic. frijoles blancos
   Spa. habas
become intoxicated (v phr)
   intoxicarse
   Chi. embriagarse
   Cub., Mex., Nic. Pan.
   emborracharse
   Spa. estar bajo la influencia del
   alcohol o de las drogas
bed, double (n phr) cama doble
   Gua., Mex., Nic. cama
   matrimonial
   Par. cama dos plazas
   Spa. cama de matrimonio
bed, king-sized (n phr) cama
   grande
   Arg. cama camera
   Col., Dom.R. cama king size
   Mex. cama king-size
   Nic. cama extra grande
   Pan., Par., Venz. cama king
bed, queen-sized (n phr) cama
   doble
   Arg., Par. cama camera
   Dom.R. cama queen size

Mex. cama queen-size
   Nic. cama grande
   Pan. cama matrimonial
   Venz. cama queen
bed, single (n phr) cama
   Chi. cama de soltero
   Col., Ecu., Nic., Pue.R. cama
   sencilla
   Gua. cama imperial
   Mex., Venz. cama individual
   Pan. cama tres cuartos
   Par. cama soltero
bedroom (n) dormitorio
   Arg., Cub., Pue.R. cuarto
   Col. cuarto, pieza
   Dom.R. aposento, cuarto
   Mex. cuarto, recámara
   Nic. aposento
   Pan. habitación
   Par. pieza
beet (n) remolacha
   Bol., Chi., Per. beterraga
   Mex. betabel
beetle (n) escarabajo
   Chi. cucaracha
   Dom.R. avejón
bell (bicycle) (n) timbre
   Arg., Chi., Dom.R., Uru.
   bocina
   Bol. campanilla
belly (n) barriga
   Arg., Cos.R., Dom.R., Mex.,
   Par., Uru. panza
   Chi. guata
   Col. pipa
   Nic. panza, timba (colloq)
   Venz. estómago
belly button (n phr) ombligo
   Chi. pupo
belt (n) cinturón
   Col., Dom.R., Pan., Pue.R.
   correa
   Cos.R., Nic. faja

Par. cinto
bench (n) banco
    Arg., Nic. banca
    Spa. banqueta
berry (n) baya
    Nic. frutilla
    Par., Pue.R. cereza
berth (n) litera
    Chi., Nic. camarote
biceps (n) bíceps
    Mex. conejos
    Nic. ratones
bifocals (n) lentes bifocales
    Arg. anteojos bifocales
    Nic. bifocales
    Pue.R. espejuelos bifocales
    Spa. gafas bifocales
big toe (n phr) dedo gordo
    Arg., Dom.R., Nic., Par., Spa.,
    Venz. dedo gordo del pie
big-nosed (adj) narizón
    Arg., Bol., Chi., Par., Uru.
    narigón
    Dom.R. narizú
bike, mountain (n phr) montañera
    Arg. bicicleta todo terreno
    Chi., Col., Venz. bicicleta de
    montaña
    Dom.R., Par., Pue.R. mountain
    bike
    ElS., Gua. bicicleta montañesa
    Mex. bicicleta de
    campotraviesa
    Spa. bicicleta de montaña,
    mountain bike
bike, road (n phr) bicicleta de
    camino
    Arg., Nic., Par., Uru. bicicleta
    Col. bicicleta para carretera
    Dom.R. bicicleta de carrera
    Mex. bicicleta turismo
    Spa. bicicleta de carreras
bike, tandem (n phr) bicicleta para

dos personas
    Col. bicicleta de dos personas,
    bicicleta doble, tándem
    Mex. bicicleta doble
    Pue.R. doblecleta
    Spa. tándem
bikini briefs (n phr) minitrusa
    Arg. bombacha
    Bol., Chi. bikini
    Col. calzoncillos
    Dom.R., Nic. tangas
    Ecu. calzón bikini
    Pan. calzoncillo corto
    Par. bikini, bombacha
    Pue.R. panticitos del bikini
    Spa. braguita de bikini
    Venz. interiores bikini
billboard (n) anuncio panorámico
    Chi., Cub., Par. cartelera
    Col. cartelera, valla
    Cos.R. rótulo
    Dom.R. valla
    Mex. anuncio
    Nic. valla, rótulo
    Pue.R. billboard
birthmark (n) marca de nacimiento
    Cub., Ecu., Per., Venz. lunar
    Dom.R., Spa. antojo
    Mex. mancha de nacimiento
    Nic. lunar de nacimiento
biscuit (n) bizcocho, galleta
    Arg. galletita
    Dom.R. bizcochito
    Mex. bisquet
    Pue.R. panecillo
black currant (n phr) casis
    Col., Mex., Nic., Par. grosella
    Pan. pasita
blackbird (n) mirlo
    Pan. talingo
blanket (n) cobija
    Arg., Bol., Col., Cub., Par.,
    Uru. frazada

Ecu. colcha
Nic. colcha, sábana
Pue.R. frisa
Spa. manta
blender (n) licuadora
Cub., Dom.R., Spa., Venz.
batidora
blimp (n) dirigible no rígido
Col., Spa. dirigible
Cub., Nic., Venz. zepelín
blinds (n) persianas
Col. cortinas
blinker (light) (n) intermitente, luz
intermitente
Arg. guiño
Bol. guiñador
Pan. luz direccional
Par. señalero
Venz. luz de cruce
blond (hair) (adj) rubio
Col. mono
Mex. güero
Nic. chele
Pan. fulo
Venz. catire
blond (person) (n) rubio/a
Col. mono/a
Cos.R. macho (person with
light hair)
Mex. güero/a
Nic. chele
Pan. fulo/a
Venz. catire/a
bloom (v) florecer
Col. dar flor
Pue.R. retollar
blowtorch (n) soplete
Pan., Pue.R. antorcha
blue (eyes) (adj) azul
Col. ojiazul
Cos.R. macho (person with
light-colored eyes)
Nic. gato (ojos claros), ojos

azules
blue jeans (n phr) jeans
Arg., Cub., Nic., Par., Uru.
vaqueros
Col. blue jeans, jeanes
Mex. pantalón de mezclilla
Pue.R. mahones
Spa. pantalones vaqueros,
vaqueros
Venz. blue jeans
blueberry (n) arándano
Mex. mora azul
Nic. frutilla
Per. mora
bluefish (n) pomátomo
Mex. anjova, pez azul
Nic. dorado
board (v) embarcarse
Chi., Col., Dom.R., Mex., Par.
abordar
Spa., Venz. embarcar
boat (n) barco
Nic.,Venz. bote
boathouse (n) caseta de botes
Col. cobertizo para las
lanchas, garaje para botes
Dom.R. casa-botes
Gua., Nic. cobertizo de
lanchas
bolt (n) perno
Col., Cos.R., Pue.R., Spa.
tornillo
Cub. cerrojo
Pan. tuerca
bookkeeper (n) contador
Cub. tenedor de libros
Spa. contable
bookstore (n) librería
Pue.R. tienda de libros
boss (n) jefe
Col., Par. patrón
bothersome (adj) molesto
Col. incómodo

ABBREVIATIONS: Arg.=Argentina Bol.=Bolivia Chi.=Chile Col.=Colombia Cos.R.=Costa Rica
Cub.=Cuba Dom.R.=Dominican Republic Ecu.=Ecuador ElS.=El Salvador Gua.=Guatemala
Hon.=Honduras Mex.=Mexico Nic.=Nicaragua Pan.=Panama Par.=Paraguay Per.=Peru
Pri.=Primary Term Pue.R.=Puerto Rico Spa.=Spain Uru.=Uruguay Venz.=Venezuela

Venz. molestoso
bottle opener (n phr) destapador
   Chi., Cos.R., Nic., Par. abridor
   Pan., Uru. abridor, saca
   corcho
   Pue.R. abridor de botellas
   Spa. abrebotellas
bow tie (n phr) corbata mariposa
   Arg., Par. moñito
   Bol. corbata de gato
   Col., Nic. corbatín
   Cub., Spa. pajarita
   Dom.R. corbata de lacito
   Mex. corbata de moñito
   Pan. corbata de gatito
   Per. corbata michi
   Pue.R. lazo
   Uru., Venz. corbata de lazo
bowl (n) plato hondo
   Chi. bol
   Col. tazón, vasija
   Mex., Par. tazón
   Pan. vasija
   Spa. cuenco
bowl, mixing (n phr) tazón para
   medir
   Arg., Par. bol
   Col. vasija para mezclar
   ElS., Gua., Venz. tazón para
   mezclar
   Mex. tazón para batir
   Pan. platón, vasija
bowl, salad (n phr) ensaladera
   Col., Pan. plato para ensalada
bowl, soup (n phr) tazón
   Col., Venz. plato de sopa
   Cub., Dom.R., Ecu. plato
   sopero
   Nic. plato hondo, plato sopero
   Pan. plato hondo, plato para
   sopa
   Par., Pue.R. sopera
box spring (n phr) colchón de

resortes
   Chi. catre
   Dom.R., Mex., Venz. box
   spring
   Nic. colchón
   Pan. esprín
   Par. somnier
   Spa. somier
boxer (n) boxeador
   Chi. pugilista
boxer shorts (n phr) calzoncillos
   Cub. calzones
   Dom.R. calzoncillos boxer
   Nic., Pan. calzoncillos largos
boy (n) niño
   Arg., Par., Pue.R., Uru. nene
   Col. chino
   Dom.R. muchachito
   Mex. chamaco
   Nic. chavalo, chigüín, cipote
boyfriend (n) novio
   Chi. pololo
   Ecu., Per. enamorado
bra, brassiere (n) sostén
   Arg. corpiño
   Col. brassiere
   Cub. ajustador
   Dom.R., Nic., Pan. brasier
   Mex. brasiere
   Par. corpiño, portaseno
   Spa. sujetador
   Uru. soutien
bracelet (n) pulsera
   Cub. pulso
   Dom.R. guillo
braid (hair) (n) trenza
   Pan. moño
   Venz. crineja
brass section (n phr) bronces
   Col. cobres
   Mex., Nic. metales
   Spa. instrumentos de metal
brat (n) mocoso

ABBREVIATIONS: Arg.=Argentina Bol.=Bolivia Chi.=Chile Col.=Colombia Cos.R.=Costa Rica
Cub.=Cuba Dom.R.=Dominican Republic Ecu.=Ecuador ElS.=El Salvador Gua.=Guatemala
Hon.=Honduras Mex.=Mexico Nic.=Nicaragua Pan.=Panama Par.=Paraguay Per.=Peru
Pri.=Primary Term Pue.R.=Puerto Rico Spa.=Spain Uru.=Uruguay Venz.=Venezuela

Col. niño/a malcriado/a
Cub., Pan. malcriado
Dom.R. carajito/a,
muchachito/a
Nic. malcriado
Par. cabezudo
Pue.R. chiquillo/a
bread, rye (n phr) pan negro
Arg., Col., Cub., Dom.R.,
Ecu., Spa., Venz. pan de
centeno
Chi. pan centeno
bread, sliced (n phr) pan de molde
Arg. pan lactal
Col. pan tajado
Cos.R. pan cortado
Dom.R., Par. pan de sandwich
Mex. pan de caja
Pue.R. pan especial
Venz. pan en rodajas
bread, white (n phr) pan blanco
tajado
Arg., Col., Dom.R., Mex.,
Spa., Venz. pan blanco
Cub. pan de molde
Nic. pan blanco de molde
Par. pan
Pue.R. pan especial
Uru. pan blanco rebanado
break up (relationship)
(v phr) romper
Arg., Dom.R. cortar
Chi., Mex., Nic. cortar,
terminar
Col. separarse
Cub. pelearse
Ecu., ElS., Gua., Hon., Venz.
terminar
breast (n) seno
Arg., Col., Cos.R., Uru. teta
Chi. pechuga
Dom.R., ElS., Gua., Nic., Spa.
pecho

Mex. busto, chiche, chichi
Pan. pecho, teta
Par. teta, titi
breaststroke (swimming) (n) estilo
braza
Arg. brazada
Chi., Col., Cub., Par., Pue.R.,
Venz. estilo pecho
Dom.R. brazado de pecho
ElS., Gua. brazada de pecho
Mex., Nic. pecho
bridal shower (n phr) despedida de
soltera
Col. shower
bridge of nose (n phr) caballete
Chi., Col., Dom.R. tabique
Mex., Nic., Venz. puente de la
nariz
Par. puente nasal, tabique
briefcase (n) portafolios
Bol. cartera, portafolio
Col., Cub., Nic., Par., Per.,
Pue.R. maletín
briefs (n) calzoncillos
Col. trusa
Dom.R. pantaloncillos
Mex., Uru. calzones
Venz. interiores
brights (headlights) (n) luces
fuertes
Arg., Chi., Dom.R., Mex.,
Nic., Pan., Venz. luces altas
Col. plenas
Cub., Pue.R., Spa. luces largas
Ecu. faros intensos
Par. luz alta
broad jump (n phr) salto de longitud
Chi., ElS., Gua., Nic., Par. salto
largo
Col. salto ancho
Pue.R. salto a lo largo
broadcast (n) emisión televisiva
Arg., Dom.R., Venz.

ABBREVIATIONS: Arg.=Argentina Bol.=Bolivia Chi.=Chile Col.=Colombia Cos.R.=Costa Rica
Cub.=Cuba Dom.R.=Dominican Republic Ecu.=Ecuador ElS.=El Salvador Gua.=Guatemala
Hon.=Honduras Mex.=Mexico Nic.=Nicaragua Pan.=Panama Par.=Paraguay Per.=Peru
Pri.=Primary Term Pue.R.=Puerto Rico Spa.=Spain Uru.=Uruguay Venz.=Venezuela

programa de televisión
Chi., Col., Cos.R., Gua., Nic.
transmisión
broadcast (v) emitir
Col., Cos.R., ElS., Gua., Hon.,
Nic.,Venz. transmitir
brown (eyes) (adj) castaño
Arg., Col., Dom.R., Par., Per.,
Spa. marrón
Bol., Chi., Cos.R., Mex., Nic.
café
brown (hair) (adj) moreno
Arg., Mex., Nic., Par., Spa.
castaño
Col. pelicastaño
Dom.R. trigueño
Uru. morocho
bruise (n) cardenal
Arg., Bol., Chi., Mex., Nic.,
Pan., Par. moretón
Col., Cub. morado
Cos.R. morete
Dom.R. chichón, hematoma,
morado
ElS., Gua., Hon. magulladura
Spa. moratón
Venz. golpe, magulladura
brunch (n) brunch
Col. onces
Mex., Par. almuerzo
Nic. comida tarde
Uru. desayuno
Venz. desayuno-almuerzo
brunette (person) (n) moreno/a
Arg., Uru. morocho/a
Col., Dom.R. trigueño/a
Spa. persona de pelo castaño
Brussels sprouts (n phr) coles de
Bruselas
Arg., Uru. repollitos de
Bruselas
Chi. repollitos italianos
Nic. repollitos

bucket (n) cubo
Arg., Bol., Chi., Cos.R., Ecu.,
Nic., Pan., Par., Per., Uru.
balde
Col., Mex., Spa. cubeta
bucksaw (n) sierra de ballesta
Nic., Uru. serrucho
Par. sierra
Spa. sierra de bastidor
bud (n) brote
Col. botón
Nic. cogollo
Spa. capullo
buddy, pal (n) compañero/a
Chi., Cub. compadre
Col. amigazo/a
Dom.R. compinche, pana
ElS., Gua., Hon. cuate
Mex. amigocho, amigote,
cuate
Nic. amigazo/a, cuate
Par. amigazo/a, che duo,
cuate, socio
Pan., Pue.R. amigo/a
buffer storage (n phr) memoria
intermediaria
Col. memoria intermedia,
memoria temporal
Mex. búfer
Nic. búfer, memoria
intermedia
Pue.R. buffer storage
Venz. memoria de reserva,
memoria intermedia, memoria
temporal
buffet (n) aparador
Col. mostrador, vitrina
Dom.R. despensa
Gua. bufetera
Mex. mesa de buffet
Par. comida sin límite, comer
hasta hartarse por un precio
fijo

ABBREVIATIONS: Arg.=Argentina Bol.=Bolivia Chi.=Chile Col.=Colombia Cos.R.=Costa Rica
Cub.=Cuba Dom.R.=Dominican Republic Ecu.=Ecuador ElS.=El Salvador Gua.=Guatemala
Hon.=Honduras Mex.=Mexico Nic.=Nicaragua Pan.=Panama Par.=Paraguay Per.=Peru
Pri.=Primary Term Pue.R.=Puerto Rico Spa.=Spain Uru.=Uruguay Venz.=Venezuela

Pue.R. chinero
bug (n) bicho, chinche
  Col., Nic., Per., Pue.R. insecto
  Dom.R. insecto, pajarito
bugle (n) clarín
  Col. corneta
  Nic. trompeta
  Spa. cornetín
building (n) edificio
  Col. edificación
bumblebee (n) abejorro
  Pue.R. avejita
bump (road) (n) bache
  Chi. lomo de toro
  Col. policia acostado
  Dom.R. hoyo
  Mex. tope
bumper (n) parachoques
  Arg., Par. paragolpes
  Col., Dom.R., Pan., Pue.R. bumper
  Mex. defensa
  Nic. bumper, guardabarro, lodera
bumper car (n phr) carro loco
  Arg., Par. autito chocador
  Col., Dom.R. carrito chocón
  Mex., Nic., Per., Venz. carro chocón
  Spa. auto de choque
bun (hair) (n) moño
  Chi. tomate
  Mex. chongo
  Pan. cebolla
bun (n) panecillo
  Arg., Par., Uru. pancito
  Bol., Spa. bollo
  Col. pan pequeño
  Cos.R. bollito
  Mex. pan para hamburgeusas, pan para hot dogs
  Nic. bollo de pan
  Pan. pan para hamburguesas

bungalow (n) casa independiente
  Arg., Par., Uru. bungalow
  Bol. cabañita
  Chi. cabaña, chalet
  Col. bungaló
  Dom.R. bungaloo
  ElS., Gua., Hon. casa campestre, casa de playa
  Mex. búngalo
  Nic. cabaña
  Pan. bungalu
  Spa. bungaló
  Venz. casa de campo
bunkbed (n) litera
  Chi., Nic. camarote
  Col., Dom.R., Pan. cama camarote
burial (n) entierro
  Chi., Mex. sepelio
  Col. exequias, sepelio
bus (n) autobús
  Arg. bus, ómnibus
  Bol. colectivo
  Chi. micro
  Col. bus, buseta, colectivo
  Cos.R. bus, lata
  Cub., Dom.R., Pue.R. guagua
  ElS., Gua. camioneta
  Mex. camión
  Nic., Pan. bus
  Par. micro, ómnibus
  Per., Uru. ómnibus
bus driver (n phr) conductor de autobús
  Arg. chofer de colectivo, chofer de micro
  Chi., Par. chofer
  Col. busetero
  Cub. guagüero
  Dom.R., Pue.R. chofer de guagua
  Mex. camionero

Nic. busero, chofer,
conductor
Pan. busero
bus stop (n phr) parada de
autobús
Arg., Per., Uru. parada del
ómnibus
Bol. parada del colectivo
Chi. parada del micro
Col., Nic., Pan. parada de
bus
Cos.R. parada de bus,
parada de lata
Cub., Dom.R., Pue.R.
parada de guagua
Par. parada
bush (n) arbusto
Cub. mata
Nic. palito
Pue.R. arbolito, palito
business district (n phr) barrio
comercial
Col., Cub., Mex., Nic.,
Pue.R. zona comercial
Dom.R. centro de
negocios
Spa. zona de negocios
businessman (n) hombre de
negocios
Arg., Chi., Nic., Par.
empresario
Col. ejecutivo

Pan. hombre profesional
businesswoman (n) mujer de
negocios
Arg., Chi., Cos.R., Nic.,
Par. empresaria
Col. ejecutiva
Pan. mujer profesional
butcher block (n phr) bloque
de carnicero
Arg. tabla de cocina
Chi., Col., Nic. tabla para
cortar
Par. tabla de picar
Pue.R. picador
butt (n) trasero
Arg. cola, traste
Chi. traste
Col. cola, culo
Cub. nalgas
buttock (n) nalga
Arg. cachete
Chi. poto
Mex. pompa, pompas
buttock (n) nalga
Arg. cachete
Chi. poto
Mex. pompa, pompas
Bye! (int) ¡Adiós!
Arg., Par. ¡Chau!
Chi. ¡Chao!
Col. ¡Ciao!
Dom.R., Nic. ¡Bye!

C

cabbage, green (n phr) repollo
verde
Cub., Ecu., Mex., Spa. col
Col., Nic. repollo
Dom.R. lechuga repollada
cabbage, white (n phr) repollo
Cub., Spa. col
Mex. col blanca
cabin (n) cabaña, choza
Chi. refugio
cable television (n phr)
televisión por cable
Arg. cable
Dom.R. telecable
Mex. cable, cablevisión
cactus (n) cacto
Arg., Chi., Col., Dom.R.,
Mex., Nic., Pan., Par.,
Pue.R., Spa. cactus
cake (n) pastel
Arg., Chi., Ecu., Par., Uru.,
Venz. torta
Bol., Cos.R., Nic. queque
Col. ponqué
Cub. cake
Dom.R., Pue.R. bizcocho
Pan. cake, dulce
Per. queque, torta
Spa. tarta
calf (n) ternera
Arg., Nic. ternero
Col., Spa. becerro, ternero
can opener (n phr) abrelatas
Chi. abridor de latas
Cos.R. abridor
canine (tooth) (n) canino

Cos.R. premolar
Cub., Mex., Nic., Par., Spa.
colmillo
canned food (n phr) alimentos
enlatados
Chi. latas de conservas
Col., Dom.R., Pan. comida
enlatada
Nic. comida enlatada,
conservas
cantaloupe (n) melón chino
Chi. melón calameño
Col. cantaloupe, melón
Cub. cantalupa
Nic., Pan., Per., Venz.
melón
cap (n) gorra
Col., Dom.R. cachucha
Par. kepi
cape (n) capa, capote
Mex. chal, quisquemel
car (n) carro
Arg., Chi., Par. auto,
coche
Col. auto
Mex. auto, automóvil,
coche
Spa. automóvil, coche
Uru. coche
car body (n phr) carrocería
Pan. chasis
car jack (crime) (v phr)
secuestrar un auto
Bol. raptar
Col. asaltar, atracar
Cub. robarse un carro

Mex. asaltar con violencia
Nic. robar con violencia
Pue.R. car jack
Spa. robar un vehículo
con alguien dentro
Uru. atracar un coche
Venz. robar un carro
car, private (n phr) carro
privado
Arg. auto particular
Chi., Ecu., Nic. carro
particular
Par., Spa., Uru. coche
particular
cardigan (n) cardigán
Arg. chaleco, saco de lana
Chi. sweater
Col. suéter abierto
Ecu., Venz. suéter
Mex. chamarra tejida,
suéter
Nic. chamarra, chaqueta
Spa. chaqueta de punto
carousel (with horses)
(n) caballitos
Arg., Par., Uru. calesita
Chi., Col., Ecu., ElS., Gua.,
Hon., Pan., Venz. carrusel
carpool (v) compartir coches
Arg. hacer pool
Col. compartir viajes en
carro
Gua. compartir carros
Mex. turnarse alternando
coches
Nic. carpool
Venz. ir juntos en un carro
cartoon (n) dibujo animado
Col., Spa. dibujos
animados
Cub., Dom.R., Nic., Pue.R.
muñequitos
Mex. caricatura

Pan. caricaturas
carving fork (n phr) trinche
Arg. tenedor
Col., ElS., Gua., Hon.,
Spa. tenedor de trinchar
Nic. tenedor para trinchar
Pan., Pue.R. tenedor para
servir
cashew (n) nuez de la India
Arg., Par., Uru. castaña de
cajú
Chi. castaña
Dom.R. semilla de cajuil
Nic. semilla de marañón
Pan. pepita de marañon
Pue.R. avellana
cast (show) (n) equipo artístico
Chi., Pan.. Par., Pue.R.
elenco
Col., Mex., Spa., Venz.
reparto
Nic. reparto, elenco
casual clothes (n phr) ropa
informal
Dom.R. ropa casual
caterpillar (n) oruga
Chi. gusano
Dom.R. larva
Pue.R. cocullo
catfish (n) bagre
Spa. barbo
cattle (n) ganado
Pue.R. vacas
cave (n) cueva
Col. caverna
celery (n) apio
Venz. cilantro
celesta (n) celesta
Col., Nic. celeste
cemetery (n) cementerio
Chi. campo santo
Mex. panteón
certified public ccountant
(CPA) (n phr) contador

ABBREVIATIONS: Arg.=Argentina Bol.=Bolivia Chi.=Chile Col.=Colombia Cos.R.=Costa Rica
Cub.=Cuba Dom.R.=Dominican Republic Ecu.=Ecuador ElS.=El Salvador Gua.=Guatemala
Hon.=Honduras Mex.=Mexico Nic.=Nicaragua Pan.=Panama Par.=Paraguay Per.=Peru
Pri.=Primary Term Pue.R.=Puerto Rico Spa.=Spain Uru.=Uruguay Venz.=Venezuela

público certificado
Chi. contador
Col. contador público
Cos.R., Nic., Pan.
contador público
autorizado, CPA
Dom.R. contable,
contador, CPA
Par. contador
Spa. contable
chainsaw (n) serrucho eléctrico
Arg., Cos.R., Nic., Par.,
Spa. motosierra
Chi., Col., Uru. sierra
eléctrica
Mex., Pue.R. sierra
de cadena
chair, director's (n phr) silla de
director, silla plegable
Mex. silla ejecutiva, sillón
ejecutivo
Par. sillón ejecutivo
chair, folding (n phr) silla
plegable
Dom.R. silla plegadiza
chair, lounging (n phr) catre,
chaise
Chi. asiento, poltrona
Col. silla de extensión
Mex., Nic. sillón reclinable
Pue.R. silla reclinable
Spa. hamaca
chair, rocking (n phr) mecedora
Arg. silla hamaca
Col. mecedor
Cub., Pue.R. sillón
chair, step (n phr) banco-
escalera
Nic. banco
Venz. silla con escalón
challenger (boxing)
(n) contrincante
Col. contendor, retador

Dom.R., Mex., Nic., Par.
retador
Uru. aspirante
Venz. retador de boxeo
change (train) (v) transbordar
Arg. hacer una conexión
Col., Cub. cambiar de tren
Venz. hacer un transbordo
de trenes
channel (n) canal
Spa. cadena
chassis (n) chasis
Dom.R., Nic., Pue.R.
chasis
Ecu., Pan., Per. bastidor
cheap (adj) barato
Col. ganga
Pan. runcho
cheater (n) tramposo
Col. embustero, estafador,
pícaro
Par. trampero
check in (baggage)
(v phr) registrar el
equipaje
Chi. despachar
Dom.R., Nic., Venz.
chequear el equipaje
cheek (n) mejilla
Chi., Col., Dom.R., Mex.,
Nic. Pan., Per., Venz.
cachete
Spa. carrillo
chef (n) chef
Col. cocinero, jefe de
cocina
Par., Spa. cocinero
Per. jefe de cocina
chest (n) pecho
Chi., Col. tórax
chestnut (n) castaña
Dom.R. pan de fruta
chicken (n) pollo

Pan. gallina
chief executive officer (CEO)
 (n phr) jefe ejecutivo
 principal
 Arg., Par. presidente
 Chi. gerente ejecutivo
 Col. gerente general
 Cos.R., Nic. director
 general, gerente general
 Dom.R. director ejecutivo
 Gua. personero ejecutivo
 de más alto rango
 Mex. director general
 Venz. oficial ejecutivo jefe
child (n) niño/a
 Arg. chico/a
 Col. chino/a
 Nic. chavalo/a, chigüín,
 cipote
chin (n) barbilla
 Arg. mentón, pera
 Chi. pera
 Col., Par. mentón
 Mex. barba
 Per. quijada
china (n) porcelana
 Chi. loza
 Col., Dom.R., Mex., Nic.
 vajilla
 Pan. loza, vajilla fina
chord (n) acorde
 Col. cuerda
christening (n) bautizo
 Arg., Col. bautismo
church (n) iglesia
 Col. basílica, capilla,
 parroquia, templo
cicada (n) cigarra
 Chi., Nic., Pue.R., Venz.
 chicharra
cigar (n) cigarro, puro
 Cub. tabaco
cigarette (n) cigarrillo

Chi. pucho
 Mex., Nic. cigarro
city (n) ciudad
 Col. metrópoli, urbe
city block (n phr) manzana
 Col., Dom.R., Ecu., Nic.,
 Pan., Par. cuadra
 Pue.R. bloque
city hall (n phr) ayuntamiento
 Bol., Nic., Pue.R. alcaldía
 Chi., Col., ElS., Gua.,
 Hon., Par. municipalidad
 Ecu. alcaldía,
 municipalidad
 Uru. intendencia
clamp (n) abrazadera
 Chi., Par., Uru., Venz.
 abrazadera
 Col. grapa
 Cos.R. prensa
 Mex. pinzas
 Nic. brida
cleft (chin) (n) hendidura
 Chi. labio leporino
 Cos.R. camanance
 Dom.R. hoyito
 Mex., Nic. barba partida
 Per. barbida partida
 Venz. barbilla hendida
click (computer) (v)
 hacer clic
 Col., Cub. pulsar
 Pue.R. apretar
cliff (n) acantilado
 Cub., Pan., Par. precipicio
 Cos.R. barranco
 Mex. barranca
 Nic. guindo
 Pue.R. risco
climbing plant
 (n phr) trepadora
 Bol., Col., Mex., Nic.,
 Pue.R. enredadera

ABBREVIATIONS: Arg.=Argentina Bol.=Bolivia Chi.=Chile Col.=Colombia Cos.R.=Costa Rica
Cub.=Cuba Dom.R.=Dominican Republic Ecu.=Ecuador ElS.=El Salvador Gua.=Guatemala
Hon.=Honduras Mex.=Mexico Nic.=Nicaragua Pan.=Panama Par.=Paraguay Per.=Peru
Pri.=Primary Term Pue.R.=Puerto Rico Spa.=Spain Uru.=Uruguay Venz.=Venezuela

cloak (n) capa
   Col. manto
clogs (n) chanclos
   Arg. ojotas
   Chi. zancos
   Col., Cub., Nic., Spa., Uru.
   zuecos
   Dom.R., Mex., Par., Pue.R.
   suecos
closet (clothes) (n) clóset
   Arg. placard
   Bol., Chi., Cos.R., Ecu.,
   Nic., Par., Uru. ropero
   Pan. estante
   Spa. armario
closet (general) (n) armario
   Chi. guardarropa
   Col., Cos.R., Cub., Mex.,
   Pan., Per. clóset
   Nic. clóset, ropero
   Par. ropero
cloudy (adj) nublado
   Chi. tapado
   Col. cerrado, encapotado
   Cos.R., Cub., Gua.
   cubierto, nuboso
cloverleaf junction
   (n phr) trébol
   Col. confluencia,
   empalme, entronque en
   forma de trébol
   Mex. paso a desnivel
coat (n) saco
   Arg. tapado
   Chi., Pue.R. chaqueta
   Col., Cub., Mex., Nic.,
   Pan., Par., Spa., Venz.
   abrigo
coat, fur (n phr) saco de piel
   Arg. tapado de piel
   Chi., Col., Dom.R., Mex.,
   Nic., Pan., Par., Pue.R., Spa.,
   Venz. abrigo de piel

   Cub. abrigo de pieles
coat, mink (n phr) saco de
   visón
   Arg. tapado de visón
   Col., Mex., Pan., Pue.R.
   abrigo de mink
   Cub., Dom.R., Nic., Spa.,
   Venz. abrigo de visón
cocaine (n) cocaína
   Col., Nic. coca
cocaine spoon (n phr) cuchara
   de cocaína
   Col. cuchara para la
   cocaína
   Mex. grapas de cocaína
   Spa. cuchara para cocaína
cockatoo (n) cacatúa
   Chi. cata
coffee bar (n phr) café
   Col., Nic., Par., Pue.R.,
   Spa. cafetería
   Cos.R. café bar
coffee maker (n phr) cafetera
   Dom.R. greca
coin purse (n phr) monedero
   Dom.R. portamonedas
colander (n) colador
   Bol., Col. coladera
   Cos.R., Dom.R., Mex.,
   Per., Spa., Uru. escurridor
   de verduras
colt (n) potro
   Chi., Nic. potrillo
comb (n) peine
   Chi. peineta
   Col., Ecu., Pan., Pue.R.
   peinilla
commercial (n) anuncio
   Arg. aviso, propaganda
   Chi., Col., Ecu., Par., Per.
   propaganda
   Dom.R., Mex. comercial
   Pan., Venz. comercial,

ABBREVIATIONS: Arg.=Argentina Bol.=Bolivia Chi.=Chile Col.=Colombia Cos.R.=Costa Rica
Cub.=Cuba Dom.R.=Dominican Republic Ecu.=Ecuador ElS.=El Salvador Gua.=Guatemala
Hon.=Honduras Mex.=Mexico Nic.=Nicaragua Pan.=Panama Par.=Paraguay Per.=Peru
Pri.=Primary Term Pue.R.=Puerto Rico Spa.=Spain Uru.=Uruguay Venz.=Venezuela

propaganda
compact disk (n phr) disco
compacto
Arg., Col., Nic., Pan. CD
Spa. CD, compact disk
compact disk player
(n phr) tocadiscos
Arg. equipo de música
para CD
Col. aparato de CD
Cos.R., Nic. CD-player
Cub. reproductor de
compact-disc
Dom.R. CD player,
tocador de discos
compactos
ElS., Gua., Venz.
reproductor de discos
compactos
Mex. tocadiscos para
discos compactos
Par. CD-player,
compactera
Spa. reproductor de CD
comptroller (n) controlador
Cos.R. auditor
Dom.R., Nic. contralor
Venz. interventor
computer (n) computadora
Col. computador
Spa. ordenador
condominium (n) condominios
ElS., Gua., Nic., Pue.R.,
Spa. condominio
conduct (music) (v) dirigir
Col. conducir
conga drum (n phr) conga
Cub. tumbadora
Venz. tambor de conga
consultant (n) consejero
Arg., Col., Mex., Pan.,
Spa. asesor
Chi., Cos.R., Dom.R.,

Ecu., Nic., Par., Per.
consultor
Venz. asesor, consultor
contestant (n) competidor
Chi., Par. concursante
Cub., Pue.R. participante
Nic. candidato,
concursante
contrabassoon (n) contrabajón
Mex. contrafagot
Nic. contrabajo
convertible (n) convertible
Spa. descapotable
cookie (n) galleta
Arg. masita
Chi., Col., Mex., Nic.,
Cos.R., Par., Pue.R., Uru.
galletita
Cub. galletica
ElS., Gua., Hon. galleta
dulce
Per. galleta de dulce
Spa. galleta, pasta
cookie cutters
(n phr) cortadores de
galletas
Arg. moldes
Chi., Dom.R., Venz.
moldes de galletas
Par. molde de galletitas
copier (n) copiadora
Nic., Par., Spa.
fotocopiadora
corkscrew (n) sacacorchos
Chi. destapador
corn (n) maíz
Bol., Chi., Ecu., Per., Uru.
choclo (choclo in Arg. is
sweet corn)
Mex. elote (fresh, on the
cob)
cornet (n) cornetín
Mex., Nic., Par., Spa.

ABBREVIATIONS: Arg.=Argentina Bol.=Bolivia Chi.=Chile Col.=Colombia Cos.R.=Costa Rica
Cub.=Cuba Dom.R.=Dominican Republic Ecu.=Ecuador ElS.=El Salvador Gua.=Guatemala
Hon.=Honduras Mex.=Mexico Nic.=Nicaragua Pan.=Panama Par.=Paraguay Per.=Peru
Pri.=Primary Term Pue.R.=Puerto Rico Spa.=Spain Uru.=Uruguay Venz.=Venezuela

corneta
cottage (n) casa de campo
  Arg. casa, casa-quinta,
  quinta
  Chi. cabaña, chalet
  Col. casita de campo
  Nic. quinta
counselor (n) consejero
  Ecu., Mex., Nic., Spa.
  asesor
counter (n) mostrador
  Arg. mesada
  Pue.R. counter
couple (n) pareja
  Arg. matrimonio
courthouse (n) tribunal de
  justicia
  Col. edificio de los
  tribunales
  Cub., Mex., Pue.R. corte
  Dom.R. palacio de justicia
  Nic. juzgado
  Par. juzgado, tribunal
  Spa. juzgado, palacio de
  justicia
crab (n) cangrejo
  Chi. jaiba, pancora
  Nic. jaiba
  Pan. jaiva
cracker (n) galleta
  Arg. galletita
  Col. galleta saltina
  Dom.R. galletica
  Nic., Venz. galleta de soda
  Par. galletitas saladas
cradle, crib (n) cuna
  Dom.R. catre
cranberry (n) arándano agrio
  Mex. mora roja
  Nic. frutilla
  Pue.R. cranberry
  Venz. cereza agria
crash (vehicle) (v) chocar

  Col. estrellar
crawl (swimming) (n) crawl
  Chi., Nic. estilo libre
  Gua., Spa. estilo crol
  Pue.R., Uru. brazada
crayfish (n) cangrejo de río
  Chi. camarón de agua
  dulce
  Col., Dom.R., Nic. jaiba
  Pue.R. juey
cream puff (n phr) repolla
  Bol., ElS., Gua., Hon., Spa.
  bollo de crema
  Chi. repollito
  Nic. relámpago
  Pan. ecler
  Uru. bomba de crema
  Venz. pastel de crema
creamer (n) cremera
  Arg. lechera
  Nic. jarrita de leche
  Spa. jarrita para leche
crease (pants) (n) raya
  Col. pliego
  Cub., ElS., Gua., Hon.,
  Nic. pliegue
  Dom.R., Pue.R. filo
  Pan. doblez
croissant (n) croissant
  Arg., Col., Par. medialuna
  Chi. media luna
  Dom.R. cruasant, pan
  camarón
  Mex. cuernito
  Per. cachito
crosswalk (n) paso de peatones
  Col., Par. cruce peatonal
  Cub. acera
  Dom.R. cruce de peatones
  Nic. paso peatonal
cuckoo (n) cuco
  Col., Nic.,Venz. cuclillo
  Mex. cucú

ABBREVIATIONS: Arg.=Argentina Bol.=Bolivia Chi.=Chile Col.=Colombia Cos.R.=Costa Rica
Cub.=Cuba Dom.R.=Dominican Republic Ecu.=Ecuador ElS.=El Salvador Gua.=Guatemala
Hon.=Honduras Mex.=Mexico Nic.=Nicaragua Pan.=Panama Par.=Paraguay Per.=Peru
Pri.=Primary Term Pue.R.=Puerto Rico Spa.=Spain Uru.=Uruguay Venz.=Venezuela

Par. cucú, cuculele
cucumber (n) pepino
   Pue.R. pepinillo
cuff (pants) (n) valenciana
   Arg. botamanga
   Bol. botapié
   Col., Spa. doblez
   Dom.R. doblado
   Nic. bastilla
   Pue.R. palasso
   Venz. ruedo doble
cufflinks (n) gemelos
   Chi. colleras
   Col., Ecu. mancornas
   Cub. yugos
   ElS., Gua., Hon., Mex.,
   Nic. mancuernillas
   Pan. mancuernas
   Pue.R., Venz. yuntas
cup (n) copa
   Arg., Col., Ecu., Gua.,
   Mex., Nic., Pan., Par., Per.,
   Spa. taza
cup, coffee (n phr) taza para
   café
   Arg. pocillo, taza de
   café
   Nic. taza de café

curly (hair) (adj) rizado
   Arg., Pan. enrulado
   Bol., Chi., Venz.
   ondulado
   Col. crespo, ondulado
   Dom.R. duro, malo
   Mex. chino
   Nic., Per. crespo
   Par. encrespado,
   enrulado
cute (adj) mono
   Arg. divino
   Bol. amoroso
   Chi. simpático
   Col. primoroso
   Cub. guapo, lindo
   Dom.R., Ecu., Pan.
   gracioso
   Mex. chulo
   ElS., Gua., Hon., Per.,
   Venz. chulo, lindo
   Nic. bonito
   Par. chalina, juky
   Pue.R. bonito, chulito
cutting board (n phr) tabla para
   cortar
   Col., Nic. tabla de cortar
   Pue.R. picador

D

Danish (n) pastelillo de fruta y
nueces
Mex. pan dulce
Nic. danés de frutas
Pan. danesa
Per. pastel
Venz. pastel danés
data (n) datos
Col. información
date (v) tener una cita
Arg. estar de novio
Col. tener compromiso
Dom.R., Gua., Mex., Nic.,
Venz. salir con
daughter or son's father-in-
law
(n phr) consuegro
Uru. suegro
daughter or son's mother-in-
law
(n phr) consuegra
Uru. suegra
daughter-in-law (n) nuera
Pue.R. yerna
daycare center (n phr) guardería
infantil
Arg., Dom.R., Nic.
guardería
Col. jardín infantil
Par. guardería, pre-jardín
Pue.R. nursery
deal (drugs) (v phr) vender
Col., ElS., Gua., Nic.
traficar con
Mex., Venz. traficar
Pue.R. distribuir

dear, darling, honey
(n) querido/a
Arg., Chi., ElS., Gua.,
Hon., Nic. mi amor
Col. amor, amorcito,
tesoro
Cub. amor, cielo
Pan. cariño
Pue.R. amor, vida
debug (computer)
(v) depurar
Dom.R. desinfectar
Pue.R., Venz. limpiar
decanter (n) licorera
Arg. jarra
Col., Nic., Spa. garrafa
Par. decantador
decelerate (v) disminuir la
velocidad
Chi., Dom.R., Nic.,
Pue.R.,
Spa. reducir la velocidad
Col., Cub., Par. desacelerar
deer (n) venado
Arg., Bol., Cos.R., ElS.,
Gua., Hon., Spa., Uru.
ciervo
delay (n) retraso
Arg., Col. demora
Chi., Par. atraso
delete (v) borrar, eliminar
Arg. deletear
demitasse (n) tacita de café
Arg. pocillo, taza de café
Col. tacita
Pue.R. pocillito de café

department store
(n phr) grandes almacenes
Cub. tienda
Col. almacén grande
Cos.R. tienda de
departamentos
Dom.R., ElS., Gua., Hon.,
Nic., Pue.R., Venz. tienda
por departamentos
Mex. tienda departamental
Pan. almacén

departure (n) salida
Chi. embarque

detour (n) desvío
Mex. desviación

dimple (n) hoyuelo
Bol. hoyo
Chi., Dom.R., Mex. hoyito
Cos.R., ElS., Gua., Hon.,
Nic. camanance

dining car (train) (n phr) coche
comedor
Col. vagón-restaurante
Spa. coche restaurante
Venz. carro comedor

dinner (n) cena
Arg., Col., Per., Pue.R.
comida

dipstick (n) indicador del nivel
de aceite
Col., Nic. varilla para
medir el aceite
Pue.R. varilla de aceite
Venz. indicador de medir
el aceite

dishes (n) platos
Pan. trastos, vajilla

dishwasher (n) lavaplatos
Arg. lavavajilla
Col., Cub., Pue.R. lavadora
de platos
Spa. lavavajillas
Uru. lava vajilla

display cabinet (n phr) vitrina
Arg. aparador
Pue.R. chinero
Nic. aparador, chinero

ditch (n) zanja
Col., Nic., Spa. cuneta
Cos.R. sanja
Uru. pozo

diver (n) buceador, buzo
Chi., Par. hombre rana

doctor (n) médico
Arg., Col., Chi., Nic.
doctor

doctor's office
(n phr) consultorio médico
Pue.R. oficina del médico,
oficina del doctor

dog tag (n phr) placa de
identificación
Mex. etiqueta

doghouse (n) perrera
Arg. cucha
Chi., Venz. casa de
perro

door-to-door salesperson
(n phr) vendedor a
domicilio
Col. vendedor puerta a
puerta
Cos.R. representante de
ventas
Nic. vendedor casa por
casa

double chin (n phr) papada
Chi. doble pera
Dom.R. doble barbilla

double feature (movies)
(n phr) doble función
Bol. película doble
Col. doble
Dom.R. doble
presentación
Mex. programa doble

ABBREVIATIONS: Arg.=Argentina Bol.=Bolivia Chi.=Chile Col.=Colombia Cos.R.=Costa Rica
Cub.=Cuba Dom.R.=Dominican Republic Ecu.=Ecuador ElS.=El Salvador Gua.=Guatemala
Hon.=Honduras Mex.=Mexico Nic.=Nicaragua Pan.=Panama Par.=Paraguay Per.=Peru
Pri.=Primary Term Pue.R.=Puerto Rico Spa.=Spain Uru.=Uruguay Venz.=Venezuela

Nic. doble tanda
Spa. sesión de dos
películas seguidas
Uru. función doble
Venz. cine continuado
doughnut (n) donut
Chi. rosca
Col., ElS., Gua., Hon.,
Mex., Pan., Par., Pue.R.
dona
dove (n) paloma
Col. palomo
Pue.R. pichón
dowel (n) clavija
Gua. tarugo
Mex. espiga, pasador
Nic. pasador
downtown (n) centro de la
ciudad
Pue.R. centro del pueblo,
pueblo
dragonfly (n) libélula
Chi. matapiojos
Cub. caballito del diablo
Dom.R. caballito de mar
Pan. caballito
draining spoon (n phr) cuchara
para escurrir
Col. cuchara de escurrir
Par., Spa. espumadera
drawer (n) gaveta
Arg., Chi., Col., Ecu.,
Mex., Nic., Par., Per., Spa.,
Uru. cajón
drawer knob (n phr) perilla
Col. pomo
Dom. R. manubrio
Nic. manigueta
Pan. agarrador
Venz. manilla
dress (woman's) (n) vestido
Arg., Col., Pan. traje
Bol. falda

Cos.R., Uru. pollera
Pue.R. traje de mujer
dress up (v phr) vestirse de
etiqueta
Arg., Nic. arreglarse
Chi., Col. vestirse
elegante
Dom.R. arreglarse,
vestirse formal
Par. arreglarse,
engalanarse
Pue.R. engalanarse
dresser (n) ropero
Arg., Chi., Col., Nic., Per.
cómoda
Cub., Venz. gavetero
Pue.R., Spa. tocador
drill bit (n phr) broca
Col. taladro
Pue.R., Venz. barrena
drill, hand (n phr) taladro de
mano
Arg., Ecu., Per., Spa., Uru.
taladradora de mano
Chi. taladro
Col., Mex. taladro manual
drive (car) (v) manejar
Chi., Col., Pan., Spa.
conducir
Pue.R. guiar
drive (computer) (n) unidad de
disco
Dom. R., Nic., Pue.R.
drive
drive-in (n) motocine
Col., Pue.R. drive-in
Dom.R. auto-cinema
Mex., Nic. autocinema
Pan., Par., Per., Venz.
autocine
driver's license (n phr) licencia
de conducir
Arg. carnet de conductor,

ABBREVIATIONS: Arg.=Argentina Bol.=Bolivia Chi.=Chile Col.=Colombia Cos.R.=Costa Rica
Cub.=Cuba Dom.R.=Dominican Republic Ecu.=Ecuador ElS.=El Salvador Gua.=Guatemala
Hon.=Honduras Mex.=Mexico Nic.=Nicaragua Pan.=Panama Par.=Paraguay Per.=Peru
Pri.=Primary Term Pue.R.=Puerto Rico Spa.=Spain Uru.=Uruguay Venz.=Venezuela

permiso de conductor
Chi. carnet de chofer
Col. pase para conducir
Cub., Venz. licensia de
manejar
Nic. licencia de manejar
Par. registro de conducir
Spa. carné de conducir
driver's seat
(n phr) asiento del
conductor
Chi., Nic. asiento del
chofer, asiento del piloto
Cub. asiento del
chofer
drizzle (n) llovizna
Col. lluvia tenue
Nic. brisa
Per. garúa
drug abuse (n phr) toxicomanía
Col., Cub., Dom.R., Nic.,
Par., Pue.R. abuso de
drogas
drug addict (n phr) drogadicto
Col. narcómano
drug addiction
(n phr) drogadicción
Col. narcomanía
Pue.R. adicción a las
drogas
drug deal (n phr) transacción de
drogas
Col., Dom.R., Gua., Nic.,
Spa., Uru. tráfico de drogas
Ecu., Venz. negocio de
drogas
Pue.R. negociación
drug dealer (n phr) traficante
de drogas
Bol., Cos.R., Cub.,
Nic.,Venz. narcotraficante
drug habit (n phr) drogadicción
Col. narcomanía

Cub. vicio de drogas
drug store (n phr) farmacia
Col. botica, droguería
Ecu., Per. botica
drug test (n phr) prueba anti-
doping
Col., Uru., Venz. prueba
anti-drogas
Cub., Mex., Pue.R.
prueba de drogas
Nic. prueba antidrogas
Pan. prueba para drogas
drug user (n phr) consumidor
de drogas
Pue.R. usuario de drogas
drum (n) tambor
Dom.R., Nic. batería
drum, tap (v) tamborilear
Col., Spa. tocar el tambor
drummer (n) tamborilero
Col. el que toca el tambor,
tambor
Dom.R. baterista
Nic. baterista, batero
(colloq), bataca (colloq)

drunk driving (v phr) manejar
borracho
Arg., Pue.R. conducir en
estado de embriaguez
Chi., Nic. manejar en
estado de ebriedad
Col. manejar embriagado
Cos.R. manejar tomado
Dom.R. manejar en estado
de embriaguez
Spa. conducir borracho,
conducir ebrio
drunkard (n) borracho
Col. beodo, borrachín
Dom.R. borrachón
dry cleaner's (n phr) tintorería
Col., Dom.R., Nic.

lavandería
   Pue.R. laundry
dryer (n) secadora
   Arg. secarropas
   Pue.R. secadora de
   ropa
duo (n) dúo

   Col. dueto
duplex (n) dúplex
   Chi. casa pareada
   Dom.R., Pue.R. casa
   dúplex
   Nic. casa doble

E

ear (n) oreja
   Col., Mex., Nic. oído
earrings (n) aretes
   Arg., Par. aros
   Nic. chapas (colloq)
   Pue.R. pantallas
   Spa. pendientes
   Venz. zarcillos
earrings, clip (n phr) aretes de
   presión
   Arg., Par. aros de presión
   Nic. aretes de prensar
   Pue.R. pantallas de clips
   Spa. pendientes de clip
   Venz. zarcillos de presión
earrings, drop
   (n phr) pendientes
   Arg. aros colgantes
   Spa. pendientes largos
earrings, pierced (n phr) aretes
   de espiga
   Arg. aros de agujero
   Dom.R. aretes de hoyito
   Nic. aretes de meter
   Pue.R. pantallas de gancho
   Spa. pendientes de tornillo
   Venz. zarcillos
earrings, screw (n phr) aretes de
   tornillo
   Arg. aros de tornillo
   Spa. pendientes de tornillo
   Venz. zarcillos de tornillo
earthquake (n) terremoto
   Chi., Mex., Nic. temblor
   Col. sismo
   Dom.R., Pue.R. temblor de

tierra
easel (n) caballete
   Chi., Col., Spa. atril
editor (n) redactor
   Col., Nic., Par., Pue.R.,
   Spa., Venz. editor
egg beater (n phr) batidor
   manual
   Chi., Nic., Pue.R. batidora
   Ecu. batidor de mano
   Par. batidor
elevator (n) ascensor
   Cub., Mex., Nic., Pan.,
   Pue.R. elevador
e-mail (n) correo electrónico
   Arg., Dom.R., Mex.,
   Pue.R., Spa. e-mail
emergency lights (n phr) luces
   de emergencia
   Arg. balizas
   Ecu. faros de emergencia
   Pue.R. luces intermitentes
encrypt (computer) (v) ocultar
   Col., Mex., Spa. encriptar
   Par. codificar
   Uru. cifrar
   Venz. cifrar, codificar
endive (n) escarola
   Arg., Col., Spa. endibia
   Col., Par. endivia
   Nic. achicoria
English horn (n phr) corno
   inglés
   Col. cuerno inglés
   Nic. corneta inglesa
entrance fee (n phr) entrada

Col. precio de la entrada
Nic., Pue.R., Venz. precio
de entrada
escalator (n) escalera mecánica
Col. escalera automática
Dom.R., Mex. escalera
eléctrica
exhaust pipe (n phr) tubo de
escape
Arg., Par. caño de
Col. exosto
Mex., Nic. escape

expressway (n) autopista
escape
Mex. vía rápida
Nic., Spa. carretera
eyeglasses (n) anteojos
Col. gafas, lentes
Cub., Pue.R.
espejuelos
Dom.R., Ecu., Pan., Par.,
Per., Venz. lentes
Spa. gafas

ABBREVIATIONS: Arg.=Argentina Bol.=Bolivia Chi.=Chile Col.=Colombia Cos.R.=Costa Rica
Cub.=Cuba Dom.R.=Dominican Republic Ecu.=Ecuador EIS.=El Salvador Gua.=Guatemala
Hon.=Honduras Mex.=Mexico Nic.=Nicaragua Pan.=Panama Par.=Paraguay Per.=Peru
Pri.=Primary Term Pue.R.=Puerto Rico Spa.=Spain Uru.=Uruguay Venz.=Venezuela

F

factory (n) fábrica
  Col. empresa, industria
  Dom.R., Pue.R. factoría
fairground (n) parque de
    atracciones
  Col. terreno para ferias
  Dom.R., Ecu. parque de
    diversiones
  Mex., Nic. feria
  Pue.R. feria, parque de
    diversiones
family member (n phr) familiar
  Arg., Chi., Ecu., Mex.,
    Nic., Par., Pue.R., Venz.
    pariente
  Col. miembro de la familia
fan belt (n phr) correa del
    ventilador
  Mex. banda del ventilador
  Pue.R. correa del abánico
farmer (n) agricultor
  Chi. ganadero
  Col. campesino
  Par. campesino, granjero
  Per. granjero
father (n) padre
  Arg., Col. papá
  Mex. papá, papi
  Nic. papa
fender (n) ala
  Arg., Par. paragolpes
  Col., Spa. guardabarro
  Cub., Ecu., ElS., Gua.,
    Venz. guardafango
  Mex. defensa
  Nic. guardabarro, lodera
  Pan. bumper trasero

  Pue.R. fender
ferris wheel (n phr) noria
  Chi., Cub. rueda gigante
  Col., Par. rueda de
    Chicago
  Dom.R., Pan. estrella
  Ecu. rueda muscovita
  Mex. rueda de la fortuna
  Nic. chicagua, rueda de
    Chicago
  Venz. rueda
ferry (n) transbordador
  Col., Cos.R., Dom.R.,
    Nic., Spa., Venz. ferry
  Cub. lancha
fiancé (male) (n) novio
  Col., Cos.R., Dom.R.,
    Nic., Pan., Par. prometido
  Mex. comprometido
fiancée (female) (n) novia
  Col., Cos.R., Dom.R.,
    Nic., Pan., Par. prometida
  Mex. comprometida
field (sports) (n) campo
  Col. cancha deportiva
  Nic., Par. cancha
file cabinet (n phr) archivo
  Chi. archivador
  Col. gavetero
  Mex., Par. archivero
film (n) película
  Arg., Cos.R., Ecu., Uru.,
    Pan. filme
  Chi., Col., Cub. cinta
  Venz. film
fire (v) despedir
  Arg., Col. echar

Cub., Dom.R botar
fire station (n phr) estación de
bomberos
Bol., Cos.R., Ecu., Spa.,
Uru. parque de bomberos
Mex. departamento de
bomberos
firefly (n) luciérnaga
Cub. cocuyo
Pue.R. cucubano
fireplace (n) chimenea
Arg. estufa, hogar
first class (adj phr) primera
clase
Arg. primera
flat tire (n phr) llanta reventada
Arg., Dom.R. goma
pinchada
Bol., Col. llanta pinchada
Chi. pneumático pinchado
Cos.R., Per. llanta
desinflada
Cub. goma ponchada
Ecu. tubo bajo
Gua. llanta pache, llanta
pinchada
Mex. llanta pinchada, llanta
ponchada
Nic. llanta ponchada
Pan. flat
Pue.R. goma vacía
Spa. neumático pinchado,
rueda pinchada
Venz. caucho pinchado
Uru. llanta desinflada,
neumático desinflado
flight attendant (n phr) auxiliar
de vuelo, azafata
Col. cabinera
Cub., Nic., Pan., Venz.
aeromozo/a
Mex. aeromosa
float (parade) (n) carroza

Chi. carro alegórico
Dom.R. balsa, flotador
flock (n) rebaño
Arg. bandada
Chi. piño
Col. manada
florist's shop (n phr) florista
Col., Dom.R., Nic., Pan.,
Pue.R., Venz. floristería
Cub., Par. florería
flounder (n) lenguado, platija
Gua. róbalo
flower bed (n phr) macizo
Arg. cantero
Bol. macetero
Gua. arriate de flores
Mex. cama de flores
Nic. jardinera
fly (pants) (n) bragueta
Chi. marrueco
Cub., Nic. portañuela
Dom.R. ziper
Par. cierre
Pue.R. zipper
foal (n) potro
Col., Nic., Venz. potrillo
fog (n) niebla
Arg., Cub., Dom.R., Mex.,
Nic., Per. neblina
Chi. camanchaca
Col. bruma, neblina
folder (n) carpeta de archivo
Bol. archivador
Dom.R., Mex., Nic., Pan.,
Pue.R. folder
Spa. archivadora, carpeta
foliage (n) follaje
Col. espesura, frondosidad
formal wear (n phr) ropa formal
Dom.R. ropa de vestir
Mex. ropa de etiqueta
four-four, common time
(n phr) compás mayor

ABBREVIATIONS: Arg.=Argentina Bol.=Bolivia Chi.=Chile Col.=Colombia Cos.R.=Costa Rica
Cub.=Cuba Dom.R.=Dominican Republic Ecu.=Ecuador ElS.=El Salvador Gua.=Guatemala
Hon.=Honduras Mex.=Mexico Nic.=Nicaragua Pan.=Panama Par.=Paraguay Per.=Peru
Pri.=Primary Term Pue.R.=Puerto Rico Spa.=Spain Uru.=Uruguay Venz.=Venezuela

Nic., Spa. compás de
cuatro por cuatro
four-wheel drive
(n phr) propulsión total
Arg., Chi., Gua., Mex.
tracción en las cuatro
ruedas
Col. tracción en las cuatro
ruedas, 4x4
Cub., Venz. tracción de
quatro ruedas
Dom.R. cuatro tracciónes
Nic. doble tracción
Par., Pue.R. 4x4
Spa. tracción a las cuatro
ruedas
fox (n) zorro
Pan. zorra
frame (movie) (n phr) imagen
Col. marco
Nic. cuadro
free admission (n phr) entrada
libre
Chi., Cub., Dom.R., ElS.,
Gua., Nic., Pan., Pue.R.
entrada gratis
Spa. entrada gratuita
freezer (n) congelador
Arg., Par., Pue.R. freezer
Bol. refrigerador
Nic. freezer, mantenedora

French fries (n phr) papas fritas
Dom.R. papitas fritas
Spa. patatas fritas
Nic. corneta francesa
Spa. trompa de pistones
fringe benefit (n phr) incentivo
Col. beneficio adicional
Cos.R. beneficio laborable
ElS., Gua. prestación
complementaria
Nic. prestaciones sociales
fruit stand (n phr) puesto de
frutas
Pue.R. frutería
fruit tree (n phr) árbol frutal
Arg. frutal
Pue.R. árbol de frutas
full-time (work) (adj) de
jornada completa
Arg. de horario completo
Col., Mex., Nic. de tiempo
completo
Cub., Dom.R., Venz. a
tiempo completo
funeral home (n phr) funeraria
Chi., Cub., Ecu., Per., Uru.
funerario
Spa. tanatorio
funicular (n) funicular
Mex., Venz. teleférico

G

game show (television)
(n phr) programa concurso
Arg. programa de
entretenimientos
Col. programa de
concurso
Cos.R. concurso
televisivo
Dom.R., Gua., Mex.,
Nic.,Venz. programa de
concursos
garage (repairs) (n) garaje
Arg. taller mecánico
Col., Nic. taller
Par. taller, taller mecánico
garage (storage) (n) garaje
Dom.R. marquesina
garbage collector
(n phr) basurero
Col., Venz. recogedor de
basura
Nic. recolector de basura
garment (n) vestido
Arg. prenda
Cub. vestidura
ElS., Gua., Nic., Spa.
prenda de vestir
Mex. ropa, traje
gas (vehicle) (n) gasolina
Arg., Par. nafta
gas pedal (n phr) acelerador
Pue.R. pedal de la gasolina
Venz. pedal de gasolina
gas tank (n phr) tanque de
gasolina
Arg. tanque de nafta

Spa. depósito de gasolina
gearbox (n) caja de cambios
ElS., Gua., Mex., Nic. caja
de velocidades
Pue.R. transmisión
gears (n) velocidades
Arg., Chi., Cub., Dom.R.,
Nic., Pan., Pue.R., Uru.,
Venz. cambios
Cos.R. marchas
get high (drugs)
(v phr) colocarse
Bol., Per. volar
Chi. volarse
Col. sollarse
Cub. cojer nota
Dom.R. darse un viaje,
ponerse high
Mex. tocarse, traer un
alucine
Nic. ponerse en onda
Pue.R. elevarse, tripear
Venz. meterse un viaje
get off (bus) (v phr) bajarse
Bol., Cos.R., Dom.R., Per.,
Uru. apearse
get on (bus) (v phr) subirse
Col. montarse
girl (n) niña
Arg., Uru. chica, nena
Col. pelada, sardina
Dom.R. muchachita
Mex. chamaca
Nic. chavala, cipota
Par. nena
girlfriend (n) novia

Chi. polola
Ecu., Per. enamorada
give birth (v phr) dar a luz
Arg. tener un/a beba/bebe/
bebé/hijo/hija
Col. alumbrar, parir
Cos.R., Dom.R., Nic., Pan.
parir
glasses, opera (n phr) gemelos
de teatro
Col. binoculares,
binóculos
Cub. anteojos de teatro
Nic. binoculares
Venz. lentes de ópera
glasses, safety (n phr) anteojos
de camino
Chi. anteojos de seguridad
Mex. gafas de protección
Nic. protectores
Pue.R. anteojos de
protección
Spa. gafas de seguridad
Venz. lentes protectores
gloomy (person) (adj) lúgubre
Col. sombrío
Dom.R. de mal humor
Mex. triste
Nic. decaído, triste
Venz. deprimido
goalie (n) portero
Arg., Chi., Par., Per.
arquero
Col. guarda-vallas
Cub. guardameta
Pan. goleador
Pue.R. porteador
Uru. golero
goatee (n) barbas de chivo
Col. candado, chivera
Dom.R. chiva, chivita
Ecu. chivita
Spa. perilla

Venz. chiva
goggles, ski (n phr) anteojos
para esquiar
Arg. antiparras
Mex. gogles para esquiar
Spa. gafas de esquí
goggles, swimming
(n phr) anteojos para nadar
Arg. antiparras
Mex. gogles
Pue.R. goggles
Spa. gafas de buceo
golf ball (n phr) pelota de golf
Col., Mex., Pue.R. bola de
golf
golf club (n phr) palo de golf
Col. taco de golf
Pan. club de golf
golf course (n phr) campo de
golf
Arg. cancha de golf
Good evening! (int phr) ¡Buenas
tardes!
Col., Ecu., Nic. ¡Buenas
noches!
Good morning! (int phr) ¡Buenos
días!
Arg. ¡Buen día!
Good night! (int phr) ¡Buenas
noches!
Ecu. ¡Hasta mañana!
Goodbye! (int) ¡Adiós!
Arg., Par. ¡Chau!
Chi. ¡Chao!
Col. ¡Hasta luego!
Dom.R., Nic. ¡Bye!
goose (n) ganso
Col. gansa
gooseberry (n) grosella
silvestre
Nic., Pue.R. grosella
grapefruit (n) toronja
Arg., Chi., Par., Spa., Uru.

ABBREVIATIONS: Arg.=Argentina Bol.=Bolivia Chi.=Chile Col.=Colombia Cos.R.=Costa Rica
Cub.=Cuba Dom.R.=Dominican Republic Ecu.=Ecuador ElS.=El Salvador Gua.=Guatemala
Hon.=Honduras Mex.=Mexico Nic.=Nicaragua Pan.=Panama Par.=Paraguay Per.=Peru
Pri.=Primary Term Pue.R.=Puerto Rico Spa.=Spain Uru.=Uruguay Venz.=Venezuela

pomelo
  Nic. grapefruit
grass (n) hierba
  Chi. césped, pasto
  Col., Mex., Par., Per. pasto
  Nic. grama
  Pue.R. yerba
grater (n) rallador
  Col. rallo
  Dom.R. guallo
  Pue.R. guayo
gray (hair) (adj) canoso
  Col. canas
  Spa. blanco
green (eyes) (adj) verde
  Col. ojiverde
  Cos.R., Nic. gato
griddle (n) asador eléctrico
  Col., Pan. sartén
  eléctrica
  Spa. plancha
grocer (n) tendero
  Arg., Par., Uru.
  almacenero
  Col. comerciante
  Cub. bodeguero
  Dom.R. dependiente de
  colmado/supermercado/
  tienda
  Ecu., Mex. abarrotero
  Nic. pulpero
grocery (n phr) tienda de
  comestibles
  Arg., Par., Uru. almacén
  Col. mercado
  Cos.R. compras
  Cub., Per. bodega

Dom.R. bodega,
supercolmado, víveres
ElS., Nic. pulpería
Gua. tienda
Mex. super, tienda de
abarrotes
Pan. abarrotería, tienda
Pue.R. colmado
Spa. supermercado
Venz. abastos, supermercado
ground floor (n phr) planta baja
  Col. piso de abajo, primer
  piso
  Dom.R. primer piso
grow up (v phr) crecer
  Col., Par. madurar
grumpy (adj) malhumorado
  Chi. andar de malas
  pulgas
  Col. gruñón
  Nic. cascarrabias, gruñón
  Pue.R. de mal humor
  Venz. cascarrabias
guardian (n) tutor
  Col., Pan., Venz. guardián
guy (n) muchacho, tipo
  Arg. pibe
  Chi. cabro
  Cos.R. fulano/a, mae
  Cub., Pue.R. chico
  Mex., Pan. fulano/a
  Nic. maje
guys (dual gender plural)
  (n) muchachos, tipos
  Arg., Ecu. chicos
  Chi. cabros, chiquillos
  Nic. majes

ABBREVIATIONS: Arg.=Argentina Bol.=Bolivia Chi.=Chile Col.=Colombia Cos.R.=Costa Rica
Cub.=Cuba Dom.R.=Dominican Republic Ecu.=Ecuador ElS.=El Salvador Gua.=Guatemala
Hon.=Honduras Mex.=Mexico Nic.=Nicaragua Pan.=Panama Par.=Paraguay Per.=Peru
Pri.=Primary Term Pue.R.=Puerto Rico Spa.=Spain Uru.=Uruguay Venz.=Venezuela

H

habit (n) vicio
  Col., Nic., Par. hábito
hacksaw (n) sierra de metal
  Col. sierra para cortar
  metal
  Cub., Nic. serrucho
  Mex., Spa. sierra para
  metal
  Pue.R. segueta
  Venz. serrucho, sierra para
  metales
hair (n) cabello, pelo
  Arg. vello
  Col. cabellera
hair dryer (n phr) secadora
  manual
  Arg., Par. secador
  Chi., Spa., Venz. secador
  de pelo
  Cub., Nic. secadora de
  pelo
  Dom.R., Pue.R. blower
  Mex. pistola de pelo,
  secadora de pelo
hair gel (n phr) gel para el pelo
  Dom.R., ElS., Gua.
  gelatina para el pelo
  Ecu. gel fijador
  Mex. jalea
  Spa. gomina para el pelo
hair mousse (n phr) mousse
  para el pelo
  Dom.R. mus para el pelo
  ElS., Gua., Spa. espuma
  para el pelo
  Mex. mouse para el pelo
hair rollers (n phr) ruleros

Chi. ondulines
  Col., Spa. rulos
  Cub., Pue.R. rolos
  ElS., Gua., Mex. tubos
  Nic. rollos, tubos
  Pan., Venz. rollos
hairdresser (n) peluquero/a
  Col. barbero
  Mex., Nic., Pan. estilista
hairdresser's shop
  (n phr) peluquería
  Dom.R., Mex., Nic., Pan.
  salón de belleza
  Pue.R. beauty parlor, salón
  de belleza
hairspray (n) laca para el pelo
  Cub., Nic. espray de pelo
  Dom.R., Mex., Pan. spray
  para el pelo
  Par., Pue.R. spray de pelo
hairy (adj) velloso
  Arg., Chi., Col., Par.,
  Pue.R., Spa., Venz. peludo
  Bol., Dom.R., Ecu., Pan.,
  Uru. velludo
  Nic. mechudo, peludo
half brother (n phr) medio
  hermano
  Chi., Nic., Spa.
  hermanastro
half sister (n phr) media
  hermana
  Chi., Nic., Spa.
  hermanastra
half-glasses (n) media luna
  Mex. lentes para leer
  Par. bifocales

ABBREVIATIONS: Arg.=Argentina Bol.=Bolivia Chi.=Chile Col.=Colombia Cos.R.=Costa Rica Cub.=Cuba Dom.R.=Dominican Republic Ecu.=Ecuador ElS.=El Salvador Gua.=Guatemala Hon.=Honduras Mex.=Mexico Nic.=Nicaragua Pan.=Panama Par.=Paraguay Per.=Peru Pri.=Primary Term Pue.R.=Puerto Rico Spa.=Spain Uru.=Uruguay Venz.=Venezuela

Venz. medios-lentes
hammock (n) hamaca
   Venz. chinchorro
handbag (n) cartera
   Col., Cos.R., Gua., Mex.,
   Pan. bolsa de mano
   Dom.R. bolso
   Spa., Venz. bolso de mano
handball (n) handbol
   ElS., Gua., Nic. balonmano
   Spa. pelota vasca
   Uru. pelota de mano
handlebar grips (bicycle)
   (n phr) puños
   Col. manillas
   Gua., Nic., Venz.
   agarraderas del manubrio
   Par., Per. mangos
handlebars (bicycle) (n) guía
   Arg., Bol., Chi., Col.,
   Mex., Nic., Par., Pue.R.,
   Venz. manubrio
   Cub., Dom.R., Pan. timón
   Ecu. manubrios
   Gua. manubrio, timón
   Spa., Uru. manillar
handsome (adj) hermoso, guapo
   Arg. buen mozo
   Bol., Par. churro
   Chi., Dom.R. buenmozo
   Col. churro, pinta
   Venz. bien parecido
hard drive (n phr) disco duro
   Pue.R. hard drive
hard drugs (n phr) drogas duras
   Col. drogas fuertes,
   drogas tóxicas
   Nic., Par. drogas fuertes
hard liquor (n phr) licor
   espiritoso
   Bol., Dom.R., Nic., Venz.
   licor fuerte
   Col. licor de alto

contenido alcohólico
   ElS., Pan. licor
   Mex., Par. bebidas fuertes
   Spa. bebida alcohólica
   fuerte
   Uru. bebida alcohólica
hare (n) liebre
   Pue.R. conejo
hat, top (n phr) sombrero de
   copa
   Arg. galera
hatchet (n) hacha
   Col. hachuela
hawk (n) halcón
   Bol. alcón
   Chi. peuco
hazelnut (n) avellana
   Dom.R. coquito
headboard (n) cabecera
   Ecu., Nic. espaldar
   Pue.R. espaldal
headlights (n) faros
   Arg. focos, luces
   Chi., Pan., Pue.R. luces
   Col. faroles delanteros
   Cub. focos
   Dom.R., Mex., Venz. luces
   delanteras
   Nic. focos delanteros
head-on collision
   (n phr) choque de frente
   Col. colisión frente a
   frente
   Nic., Spa., Uru. choque
   frontal
   Per. choque frente a frente
hedge (n) seto
   Col., Nic. matorral
   Mex. cercado de arbustos
heel (shoe) (n) taco
   Col., Cub., Gua., Hon.,
   Mex., Nic., Pan., Spa.,
   Venz. tacón

heel, high (shoe) (n phr) taco
  alto
  Col., Cub., ElS., Gua.,
  Hon., Mex., Nic., Pan.,
  Spa., Venz. tacón alto
Hello? (answering telephone)
  (int) ¿Dígame?
  Arg., Bol., Par. ¿Hola?
  Cub. ¿Oigo?
  Col., Cos.R., Dom.R.,
  Ecu., ElS., Gua., Hon.,
  Nic., Per., Venz. ¿Aló?
  Mex. ¿Bueno?
  Pan., Pue.R. ¿Haló?
  Uru. ¿Aló?, ¿Hola?
herbalist's shop (n) botánica
  Col. tienda botánica
  Mex., Nic. tienda naturista
  Par. tienda naturalista
  Spa. tienda de botánica
  Uru. herbolario
hibiscus (n) hibisco
  Nic. flor de avispa
  Pan. papo
high jump (n phr) salto de altura
  Chi., Col., ElS., Gua.,
  Hon., Nic., Par. salto alto
  Pue.R. salto a lo alto
hill (n) colina
  Chi. cerro, loma
  Cub., Pan. loma
  Nic., Par. cerro
  Pue.R. cuesta
hit (song) (n) canción de moda
  Col. éxito
  Cos.R. , Nic. éxito, hit
  Dom.R. hit
hitchhike (v) hacer autostop
  Arg., Chi., Par. hacer dedo
  Col. echar dedo
  Cos.R., Nic. pedir ride
  Dom.R. pedir bola
  ElS., Gua., Hon. pedir

  jalón a dedo
  Per. tirar dedo
  Pue.R. pedir pon
  Venz. pedir cola
hoe (n) azada
  Bol. azador
  Col., Pan. asadón
  Dom.R., Gua., Nic. azadón
  Mex. talacho
  Venz. azadón, pico
hole in one (n phr) hoyo en uno
  Pue.R. bola en uno
holiday (n) día feriado
  Arg., Nic. feriado
  Col., Spa. día festivo
  Mex. día de fiesta, día de
  vacaciones
hood (n) capucha
  Chi. capuchón
  Cub. caperuza
horizontal bar (n phr) barra fija
  Col., Nic., Pan., Par.,
  Pue.R., Venz. barra
  horizontal
horseback riding
  (n phr) equitación
  Col., Par. cabalgar,
  montar a caballo
  Cub. ir a caballo
  Nic. montar a caballo
horsefly, gadfly (n) tábano
  Col. moscardón
  Pue.R. caballito de San
  Pedro
hospital (n) hospital
  Col. clínica
host (show) (n) presentador
  Col. animador
  Dom.R., Mex., Venz.
  anfitrión/a
  Per. maestro de
  ceremonias
hot air balloon (n phr) globo

ABBREVIATIONS: Arg.=Argentina Bol.=Bolivia Chi.=Chile Col.=Colombia Cos.R.=Costa Rica
Cub.=Cuba Dom.R.=Dominican Republic Ecu.=Ecuador ElS.=El Salvador Gua.=Guatemala
Hon.=Honduras Mex.=Mexico Nic.=Nicaragua Pan.=Panama Par.=Paraguay Per.=Peru
Pri.=Primary Term Pue.R.=Puerto Rico Spa.=Spain Uru.=Uruguay Venz.=Venezuela

aerostático
Chi., Col., Nic. globo
Venz. globo de aire
caliente
house robe (n phr) túnica
Col. vestido casero
Cub., Dom.R., Spa., Venz.
bata de casa
Nic., Par. bata
Pan. bata de estar en casa
How's it going? (phr) ¿Cómo te
(le) va?
Arg., Mex., Pue.R., Uru.
¿Qué tal?
Bol. ¿Cómo estás?
Dom.R. ¿Cómo tú estás?
Ecu. ¿Qué ha habido?,
¿Qué tal?
Nic. ¿Qué tal? ¿Cómo
estás?
hubcap (n) tambora
Chi. taparuedas
Col. copa de la rueda
Ecu., Spa. tabacubo
Mex. tapón
Nic. plato
Pan. rin
Pue.R. tapabocina
Uru. embellecedor
Venz. taza del caucho

hum (n) zumbido
Col. susurro
hummingbird (n) colibrí
Arg., Col., Pan. picaflor
Ecu. chupaflor
hurdles race (n phr) vallas
Chi. obstáculos
Col. competencia de
obstáculos
Cub., Dom.R., ElS., Gua.,
Hon., Nic., Venz. carrera
de obstáculos
hurricane (n) huracán
Dom.R. ciclón
husband (n) esposo, marido
Col. compañero,
cónyuge, pareja
hut (n) choza
Arg. albergue, cabaña,
casilla
Dom.R. casita de paja
hydrofoil boat (n phr) hidroala
Chi., Nic., Par. hidroavión
Col. aereodeslizador
Mex. hidrofoil
hymn (n) cántico
Bol., Col., Dom.R., Mex.,
Nic., Par., Spa., Venz.
himno
Pue.R. canción, himno

ABBREVIATIONS: Arg.=Argentina Bol.=Bolivia Chi.=Chile Col.=Colombia Cos.R.=Costa Rica
Cub.=Cuba Dom.R.=Dominican Republic Ecu.=Ecuador ElS.=El Salvador Gua.=Guatemala
Hon.=Honduras Mex.=Mexico Nic.=Nicaragua Pan.=Panama Par.=Paraguay Per.=Peru
Pri.=Primary Term Pue.R.=Puerto Rico Spa.=Spain Uru.=Uruguay Venz.=Venezuela

I

ice bucket (n) balde de hielo
　　Dom.R., Ecu., Gua., Mex.,
　　Par., Venz. hielera
　　Nic., Pue.R. cubeta de
　　hielo
ice cream parlor
　　(n phr) heladería
　　Mex. nevería
　　Nic. sorbetería
ice cream truck
　　(n phr) heladero
　　Col. camión del helado,
　　carrito de helados
　　Mex. carro de helados
　　Nic. carrito de helados
　　Par. camión de helados
　　Spa. camión del helado
ice skating (n phr) patinaje
　　sobre hielo
　　Chi., Cub. patinaje en hielo
　　Col. patinaje en el hielo
iceberg (n) iceberg
　　Chi. témpano de hielo
icing syringe (n) jeringuilla de
　　decoración
　　Col. jeringuilla para
　　decorar
　　Nic. decorador de pasteles
　　Venz. decorador para
　　pasteleros
icon (computer) (n) ícono
　　Cub. símbolo gráfico
　　Pue.R. icon
impolite (adj) descortés, mal
　　educado
　　Col. grosero

Nic. malcriado,
　　maleducado
　　Spa. maleducado
index card (n phr) ficha
　　Col., Pue.R. tarjeta
infant (n) niño/a
　　Arg., Uru. chico/a, nene/a
　　Col., Gua., Par. criatura
　　Cub., Mex., Spa. bebé
　　Nic. bebé, nene
infomercial (n) comercial
　　informativa
　　Col. anuncio informativo,
　　programa comercial para
　　promocionar algo
　　Cos.R. boletín informativo
　　Nic. comercial
　　Spa. telepromoción
　　Uru. información de
　　interés
inhale (drugs) (v phr) aspirar
　　Arg., Col., Mex., Nic.,
　　Pue.R. inhalar
　　Cub., Dom.R. oler
inmate (n) preso
　　Col. prisionero, recluso
　　Nic. recluso
　　Pan. reo
inner tube (bicycle tire)
　　(n phr) tubo
　　Chi., Par., Spa. cámara
　　Cos.R., Nic. neumático
　　Venz. tripa del caucho
instructor (sports) (n) instructor
　　de deportes
　　Arg., Bol., Chi., Cub., Nic.

---

entrenador
Col. instructor
deportivo
Pue.R. maestro de
educación física
Venz. entrenador de
deportes
interviewee (n) entrevistado/a
Arg., Cos.R., Cub., Ecu.,
ElS., Gua., Hon., Per. Pue.R.

encuestado/a
interviewer (n)
entrevistador/a
Arg., Cos.R., Cub., Ecu.,
Pue.R. encuestado/a
ElS., Gua., Hon., Per.,
Pue.R. encuestador/a
iris (n) lirio
Nic., Par., Venz. iris

J

jack (car) (n) gato
    Bol., Chi., Nic., Per. gata
    Gua. triquet
jacket (n) chaqueta
    Arg. campera
    Dom.R., Pan. saco
    Mex., Nic. chamarra
    Per. casca
    Pue.R. blazer (women),
    gabán (men)
jam session (n phr) descarga
    Chi., Nic. ensayo
    Col. sesión de música
    improvisado
    Pue.R. jameo
    Spa. jam session
janitor (n) conserje
    Chi. limpiador
    Cub. barrendero
jaw (n) mandíbula
    Col., Nic. quijada
jazz music (n phr) música jazz
    Col., Nic. música de jazz
    Dom.R., Spa. jazz

jersey (n) jersey
    Bol. saco
    Col. chompa
    Mex. playera de punto
    Nic.,Venz. suéter
jet (n) jet
    Chi. avión a chorro
jet-lag, to have (phr) tener jet
    lag
    Dom.R. estar desorientado
    por desfase de horarios
    Mex. sentirse mal por la
    altura, sentirse mal por el
    vuelo
    Nic., Spa. tener desfase
    horario
joint (n) articulación
    Dom.R., Spa. coyuntura
journalist (n) periodista
    Col. corresponsal,
    redactor, reportero
jungle (n) selva
    Chi., Col., Dom.R., Pue.R.,
    Venz. jungla

K

kettle (n) marmita
   Arg., Uru. pava
   Bol. caldera
   Chi., Col., Per., Spa.
   tetera
   Cub. caldero
   Ecu. cantina de agua
   Mex. olla grande
   Nic. jarrilla
key (music) (n) tono
   Col. tonalidad
keyboard (computer)
   (n) teclado
   Pue.R. keyboard
kid (n) chico/a

   Cub. chiquito/a
   Col. niño/a, peladito/a
   Dom.R. muchacho/a
kiwi (n) kiwi
   Uru. quivi
knife, butter (n phr) cuchillo para
   mantequilla
   Arg. cuchillo para manteca
knife sharpener (n phr) afilador de
   cuchillo
   Dom.R. amolador
knit shirt (n phr) polo
   Dom.R., Pan. suéter
   Mex. playera
   Per. camiseta

ABBREVIATIONS: Arg.=Argentina Bol.=Bolivia Chi.=Chile Col.=Colombia Cos.R.=Costa Rica Cub.=Cuba Dom.R.=Dominican Republic Ecu.=Ecuador ElS.=El Salvador Gua.=Guatemala Hon.=Honduras Mex.=Mexico Nic.=Nicaragua Pan.=Panama Par.=Paraguay Per.=Peru Pri.=Primary Term Pue.R.=Puerto Rico Spa.=Spain Uru.=Uruguay Venz.=Venezuela

L

label (n) etiqueta
  Dom.R., Pue.R. label
label, adhesive (n phr) etiqueta
  adhesiva
  Dom.R., Pue.R. label
  adhesiva
ladybug (n) mariquita
  Arg. vaquita de San Antonio
  Chi. chinita
  Mex. catarina
  Par. escarabajo
  Venz. coquito
LAN (local area network)
  (n phr) LAN
  Mex. red local LAN
  Par., Spa., Venz. red de área
  local
lane (n) carril
  Cub. línea
  Venz. canal
laundry (n) lavandería
  Arg. lavadero
lawn (n) césped
  Arg., Bol., Col., Mex., Par.,
  Per. pasto
  Cub., Dom.R. yerba
  Dom.R., ElS., Gua., Hon.,
  Nic., Venz. grama
  Pue.R. grama, pasto
lawn mower
  (n phr) cortacéspedes
  Arg. máquina de cortar pasto
  Bol. cortadora
  Chi. cortapasto
  Col. máquina para cortar el
  pasto

Cub. máquina de cortar
hierba
ElS., Gua., Hon. cortagrama
Mex. podadora de pasto
Nic. podadora de césped /
grama
Par. cortacésped, corta-
pasto
Per. cortador de césped,
cortador del pasto
Pue.R. cortadora de grama
Spa. cortacésped
Venz. cortagrama, segadora
lawn rake (n phr) barredora
  Arg., Chi., Col., Cub.,
  Dom.R., Mex., Nic., Pan.,
  Par. rastrillo
lawyer (n) abogado
  Col. jurista
lawyer's office (n phr) bufete de
  abogados
  Arg. estudio de abogados
  Col., Pue.R. oficina de
  abogados
  Ecu., Par. estudio juridico
lazy (adj) perezoso
  Arg., Cub., Par. vago
  Bol., Chi., Venz. flojo
  Col., Uru. haragán
  Dom.R., Nic. haragán, vago
  Mex. flojo, holgazán,
  huevón
leek (n) porro
  Arg., Col., Dom.R., Ecu.,
  ElS., Gua., Hon., Nic., Spa.,
  Uru. puerro

Mex., Per. poro
leotard (n) leotardo
   Chi., Par. malla
   Venz. mallas de ejercicio
level (n) nivel
   Chi. nivelador
   Par., Uru. plomada
liar (n) mentiroso
   Chi. chamullento
   Col., Nic. embustero
librarian (n) bibliotecario/a
   Dom.R. bibliotecólogo
lighter (n) encendedor
   Cub. fosforera
lightning (n) rayo, relámpago
   Col. centella
lime (n) lima
   Pan. limón
lip synch (v phr) doblar
   Dom.R., Nic. hacer mímica
   Dom.R. hacer mímica
lipstick (n) lápiz labial
   Arg., Bol., Chi. rouge
   Col. colorete
   Cub., Dom.R., Spa. pintalabios
   Mex. bile
   Nic. lápiz de libios
   Pan. lipstick
   Pue.R. lipstic
   Spa., Uru. lápiz de labios
liquor (n) bebidas fuertes
   Col., ElS., Gua., Hon., Mex., Pan., Venz. licor
   Nic. guaro
   Par. bebidas alcóholicas
   Spa. bebida alcohólica fuerte
liquor store (n phr) tienda de bebidas alcohólicas
   Bol., Mex., Nic. licorería
   Col. cigarrería, licorería
   Dom.R., Pue.R. liquor store
   Pan. bodega

Par. bodega, licorería
live broadcast
   (n phr) transmisión en directa
   Arg. programa en vivo, transmisión en directo
   Bol., Col., ElS., Gua., Uru. transmisión en directo
   Chi., Nic., Per. transmisión en vivo y en directo
   Cos.R., Cub., Dom.R., Ecu., Pan., Spa., Venz. transmisión en vivo
   Mex. transmisión directa, transmisión en vivo
   Par. transmisión en directo, transmisión en vivo
living room (n phr) cuarto de estar, sala
   Arg. living
loading dock (n phr) plataforma de carga
   Col., Nic. muelle de carga
   Par. puerto de carga
loafers (n) zapatos de andar
   Chi., Col., Ecu., Nic., Par., Venz. mocasines
   Dom.R. zapatos bajitos
   ElS., Gua., Spa. zapatos estilo mocasín
   Mex. zapatos de casa
lobby (n) foyer
   Arg. hall de entrada, lobby, recepción
   Chi. hall de entrada, recepción
   Col. pasillo
   Cub., ElS., Gua., Spa. vestíbulo
   Dom.R., Mex., Pue.R. lobby
   Nic., Par. recepción
   Pan. loby
   Venz. sala de espera,

ABBREVIATIONS: Arg.=Argentina Bol.=Bolivia Chi.=Chile Col.=Colombia Cos.R.=Costa Rica
Cub.=Cuba Dom.R.=Dominican Republic Ecu.=Ecuador ElS.=El Salvador Gua.=Guatemala
Hon.=Honduras Mex.=Mexico Nic.=Nicaragua Pan.=Panama Par.=Paraguay Per.=Peru
Pri.=Primary Term Pue.R.=Puerto Rico Spa.=Spain Uru.=Uruguay Venz.=Venezuela

vestíbulo
local train (n phr) tren local
   Mex. metro
   Spa. tren de cercanías
locket (n) relicario
   Cub. guardapelo
   Dom.R., Par. medallón
locust (n) langosta
   Col. cigarra, saltamontes
   Nic. chapulín , cigarra
loud (noise) (adj) ruidoso
   Chi. fuerte
love seat (n) confidente
   Arg. silloncito
   Col., ElS., Gua., Nic., Venz.
   sofá para dos personas
   Dom.R., Mex. love seat
   Pue.R., Spa. sofá

Col., Nic., Par., Pue.R.
   canción romántica
love, lovey (n) amor
   Chi. tesoro
   Col. amorcito, cariño
   Cos.R. , Nic. amorcito
LSD (n) LSD
   Cos.R., Cub., Nic. ácido
lubrication (n) engrase
   Chi. lubrificación
   Col., Dom.R., Gua., Nic.,
   Pan. lubricación
   Mex. engrasado
lunch (n) almuerzo
   Dom.R., Mex., Spa. comida
lyrics (n) letra de una canción
   Dom.R. letras de una
   canción

M

Ma'am, Madam (n) Señora
    Cos.R., Pan. Doña
    Nic. Doña, Doñita
    Par. Doña, Ña
macaw (n) guacamayo
    ElS., Gua., Mex. guacamaya
    Nic. lapa
mail room (n phr) cuarto de
    correos, sala de correos
    Par. correo
    Spa. cuarto del correo
main course (n) plato fuerte
    Arg., Chi., Dom.R., Nic.,
    Par., Per., Pue.R., Spa., Uru.,
    Venz. plato principal
    Col. entrada
    Mex. platillo principal
makeup kit (n phr) estuche de
    maquillaje
    Col. juego de maquillaje
    Pue.R. cartera de maquillaje
manager (n) gerente
    Col. administrador, director
manager (sports) (n) manager
    deportivo
    Col., Pan. administrador
    deportivo
    Mex., Par. técnico
    Venz. administrador
    deportivo, gerente deportivo
mandarine orange
    (n phr) mandarina
    Pue.R. china mandarina
mandolin (n) mandolina
    Chi. mandolín
manicurist (n) manicuro/a

    Chi. manicure
    Dom.R., Ecu., Mex., Nic.,
    Pan., Per., Venz. manicurista
maple (tree) (n) arce
    Gua., Mex., Nic. maple
    Gua., Mex. maple
marijuana (n) marihuana
    Col. yerba
    Cos.R. monte, mota
    Nic. Hierba, monte
marijuana cigarette
    (n phr) cigarrillo de
    marihuana
    Arg., Par. porro
    Chi. pito
    Col. varillo
    Cos.R., Nic. puro
    Cub., Pue.R. pitillo de
    marihuana
    Dom.R. joint, tabaco de
    marihuana
marker (n) marcador
    Cub., Mex. plumón
    Spa. rotulador
marry (v) casarse
    Col. contraer nupcias,
    desposarse
matchstick (n) cerilla, fósforo
    Mex., Nic. cerillo
mattress (n) colchón
    Pue.R. matres
mayor (n) alcalde/alcaldesa
    Chi. prefecto
    Dom.R. síndico
    Mex. presidente municipal
    Nic. edil

ABBREVIATIONS: Arg.=Argentina Bol.=Bolivia Chi.=Chile Col.=Colombia Cos.R.=Costa Rica Cub.=Cuba Dom.R.=Dominican Republic Ecu.=Ecuador ElS.=El Salvador Gua.=Guatemala Hon.=Honduras Mex.=Mexico Nic.=Nicaragua Pan.=Panama Par.=Paraguay Per.=Peru Pri.=Primary Term Pue.R.=Puerto Rico Spa.=Spain Uru.=Uruguay Venz.=Venezuela

Par., Uru. intendente
Uru. intendente
measure (music) (n) compás
Col. medida, ritmo
measuring cups (n phr) tazas
para medir
Dom.R. tazas medidoras
Nic. taza de medida
measuring spoons
(n phr) cucharas para medir
Dom.R. cucharas medidoras
Nic. cucharas de medida
meat grinder (n phr) molino de
carne
Arg., Col., Dom.R. moledora
de carne
Cub. molidora
Pan., Pue.R. moledor de
carne
median (n) centro de la calle
Col. isla de tráfico,
separador
Nic. boulevard
Par. carril
Pue.R. carril del centro
Spa. mediana
Venz. isla
men's (bathroom) (n) hombres
Chi., Col., Cub., Dom.R.,
Mex., Nic., Venz. caballeros
microwave (oven) (n) micro
Arg., Col., Cub., Par., Uru.
microonda
Chi., Mex., Nic., Pue.R.,
Spa., Venz. microondas
middle finger (n phr) dedo del
corazón
Arg. medio
Col. dedo corazón
Cub., Dom.R., Venz. dedo del
medio
Mex., Nic., Par., Uru. dedo
medio

midwife (n) partera
Col., Dom.R., ElS., Gua.,
Hon., Nic., Spa. comadrona
miniskirt (n) minifalda
Col., Pue.R. falda corta
mist (n) neblina
Arg., Pue.R. niebla
Col. bruma
Pan. bajareque
mistress (n) amante
Col. mosa
Cub., Nic. querida
Mex. concubina
Pue.R. chilla
mixer (n) batidora
Cub. mezclador
modular office (n phr) oficina
modular
Dom.R., Nic. módulo
molar (n) muela
Col. molar
monitor (computer) (n) monitor
Arg., Chi. pantalla
monkey (n) mono
Col. mico
Mex. chango
moose (n) anta
Arg., Nic., Par., Spa., Venz.
alce
Chi. ante
Col., Mex. alce, ante
moss (n) musgo
Dom.R, Par. moho
mother (n) madre
Arg. mamá, vieja
Col., Par. mamá
Nic. mama, vieja
motherboard (n) placa madre
Col., Nic., Spa. tarjeta
madre
Mex. tarjeta principal
Pan. mother board
Venz. placa base

motorcycle, motorbike
(n) motocicleta, moto
Pue.R. motora
mouse (n) ratón
Chi. laucha
move (v) mudarse
Bol. trasladarse
Col. cambiarse de casa,
trastiar
Nic. cambiarse de casa
movie theater (n phr) sala de
cine
Col., Ecu. teatro de cine
movie theater (n) sala de cine
Col., Ecu. teatro de cine
Nic. cine
movie, G-rated (n phr) película
para todo público
Mex. película para todo
público clasificación A
Nic. apta para todo público
movie, horror (n phr) película de
miedo
Arg., Col., Cos.R., Dom.R.,
Nic., Par. película de terror
Mex., Uru. película de
horror
Pue.R., Venz. película de
horror, película de terror
movie, PG-rated (n phr) película
para todo público
Mex. película para
adolescentes y adultos
clasificación B
Nic. apta para todo público
ue.R. película público general
Spa. película apta para todos
los públicos
enz. película censura B
movie, western (n phr) película
de vaqueros
Arg. película de cowboys
Spa. western

movie, X-rated (n phr) película
para adultos
Col. película porno
Cub., Par. película
pornográfica
Mex. película sólo para
adultos clasificación C
Nic. película sólo para
adultos
Pue.R. película X
muffin (n) panecillo
Arg., Col. muffin
Bol., Par. pancito
Gua. mollete
Mex. mufin, panque,
pastelito
Nic. bollo
Per. quequito
Spa. magdalena
muffin pan (n phr) molde para
panecillos
Arg. molde para muffin
Bol. molde para pancitos
Mex. molde para mufin,
molde para pastelitos
Nic. molde para bollos
Par. molde para pan
Per. molde para quequitos
Spa. molde para magdalenas
muffler (n) mofle
Arg., Col., Ecu., Par., Spa.,
Uru. silenciador
Dom.R. muffler
Mex. muffler
Nic. escape
Venz. amortiguador
mug (n) jarro
Arg. jarrita, jarrito
Chi. jarra, tazón
Cub. vaso
ElS.,Gua. pocillo
Nic. jarra, pocillo
Pue.R., Spa., Venz. Jarra

mug, beer (n phr) jarra para cerveza
  Arg. porrón
  Mex. jarro de cerveza
  Nic., Pue.R., Spa., Venz.
  jarra de cerveza
  Par. manija
mug, coffee (n phr) jarra para
  café
  Arg. jarrito, jarrita
  ElS., Gua., Nic. pocillo para
  café
  Mex. jarro para café
  Par. cafetera
  Mex. jarro para café

  Pue.R. tazón de café
  Venz. jarrita para café
mushroom (n) hongo
  Col., Mex., Par. champiñón
  Spa. champiñón, seta
musical (movie) (n) película
  musical
  Dom.R., Nic., Pue.R.
  músical
mussel (n) mejillón
  Chi. choro
mustang (n) mustango
  Arg., Par. potro
  Nic. mustang

N

nail polish (n) esmalte de uñas
 Chi. cutex
 Col., Spa. pintauñas
 Cub., Nic., Venz. pintura de
 uñas
 Dom.R. cute
 Par. pinta uña
nanny (n) niñera
 Chi., Col., Mex., Venz. nana
nape (n) nuca
 Col., Nic. cogote
naughty (adj) travieso
 Arg. liero
 Chi. malvado
 Col. juguetón
 Cub. pillo
 Dom.R. bellaco
 Nic., Pue.R. necio
navel (n) ombligo
 Arg., Chi. pupo
neck (guitar) (n) mástil
 Chi. cuello
 Nic. brazo
neck (n) cuello
 Col., Nic. pescuezo
necklace, pendant
 (n phr) collar con medallón
 Chi. medallón
 Dom.R. pendiente con
 medalla
 Mex. pendiente con cadena
 Nic. collar con colgante
 Par. collar
 Spa. colgante con cadena
nectarine (n) ciruela de negra
 Chi. durazno pelado

 Col., Cub., Nic. nectarina
 Cos.R., Dom.R. ciruela
 ElS., Gua. nectarino
 Mex. nectarín
 Pan. ciruela negra
 Par., Uru. pelón
 Pue.R., Venz. nectarine
 Spa. briñón
neighborhood (n) vecindad
 Arg., Ecu., Pan., Par., Uru.
 barrio
 Bol., Gua., Pue.R., Venz.
 vecindario
 Col., Dom.R., Nic., Per.,
 Spa. barrio, vecindario
neon sign (n phr) anuncio de
 neón
 Arg. cartel de néon
 Col. aviso con luz de neón
 Dom.R. letrero de neon
 Par. cartel lumínico
network (television) (n) cadena
 Dom.R. telecadena
news brief (n phr) breves
 Chi. breves informativos
 Col. informativo breve
 Cos.R. resúmen noticioso
 Dom.R. titulares
 Gua., Par. resúmen de
 noticias
 Mex. noticiero breve
 Nic. breves informativos,
 resúmen noticioso , tips
 informativos
 Mex. noticiero breve
 Venz. resúmen de

ABBREVIATIONS: Arg.=Argentina Bol.=Bolivia Chi.=Chile Col.=Colombia Cos.R.=Costa Rica Cub.=Cuba Dom.R.=Dominican Republic Ecu.=Ecuador ElS.=El Salvador Gua.=Guatemala Hon.=Honduras Mex.=Mexico Nic.=Nicaragua Pan.=Panama Par.=Paraguay Per.=Peru Pri.=Primary Term Pue.R.=Puerto Rico Spa.=Spain Uru.=Uruguay Venz.=Venezuela

noticias
Spa. rueda de prensa
newscast (n) telediario
Arg., Chi., Col., Ecu., Pan.
noticiero
Cos.R., Nic. telenoticiero
Cub. reporte
Dom.R. noticiero,
telenoticiero
Mex. noticias, noticiero
Par. noticiero, telenoticias
Spa. noticiario
newsstand (n) puesto de
periódicos
Arg. puesto de diarios
Col. puesto de periódicos y
de revistas
Nic., Par. quiosco
nice (adj) simpático
Col., Cub., Nic., Spa.
amable
Dom.R. chulo
Pue.R. chévere
Venz. agradable
nightgown (n) camisón

Chi., Col. camisa de dormir
Cub., Pue.R. bata de dormir
Dom.R. pijama
Ecu. camisa de noche
Nic. bata
nipple (n) pezón
Col. tetilla
nostril (n) ventanilla
Chi. narina
Cub. ventana de la nariz
Dom.R. hoyo de la nariz
Mex. poro de la nariz
Nic. fosanasal
Pue.R. roto de la nariz
Venz. orificio nasal
notebook (n) cuaderno
Cub. carpeta
Dom.R. libreta, mascota
Pue.R. libreta
nursery (plants) (n) semillero
Arg., Col., Dom.R., Nic., Par.
vivero
Mex. invernadero
nutmeg (n) nuez moscada
Par., Pue.R. nuez

ABBREVIATIONS: Arg.=Argentina Bol.=Bolivia Chi.=Chile Col.=Colombia Cos.R.=Costa Rica
Cub.=Cuba Dom.R.=Dominican Republic Ecu.=Ecuador ElS.=El Salvador Gua.=Guatemala
Hon.=Honduras Mex.=Mexico Nic.=Nicaragua Pan.=Panama Par.=Paraguay Per.=Peru
Pri.=Primary Term Pue.R.=Puerto Rico Spa.=Spain Uru.=Uruguay Venz.=Venezuela

O

odd (adj) curioso, raro
  Chi. extraño
  Col. extraño, insólito,
  inusitado
  Nic. estrafalario, extraño
office cubicle (n phr) recinto
  Bol. oficina
  Col., Dom.R., Gua., Mex.,
  Nic., Pan., Pue.R., Venz.
  cubículo
office divider (n phr) partidor
  Bol., Ecu., Par. divisor
  Col. separador
  Dom.R. división
  Mex. biombo separador
office hours (n phr) horas de
  oficina
  Cub. horas de trabajo
  Nic. horas hábiles
office manager (n phr) jefe de
  oficina
  Col. administrador, gerente
  Cub., Mex., Nic., Pue.R.,
  Venz. gerente de oficina
  Par. gerente
office suite (n phr) oficina
  Venz. suite de oficinas
office supplies (n phr) artículos
  de oficina
  Cub. materiales de oficina
  Ecu., Par. útiles de oficina
offside (n) fuera de juego
  Arg. offside
  Col., ElS., Gua., Hon. de
  posición adelantada
  Mex. lateral

  Par. posición adelantada
  Pue.R. fuera de posición
oil can (n phr) aceitera
  Arg., Cub., Nic., Venz. lata
  de aceite
  Col. tarro de aceite
okra (n) quimbombó
  Dom.R. molondrón
  Mex., Nic. okra
  Par. malva
old (adj) viejo
  Col., Par. anciano
  Nic. roco, vetarro
olive (n) aceituna
  Cos.R. oliva
omelet (n) omelete
  Bol., Col., Cub., Par., Per.,
  Pue.R., Spa., Venz. tortilla
  Dom.R. tortilla española
  Nic. torta de huevo
one-way ticket (n phr) billete
  sencillo
  Arg. boleto de ida, pasaje de
  ida
  Bol. billete de ida, billete de
  una sola vía
  Chi., Mex., Nic., Pan., Venz.
  boleto de ida
  Col. tiquete de una sola vía
  Cos.R., Dom.R., Par. pasaje
  de ida
  Ecu., Spa. billete de ida
  Per. boleto en un solo
  sentido
onion, pickling
  (n phr) cebollino

ABBREVIATIONS: Arg.=Argentina Bol.=Bolivia Chi.=Chile Col.=Colombia Cos.R.=Costa Rica
Cub.=Cuba Dom.R.=Dominican Republic Ecu.=Ecuador ElS.=El Salvador Gua.=Guatemala
Hon.=Honduras Mex.=Mexico Nic.=Nicaragua Pan.=Panama Par.=Paraguay Per.=Peru
Pri.=Primary Term Pue.R.=Puerto Rico Spa.=Spain Uru.=Uruguay Venz.=Venezuela

Chi., Nic. cebollín
Col. cebollina
Dom.R. escabeche
Mex. cebolla de cambray
Par. cebollit
Spa. cebolleta
onion, red (Bermuda)
(n phr) cebolla roja
Ecu., Par. cebolla colorada
Mex., Nic. cebolla morada
onion, vidalia (n phr) vidalia
Bol., Par. cebolla
Col., Nic. cebolla vidalia
orange (n) naranja
Dom.R., Pue.R. china
orchard (n) huerto
Pue.R. hortaliza
ostrich (n) avestruz
Col., Par. ñandú
ottoman (n) otomana
Mex., Par. taburete
Nic. diván
Pan. banquillo
Pue.R. banquillo , ottomán
utfit (n) conjunto

Chi., Nic., Par. traje
Col. vestimenta
outgoing (adj) extrovertido
Arg. dado
Cub., Nic., Par. sociable
overalls (n) mono
Arg., Dom.R., Pue.R.
mameluco
Chi., Col., Pan. overol
Cub. guardapolvo
Mex. overales, pantalones
de peto
Per. coverall
Uru. entero
overcoat (n) abrigo
Arg. sobretodo
Col. garbardina
overwhelming (adj) abrumador
Chi., Col., Nic. agobiante
owl (n) búho
Arg., Col., Cub., Dom.R.,
Par. lechuza
Chi. chuncho
oyster (n) ostra
Mex. ostión

ABBREVIATIONS: Arg.=Argentina Bol.=Bolivia Chi.=Chile Col.=Colombia Cos.R.=Costa Rica
Cub.=Cuba Dom.R.=Dominican Republic Ecu.=Ecuador ElS.=El Salvador Gua.=Guatemala
Hon.=Honduras Mex.=Mexico Nic.=Nicaragua Pan.=Panama Par.=Paraguay Per.=Peru
Pri.=Primary Term Pue.R.=Puerto Rico Spa.=Spain Uru.=Uruguay Venz.=Venezuela

P

pad (paper) (n) cuaderno
  Arg., Mex., Per. bloc
  Bol., Pan., Pue.R., Venz. libreta
  Col. bloc, cuaderno de notas
  Nic. bloc, libreta
  Spa. bloc de notas
pad, legal (n phr) cuaderno legal
  Arg., Chi. bloc
  Bol. libreta legal
  Dom.R., Pan., Pue.R., Venz.
  libreta tamaño legal
  Mex. bloc tamaño oficio
  Nic. bloc legal
  Par., Spa. bloc tamaño legal
pad, writing (n phr) cuaderno
  Arg., Chi. bloc
  Col., Dom.R., Pue.R., Venz.
  libreta
  Mex., Par. bloc tamaño
  carta
  Nic. bloc, libreta
  Spa. bloc de notas
pad, yellow (n phr) cuaderno
  amarillo
  Arg., Chi. bloc
  Bol., Col. Dom.R. libreta
  amarilla
  Mex., Spa. bloc Amarillo
  Nic. bloc /libreta amarilla
  Pue.R., Venz. libreta de
  papel amarilla
pail (n) balde
  Mex., Pue.R. cubeta
  Venz. balde, tobo
painter's knife (n phr) navaja
  de pintor

Mex. espátula, raspa
  Nic., Par. espátula
pajamas (n) piyamas
  Col. pijama, piyama
  Dom.R., Pue.R. pajamas
  Nic. piyama
  Spa. pijama
pallet (n) paleta
  Chi. palé
  Mex. palet, tarima
  Par., Uru. plataforma
palm (tree) (n) palma
  Arg., Col., Mex., Nic.
  palmera
pancake (n) panqueque
  Dom.R., Pan., Pue.R.
  pancake
  Mex. hotcake
  Venz. panqueca
panties (n) calzones
  Arg., Par., Uru. bombachas
  Col. tangas
  Cub., Pan. blúmer, pantis
  Dom.R., Pue.R. panties
  Mex. pantaleta
  Nic. blúmer, calzón
  Spa. bragas
  Venz. pantaletas
pantry (n) despensa
  Bol., Col., Mex. alacena
  Dom.R., Nic. pantry
  ElS., Gua., Hon. comedor
  auxiliar, pantry
  Pue.R. gabinete
pantyhose (n) media pantalón
  Arg. medias largas

Dom.R. media panty,
pantyhose
Mex. pantimedia
Nic. medias, pantyhose
Pan. pantihose
Per. media nylon
Pue.R. medias nylon
Spa. panty
Par. media fina, media
nylon, pantimedias
Uru. pantimedias
Venz. medias panty
papaya (n) papaya
Cub. fruta bomba
Dom.R. lechoza
Pue.R. lechosa
Venz. lechoso
paperclip (n) clip
Arg., Uru. ganchito
Bol., Cos.R., Cub., ElS.,
Gua., Hon. sujetapapel
Col. clip
parakeet (n) perico
Nic. chocoyo
Par. cotorra
Spa. periquito
parents (n) padres
Arg., Uru. viejos
Col., Nic. papás
park (n) parque
Arg., Par. plaza
park (v) estacionar
Bol., Col., Cos.R., Cub.,
Dom.R., ElS., Gua., Hon.,
Nic., Pan. parquear
Spa. aparcar
parka (n) parka
Nic. capote
Par., Pue.R. capa
parking lot
(n phr) estacionamiento
Arg. playa de
estacionamiento

Bol., Cos.R., Cub., Dom.R.
ElS., Gua., Hon., Nic.
parqueo
Col., Pan. parqueadero
Pue.R. parking
Spa. parking, aparcamiento
parrot (n) loro
Col., Dom.R. cotorra
parsnip (n) chiriva
Col. chirivia, chirivía
Gua. chiviría
Uru. pastinaca
part (hair) (n) raya
Chi., Pan. partidura
Dom.R., Mex., Nic., Venz.
partido
part-time (work) (adj) por parte
de la jornada
Mex. de medio tiempo,
parte de tiempo
Nic. medio tiempo
Par. de medio tiempo
Per., Spa. a tiempo parcial
Pue.R. part-time
pass (traffic) (v) pasar
Chi. ultrapasar
Cos.R. adelantarse
Dom.R., Mex. rebasar
Nic. adelantar , aventajar,
rebasar
Spa. adelantar
pastry brush (n phr) pincel de
repostería
Col., Gua., ElS., Nic., Pan.
brocha de repostería
pastry cutting wheel
(n phr) cortapastas
Col. rodete para cortar masa
Nic. rueda para cortar masa
patient (n) paciente
Arg., Bol., Cub., Cos.R.,
Ecu., Gua., Uru. enfermo/a
Col. doliente

ABBREVIATIONS: Arg.=Argentina Bol.=Bolivia Chi.=Chile Col.=Colombia Cos.R.=Costa Rica
Cub.=Cuba Dom.R.=Dominican Republic Ecu.=Ecuador ElS.=El Salvador Gua.=Guatemala
Hon.=Honduras Mex.=Mexico Nic.=Nicaragua Pan.=Panama Par.=Paraguay Per.=Peru
Pri.=Primary Term Pue.R.=Puerto Rico Spa.=Spain Uru.=Uruguay Venz.=Venezuela

PC (n) PC
    Arg., Gua., Mex., Nic., Venz.
    computadora personal
    Bol. computador personal
    Spa. ordenador personal
peach (n) durazno
    Cub., Dom.R., Nic., Par.,
    Per., Pue.R., Spa. melocotón
peak (mountain) (n phr) pico
    Chi. cima
    Nic. cima, cumbre
peanut (n) maní
    Mex. cacahuate
    Spa. cacahuete
peas, green (n phr) arvejas
    Cub., Mex. chícharos
    Nic., Pan. petit pois
    Per. arvejitas
    Pue.R., Spa. guisantes
pecan (n) pacana
    Bol., ElS., Gua., Hon. pecana
    Mex., Nic., Par. nuez
peeler (n) pelador
    Mex. pelapapas
pen (n) pluma
    Arg., Chi., Uru. lapicera
    Nic., Per. lapicero
    Spa. bolígrafo
pen, ball-point (n phr) bolígrafo
    Bol. punta bola
    Chi. lapicera de pasta
    Col. esfero
    Per. lapicero
pen, fountain (n phr) pluma de
    fuente
    Arg., Par. lapicera fuente
    Bol., Mex., Pue.R., Venz.
    pluma fuente
    Chi. lapicera a fuente
    Per. lapicero de tinta
    Spa. pluma, pluma
    estilográfica
    Uru. estilográfica

penis (n) pene
    Col. falo, verga
    Nic. verga
    Par. pilin
penknife (n) navaja
    Chi., Spa., Venz.
    cortaplumas
    Pue.R. cuchilla
pepper shaker
    (n phr) pimentera
    Arg., Col., Gua., Mex., Nic.,
    Per. pimentero
    Pue.R. pimienta
    Venz. pimientero
pepper, hot (n phr) chile
    Bol., Chi., Venz., Par., Per.
    ají
    Col., Cub., Pan., Pue.R. ají
    picante
    Cos.R., Nic. chile picante
    Ecu. pimiento picante
    Spa. guindilla
pepper, sweet (n phr) pimiento
    morrón
    Col. pimentón rojo,
    pimentón verde
    Cos.R. chile dulce
    Nic. chiltoma
    Pan. ají dulce, pimentón
    Par. locote, pimiento
    Per., Venz. pimentón
    Spa. pimiento
perennial (plant) (n) perenne
    Pue.R. permanente
performer (n) artista
    Col. intérprete
    Mex. intérprete, músico
    Nic. actor, actriz
perfume (n) perfume
    Spa. colonia
pest (person) (n) machaca
    Bol. cargoso
    Chi. insoportable

Col., Pan. peste
Cub. chivón, ladilla
Dom.R. pesta, plaga
Ecu. necio/a
ElS., Gua. tipo/a pesado/a
Mex., Venz. fastidioso
Nic. necio, pesado
Par. pesado, pelmazo
Pue.R. sabandija
Spa. pelma, pelmazo
pet shop (n phr) pajarería
Col. almacén de mascotas
Dom.R. pet shop, tienda de
mascotas
ElS., Gua. tienda de mascotes
Mex. tienda de animales
domésticos, veterinaria
Nic., Par. tienda de
mascotas
Pue.R. pet shop, tienda de
animales
Spa. tienda de animales
petticoat (n) combinación
Chi. enagüa
Cub. sayuela
Dom.R. mediofondo, refajo
Mex. enaguas
Nic. fustán
Pan. peticote
Par. enagua
Pue.R. refajo
Venz. enaguas, fondo
pharmacist (n) farmacéutico
Col. boticario, farmaceuta
Venz. farmaceuta
piccolo (n) pícolo
Col., Mex., Par., Spa. flautín
pickle (n) pepino encurtido
Cub. pepino
Dom.R., Mex., Par., Pue.R.
pepinillo
Spa. pepinillo en vinagre
Venz. encurtido

pickup truck (n phr) camioneta
Cos.R., ElS., Gua., Hon.,
Pan., Per. pickup
Mex., Venz. camioneta
pickup
pie (n) tarta
Bol. pie
Chi., Cos.R. torta
Col. ponqué
Dom.R., Nic. pastel, pie
Mex. pay
Pan., Per., Pue.R. pastel
Venz. tartaleta
pie pan (n phr) molde para pastel
Arg. molde para tartas
Chi. molde para pie
Dom.R. molde de bizcocho
Mex. molde para pay
Nic. model para pastel / pie
pig (n) puerco
Arg., Chi., Ecu., Uru.
chancho
Bol. chancho, cuchi
Col. cerdo, marrano
Cos.R. chancho, cochino
Cub. cochino
Dom.R., Pue.R., Spa. cerdo
ElS., Gua., Hon. coche,
marrano
Mex. cochino, marrano
Nic. cerdo, chancho,
marrano
Pan. marrano
Per. cerdo, chancho
Venz. cerdo, cochino
pigtail (n) trenza
Bol., Cos.R. cola
Chi. colita, moño
Col., Dom.R., Mex., Venz.
colita
Per. cachito
Spa., Uru. coleta
pillowcase (n) funda

Gua. sobrefunda

pilot (n) piloto
   Col. aviador

pimp (n) chulo
   Chi. cafiche
   ElS., Gua., Hon. alcahuete
   Nic. chivo
   Par. caficho

pimple (n) grano
   Chi., Cos.R., Dom.R., Spa.
   espinilla
   Col., Nic., Venz. barro,
   espinilla
   Mex. barro
   Par., Per. barrito

pincers (n) tenazas
   Col., Mex. pinzas

pine cone (n phr) piña
   Nic. piña de pino
   Per. piñón

pineapple (n) piña
   Uru. ananá

pinkie finger (n phr) dedo
   meñique
   Cub. dedo chiquito
   Nic. meñique

pistachio (n) pistacho
   Mex. pistache

pitcher (n) jarra
   Chi. jarrón
   Gua., Nic. pichel

plain (topography) (n) llanura
   Col., Dom.R. llano
   Mex. esplanada, planicie
   Pue.R. planicie

plane (carpentry) (n) plano
   Arg., Col., Dom.R., Mex.,
   Nic., Spa., Uru. cepillo

plantar arch (foot) (n phr) arco
   plantar
   Arg., Mex., Nic., Par., Venz.
   arco del pie
   Col. arco de la planta del pie

Dom.R. puente

platform (train) (n) andén
   Col., Cub., Par., Per. plataforma
   Col., Cub., Per. plataforma

platter (n) fuente de servir
   Col., Nic., Pan., Par. bandeja
   Mex. platón

pliers (n) pinzas
   Chi., Cos.R., Dom.R., Nic.,
   Per., Pue.R., Venz. alicate
   Col., Pan., Spa. alicates
   Mex. alicatas

plumber (n) plomero
   Chi. gáfiter [from "gas fitter"]
   Chi. gáfiter [from gasfitter]
   Ecu. gasfitero
   Nic., Spa. fontanero

pocket, back (n phr) bolsillo
   trasero
   Dom.R. bolsillo de atrás

pocket, breast (n phr) bolsillo
   superior
   Dom.R., Nic. bolsillo de la
   camisa

pole vault (n phr) salto con
   garrocha
   Nic., Pue.R. salto con
   pértiga
   Spa. salto de pértiga
   Venz. salto de garrocha

police detective (n) agente
   Chi., Mex., Pan., Venz.
   detective
   Col. agente de policía,
   detective policíaco
   Dom.R. detective policial
   ElS., Gua., Hon., Nic.
   detective de la policía
   Spa. investigador

police officer (n phr) policía
   Chi. carabinero
   Col., Spa. agente de policía
   Dom.R. agente policial

Venz. oficial de policía
police station (n phr) comisaría
Col., Cub., Gua., Nic., Pan.,
Pue.R. estación de policía
Dom.R. destacamento
policial
polite (adj) cortés, educado
Col. atento, culto
Mex. caballeroso
politician (n) político
Col. hombre público
pollution (n) contaminación
Col. polución
pomegranate (n) granada
Cos.R. granadilla
pond (n) charca
Arg., Par., Uru. charco
Chi. charco, laguna
Col., ElS., Gua., Hon., Mex.
estanque
Dom.R. laguna
Nic., Venz. estanque, laguna
pony (n) jaca
Col., Dom.R., Mex., Nic.,
Pan., Par. pony
Cub., Ecu. caballito
Pue.R., Venz. caballito, pony
Arg., Spa. poni
Uru. poney
ponytail (hair) (n) cola de
caballo
Arg. cola, colita
Pue.R. rabo de caballo
Spa. coleta
porch (n) pórtico
Cub., Nic. porche
Dom.R. galería
Gua. terraza cubierta
Pan. porch
porpoise (n) marsopa
Chi., Ecu., Par. delfín
porter (n) maletero
Bol. maletera

Col., Cub. portero
Spa. mozo
Venz. cargador de maletas
post office (n phr) oficina de
correos
Arg., Cub. correo
Col. oficina postal
Nic. bedel
post office box (n phr) apartado
postal
Bol. casilla
Chi. casilla postal
Col. buzón postal
Spa. apartado de correos
pot (n) olla
Arg., Par. cacerola
Nic. porra
Spa. puchero
potato (n) papa
Cub., Spa. patata
potato masher (n phr) majador
de papas
Chi. moledor de papas
Mex. prensapapas
Nic. colador de papas
Par., Uru. triturador de papas
Per. machucador de papas
pothole (n) pozo
Arg., Cub., Gua., Mex., Nic.,
Spa. bache
Chi., Dom.R. hoyo
Col., Cos.R., Ecu., Pan.
hueco
prairie (n) pradera
Dom.R., Nic. valle
prawn (n) gamba
Arg. camarón, langostino
Chi. camarón gigante
Col., Cub., Mex., Pan., Spa.
langostino
Ecu., Nic., Par., Uru.
camarón
praying mantis (n phr) manta

ABBREVIATIONS: Arg.=Argentina Bol.=Bolivia Chi.=Chile Col.=Colombia Cos.R.=Costa Rica
Cub.=Cuba Dom.R.=Dominican Republic Ecu.=Ecuador ElS.=El Salvador Gua.=Guatemala
Hon.=Honduras Mex.=Mexico Nic.=Nicaragua Pan.=Panama Par.=Paraguay Per.=Peru
Pri.=Primary Term Pue.R.=Puerto Rico Spa.=Spain Uru.=Uruguay Venz.=Venezuela

religiosa
Nic. rezadora
Pan. maría palito
Par., Spa. mantis religiosa
Pue.R. mantilla
pregnant (adj) embarazada
Col. encinta, esperando,
preñada
Nic. panzona
Pan., Per. encinta
Venz. en estado
preserves (n) conserva (de
alimentos)
Chi., Col., Nic. conservas
Dom.R. preservas
Per., Spa. mermelada
pretty (adj) guapa
Arg., Cub., Pue.R. linda
Chi. bonita, preciosa
Col. bella, bonita, linda
Dom.R., Ecu., ElS., Gua.,
Nic., Pan., Uru. bonita
priest (n) sacerdote
Chi., Mex. padre
Col. capellán, clérigo, cura,
padre, religioso
Nic. cura, padre
Pue.R., Spa., Venz. cura
print shop (n phr) imprenta
Col. taller tipográfico,
talleres gráficos
printer (computer) (n) impresora
Pue.R. printer
prison (n) cárcel
Col. calabozo, cana,
correccional, penal,
penitenciaría, prisión
Pue.R., Venz. prisión
prisoner (n) preso
Chi. reo
Col. encarcelado, prisionero,
recluso
Nic. recluso

Pan. prisionero
professor (n) profesor/a
Chi. maestro/a
Col. catedrático, educador,
maestro/a
program (n) programa
Dom.R. show
props (n) accesorios
Col. ayudas de escenario,
soporte
Mex. adornos
prostitute (n) prostituta, puta
Col. cortesana, mujer de
mala vida, mujerzuela,
ramera
Nic. playo
pruning shears
(n phr) podadera
Arg., Dom.R., Nic., Spa.
tijeras de podar
Bol., Ecu., Pue.R. podadora
Col. tijeras para podar
Mex. podadoras
Par. podadora, tijera de
podar
Venz. tijera podadora
pubic hair (n phr) vello
pubiano
Col., Cos.R., ElS., Gua.,
Mex., Nic., Par., Venz. vello
púbico
Cub. pendejo
Dom.R. vello
Uru. vello del pubis
puff pastry (n phr) hojaldre
Chi. masa de mil hojas
Nic. hojaldra
Venz. milhoja
pullover (n) pulóver
Arg. sweater
Bol. saco
Col., Mex. suéter cerrado
Nic. suéter

Per. chompa
Spa. jersey
Venz. suéter

pumpkin (n) calabaza
Bol., Chi., Pan. zapallo
Col., Venz. ahuyama

ABBREVIATIONS: Arg.=Argentina Bol.=Bolivia Chi.=Chile Col.=Colombia Cos.R.=Costa Rica
Cub.=Cuba Dom.R.=Dominican Republic Ecu.=Ecuador ElS.=El Salvador Gua.=Guatemala
Hon.=Honduras Mex.=Mexico Nic.=Nicaragua Pan.=Panama Par.=Paraguay Per.=Peru
Pri.=Primary Term Pue.R.=Puerto Rico Spa.=Spain Uru.=Uruguay Venz.=Venezuela

Q

quick (adj) rápido
    Chi., Col. veloz
quiet (adj) silencioso
    Chi., Col., Venz. callado
    Dom.R., Pan. tranquilo

    Nic. callado, tranquilo
quit using drugs (v) dejar las
    drogas
    Col., Nic. cortar con el
    vicio

R

rabbi (n) rabino
    Spa. rabí
racecar (n phr) coche de carrera
    Arg., Chi. auto de carrera
    Cub., ElS., Gua., Hon., Nic.,
    Pan., Pue.R. carro de carrera
    Col., Per., Venz. carro de
    carreras
    Dom.R. auto de carrera,
    carro de carrera
    Spa. coche de carreras
radiator grill (n phr) rejilla del
    radiador
    Arg., Col., Par. parrilla del
    radiador
rain forest (n phr) selva tropical
    Col., Nic. bosque tropical
raincoat (n) impermeable
    Arg., Par. piloto
    Col., Spa. gabardina
    Cub. capa de agua
    Nic. capote para la lluvia
    Pan. capote
    Pue.R. capa
raise (children) (n) criar
    Col. educar, enseñar, formar
range (mountain) (n phr) sierra
    Chi., Nic. cordillera
    Col. cadena
razor (n) rasuradora
    Arg., Chi. gillette
    Col., Nic. máquina de afeitar
    Cub., Spa. cuchilla de afeitar
    Dom.R., Pue.R. afeitadora
    Mex. rastrillo Mex.

    rastrillo
    Pan. navaja
    Venz. hojilla de afeitar
realtor (n) corredor de bienes
    raíces
    Arg. inmobiliario
    Col. corredor de bienes de finca
    raíz
    Nic. agente
reamer (n) escariador
    Mex. escariadora
    Par., Pue.R. arado
    Spa. fresadora
    Uru. escardador
rear window (n phr) ventana
    trasera
    Arg. luneta
    Col. ventanilla trasera
    Pue.R. cristal trasero
rear-view mirror (n phr) espejo
    retrovisor
    Nic. retrovisor
    Uru. espejo trasero
record album (n phr) álbum
    Col. disco
recreational vehicle
    (n phr) vehículo de recreo
    Bol. vagoneta
    Chi., Par. casa rodante
    Mex., Nic. camper
    Pue.R. RV
    Spa. caravana
    Venz. vehículo recreacional
referee (n) árbitro
    Arg. referee

ABBREVIATIONS: Arg.=Argentina Bol.=Bolivia Chi.=Chile Col.=Colombia Cos.R.=Costa Rica
Cub.=Cuba Dom.R.=Dominican Republic Ecu.=Ecuador ElS.=El Salvador Gua.=Guatemala
Hon.=Honduras Mex.=Mexico Nic.=Nicaragua Pan.=Panama Par.=Paraguay Per.=Peru
Pri.=Primary Term Pue.R.=Puerto Rico Spa.=Spain Uru.=Uruguay Venz.=Venezuela

Bol., Col., Ecu., Per. juez
Mex. refere
Nic. juez, réferi
Pan. referí
reflector (bicycle) (n) reflector
Arg. faro, luz
Nic. luz
refrigerator (n) refrigerador
Arg., Par. heladera
Col., Dom.R., Pue.R., Venz.
nevera
Cos.R. refrí
Ecu., nevera, refrigeradora
Nic., Per. refrigeradora
Spa. frigorífoco, nevera
reindeer (n) reno
Dom.R. cervatillo
remote control (n phr) control
remoto
Spa. mando a distancia
rent (housing) (v) alquilar
Chi., Col. arrendar
Mex., Pue.R. rentar
reporter (n) locutor
Arg., Chi. periodista
Col., Cos.R., Dom.R., Mex.,
Nic., Pan., Pue.R., Venz.
reportero
request stop (bus) (n phr) parada
facultativa
Col. solicitud para hacer
detener el bus
Mex. parada solicitada
Nic. pedir parada
Par. parada de omnibus
Spa. parada discrecional
Venz. parada pedida
residencial area (n phr) zona
residencial
Arg., Par. barrio residencial
Col. área residencial
Pue.R. área residencial,
sector residencial

resonant (adj) sonoro
Col. estruendoso
Mex. resonante
Nic. estruendoso, ruidoso
résumé (work history)
(n) currículum (vitae)
Col. hoja de vida
Mex. currículo
Pue.R. resumé
retirement home (n phr) hogar
de ancianos
Arg., Nic. asilo de ancianos
Col. ancianato
Mex., Par. asilo
Pan. retiro para ancianos
reverse (n) marcha atrás
Col., Dom.R., Mex., Pan.,
Par. reversa
Nic., Venz. retroceso
Pue.R. riversa
ride, bicycle (v phr) montar en
bicicleta
Arg., Chi., Cos.R., Mex.,
Par. andar en bicicleta
Col. montar cicla
Nic. montar bicicleta
Pue.R. correr bicicleta
right of way (n phr) prioridad
Arg., Cub., Pue.R. derecho
de paso
Chi., Mex. paso
Col. derecho a la vía
Dom.R., Ecu., Spa.
preferencia
ElS., Gua., Pan. derecho de
vía
Nic. preferencia,
servidumbre
Par. preferencial
Venz. prioridad de
circulación
rim (bicycle wheel) (n) llanta
Chi., Col., Cos.R. aro

Mex., Nic. rin
Par., Venz. rueda
ring (boxing) (n) ring de boxeo
Chi., Par. cuadrilátero
Col., Nic., Pue.R., Uru.
cuadrilátero de boxeo
ring (n) anillo
Pan., Pue.R. sortija
ring, class (n phr) anillo de
graduación
Pue.R. sortija de graduación
ring, diamond (n phr) anillo de
diamante
Pue.R. sortija de diamante
Spa. anillo de diamantes
ring, signet (n phr) sortija de
sello
Col. anillo de sello
Spa. sello
ring, wedding (n phr) anillo de
matrimonio
Arg., Par. alianza, anillo de
casamiento
Nic. anillo de casamiento/
boda
Per., Pue.R. aro de
matrimonio
rise (bread) (v) leudarse
Bol., Chi., ElS., Gua., Hon.,
Mex., Spa. levantarse
Col. inflarse, levantarse
Cos.R., Dom.R., Ecu., Nic.,
Pan., Pue.R. crecer
road shoulder (n phr) lomo
Arg., Par. banquina
Col., Cos.R. orilla de la
carretera
ElS., Gua., Nic. borde de la
carretera
Pue.R. paseo
Spa., Uru. arcén
Venz. hombrillo
road sign (n phr) letrero de

carretera
Arg. cartel
Chi. señalización en la
carretera
Col. aviso vial
Dom.R., Spa., Uru. señal de
tráfico
Nic., Par., Venz. señal de
tránsito
Per. señal del camino
road works (n phr) obras
Arg., Pue.R. construcción
Col. arreglos en la vía
Nic. obras viales
Venz. mantenimiento de
calles
roasting pan (n phr) sartén para
asar
Col., Nic. bandeja para
hornear
Spa. bandeja para el horno
Venz. olla para hornear
rock music (n phr) música rock
Col., Par. música de rock
Dom.R., Spa. rock
roll (n phr) pancito
Col., Pan. panecillo
ElS., Gua., Nic., Spa. bollo
Pue.R. pan
rolling pin (n phr) rodillo
Arg. palo de amasar
Bol., Chi. fuslero
Per. amasador
rolodex (n) fichero giratorio
Nic. fichero rolodex
Pue.R. rolodex
root (hair) (n) raíz
Dom.R. crecimeinto
rotten (food) (adj) podrido
Mex. echado a perder
round trip ticket (n phr) billete
de ida y vuelta
Arg. boleto de ida y vuelta,

pasaje de ida y vuelta
Chi., Pan., Per., Venz. boleto
de ida y vuelta
Col. tiquete de ida y vuelta
Cos.R., Dom.R., Par. pasaje
de ida y vuelta
Mex. boleto de ida y vuelta,
boleto de viaje Redondo
Nic. boleto de ida y vuelta,
ticket de idea y vuelta
rubber band (n phr) cinta
elástica
Arg., Dom.R., Pue.R. gomita
Bol., Chi. elástico
Col. caucho
Cub., Mex., Pan., Per., Venz.
liga
ElS., Gua., Hon., Nic. hule
Spa., Uru. goma elástica
rubbers (shoes) (n) chanclos de
goma
Arg. ojotas de goma
Chi., Uru. zapatos de

goma
Col. zapatos de caucho
Cub., Pue.R. chancletas de
goma
ElS., Gua., Hon. chanclas de
hule
Mex. chanclas de plástico,
huaraches de plástico,
sandalias de plástico
Nic. chinelas
Par. zapatillas
Spa. chanclas
rush hour (n phr) hora pico
Arg. rush hour
Cub., Mex. hora de tráfico
Per. hora de entrada o salida
a los trabajos
Pue.R. hora del tapón
Spa. hora punta
rutabaga (n) nabo sueco
Col. nabo de suecia, rutabaga
Nic. colinabo
Par. nabo

S

sailboat (n) barco de vela
   Col. bote de vela
   Dom.R., Nic. velero
   Par. barcode vela, velero
salary (n) sueldo
   Col., Mex., Nic., Pan., Par.
   salario
salesperson (n) dependiente
   Chi. promotor/a, vendedor/a
   Col., Dom.R., Ecu., ElS.,
   Gua., Hon., Mex., Nic., Par.,
   Venz. vendedor/a
sandals (n) sandalias
   Cub., Nic. chancletas
sandbar (n) barra de arena
   Mex., Par. banco de arena
satellite television
   (n phr) televisión por
   satélite
   Nic. parabolica
   Par. televisión satelital
   Spa. televisión vía satélite
saucepan (n) cacerola
   Arg., Pue.R. olla
   Col. perol
   Nic. olla, perol, porra
   Spa. cazo
saw (n) sierra
   Arg., Cub., Nic., Per.
   serrucho
scab (n) costra
   Cub., Dom.R. postilla
scallion (n) cebolla verde
   Bol. cebollita verde
   Col. cebolla larga
   ElS., Gua., Hon., Nic., Venz.
   cebollín

Pan. cebollina
   Mex. cebollino
   Par. cebollita
scallop (n) venera
   Arg., Venz. vieira
   Chi. ostión
   ElS., Gua., Nic. concha,
   escalope
   Pan. conchuela
   Par., Spa. concha
scanner, optical
   (n phr) explorador óptico
   Arg., Dom.R., Par., Pue.R.
   scanner
   Chi., Cub., Mex., Nic., Pan.,
   Spa. escáner
   Venz. copiador óptico
scared (adj) asustado
   Col. atemorizado
school (n) escuela
   Arg., Col., Gua., Nic. colegio
school day (n phr) día lectivo
   Col. día de colegio
   Dom.R., Nic., Per. día de
   clases
   Mex., Venz. día de escuela
   Par., Pue.R. día de clase
scorpion (n) alacrán
   Arg., Chi., Col., Cos.R.,
   Nic., Pan., Spa., Uru., Venz.
   escorpión
scraper (n) rascador
   Chi. raspadora
   Col. cuchilla raspadora
   Mex. raspa
   Nic., Pue.R. espátula
   Par., Venz. raspador

ABBREVIATIONS: Arg.=Argentina Bol.=Bolivia Chi.=Chile Col.=Colombia Cos.R.=Costa Rica
Cub.=Cuba Dom.R.=Dominican Republic Ecu.=Ecuador ElS.=El Salvador Gua.=Guatemala
Hon.=Honduras Mex.=Mexico Nic.=Nicaragua Pan.=Panama Par.=Paraguay Per.=Peru
Pri.=Primary Term Pue.R.=Puerto Rico Spa.=Spain Uru.=Uruguay Venz.=Venezuela

screenplay (n) guión
cinematográfico
  Bol. telón
  Dom.R., ElS., Gua., Hon.
  libreto
  Nic. guión
  Par. guión , libreto
  Spa. argumento
screwdriver (n) destornillador
  Chi. llave
  Mex., Per. desarmador
  Nic. desarmador,
  desatornillador
scroll (computer) (v) desplazar
  Pan. mover
  Pue.R. scroll
scythe (n) guadaña
  Mex. zapapico
  Par. hoz
seamstress (n) costurera
  Arg., Chi., Col., Nic., Pan.,
  Spa. modista
seashore (n) orilla del mar
  Chi., Nic., Par., Pue.R. costa
  Col. costa, litoral, ribera del
  mar
seat (bicycle) (n) asiento
  Bol., Col. silla
  Chi., Dom.R., Ecu., Pue.R.,
  Spa., Uru. sillín
second class (adj phr) segunda
clase
  Arg. segunda
  Dom.R. clase económica
sedan (n) sedán
  Par., Spa. turismo
See you later! (int phr) ¡Hasta
luego!
  Col. ¡Te veo luego!, ¡Te veo
  más tarde!, ¡Hasta pronto!
  Dom.R., ElS., Gua., Nic.,
  Pan. ¡Nos vemos!
  Par. ¡Nos vemos!, ¡Nos

vemos mas tarde!
  Pue.R. ¡Hasta la vista!
seedling (n) planta de semillero
  Chi. brote
  Col. planta de vivero
  Cos.R., Nic., Par. almácigo
  Mex. plantita
selfish (adj) egoísta
  Col. ególatra
sell drugs (v phr) vender drogas
  Pue.R. tirar drogas
set (movie) (n) escenario
  Chi. estudios
  Col. decorado
  Spa. plató
shallot (n) chalote
  Mex. cebollino, cebollita
  Nic. cebollín
  Par. cebollita
shampoo (n) champú
  Arg., Nic. shampoo
share needles (v phr) compartir
agujas
  Col., Nic. compartir jeringas
  Mex. prestarse jeringas
  Venz. compartir
  inyectadoras
shed (n) cobertizo
  Chi. galpón
  Nic. bajareque
  Par. galpón
  Pue.R. casita de
  herramientas
sheep (n) oveja
  Mex. borrego
sheet, contour (n phr) sábana de
cajón
  Arg. sábana de elástico
  Col. sábana de forro
  Nic. cubrecama
  Par. sábana elástica
  Spa. sábana bajera ajustable
  Venz. sábana de esquinera

ABBREVIATIONS: Arg.=Argentina Bol.=Bolivia Chi.=Chile Col.=Colombia Cos.R.=Costa Rica
Cub.=Cuba Dom.R.=Dominican Republic Ecu.=Ecuador ElS.=El Salvador Gua.=Guatemala
Hon.=Honduras Mex.=Mexico Nic.=Nicaragua Pan.=Panama Par.=Paraguay Per.=Peru
Pri.=Primary Term Pue.R.=Puerto Rico Spa.=Spain Uru.=Uruguay Venz.=Venezuela

shift gear (v phr) cambiar la
velocidad
  Arg. hacer un cambio
  Chi. pasar la marcha, reducir la
  marcha
  Col., Nic. meter un cambio
  Pue.R. cambiar de cambios
  Spa. cambiar la marcha
shin (n) espinilla
  Chi. canilla
  Nic. chinpinilla
ship (n) buque
  Arg., Cos.R., Nic., Pan.,
  Uru., Venz. barco
  Chi. barco, navío
  Col. barco, embarcación
shirt, dressy (n phr) camisa
formal
  Arg., Dom.R., Mex., Nic.,
  Pan., Par., Uru., Venz.
  camisa de vestir
shirt, long-sleeved
  (n phr) camisa de manga
  larga
  Arg. remera de manga larga
shirt, short-sleeved
  (n phr) camisa de manga
  corta
  Arg. remera de manga corta
shoe rack (n phr) zapatera
  Col. repisa para zapatos,
  zapatero
  Par. zapatero
shoelace (n) cordón
  Mex. agujeta
  Pue.R. gabete
shoes, hiking (n phr) botas
  Chi. bototos
  Col. zapatos de caminar
  Mex. botas de alpinismo
  Spa. botas de monte
shoes, patent leather
  (n phr) zapatos de

charol
  Arg., Bol., Cos.R., Ecu.,
  Per., Pue.R. zapatos de cuero
  barnizado
  Dom.R. zapatos de cuero,
  zapatos de piel
  Venz. zapatos de cuero,
  zapatos de patente
shoes, tennis (n phr) zapatos de
tenis
  Arg., Chi., Pan. zapatillas
  Col., Nic. zapatos tenis
  Dom.R., Mex. tenis
  Spa. zapatillas de deporte
  Venz. zapatos de goma
shoot (movie) (v) rodar
  Nic., Venz. filmar
shooting (movie) (n) rodaje
  Nic., Venz. filmación
shop sign (n phr) letrero
comercial
  Arg. cartel
  Col. anuncio de almacén
shop window (n phr) vitrina
  Arg. vidriera
  Cos.R., Cub., Per., Spa.
  escaparate
  Mex. aparador
  Nic. escaparate, exhibidor
shoreline (n) costa
  Col. litoral, orilla
short (adj) pequeño
  Arg., Per., Spa. bajo
  Chi., Pan., Pue.R. corto
  Col., Dom.R. bajito
  Mex. bajo, chaparro, corto
  Nic. corto, chingo
short (person) (adj) pequeño
  Arg., Uru. bajito, petiso
  Col. bajito, bajo
  Dom.R. bajito
  Mex. de estatura baja,
  chaparro

Nic. bajo, chaparro
Venz. bajo

shorts (n) pantalones cortos
Arg., Chi., Col., Dom.R.,
Mex., Nic., Venz. shorts
Cub. bermudas
Pan. pantaloncitos cortos
Par. bermudas, pantalones
corto
Pue.R. pantalón corto

shot glass (n phr) copa de trago
Chi. medida para bebida
Col. copita
Dom.R. vaso de trago corto
Mex. caballo (big), caballito
(small), vaso tequilero
Nic. copita
Pue.R. vasito
Spa. chupito

shot put (n phr) lanzamiento de
peso
Nic. la nzamiento de bala
Par., Pue.R. lanzamiento de
pesa

shovel (n) pala
Per. palana

show (movie) (v) proyectar
Arg. dar, pasar
Col. presentar
Dom.R. pasar
Nic. exhibir, presentar
Venz. mostrar

shredder (n) trituradora
Mex. picadora de papel

shrimp (n) camarón
Chi. langostino
Spa. gamba

shrub (n) arbusto
Cub. mata

shutters (n) postigos
Col., Ecu., Gua., Nic., Par.
persianas
Mex. contraventanas

shy (adj) tímido
Cub., Nic., Pan. penoso

sick leave (n phr) permiso de
convalecencia
Arg., Bol., ElS., Gua., Hon.,
Par. permiso por enfermedad
Col., Dom.R. licencia por
enfermedad
Cub. días de enfermedad
Nic. subsidio por enfermedad
Venz. permiso de
convalescencia

sickle (n) hoz
Mex., Par. pico
Pue.R. yunta

side entrance
(n phr) puerta lateral
Arg., Par. puerta de servicio
Col., Nic. entrada lateral
Cub. puerta del costado
Mex. puerta del lado

sidewalk (n) acera
Arg., Chi., Cos.R., Ecu.,
Per., Uru. vereda
Col., Nic. andén
Mex. banqueta

sieve (n) cedazo
Arg., Spa. tamiz
Chi., Cub., Venz. colador
Col. coladera, tamiz
Mex. coladera
Nic. zaranda

silverware (n) cubiertos
Col. platería

sing harmony (v phr) cantar en
armonía
Par. cantar afinado
Pue.R. cantar afinados

single (unmarried) (adj) soltero
Col. célibe, solterón

sinus (n) seno
Mex., Spa. seno nasal
Venz. cavidad

sitar (n) sitar
  Nic. cítara
  Venz. guitarra oriental
sitcom, situation comedy
  (n phr) comedia de situación
  Chi., Col., Dom.R., Nic.,
  Spa. comedia
skeleton (n) esqueleto
  Col. osamenta Mex. calaca
ski jump (n phr) trampolín
  Venz. salto en esquíes
skid (traffic) (v) patinar
  Cos.R. resbalar
skimmer (n) espumadera
  Col. desnatadora
  Mex. desnatador
skinny (adj) delgado, flaco
  Col. enjuto
skirt (n) falda
  Arg., Par., Uru. pollera
  Cub. saya
skull (n) cráneo
  Col., Cos.R., Mex. calavera
sledgehammer (n) almádena
  Chi., Dom.R., Mex., Nic.,
  Par. mazo
  Pue.R. marrón
sleeping car (train)
  (n phr) coche cama
  Col. litera
sleepy (adj) soñoliento
  Dom.R. asueñado
  Mex., Nic., Par. adormilado
slip (n) combinación
  Chi., Pue.R. enagua
  Cub. sayuela
  Dom.R. mediofondo
  Nic. fustán
  Pan. peticote
  Par. enagua
  Mex., Venz. fondo
slippers (n) pantuflas
  Arg. chinelas

  Col. babuchas
  Cos.R., Cub., Pan.
  Chancletas
  Nic. chinelas, chancletas
  Spa. zapatillas de casa
slow (adj) lento
  Col. despacioso, lerdo
small (adj) chiquito, pequeño
  Arg., Chi. chico
  Col. chico, corto, menudo
smelt (n) eperlano
  Chi., Nic., Par. pejerrey
snack (n) merienda
  Col., Nic. bocadillo,
  refrigerio
  Dom.R. picadera
  Mex. botana
  Spa. snack
snail (n) caracol
  Dom.R., Nic. babosa
snake (n) culebra
  Arg., Bol., Mex., Uru. víbora
  Chi., Cub. serpiente
snapper (n) pargo
  Dom.R., Pue.R. chillo
  Mex. guachinango,
  huachinango
snare (of drum) (n) cuerdas
  Col. bordón, tirante
  Nic. bordón
snare drum (n phr) tarola
  Col. tambor militar pequeño
  Cos.R., Nic. redoblante
sneakers (n) snikers
  Arg., Chi., Pan., Per., Uru.
  zapatillas
  Col., Cos.R., Dom.R., Nic.,
  Par., Pue.R. tenis
  Ecu. zapatos de caucho
  ElS., Gua., Hon. zapatos de
  lona con suela de hule
  Mex. tenis de lona
  Spa. zapatillas de lona

ABBREVIATIONS: Arg.=Argentina Bol.=Bolivia Chi.=Chile Col.=Colombia Cos.R.=Costa Rica
Cub.=Cuba Dom.R.=Dominican Republic Ecu.=Ecuador ElS.=El Salvador Gua.=Guatemala
Hon.=Honduras Mex.=Mexico Nic.=Nicaragua Pan.=Panama Par.=Paraguay Per.=Peru
Pri.=Primary Term Pue.R.=Puerto Rico Spa.=Spain Uru.=Uruguay Venz.=Venezuela

Venz. zapatos de goma
snifter (n) copa ancha de boca
estrecha
Chi. copa de cognac
snoop (n) fisgón
Chi. intruso
Col. entremetido, metiche,
metido
Cub. metiche, metido
Dom.R. curioso, entrometido,
metiche Dom.R.
Ecu., Mex. metiche
Gua. entrometido, shute
Pan. vidajeno/a
Par. entrometido, metiche
Pue.R. ligón
Venz. averiguador
soap opera (n phr) telenovela
Arg., Cub. novela
soccer (n) fútbol
Pue.R. balompié
sock (n) calcetín
Arg., Uru. media (tres
cuartos), soquete
Col., Cub., Dom.R., Ecu.,
Pan., Pue.R., Venz. media
Par. medias
soft (adj) blando
Col. flojo, suave
Nic. Suave
soft drugs (n phr) drogas blandas
Col. drogas más suaves,
drogas menos fuertes, drogas
no tan dañinas
Mex., Nic., Par. drogas
suaves
software (n) software
Nic., Spa. programas
soil (n) tierra
Nic. suelo
Pue.R. terreno
soldier (n) soldado
Col. militar, recluta

song (n) canción
Arg. tema
Col. canto
sound effects (n phr) efectos \
sonoros
Arg., Col., Mex., Nic., Pan.,
Pue.R., Spa., Venz. efectos
de sonido
sound track (n phr) banda
sonora
Arg. banda de sonido
Mex., Pue.R. música
Nic. pista
Venz. pista de sonido
sour (adj) agrio
Col. ácido, amárgo
Nic., Pan. ácido
soybeans (n) frijoles de soja
Chi., Spa. soja
Col., Gua. semillas de soya
Cub., Venz. soya
Nic. frijol de soya
Par., Uru. porotos de soja
spade (n) pala
Chi. pica
Venz. pico
spare parts (n phr) repuestos
Cub., Spa. piezas de repuesto
Mex. refacciones
Pue.R. repuestas
spare tire (n phr) rueda de
repuesto
Arg. goma de auxilio, rueda
de auxilio
Bol., Ecu., Gua., Nic., Pan.
llanta de repuesto
Dom.R. goma de repuesto
Mex. llanta de refacción
Par. llanta de repuesto, rueda
de auxilio
Pue.R. goma de repuesta
Venz. caucho de repuesto
spectacles (n) anteojos

ABBREVIATIONS: Arg.=Argentina Bol.=Bolivia Chi.=Chile Col.=Colombia Cos.R.=Costa Rica
Cub.=Cuba Dom.R.=Dominican Republic Ecu.=Ecuador EIS.=El Salvador Gua.=Guatemala
Hon.=Honduras Mex.=Mexico Nic.=Nicaragua Pan.=Panama Par.=Paraguay Per.=Peru
Pri.=Primary Term Pue.R.=Puerto Rico Spa.=Spain Uru.=Uruguay Venz.=Venezuela

Col. gafas, lentes
Venz. espejuelos
speed limit (n phr) límite de
velocidad
Mex., Pue.R. velocidad
máxima
speedometer (n) velocímetro
Chi. cuenta kilómetros
Cub. cuentakilómetro
spider (n) araña
Dom.R. cacata
spine (n) columna vertebral
Col. espinazo
Ecu. espina dorsal, espinaso
Gua. espina dorsal
spoiled (child) (adj) mimado
Arg., Cub., Pan., Pue.R.
malcriado
Chi. regalón
Col. consentido,
malacostumbrado, malcriado
Cos.R. chineado
Dom.R. ñoño
Ecu. consentido
Mex. chiqueado, consentido
Nic. consentido, malcriado
Per. engreído
spoke (bicycle wheel) (n) faro
Arg., Cub., Gua., Mex., Nic.
rayo
Col. radio, rayo
Spa., Venz. radio
sports car (n phr) carro
deportivo
Arg., Chi., Par. auto
deportivo
Bol. coche sport
Cub. carro de deporte
Spa., Uru. coche deportivo
spouse (n) cónyuge
Col., Nic. esposo/a, media
naranja
Cos.R., Cub., Dom.R., Mex.

esposo/a
sprinkler (n) rociador
Arg. regador
Cub., Par. regadera
Mex. regilete
Nic., Spa. aspersor
sprint (v) esprintar
Chi. picar
Col., Dom.R., Par. correr a
toda velocidad
Cub. correr
Nic. balacearse, correr a toda
velocidad
squash (n) chilacayote
Bol. zapallito
Col., Cos.R., Cub., Ecu.,
Par., Spa. calabaza
Dom.R., Venz. Auyama
Nic. ayote
Pan. chayote
Uru. zapallo
squid (n) calamar
Chi. jibia
stadium (n) estadio
Pue.R. parque
stair machine
(n phr) escaladora
Cos.R. máquina escalera
Dom.R., Par. máquina de
hacer ejercicios
Mex. escalera
stall (car) (v) calar
Arg., Cub., Ecu., Mex., Pan.
parar
Chi. pararse
Col. vararse
Cos.R. quedar varado
Pue.R. inundar
Nic. ahogarse, pararse
Par. ahogarse
Spa. calarse
Venz. apagarse el carro
stallion (n) padrillo

Arg., Col., Dom.R., Par.,
Spa., Venz. semental
Chi. garañón
Gua. garañón, semental
Nic. garañón, padrote,
semental
staple (n) grapa
Arg. ganchito
Chi. corchete
Cub. presilla
Par., Per. grampa
staple remover (n phr) uñas
Bol., Ecu., ElS., Gua., Hon.,
Nic. sacagrapas
Chi. saca corchetes
Col. removedor de grapas
Dom. R. uñas saca grapas
Mex. uña quitagrapas
Par. saca grampas
Spa. quitagrapas
Venz. saca-grapas
stapler (n) engrapadora
Arg. abrochadora
Chi. corchetera
Cub., Par. pressilladora
Per. engrampador
Pue.R., Spa. grapadora
start (car) (v) arrancar
Chi., Dom.R. encender,
prender
Col. poner en marcha,
prender
Nic. encender
Pue.R. prender
starter (n) arranque
Chi. salir
Cos.R., Mex. arrancador
Par., Spa. motor de arranque
Pue.R. estarter
station wagon
(n phr) camioneta
Cos.R., Ecu., Per., Spa.
combinable

Bol. vagoneta
Cub. pisicorre
Dom.R. station, van
Pue.R. guagüita
stationary bicycle
(n phr) bicicleta estacionaria
Mex. bicicleta fija
Pan. bicicleta estable
Par. bicicleta
Spa. bicicleta estática
steering wheel (n phr) volante
Chi., Par. manubrio
Col., Cub., Gua., Nic., Pan.
timón
Dom.R., Pue.R. guía
stick shift (n phr) palanca de
cambios
Arg. cambio
Cos.R. marcha
Mex. palanca de velocidades
Spa. cambio manual
stomach (n) estómago
Col. aparato digestivo
stool (n) banco
Chi. piso
Dom.R. banqueta, banquito
Nic. banquito, pata de gallina
stop (sign) (n) alto
Arg., Chi., Col., Pue.R. pare
Par., Spa. stop
storage room
(n phr) almacenaje
Arg., Col. depósito
Bol., Dom.R., Pue.R., Spa.
almacén
Chi. despensa
Cos.R., Ecu., Gua., Nic.
bodega
Mex. almacén, bodega
store (computer data)
(v) almacenar
Arg., Nic. grabar, guardar
Dom.R. archivar

Mex., Pan. guardar
Venz. guarder
storm (n) tormenta
Col. aguacero, borrasca
stove (n) estufa
Arg., Bol., Chi., Nic., Per.,
Spa., Uru. cocina
straight (hair) (adj) lacio
Chi., Col., Spa., Venz. liso
Dom.R. bueno
Nic. liso, chiriso
strange (adj) extraño, raro
Col. insólito, singular
strawberry (n) fresa
Arg., Par. frutilla
stream (n) arroyo
Col., Dom.R., Pue.R.
riachuelo
Nic. crique, quebrada
street lamp (n phr) farol
Dom.R. palo de luz
Nic. luminaria, poste de luz
Pan. poste de luz
Spa. farola
street, cobblestone (n phr) calle
de guijarro
Arg., Bol., Col., Ecu., Venz.
calle empedrada
Chi. calle de adoquines, calle
de paralelepípedos
Gua. calle de adoquín
Mex., Nic. calle adoquinada
Pan. calle de ladrillo
Per. calle de piedras
Pue.R., Spa., Uru. calle de
adoquines
street, dead-end (n phr) calle
sin salida
Col., Mex. calle cerrada
Dom.R. cul de sac
Venz. calle ciega
street, one-way (n phr) calle de
una mano

Chi. vía única
Col., Mex., Per. calle de un
solo sentido
Cos.R., Dom.R., Nic.,
Pue.R., Venz. calle de una
vía
Ecu. calle de una sola
dirección
ElS., Gua., Hon. calle de una
sola vía
Pan. calle de una vía, one
way
Par. calle sentido único
Spa. calle de dirección única
string quartet (n phr) cuarteto
de cuerdas
Spa. cuarteto de cuerda
strum (v) guitarrear
Col., Nic., Spa. rasguear
Cos.R. rasgar
strumming (n) guitarreo
Col., Spa. rasgueado
Cos.R. rasgueo
Nic. rasgueado, rasgueo
stud (n) tachuela
Col. chinche
Mex. espárrago, espiga,
pasador, viga vertical
Nic. ojo de gato (reflectante
en la calle), semental
stump (n) tocón
Dom.R. cabo
Mex. parte del tronco
Nic. cabo, cabito, muñón,
tuco
stunt (n) acrobática
Col., Mex. truco
Dom.R., Pue.R. doblaje
Nic., Spa., Venz. acrobacia
stuntman (n) acróbata
Arg. extra Arg. extra
Col. aquel que realiza los trucos
Dom.R., Mex., Pue.R. doble

Nic. doble, extra
Spa. doble, especialista
Venz. especialista en
acrobacias
subtitles (n) subtítulos
Cub., Pan., Uru. leyendas
suburb (n) barrio
Col. barrio en las afueras,
suburbio
Dom.R., Gua. suburbio
Mex. colonia,
fraccionamiento
Nic. residencial
succulent (plant) (n) suculenta
Mex. carnosa
suit (n) traje
Bol., Per. terno
Col., Pan. vestido
suit, double-breasted
(n phr) traje cruzado
Gua. traje traslapado
Nic. traje con traslape
suit, tailored (n phr) traje sastre
Col. vestido hecho a la
medida
Pan. vestido sastre
Par. traje a medida
Nic., Venz. traje a la medida
suit, three-piece (n phr) terno
Bol., Dom.R., Mex., Nic.,
Par., Pue.R., Venz. traje de
tres piezas
Pan. vestido de tres piezas
suitcase (n) maleta
Arg., Nic., Par. valija
sunroof (n) sunroof
Chi., Spa. techo solar
Col., Par. techo corredizo
Mex. quemacocos
Nic. techo convertible,
techo descapotable
Venz. techo corredizo, techo
descapotable

sunscreen (n) loción solar
Arg. pantalla solar,
protector
Chi., Cos.R., Nic. protector
solar
Dom.R. bloqueador solar
Mex., Per. bronceador
Par. bronceador, protector
solar
Spa. crema de protección
solar
Venz. protector de sol
surf the net (v phr) surfear la
Internet
Arg. navegar la red
Bol., Ecu. navegar en el
Internet
Chi., Gua. navegar por la
Internet
Col. navegar por Internet
Dom.R. surfear en el
Internet
Mex. accesar a la red, buscar
en la red, usar la red
Nic. navegar por Internet
Par., Spa., Uru. navegar por
la red
Venz. explorar el Internet
suspenders (n) ligas
Chi. suspensores
Dom.R. breteles
Gua., Nic., Pan., Spa., Venz.
tirantes
Mex. ligeros
swamp (n) marisma
Chi. ciénaga, pantano
Col., Dom.R., Ecu., Mex.,
Par., Venz. pantano
Nic. swampo
Uru. terreno pantanoso
sweater (n) suéter
Arg. pulover
Chi. chomba

ABBREVIATIONS: Arg.=Argentina Bol.=Bolivia Chi.=Chile Col.=Colombia Cos.R.=Costa Rica
Cub.=Cuba Dom.R.=Dominican Republic Ecu.=Ecuador EIS.=El Salvador Gua.=Guatemala
Hon.=Honduras Mex.=Mexico Nic.=Nicaragua Pan.=Panama Par.=Paraguay Per.=Peru
Pri.=Primary Term Pue.R.=Puerto Rico Spa.=Spain Uru.=Uruguay Venz.=Venezuela

Per. chompa
Spa. jersey
sweatshirt (n) camisa de trabajo
Arg. buzo
Chi., Col., Mex., Nic.,
Pue.R. sudadera
Dom.R. abrigo, sudadera
Gua. sudadero
Par. buzo, sudadera
Spa. jersey
sweet potato (n phr) batata
Bol., Ecu., Gua., Mex., Nic.,
Pan., Per. camote
Chi. papa dulce
Cub., Uru. boniato

sweetheart (n) enamorado/a
Chi. pololo/a
Mex. corazón
Nic. amor, corazón
Spa. cariño, querido
swimming pool
(n phr) piscina
Arg., Par. pileta
Mex. alberca
Swiss roll (n phr) rollo
Nic., Spa. brazo de gitano
Uru. rosca
Venz. bollo de pan
swordfish (n) pez espada
Chi. albacora

ABBREVIATIONS: Arg.=Argentina Bol.=Bolivia Chi.=Chile Col.=Colombia Cos.R.=Costa Rica
Cub.=Cuba Dom.R.=Dominican Republic Ecu.=Ecuador ElS.=El Salvador Gua.=Guatemala
Hon.=Honduras Mex.=Mexico Nic.=Nicaragua Pan.=Panama Par.=Paraguay Per.=Peru
Pri.=Primary Term Pue.R.=Puerto Rico Spa.=Spain Uru.=Uruguay Venz.=Venezuela

T

table leaf (n phr) tablero
  Chi. tabla
  Col. hoja Col. hoja, lámina
  Mex. tablón de extensión
  Nic. tabla de extensión
table, kitchen (n phr) mesa de
  cocina
  Pan. mesita de cocina
table, night (n phr) mesilla de
  noche
  Arg. mesa de luz, mesita de
  luz
  Bol. mesita de noche,
  velador
  Chi. velador
  Col., ElS., Gua., Hon., Nic.,
  Pue.R., Venz. mesa de noche
  Dom.R., Pan., Par. mesita de
  noche
table, serving (n phr) mesita de
  servicio
  Arg. mesita rodante
  Col., Nic. mesa de servicio
  Par. meza de servir
  Venz. mesa de servir
tack (n) tachuela
  Nic. chinche
  Spa. chincheta
tailcoat (n) frac
  Nic., Par., Venz. smoking
tailor (n) sastre
  Col., Spa. costurero
talk show (n phr) programa de
  entrevistas
  Col. programa de charlas
  Nic. programa en vivo

talkative (adj) hablador, locuaz
  Arg., Par. charlatán
  Col. charlatán, dicharachero,
  garlador
  Nic. hablantín
  Pan. conversador
tambourine (n) pandero
  Chi., Col., Cub., Dom.R.,
  Ecu., Nic., Pue.R., Spa.
  pandereta
tan (skin) (adj) bronceado
  Arg., Chi., Dom.R. quemado
  Col. tostado
tan (v) broncearse
  Arg., Chi., Dom.R. quemarse
  Col. dorarse al sol
tape (cassette) (n) cinta
  Arg., Col., Venz. casete
  Dom.R., Mex., Nic., Par.
  cassette
tape (n) cinta adhesiva
  Ecu. cinta pegante
  Mex. durex
  Nic., Pue.R. tape
  Spa. celo
tape dispenser (n phr) carrete
  de cinta
  Col. dispensador de cinta
  pegante
  Dom.R., Nic. rollo de tape
  Mex. dispensador de durex,
  portarrollo
  Par. rollo cinta adhesiva
  Spa. carrete de celo
  Venz. dispensador de cinta
  adhesiva

tape measure (n phr) metro
  Arg., Col., Dom.R., Mex.,
  Nic., Spa. cinta métrica
  Chi. huincha
  Cub. centímetro
  Pan. cinta de medir
taro (n) taro
  Cub. malanga
  Dom.R. yautía
  Nic. quequisque
tart (n) moldecito
  Bol., Chi., Pue.R., Uru.,
  Venz. tarta
  Col. torta
  Dom.R. dulcito relleno
  Gua. pastelito
  Mex. tartaleta
  Nic. pastelito, torta
  Par. molde
  Spa. pastel de frutas
attler (n) charlatán
  Chi., Cub., Gua. chismoso/a
  Dom.R., Pue.R.
  sinvergüenza
  Mex. hablador
  Nic. tapudo
  Spa. chivato
taxi (n) taxi
  Venz. libre
taxi driver (n phr) conductor de
  taxi
  Arg., Cub., Dom.R., Gua.,
  Mex., Per., Spa. taxista
  Chi., Cos.R. chofer de taxi
  Col. chofer de taxi,
  taxista
  Nic. taxista, taxero
  Venz. conductor de libre
taxi stand (n phr) parada de taxi
  Venz. parada de libres,
  parada de taxis
teacher (n) profesor/a
  Chi., Mex., Pan., Spa., Venz.

maestro/a
  Col. educador, maestro/a
  Cub. profe
  Nic. docente, maestro/a
teenager (n) adolescente
  Dom.R. teenager
  Nic. chavalo
teeth (n) dientes
  Col. dentadura
telecommute (v) teletrabajar
  Nic. trabajo a distancia
  Par. tener oficina a
  domicilio
  Venz. tener oficina
  domiciliaria, tener oficina a
  domicilio
telephone booth (n phr) cabina
  telefónica
  Mex., Nic. teléfono público
television set (n phr) televisor
  Col., Mex., Spa. televisión
television viewer
  (n phr) televidente
  Col. teleaudiencia
temporary worker
  (n phr) temporero
  Bol. temporal
  Chi., Par. jornalero
  Col., Cos.R., Gua., Venz.
  empleado/a temporal
  Mex. trabajador eventual
  Nic. jornalero, trabajador
  temporal
  Uru. temporario
tenor drum (n phr) teno
  Col. tambor de tenor
  Nic. tambor tenor
  Par., Spa. tenor
tent (n) carpa
  Chi., Cos.R., Dom.R., Mex.,
  Nic., Spa., Venz. tienda de
  campaña
  Pan. tolda

ABBREVIATIONS: Arg.=Argentina Bol.=Bolivia Chi.=Chile Col.=Colombia Cos.R.=Costa Rica
Cub.=Cuba Dom.R.=Dominican Republic Ecu.=Ecuador ElS.=El Salvador Gua.=Guatemala
Hon.=Honduras Mex.=Mexico Nic.=Nicaragua Pan.=Panama Par.=Paraguay Per.=Peru
Pri.=Primary Term Pue.R.=Puerto Rico Spa.=Spain Uru.=Uruguay Venz.=Venezuela

termite (n) termita
  Cos.R., Cub., Dom.R., Pan.,
  Pue.R. comején
  Chi. polilla
  Ecu., ElS., Gua., Hon.
  Comején
  Nic. comején, polilla
three-ring binder
  (n phr) carpeta de argollas
  Arg. carpeta con ganchos
  Chi. archivador
  Col. folder de argollas
  Dom.R. carpeta de tres
  hoyos
  Nic. folder de tres anillos
  Pan. portafolio
  Spa. carpeta de tres anillos
through train (n phr) tren
  directo
  Par., Venz. tren expreso
thumb (n) pulgar
  Arg. dedo gordo
ticket (n) billete
  Arg., Cub. boleto, pasaje
  Chi., Mex., Pan., Per.,
  Pue.R. boleto
  Col. tiquete, voleto
  Cos.R. pasaje
  Dom.R., Nic. pasaje, ticket
  Par., Venz. boleto, ticket
ticket collector (n phr) revisor
  Chi., Ecu. conductor
  Col. recolector de tiquetes
  Mex. persona que recoge los
  boletos
  Nic. cobrador
  Par. guarda
  Per. boletero
  Venz. chequeador de boletos,
  chequeador de tickets
ticket, speeding (n phr) multa
  por exceso de velocidad
  Mex., Nic. infracción por

  exceso de velocidad
  Pan. boleta por velocidad
  Par. multa por infracción
ticket, traffic (n phr) multa
  Mex. infracción
  Pan. boleta
tights (n) leotardo
  Chi. medias gruesas
  Col. media pantalón
  Mex., Nic., Venz. mallas
  Par. malla
  Pue.R. tights
  Spa. leotardos, medias
timetable (n) horario
  Col. itinerario
timpani (n) timbal
  Col., Cub. tímpanos
tip of nose (n phr) lóbulo
  Chi., Col., Mex., Nic., Spa.,
  Venz. punta de la nariz
tire (bicycle) (n) neumático
  Arg., Dom.R., Pue.R. goma
  Bol., Col., Cos.R., Gua., Mex.,
  Pan., Per. llanta
  Cub. rueda
  Venz. caucho
tire (car) (n) llanta
  Arg., Cub. goma, rueda
  Chi., Col. pneumático
  Dom.R., Pue.R. goma
  Spa. rueda
  Venz. caucho
tired (adj) cansado
  Col. fastigado
toast (n) tostada
  Mex., Pan. pan tostado
toaster (n) tostador
  Chi., Col., Cub., Dom.R.,
  Ecu., Pue.R., Spa., Venz.
  tostadora
toddler (n) pequeñito/a
  Arg. beba, bebe, bebé
  Col. niño/a chiquito/a

ElS., Gua., Hon., Nic. niño/a
que empieza a andar
Mex. niño/a de edad pre-
escolar, niño/a que empieza
a andar
Spa. niño/a
Venz. niñito/a
toenail (n) uña del pie
Col. uña del dedo del pie
tomato (n) tomate
Mex. jitomate
tom-tom (n) tam-tam
Col. tantán
Spa. tamtan
tone (n) sonoridad
Col., Dom.R., Mex., Nic.
tono
toner (n) tinta
Dom. R., Nic., Par. toner
Mex. tonificador
toner cartridge (n phr) cartucho
de tinta
Dom.R. cartucho del toner
Dom.R. cartucho del toner
Mex. cartucho tonificador
Nic., Par. cartucho de toner
Mex. cartucho tonificador
tongs (n) tenazas
Arg., Col., Spa. pinzas
tonsil (n) amígdala
Mex. angina
toothpaste (n) dentífrico, pasta
de dientes
Col. crema dental
Per., Pue.R. pasta dental
town (n) pueblo
Col. población
townhouse (n) casa en hilera
Bol., Uru. casa pegada
Col. casa de ciudad, casa
particular en la ciudad
Dom.R., Nic., Pue.R.
townhouse

Gua. casa particular en
complejos residenciales
Mex. dúplex horizontal
Par. duplex
Spa. casa adosada
traffic (n) tráfico
Chi., Cos.R., Dom.R.
tránsito
traffic island (n phr) isleta
Arg., Col., Par., Venz. isla
Nic. bahía peatonal
traffic jam
(n phr) congestionamiento
Arg., Nic., Par., Per., Uru.
embotellamiento
Chi. atascamiento,
congestión, taco
Col. trancón
Cos.R. atasco, presa
Cub. tráfico
Dom.R., Pue.R. tapón
Pan. tranque
Spa. atasco
trailer (n) remolque
Chi., Cos.R., Dom.R., Nic.,
Pan. trailer
train (for job) (v) capacitar
Col., Cub., Dom.R., Ecu., Pan.,
Venz. entrenar
tread (tire) (n) ranuras
Mex. dibujo de llanta
Nic. grabado de la llanta
Spa. cubierta
Venz. huella del caucho
treadmill (n) rueda de andar
Col. caminador
Cos.R., Nic. banda sin fin
Dom.R. máquina de caminar
Mex., Uru. caminadora
Par. caminor
Pue.R. máquina de correr
treble (stereo) (n) de agudos
Col., Nic., Par. tonos agudos

Spa. agudos
tree (n) árbol
  Dom.R. mata
tremendous (adj) imponente
  Arg., Chi., Cub., Mex., Nic,
  Venz. tremendo
  Col. asombroso
trench coat (n phr) trinchera
  Col., Spa. impermeable
  Mex. gabardina
  Nic. gabán
trifocals (n) trifocales
  Spa. gafas trifocales
  Venz. lentes trifocales
triple jump (n phr) salto triple
  Arg., Col. triple salto
trolley (n) tranvía
  Chi. trole
  Dom.R. carrito
  Mex. trolebús
trowel (n) desplantador
  Chi., Nic. paleta
  Mex. palustre
  Par., Venz. aplanadora
  Pue.R. palaustre
trunk (car) (n) baúl
  Bol., Per. maletera
  Chi. porta equipaje
  Cub., Pan., Spa. maletero
  Mex. cajuela
  Nic. maletero, valijera
  Par., Venz. maleta
t-shirt (n) camiseta
  Arg. remera
  Chi. polera
  Dom.R. polo-shirt
tumbler (n) vaso para whiskey
  Arg., Nic. vaso
tuna (n) atún
  Pue.R. tuna
tune up (v phr) revisar
  Cub. reglar
  Dom.R. arreglar

Gua., Mex., Nic. afinar
  Venz. entonar
turkey (n) pavo
  Cub. guanajo
  Mex. guajolote
  Nic. chompipe
turn on (television) (v phr) prender
  Bol., Chi., Cub., Ecu., Gua.,
  Nic., Par., Spa., Uru. encender
turn right, left (v phr) doblar a la
  derecha, izquierda
  Cos.R. virar a la derecha,
  izquierda
  Mex. dar vuelta a la derecha,
  izquierda
  Nic. girar
  Spa. torcer a la derecha,
  izquierda
turner (n) pala
  Nic. tornero/a
  Pan. espátula
  Venz. paleta
turning light (n phr) luz
  direccional
  Arg. guiño
  Chi. luz del indicador
  Col. luz para doblar
  Cub., Spa. intermitente
  Dom.R. luz de doblar
  Gua., Nic. pidevías
  Mex. dirrecional
  Per. luz para voltear
  Uru. señal intermitente
  Venz. señal de cruce
turtleneck (n) cuello vuelto
  Arg., Par. polera
  Chi. beatle
  Col. buzo, cuello de tortuga
  Dom.R., Nic., Pan., Venz.
  cuello tortuga
  Mex., Pue.R. cuello de
  tortuga
  Per. cuello Jorge Chavez

Spa. polo de cuello alto
Uru. rompeviento
tuxedo (n) smoking
Pan. toxido
Pue.R. tuxedo

two-four time
(n phr) compás
menor, compasillo
Nic., Par., Spa. compás de
dos por cuatro

ABBREVIATIONS: Arg.=Argentina Bol.=Bolivia Chi.=Chile Col.=Colombia Cos.R.=Costa Rica
Cub.=Cuba Dom.R.=Dominican Republic Ecu.=Ecuador ElS.=El Salvador Gua.=Guatemala
Hon.=Honduras Mex.=Mexico Nic.=Nicaragua Pan.=Panama Par.=Paraguay Per.=Peru
Pri.=Primary Term Pue.R.=Puerto Rico Spa.=Spain Uru.=Uruguay Venz.=Venezuela

U

umpire (baseball) (n) umpire
    Cub., Ecu., Uru., Venz.
    árbitro
    Mex. ampayer
    Nic. árbitro, juez
underpass (n) paso subterráneo
    Chi. paso nivel
    Col., Par. pasadizo
    subterráneo
    Nic. paso a desnivel
    Spa. paso inferior
underwear (n) ropa interior
    Cos.R., Bol. ropa blanca
    Cub. ropa de interior

undress (v) desvestirse
    Col., Venz. quitarse la ropa
upper floor (n phr) planta alta
    Col. piso superior
    Dom.R., Nic. piso de arriba
    Spa. planta superior
uptown (n) distrito residencial
    Dom.R. área residencial
    Nic. zona residencial
    Par. barrio residencial
use drugs (v phr) drogarse
    Col. consumir drogas, usar
    drogas
    ElS., Gua. consumir drogas

V

vacant (adj) libre
    Col. desocupado
    Dom.R. vacante
    Mex., Venz. vacío
    Nic. desocupado, vacío
vacuum cleaner
    (n phr) aspiradora
    Cub., Cos.R. aspirador
valve (trumpet) (n) pistón
    Mex. llave
van (n) camión
    Arg., Chi., Dom.R., Pue.R.
    van
    Col., Uru. furgón
    Cos.R., Mex., Nic.
    camioneta
    Ecu. buseta
    Pan. busito, van
    Per. microbus
    Spa. furgoneta
    Venz. camioneta, furgoneta
vegetable garden
    (n phr) huerto
    Arg. huerta, quinta
    Spa. huerta
vest (n) chaleco
    Arg. camiseta, musculosa
videocassette (n) videocasete
    Col. casete para vídeo
    Dom.R. casette
    Spa. cinta de vídeo
videocassette recorder (VCR)
    (n phr) videograbadora

Arg., Mex., Nic.
videocasetera
Chi. VCR
Col. grabadora de vídeo,
VCR
Spa. vídeo
videogame (n) videojuego
    Col., Cos.R., Dom.R., Mex.,
    Nic., Venz. juego de vídeo
village (n) aldea
    Arg. pueblo
    Col. población, poblado,
    pueblo, villorrio
    Dom.R., Par. pueblito
    Nic. caserío
violoncello (n) violoncelo
    Spa. violonchelo
vise (n) prensa
    Mex., Nic., Uru. torno
v-neck (n) cuello de pico
    Arg., Chi., Col., Gua., Mex.,
    Venz. cuello en V
    Dom.R., Pan., Per., Pue.R.
    cuello V
    Par. escote V
    Uru. escote en V
volleyball (n) voleibol
    Cub. volibol
    Par. volley
vulture (n) buitre
    Chi. jote
    Cub. aura tiñosa

W

waffle (n) gofre
    Col. barquillo, waffle
    Gua., Nic. wafle
    Mex., Par. waffle
wagon (n) carreta
    Bol., Ecu., Gua., Nic., Spa.
    vagón
waist (n) cintura
    Col., Nic. talle
waiter (n) camarero
    Arg., Bol., Cos.R., Dom.R.,
    Uru. mozo
    Chi. garzón, mesero, mozo
    Col., Cub., Dom.R., ElS.,
    Gua., Mex., Nic., Pan.,
    Pue.R. mesero
    Venz. mesonero
wake (n) velorio
    Col. velación
    Cos.R., Nic. vela
    Dom.R. funeral
    Spa. velatorio
wallet (n) billetera, cartera
    Dom.R. cartera de hombre
walnut (n) nuez del nogal
    Nic., Pan., Par. nuez
    Pue.R. avellana
walrus (n) morsa
    Dom.R. foca marina
WAN (wide area network)
    (n phr) WAN
    Col., Par. red de área
    extendida
    Mex., Spa. red de área
    amplia
    Uru. red de área ancha
    Venz. red de área extensa

warden (prison) (n) director/a de
    la cárcel
    Nic. alcaide
    Venz. carcelero, guardián de
    la cárcel
wart (n) verruga
    Mex., Nic. mezquino
    Per. callo
washer (n) arandela
    Mex. rodana
wasp (n) avispa
    Pan. abejorro
watch television (v phr) ver
    tele(visión)
    Col., Nic. mirar televisión
    Spa. ver la televisión
water fountain (n phr) fuente de
    agua
    Arg., Chi., Mex., Venz.
    bebedero
    Dom.R. neverita
water skiing (n phr) esquí
    acuático
    Chi., Par. ski acuático
    Cos.R., Ecu., ElS., Gua., Per.,
    Venz. esquí náutico
waterfall (n) cascada
    Dom.R. caída de agua
    Spa. catarata
watering can (n phr) regadera
    Mex. regador de plantas
    Nic. pascón
    Venz. lata de regar
watermelon (n) sandía
    Col., Venz. patilla
    Cub. melón de agua
    Dom.R. pastilla

ABBREVIATIONS: Arg.=Argentina Bol.=Bolivia Chi.=Chile Col.=Colombia Cos.R.=Costa Rica
Cub.=Cuba Dom.R.=Dominican Republic Ecu.=Ecuador ElS.=El Salvador Gua.=Guatemala
Hon.=Honduras Mex.=Mexico Nic.=Nicaragua Pan.=Panama Par.=Paraguay Per.=Peru
Pri.=Primary Term Pue.R.=Puerto Rico Spa.=Spain Uru.=Uruguay Venz.=Venezuela

wavy (hair) (adj) ondulado
   Nic., Venz. crespo
wear (clothing) (v) llevar
   Arg., Bol., Gua., Pan., Venz.
   usar
   Chi. ponerse, vestir
   Col. tener puesto
   Cub. llevar puesto, tener
   puesto
   Dom.R. llevar puesto,
   ponerse
   Mex., Nic. ponerse
   Par. llevar puesto, vestir
weather report (n phr) boletín
   meteorológico
   Arg., Nic., Par. pronóstico
   del tiempo
   Col. reporte del estado del
   tiempo
   Venz. reporte del tiempo,
   reporte meteorológico
weather reporter
   (n phr) meteorólogo
   Venz. reportero del tiempo,
   reportero meteorológico
website (n) sitio web
   Arg. página principal
   Dom.R., Pue.R. web-site
   Gua. sitio de la red
   Nic. página Web
   Venz. lugar del Web, página
   del Web
wedding (n) boda
   Arg. casamiento
   Col. casamiento, enlace,
   nupcias, matrimonio, union
   Nic. casamiento,
   matrimonio
   Pan. matrimonio
weed (n) mala hierba
   Arg. maleza, yuyo
   Chi., Ecu., Nic. maleza
   Dom.R. maleza, pajón

   Mex. hierba silvestre
   Par. yuyo
   Pue.R. yerba mala
weekday (n) día de entre semana
   Arg., Col., Dom.R., Pue.R.,
   Venz. día de semana
   Gua., Nic., Spa. día entre
   semana
weight lifting
   (n phr) levantamiento de
   pesas
   Chi. alterofilismo
wetlands (n) pantano
   Chi. marisma
   Mex. terreno pantanoso
   Nic. humedales
What's up? (int phr) ¿Qué pasa?
   Chi., Par. ¿Qué hay?
   Col. ¿En qué andas/an?,
   ¿Qué hay?
   Dom.R. ¿Qué hay de nuevo?
   Nic. ¿Qué onda? ¿Qué pasó?
   Pan. ¿Quiubo?
wife (n) esposa, mujer
   Col. compañera, cónyuge,
   pareja
   Dom.R., Par. señora
   Nic. compañera, cónyuge,
   pareja, señora
wine shop (n phr) bodega
   Col. taberna
   Dom.R. tienda de vinos
   Ecu. tienda de licores
   Mex., Nic., Pue.R. vinatería
   Uru. vinería
wipers (windshield)
   (n) limpiaparabrisas
   Col. limpiabrisas
   Dom.R. limpiavidrios
   Nic., Per. parabrisas
   Pue.R. wipers
   Venz. limpia-parabrisas
women's (bathroom) (n) mujeres

Chi., Col., Cub., Dom.R.,
Mex., Nic., Pue.R., Venz.
damas
woodcock (n) chocha
Col. gallineta
ElS., Gua. gallina sorda,
gallineta
Nic., Venz. perdiz
word processing
(n phr) procesamiento de
palabras
Arg., Mex., Par. procesamiento
de textos

Cub., Ecu. procesamiento
de texto
Pue.R. word processing
work day (n phr) día hábil
Col. día laborable, día de
trabajo
Dom.R., Spa. día
laborable
Per., Pue.R. día de trabajo
wrong (adj) equivocado
Col. erróneo
Nic. erróneo, incorrecto
Pue.R., Spa. incorrecto

X-Y-Z

xylophone (n) xilófono
    Cub., Par. marimba
yacht (n) yate
    Dom.R. bote
yellow jacket (n phr) avispa con
    pintas amarillas
    Nic. avispa chaqueta

    amarilla
    Pan., Par. abispa
zucchini (n) calabacín
    Chi. zapallito italiano
    Mex. calabacita
    Nic. zucchini
    Par. calabaza

PART II: SPANISH—ENGLISH

A

a tiempo completo Cub., Dom.R.,
Venz. (adj phr) full-time
(work)
a tiempo parcial Cub., Per., Spa.
(adj phr) part-time (work)
abarrotería Pan. (n) grocery
abarrotero Ecu., Mex. (n) grocer
abastos Venz. (n) grocery
abdomen Pri. (n) abdomen
abejorro 1. Pri. (n) bumblebee
2. Pan. (n) wasp
abispa Cub., Pan., Par. (n) yellow
jacket
abogado Pri. (n) lawyer
abordar Chi., Col., Dom.R., Mex.,
Par. (v) board
abrazadera Pri. (n) clamp
abreboca Pan. (n) appetizer
abrebotellas Spa. (n) bottle opener
abrelatas Pri. (n) can opener
abridor 1. Chi., Cos.R., Nic., Pan.,
Uru (n) bottle opener
2. Cos.R. (n) can opener
abridor de botellas Pue.R.
(n phr) bottle opener
abridor de latas Chi. (n phr) can
opener
abrigo 1. Pri. (n) overcoat 2. Col.,
Cub., Mex., Nic., Pan., Par.,
Spa., Venz. (n) coat 3. Dom.R.
(n) sweatshirt
abrigo de mink Col., Mex., Pan.,
Pue.R. (n phr) coat, mink
abrigo de piel Chi., Col., Dom.R.,
Mex., Nic., Pan., Par., Pue.R.,
Spa., Venz. (n phr) coat, fur

abrigo de pieles Cub. (n phr) coat,
fur
abrigo de visón Cub., Dom.R.,
Nic., Spa., Venz. (n phr) coat,
mink
abrochadora Arg. (n) stapler
abrumador Pri. (adj) overwhelming
aburrido Pri. (adj) boring
abuso de drogas Col., Cub.,
Dom.R., Nic., Par., Pue.R.
(n phr) drug abuse
acantilado Pri. (n) cliff
accesar a la red Mex. (v phr) surf
the net
accesorios Pri. (n) props
aceitera Pri. (n) oil can
aceituna Pri. (n) olive
acelerador Pri. (n) gas pedal
acera 1. Pri. (n) sidewalk 2. Cub.
(n) crosswalk
achicoria Nic. (n) endive
ácido 1. Col., Nic., Pan. (adj) sour
2. Cos.R., Cub., Nic. (n) LSD
acorde Pri. (n) chord
acrobacia Nic., Spa., Venz.
(n) stunt
acróbata Pri. (n) stuntman
acrobática Pri. (n) stunt
actor 1. Pri. (n) actor 2. Nic.
(n) performer
actriz 1. Pri. (n) actress 2. Nic.
(n) performer
adelantar Nic., Spa. (v) pass
(traffic)
adelantarse Cos.R. (v) pass
(traffic)

ABBREVIATIONS: Arg.=Argentina Bol.=Bolivia Chi.=Chile Col.=Colombia Cos.R.=Costa Rica
Cub.=Cuba Dom.R.=Dominican Republic Ecu.=Ecuador ELS.=El Salvador Gua.=Guatemala
Hon.=Honduras Mex.=Mexico Nic.=Nicaragua Pan.=Panama Par.=Paraguay Per.=Peru
Pri.=Primary Term Pue.R.=Puerto Rico Spa.=Spain Uru.=Uruguay Venz.=Venezuela

adicción Col., Cos.R., Dom.R.,
Mex., Nic., Pan., Pue.R.
(n) addiction
adicción a las drogas Pue.R.
(n phr) drug addiction
adicto Pri. (adj) addicted
¡Adiós! Pri. (int) Bye!; Goodbye!
administrador Col. (n) office
manager
administrador deportivo Col.,
Pan., Venz. (n phr) manager
(sports)
adolescente Pri. (n) teenager
adormilado Mex., Nic., Par.
(adj) sleepy
adornos Mex. (n) props
adulto Pri. (n) adult
aereodeslizador Col. (n) hydrofoil
boat
aerobic Spa. (n) aerobics
aeróbicos Dom.R., ElS., Gua.,
Hon., Nic., Pan., Pue.R., Uru.
(n) aerobics
aerobics Col., Mex. (n) aerobics
aerobismo Pri. (n) aerobics
aerolínea Pri. (n) airline
aeromozo/a Cub., Nic., Mex., Pan.,
Venz.(n) flight attendant
aeronave Col. (n) airplane
afeitadora Dom.R., Pue.R.
(n) razor
aficionado Col., Nic., Mex., Venz.
(n) amateur
afilador de cuchillo Pri.
(n phr) knife sharpener
afinar Gua., Mex., Nic. (v) tune up
agarraderas del manubrio Gua.,
Nic., Venz. (n phr) handlebar
grips (bicycle)
agarrador Pan. (n) drawer knob
agente 1. Pri. (n) police detective
2. Nic. (n) realtor
agente de policía 1. Col. (n phr) police

detective 2. Col., Spa.
(n phr) police officer
agente policial Dom.R.
(n phr) police officer
agobiante Chi., Col., Nic.
(adj) overwhelming
agradable Venz. (adj) nice
agricultor Pri. (n) farmer
agrio Pri. (adj) sour
aguacate Pri. (n) avocado
aguacero Col. (n) storm
agudos Spa. (n) treble (stereo)
agujeta Mex. (n) shoelace
ahogarse Nic., Par. (v) stall (car)
ahuyama Col., Venz. (n) pumpkin
aire acondicionado Pri.
(n phr) air conditioning
airecondicionado Cos.R. (n) air
conditioning
ají Bol., Chi., Venz., Par., Per.
(n) pepper, hot
ají dulce Pan. (n phr) pepper,
sweet
ají picante Col., Cub., Pan., Pue.R.
(n phr) pepper, hot
ajustador Cub. (n) bra, brassiere
al revés Cub. (adv phr) backstroke
(swimming)
ala Pri. (n) fender
alacena Bol., Col., Mex. (n) pantry
alacrán Pri. (n) scorpion
albacora Chi. (n) swordfish
albaricoque Pri. (n) apricot
alberca Mex. (n) swimming pool
albergue Arg. (n) hut
albornoz Spa. (n) bathrobe
álbum Pri. (n) record album
alcachofa Pri. (n) artichoke
alcahuete ElS., Gua., Hon.
(n) pimp
alcaide Nic. (n) warden
(prison)
alcalde/sa Pri. (n) mayor

alcaldía Bol., Ecu., Nic., Pue.R.
(n) city hall
alcaucil Arg., Uru. (n) artichoke
alce Arg., Col., Mex., Nic., Par.,
Spa., Venz. (n) moose
alcón Bol. (n) hawk
aldea Pri. (n) village
alianza Arg., Par. (n) ring, wedding
alicatas Mex. (n) pliers
alicate Chi., Cos.R., Dom.R., Nic.,
Per., Pue.R., Venz. (n) pliers
alicates Col., Pan., Spa. (n) pliers
alimentos enlatados Pri.
(n phr) canned food
almacén 1. Arg., Par., Uru.
(n) grocery 2. Bol., Dom.R.,
Mex., Pue.R., Spa. (n) storage
room 3. Pan. (n) department
store
almacenaje Pri. (n) storage room
almacenar Pri. (v) store computer
data)
almacén de mascotas Col.
(n phr) pet shop
almacenero Arg., Par., Uru.
(n) grocer
almacén grande Col.
(n phr) department store
almácigo Cos.R., Nic., Par.
(n) seedling
almádena Pri. (n) sledgehammer
almuerzo 1. Pri. (n) lunch 2. Mex.
(n) brunch
¿Aló? Col., Cos.R., Dom.R., Ecu.,
ElS., Gua., Hon., Nic., Per.,
Uru.,Venz. (int) Hello?
(answering telephone)
alquilar Pri. (v) rent (housing)
alterofilismo Chi. (n) weight
lifting
alto Pri. (int) stop (sign)
alubias Spa. (n) beans
alubias negras Spa. (n phr) beans,

black
alubias rojas Spa. (n phr) beans,
kidney
alumbrar Col. (v phr) give birth
amable Col., Cub., Nic., Spa.
(adj) nice
amador Chi. (n) amateur
amante Pri. (n) mistress
amárgo Col. (adj) sour
amasador Per. (n) rolling pin
amateur Pri. (n) amateur
amigable Col., Mex., Pue.R.
(adj) friendly
amigazo/a Col., Nic., Par.
(n) buddy, pal
amígdala Pri. (n) tonsil
amigo/a Pan., Pue.R. (n) buddy, pal
amigocho Mex. (n) buddy, pal
amigote Mex. (n) buddy, pal
amistoso Pri. (adj) friendly
amolador Dom.R. (n) knife
sharpener
amor, mi 1. Pri. (n phr) love,
lovey 2. Arg., Chi., Col., Cub.,
ElS., Gua., Hon., Nic., Pue.R.
(n phr) dear, honey, sweetheart
amorcito 1. Col. (n) dear, darling,
honey 2. Col., Cos.R., Nic.
(n) love, lovey
amoroso Bol. (adj) cute
amortiguador Venz. (n) muffler
ampayer Mex. (n) umpire
(baseball)
anacardo Cub. (n) cashew
ananá Uru. (n) pineapple
anchoa Pri. (n) anchovy
anchoveta Chi., Per.
(n) anchovy
ancianato Col. (n) retirement
home
anciano Col., Par. (adj) old
andar de malas pulgas Chi.
(adj phr) grumpy

andar en bicicleta Arg., Chi.,
   Cos.R.,
   Mex., Par. (v phr) ride
   (bicycle)
andén 1. Pri. (n) platform (train)
   2. Col., Nic. (n) sidewalk
anfitrión/a Dom.R., Mex., Venz.
   (n) host (show)
angina Mex. (n) tonsil
anillo Pri. (n) ring
anillo de boda Nic. (n phr) ring,
   wedding
anillo de casamiento Arg., Nic.,
   Par. (n phr) ring, wedding
anillo de diamante Pri.
   (n phr) ring, diamond
anillo de diamantes Spa.
   (n phr) ring, diamond
anillo de graduación Pri.
   (n phr) ring, class
anillo de matrimonio Pri.
   (n phr) ring, wedding
anillo de sello Col. (n phr) ring,
   signet
animador Col. (n) host (show)
anjova Mex. (n) bluefish
anta Pri. (n) moose
ante Chi., Col. (n) moose
anteojos Pri. (n) eyeglasses;
   spectacles
anteojos bifocales Arg.
   (n phr) bifocals
anteojos de camino Pri.
   (n phr) glasses, safety
anteojos de protección
   Pue.R. (n phr) glasses,
   safety
anteojos de seguridad Chi.
   (n phr) glasses, safety
anteojos de teatro Cub.
   (n phr) glasses, opera
anteojos para esquiar Pri.
   (n phr) goggles, ski

anteojos para nadar Pri.
   (n phr) goggles, swimming
antiparras 1. Arg. (n) goggles, ski
   2. Arg. (n) goggles, swimming
antiperspirante ElS., Gua., Hon.,
   Mex., Pue.R.
   (n) antiperspirant
antojitos Col. (n) appetizer
antojo Dom.R., Spa. (n) birthmark
antorcha Pan., Pue.R.
   (n) blowtorch
anuncio 1. Pri. (n) commercial
   2. Mex. (n) billboard
anuncio de almacén Col.
   (n phr) shop sign
anuncio de neón Pri. (n phr) neon
   sign
anuncio informativo Col.
   (n phr) infomercial
anuncio panorámico Pri.
   (n phr) billboard
apagarse el carro Venz.
   (v phr) stall (car)
aparador 1. Pri. (n) buffet 2. Arg.,
   Nic. (n) display cabinet
   3. Mex. (n) shop window
aparato de CD Col.
   (n phr) compact disk player
aparcamiento Spa. (n) parking lot
aparcar Spa. (v) park
apartado de correos Spa.
   (n phr) post office box
apartado postal Pri. (n phr) post
   office box
apartamento Pri. (n) apartment
apearse Bol., Cos.R., Dom.R., Per.,
   Uru. (v) get off (bus)
aperitivo Pri. (n) appetizer
aplanadora Par., Venz. (n) trowel
aposento Dom.R., Nic.
   (n) bedroom
apretar Pue.R. (v) click
   (computer)

arado Par., Pue.R. (n) reamer

araña Pri. (n) spider

arándano Pri. (n) blueberry

arándano agrio Pri.
(n phr) cranberry

arandela (n) washer

árbitro 1. Pri. (n) referee 2. Cub.,
Ecu., Nic., Uru., Venz.
(n) umpire (baseball)

árbol Pri. (n) tree

árbol de frutas Pue.R. (n phr) fruit
tree

árbol frutal Pri. (n phr) fruit tree

arbolito Pue.R. (n) bush

arbusto Pri. (n) bush; shrub

arce Pri. (n) maple (tree)

arcén Spa., Uru. (n) road shoulder

archivador 1. Bol. (n) folder
2. Chi. (n) file cabinet; three-
ring binder

archivadora Spa. (n) folder

archivar Dom.R. (v) store
computer data)

archivero Mex., Par. (n) file
cabinet

archivo Pri. (n) file cabinet

arco de la planta del pie Col.
(n phr) plantar arch (foot)

arco del pie Arg., Mex., Nic., Par.,
Venz. (n phr) plantar arch
(foot)

arco plantar Pri. (n phr) plantar
arch (foot)

área residencial 1. Col., Pue.R.
(n phr) residencial area
2. Dom.R. (n phr) uptown

aretes Pri. (n) earrings

aretes de espiga Pri.
(n phr) earrings, pierced

aretes de hoyito Dom.R.
(n phr) earrings, pierced

aretes de meter Nic.
(n phr) earrings, pierced

aretes de presión Pri.
(n phr) earrings, clip

aretes de tornillo Pri.
(n phr) earrings, screw

argumento Spa. (n) screenplay

armario 1. Pri. (n) closet (general)
2. Spa. (n) closet (clothes)

aro Chi., Col., Cos.R. (n) rim
(bicycle wheel)

aro de matrimonio Per., Pue.R.
(n phr) ring, wedding

aros Arg., Par. (n) earrings

aros colgantes Arg.
(n phr) earrings, drop

aros de agujero Arg.
(n phr) earrings, pierced

aros de presión Arg., Par.
(n phr) earrings, clip

aros de tornillo Arg.
(n phr) earrings, screw

arquero Arg., Chi., Par., Per.
(n) goalie

arrancador Cos.R., Mex.
(n) starter

arrancar Pri. (v) start (car)

arranque Pri. (n) starter

arrecho Nic. (adj) angry

arreglar Dom.R. (v) tune up

arreglarse Arg., Dom.R., Nic., Par.
(v) dress up

arreglos en la vía Col. (n phr) road
works

arrendar Chi., Col. (v) rent
(housing)

arriate de flores Gua.
(n phr) flower bed

arroyo Pri. (n) stream

arruga Col. (n) crease
(pants)

articulación Pri. (n) joint

artículos de oficina Pri.
(n phr) office
supplies

ABBREVIATIONS: Arg.=Argentina Bol.=Bolivia Chi.=Chile Col.=Colombia Cos.R.=Costa Rica
Cub.=Cuba Dom.R.=Dominican Republic Ecu.=Ecuador EIS.=El Salvador Gua.=Guatemala
Hon.=Honduras Mex.=Mexico Nic.=Nicaragua Pan.=Panama Par.=Paraguay Per.=Peru
Pri.=Primary Term Pue.R.=Puerto Rico Spa.=Spain Uru.=Uruguay Venz.=Venezuela

artista Pri. (n) performer
arvejas 1. Pri. (n) peas, green
    2. Par. (n) beans, green
arvejitas Per. (n) peas, green
asadón Col., Pan. (n) hoe
asador eléctrico Pri.
    (n phr) griddle
asaltar Col. (v) car jack (crime)
asaltar con violencia Mex.
    (v phr) car jack (crime)
ascensor Pri. (n) elevator
asentaderas Mex. (n) butt
asesor 1. Arg., Col., Mex., Pan.,
    Spa., Venz. (n) consultant
    2. Ecu., Mex., Nic., Spa.
    (n) counselor
asiento 1. Pri. (n) seat (bicycle)
    2. Chi. (n) chair, lounging
asiento del chofer Chi., Cub., Nic.
    (n phr) driver's seat
asiento del conductor Pri.
    (n phr) driver's seat
asiento del piloto Chi., Nic.
    (n phr) driver's seat
asilo Mex., Par. (n) retirement
    home
asilo de ancianos Arg., Nic.
    (n phr) retirement home
asombroso 1. Pri. (adj) amazing
    2. Col. (adj) tremendous
aspersor Nic., Spa. (n) sprinkler
aspirador Cub., Cos.R. (n) vacuum
    cleaner
aspiradora Pri. (n) vacuum cleaner
aspirante Uru. (n) challenger
    (boxing)
aspirar Pri. (v) inhale (drugs)
asueñado Dom.R. (adj) sleepy
asustado Pri. (adj) scared
atascamiento Chi. (n) traffic jam
atasco Cos.R., Spa. (n) traffic jam
atemorizado Col. (adj) scared
atento Col. (adj) polite

aterrador Pri. (adj) terrifying
aterrorizante Col. (adj) terrifying
atleta Pri. (n) athlete
atracar Col. (v) carjack (crime)
atracar un coche Uru. (v phr) car
    jack (crime)
atraso Chi., Par. (n) delay
atril Chi., Col., Spa. (n) easel
atún Pri. (n) tuna
auditor Cos.R. (n) comptroller
aura tiñosa Cub. (n phr) vulture
autito chocador Arg., Par.
    (n phr) bumper car
auto Arg., Chi., Col., Mex., Par.
    (n) car
auto de carrera Arg., Chi., Dom.R.
    (n phr) racecar
auto de choque Spa.
    (n phr) bumper car
auto deportivo Arg., Chi., Par.
    (n phr) sports car
auto particular Arg. (n phr) car,
    private
autobús Pri. (n) bus
autocine Pan., Par., Per., Venz.
    (n) drive-in
auto-cinema Dom.R. (n) drive-in
autocinema Mex., Nic.
    (n) drive-in
automóvil Mex., Spa. (n) car
autopista Pri. (n) expressway
auxiliar de vuelo Pri.
    (n phr) flight
    attendant
auyama Dom.R., Venz. (n) squash
avejita Pue.R. (n) bumblebee
avejón Dom.R. (n) beetle
avellana Pri. (n) hazelnut
aventajar Nic. (v) pass (traffic)
averiguador Venz. (n) snoop
avestruz Pri. (n) ostrich
aviador Col. (n) pilot
avión Pri. (n) airplane

ABBREVIATIONS: Arg.=Argentina Bol.=Bolivia Chi.=Chile Col.=Colombia Cos.R.=Costa Rica
Cub.=Cuba Dom.R.=Dominican Republic Ecu.=Ecuador ElS.=El Salvador Gua.=Guatemala
Hon.=Honduras Mex.=Mexico Nic.=Nicaragua Pan.=Panama Par.=Paraguay Per.=Peru
Pri.=Primary Term Pue.R.=Puerto Rico Spa.=Spain Uru.=Uruguay Venz.=Venezuela

avión a chorro Chi.
  (n phr) jet
aviso Arg. (n) commercial
aviso con luz de neón Col.
  (n phr) neon sign
aviso vial Col. (n phr) road
  sign
vispa (n) wasp
avispa chaqueta amarilla Nic.
  (n phr) yellowjacket
avispa con pintas amarillas

axila Pri. (n) armpit
ayote Nic. (n) squash
ayudas de escenario Col.
  (n phr) props
ayuntamiento Pri. (n) city hall
azada Pri. (n) hoe
azadón Dom.R., Gua., Nic., Venz.
  (n) hoe
azador Bol. (n) hoe
azafata Pri. (n) flight attendant
azul Pri. (adj) blue (eyes)

  (n phr) yellow jacket

ABBREVIATIONS: Arg.=Argentina Bol.=Bolivia Chi.=Chile Col.=Colombia Cos.R.=Costa Rica
Cub.=Cuba Dom.R.=Dominican Republic Ecu.=Ecuador EIS.=El Salvador Gua.=Guatemala
Hon.=Honduras Mex.=Mexico Nic.=Nicaragua Pan.=Panama Par.=Paraguay Per.=Peru
Pri.=Primary Term Pue.R.=Puerto Rico Spa.=Spain Uru.=Uruguay Venz.=Venezuela

B

babosa Dom.R., Nic. (n) snail
babuchas Col. (n) slippers
babysitter Arg. (n) babysitter
bache 1. Pri. (n) bump (road)
    2. Arg., Cub., Gua., Mex., Nic.,
    Spa. (n) pothole
bagel Bol., Col., Pue.R. (n) bagel
bagre Pri. (n) catfish
baguette Pri. (n) baguette
bahía peatonal Nic. (n phr) traffic
    island
bajareque 1. Pan. (n) mist 2. Nic.
    (n) shed
bajarse Pri. (v) get off (bus)
bajito 1. Col., Dom.R. (adj) short
    2. Col., Dom.R., Uru.
    (adj) short (person)
bajo 1. Pri. (n) bass (voice) 2. Arg.,
    Mex., Per., Spa. (adj) short
    3. Col., Venz. (adj) short
    (person) 4. Col., Nic., Par.
    (n) bass (stereo)
bajo la influencia Spa.
    (adj phr) intoxicated
balacearse Nic. (n) sprint
balcón Pri. (n) balcony
balconcillo Col. (n) balcony
balde Pri. (n) bucket; pail
balde de hielo Pri. (n phr) ice bucket
balizas Arg. (n) emergency lights
balompié Pue.R. (n) soccer
balón Col., Spa. (n) ball (soccer)
baloncesto Pri. (n) basketball
balonmano ElS., Gua., Nic.
    (n) handball
bañador Spa. (n) bathing suit

banana Arg., Uru. (n) banana
banano Col., Cos.R., Ecu., Nic.
    (n) banana
banca Arg., Nic. (n) bench
banco 1. Pri. (n) bench 2. Pri.
    (n) stool 3. Nic. (n) chair, step
banco de arena Mex., Par.
    (n phr) sandbar
banco-escalera Pri. (n) chair, step
banda de sonido Arg.
    (n phr) sound track
banda del ventilador Mex.
    (n phr) fan belt
banda sin fin Cos.R., Nic.
    (n phr) treadmill
banda sonora Pri. (n phr) sound
    track
bandada Arg. (n) flock
bandeja Col., Cub., Pan., Par.
    (n) platter
bandeja para el horno Spa.
    (n phr) roasting pan
bandeja para hornear Col., Nic.
    (n phr) roasting pan
banjo Pri. (n) banjo
baño Pri. (n) bathroom
banqueta 1. Dom.R. (n) stool
    2. Mex. (n) sidewalk 3. Spa.
    (n) bench
banquillo Pan., Pue.R.
    (n) ottoman
banquina Arg., Par. (n) road
    shoulder
banquito Dom.R., Nic. (n) stool
banyo Spa. (n) banjo
bar Pri. (n) bar

barato Pri. (adj) cheap

barba Mex. (n) chin

barba partida Mex., Nic.
(n phr) cleft (chin)

barbas de chivo Pri. (n phr) goatee

barbero 1. Pri. (n) barber 2. Col.
(n) hairdresser

barbida partida Per. (n phr) cleft
(chin)

barbilla hendida Venz.
(n phr) cleft (chin)

barbilla Pri. (n) chin

barbo Spa. (n) catfish

barco 1. Pri. (n) boat 2. Arg., Chi.,
Col., Cos.R., Nic., Pan., Uru.,
Venz. (n) ship

barco de vela Pri. (n phr) sailboat

barman Pri. (n) bartender

barquillo Col. (n) waffle

barra (entre compases) Col. (n) bar
(music)

barra de arena Pri.
(n phr) sandbar

barra de pan Spa. (n phr) baguette

barra fija Pri. (n phr) horizontal
bar

barra horizontal Col., Nic., Pan.,
Par., Pue.R. Venz.
(n phr) horizontal bar

barraca Pue.R. (n) barracks

barracas Pan. (n) barracks

barranca Mex. (n) cliff

barranco Cos.R. (n) cliff

barredora Pri. (n) lawn rake

barrena Pue.R., Venz. (n) drill bit

barrendero Cub. (n) janitor

barriga 1. Pri. (n) belly 2. Par.,
Per. (n) abdomen

barrio 1. Pri. (n) suburb 2. Arg.,
Col., Dom.R., Ecu., Nic., Pan.,
Par., Per., Spa., Uru.
(n) neighborhood

barrio comercial Pri.

(n phr) business district

barrio en las afueras Col.
(n phr) suburb

barrio residencial 1. Arg., Par.
(n phr) residencial area 2. Par.
(n phr) uptown

barrito Par., Per. (n) pimple

barro Col., Mex., Nic., Venz.
(n) pimple

bartender Dom.R., Nic. (n) bartender

basket Nic. (n) basketball

basketball Mex., Pan., Par.
(n) basketball

basketbol Arg., Per., Uru.
(n) basketball

bastidor Ecu., Pan., Per. (n) chassis

bastilla Nic. (n) cuff (pants)

basurero Pri. (n) garbage collector

bata 1. Par. (n) bathrobe 2. Nic.
(n) nightgown 3. Nic., Par.
(n) house robe

bataca Nic. (n) drummer

bata de baño Pri. (n phr) bathrobe

bata de casa Cub., Dom.R., Spa.,
Venz. (n phr) house robe

bata de dormir Cub., Pue.R.
(n phr) nightgown

bata de estar en casa Pan.
(n phr) house robe

batata Pri. (n) sweet potato

batería Dom.R., Nic. (n) drum

baterista Dom.R., Nic.
(n) drummer

batero Nic. (n) drummer

bathing suit Pri. (n phr) traje de
baño

batidor Par. (n) egg beater

batidor de mano Ecu. (n phr) egg
beater

batidor manual Pri. (n phr) egg
beater

batidora 1. Pri. (n) mixer 2. Chi.,
Nic., Pue.R. (n) egg beater

3. Cub., Dom.R., Spa., Venz.
    (n) blender
batón Bol. (n) bathrobe
baúl Pri. (n) trunk (car)
bautismo Arg., Col. (n) christening
bautizo Pri. (n) christening
baya Pri. (n) berry
beatle Chi. (n) turtleneck
beauty parlor Pue.R.
    (n phr) hairdresser's shop
beba 1. Arg. (n) toddler 2. Arg.,
    Uru. (n) baby
bebé 1. Pri. (n) baby 2. Cub., Mex.,
    Nic., Spa. (n) infant 3. Arg.
    (n) toddler
bebedero Arg., Chi., Mex., Venz.
    (n) water fountain
bebida alcohólica 1. Pri.
    (n phr) alcoholic beverage
    2. Uru. (n phr) hard liquor
bebida alcohólica fuerte Spa.
    (n phr) hard liquor
bebidas fuertes 1. Pri.
    (n phr) liquor 2. Mex., Par.
    (n phr) hard liquor
bebido Col. (adj) drunk
becerro Col., Spa. (n) calf
bedel Nic. (n) post office
bella Col. (adj) pretty
bellaco Dom.R. (adj) naughty
bello Chi., Col., Cos.R., Cub.,
    Dom.R. (adj) beautiful
beneficio adicional Col.
    (n phr) fringe benefit
beneficio laborable Cos.R.
    (n phr) fringe benefit
beodo Col. (n) drunkard
berbiquí Mex. (n) awl
bermudas Cub., Par. (n) shorts
betabel Mex. (n) beet
beterraga Bol., Chi., Per. (n) beet
bibliotecario/a Pri. (n) librarian
bibliotecólogo Dom.R. (n)librarian

bíceps Pri. (n) biceps
bicho Pri. (n) bug
bicicleta Arg., Nic., Par., Uru.
    (n) bike, road
bicicleta de camino Pri.
    (n phr) bike, road
bicicleta de campotraviesa Mex.
    (n phr) bike, mountain
bicicleta de carrera Dom.R.
    (n phr) bike, road
bicicleta de carreras Spa.
    (n phr) bike, road
bicicleta de dos personas Col.
    (n phr) bike, tandem
bicicleta de montaña Chi., Col.,
    Spa., Venz. (n phr) bike,
    mountain
bicicleta doble Col., Mex.
    (n phr) bike, tandem
bicicleta estable Pan.
    (n phr) stationary bicycle
bicicleta estacionaria Pri.
    (n phr) stationary bicycle
bicicleta estática Spa.
    (n phr) stationary bicycle
bicicleta fija Mex.
    (n phr) stationary
    bicycle
bicicleta montañesa ElS., Gua.,
    Hon. (n phr) bike,
    mountain
bicicleta para carretera Col.
    (n phr) bike, road
bicicleta para dos personas Pri.
    (n phr)bike, tandem
bicicleta todo terreno Arg.
    (n phr) bike, mountain
bicicleta turismo Mex.
    (n phr) bike, road
bien parecido Venz.
    (adj phr) handsome
bifocales 1. Nic. (n) bifocals 2. Par.
    (n) half-glasses

ABBREVIATIONS: Arg.=Argentina Bol.=Bolivia Chi.=Chile Col.=Colombia Cos.R.=Costa Rica
Cub.=Cuba Dom.R.=Dominican Republic Ecu.=Ecuador ElS.=El Salvador Gua.=Guatemala
Hon.=Honduras Mex.=Mexico Nic.=Nicaragua Pan.=Panama Par.=Paraguay Per.=Peru
Pri.=Primary Term Pue.R.=Puerto Rico Spa.=Spain Uru.=Uruguay Venz.=Venezuela

bikini Bol., Chi., Par. (n) bikini
briefs
bilé Mex. (n) lipstick
billboard Pue.R. (n) billboard
billete Pri. (n) ticket
billete de ida Bol., Ecu., Spa.
(n phr) one-way ticket
billete de ida y vuelta Pri.
(n phr) round trip ticket
billete de una sola vía Bol.
(n phr) one-way ticket
billete sencillo Pri. (n phr) one-
way ticket
billetera (n) wallet
binoculares Col., Nic. (n) glasses,
opera
binóculos Col. (n) glasses, opera
biombo separador Mex.
(n phr) office divider
bisquet Mex. (n) biscuit
bizcochito Dom.R. (n) biscuit
bizcocho 1. Pri. (n) biscuit
Dom.R., Pue.R. (n) cake
blanco Spa. (adj) gray (hair)
blazer Pue.R. (n) jacket (women's)
bloc 1. Arg., Chi. (n) pad, legal
2. Arg., Chi., Nic. (n) pad,
writing 3. Arg., Chi. (n) pad,
yellow 4. Arg., Col., Mex.,
Nic., Per. (n) pad (paper)
bloc amarillo Mex., Nic., Spa.
(n phr) pad, yellow
bloc de notas Spa. (n phr) pad
(paper); pad, writing
bloc legal Nic. (n phr) pad, legal
bloc tamaño carta Mex., Par.
(n phr) pad, writing
bloc tamaño legal Par., Spa.
(n phr) pad, legal
bloc tamaño oficio Mex.
(n phr) pad, legal
bloque Pue.R. (n) city
block

bloque de carnicero Pri.
(n phr) butcher block
bloqueador solar Dom.R.
(n phr) sunscreen
blower Dom.R., Pue.R. (n) hair
dryer
blue jeans Col., Venz. (n phr) blue
jeans
blúmer Cub., Nic., Pan. (n) panties
bocadillo Col., Nic. (n) snack
bocaditos Per. (n) appetizer
bocas Cos.R., Nic. (n) appetizer
bocina Arg., Chi., Dom.R., Uru.
(n) bell (bicycle)
bodega 1. (n) wine shop 2. Cos.R.,
Ecu., Gua., Mex., Nic.
(n) storage room 3. Cub.,
Dom.R., Per. (n) grocery
4. Pan.,
Par. (n) liquor store
bodeguero Cub. (n) grocer
bol 1. Arg., Par. (n) bowl, mixing
2. Chi. (n) bowl
bola de balompié Pue.R.
(n phr) ball (soccer)
bola de golf Col., Mex., Pue.R.
(n phr)golf ball
bola en uno Pue.R. (n phr) hole in
one
boleta Pan. (n) ticket, traffic
boleta por velocidad Pan.
(n phr) ticket, speeding
boletero Per. (n) ticket collector
boletín informativo Cos.R.
(n phr) infomercial
boletín meteorológico
(n phr) weather report
boleto Arg., Chi., Cub., Mex.,
Pan., Per., Pue.R., Venz.
(n) ticket
boleto de ida Arg., Chi., Mex.,
Nic., Pan., Venz. (n phr) one-
way ticket

boleto de ida y vuelta Arg., Chi.,
Mex., Nic., Pan., Per., Venz.
(n phr) round trip ticket
boleto de viaje redondo Mex.
(n phr) round trip ticket
boleto en un solo sentido Per.
(n phr) one-way ticket
bolígrafo 1. Pri. (n) pen, ball-point
2. Spa. (n) pen
bollito Cos.R. (n) bun
bollo 1. Bol., Spa. (n) bun 2. ElS.,
Gua., Nic., Spa. (n) roll 3. Nic.
(n) muffin
bollo de crema Bol., ElS., Gua.,
Hon., Spa. (n phr) cream puff
bollo de pan 1. Venz. (n phr) Swiss
roll 2. Nic. (n phr) bun
bolsa de mano Col., Cos.R., Gua.,
Mex., Pan. (n phr) handbag
bolsas Dom.R. (n) bags (under
eyes)
bolsillo de atrás Dom.R., Nic.
(n phr) pocket, back
bolsillo de la camisa Dom.R.
(n phr) pocket, breast
bolsillo superior Pri.
(n phr) pocket, breast
bolsillo trasero Pri.
(n phr) pocket, back
bolso Dom.R. (n) handbag
bolso de mano Spa., Venz.
(n phr) handbag
bomba de crema Uru.
(n phr) cream puff
bombacha Arg., Par. (n) bikini
briefs
bombachas Arg., Par., Uru.
(n) panties
boniato Cub., Uru. (n) sweet
potato
bonita Chi., Col., Dom.R., Ecu.,
ElS.,Gua., Nic., Pan., Uru.

(adj) pretty
bonito Nic., Pue.R. (adj) cute
bonito Pri. (adj) beautiful
boquerón Cos.R., Dom.R., Per.,
Pue.R. (n) anchovy
boquitas Nic. (n) appetizer
borde de la carretera ElS., Gua.,
Nic.(n phr) road shoulder
bordón Col., Nic. (n) snare (of
drum)
borrachín Col. (n) drunkard
borracho 1. Pri. (n) drunkard
2. Nic., Pan. (adj) drunk,
intoxicated
borrachón Dom.R. (n) drunkard
borrar Pri. (v) delete
borrasca Col. (n) storm
borrego Mex. (n) sheep
bosque tropical Col., Nic.
(n phr) rain forest
botamanga Arg. (n) cuff (pants)
botana Mex. (n) snack
botánica Pri. (n) herbalist's shop
botapié Bol. (n) cuff (pants)
botar Cub., Dom.R (v) fire
botas Pri. (n) shoes, hiking
botas de alpinismo Mex.
(n phr) shoes,hiking
botas de monte Spa. (n phr) shoes,
hiking
bote Nic., Venz. (n) boat
bote de vela Col. (n phr) sailboat
botica Col., Ecu., Per. (n) drug store
boticario Col. (n) pharmacist
botón Col. (n) bud
bototos Chi. (n) shoes, hiking
boulevard Nic. (n) median
box spring Dom.R., Mex., Venz.
(n phr) box spring
boxeador Pri. (n) boxer
bragas Spa. (n) panties
bragueta Pri. (n) fly (pants)

braguita de bikini Spa.
  (n phr) bikini briefs
brasier Dom.R., Nic., Pan. (n) bra,
  brassiere
brasiere Mex. (n) bra, brassiere
brassiere Col. (n) bra, brassiere
bravo Col., Cub., Venz. (adj) angry
brazada 1. Arg. (n) breaststroke
  (swimming) 2. Pue.R., Uru.
  (n) crawl (swimming)
brazada de pecho Dom.R., ElS.,
  Gua., Hon.
  (n phr) breaststroke
  (swimming)
brazo Nic. (n) neck (guitar)
brazo de gitano Nic., Spa.
  (n phr) Swiss roll
breteles Dom.R. (n) suspenders
breves Pri. (n) news brief
breves informativos Chi., Nic.
  (n phr) news brief
brida Nic. (n) clamp
briñón Spa. (n) nectarine
broca Pri. (n) drill bit
brocha de repostería Col., Gua.,
  ElS., Hon., Nic., Pan.
  (n phr) pastry brush
broche para el pelo Pri.
  (n phr) barrette
bronceado Pri. (adj) tan (skin)
bronceador Mex., Par., Per.
  (n) sunscreen
broncearse Pri. (v) tan
bronces Pri. (n) bronze section
brote 1. Pri. (n) bud 2. Chi.
  (n) seedling
brotes de soja Arg., Uru.
  (n phr) bean sprouts
brotes de soje Par. (n phr) bean
  sprouts
bruma Col. (n) fog; mist
brunch Pri. (n) brunch
buceador Pri. (n) diver

¡Buen día! Arg. (int phr) Good
  morning!
¡Buenas noches! 1. Pri.
  (int phr) Good night! 2. Col.,
  Ecu., Nic. (int phr) Good
  evening!
¡Buenas tardes! Pri.
  (int phr) Good evening!
buen mozo Arg.
  (adj phr) handsome
buenmozo Chi., Dom.R.
  (adj) handsome
bueno Dom.R. (adj) straight (hair)
¿Bueno? Mex. (int) Hello?
  (answering telephone)
¡Buenos días! Pri. (int phr) Good
  morning!
búfer Mex., Nic. (n) buffer storage
bufete de abogados Pri.
  (n phr) lawyer's office
bufetera Gua. (n) buffet
buffer storage Pue.R.
  (n phr) bufferstorage
búho Pri. (n) owl
buitre (n) vulture
bumper Col., Dom.R., Nic., Pan.,
  Pue.R. (n) bumper
bungaló Col., Spa. (n) bungalow
búngalo Mex. (n) bungalow
bungaloo Dom.R. (n) bungalow
bungalow Arg., Par., Uru.
  (n) bungalow
bungalu Pan. (n) bungalow
buque Pri. (n) ship
bus Arg., Cos.R., Nic., Pan. (n) bus
buscar en la red Mex. (v phr) surf
  thenet
busero Nic., Pan. (n) bus
  driver
buseta 1. Col. (n) bus 2. Ecu. (n) van
busetero Col. (n) bus driver
busito Pan. (n) van
busto Mex. (n) breast
butaca Cub., Dom.R., Pue.R.

ABBREVIATIONS: Arg.=Argentina   Bol.=Bolivia   Chi.=Chile   Col.=Colombia   Cos.R.=Costa Rica
Cub.=Cuba   Dom.R.=Dominican Republic   Ecu.=Ecuador   ElS.=El Salvador   Gua.=Guatemala
Hon.=Honduras   Mex.=Mexico   Nic.=Nicaragua   Pan.=Panama   Par.=Paraguay   Per.=Peru
Pri.=Primary Term   Pue.R.=Puerto Rico   Spa.=Spain   Uru.=Uruguay   Venz.=Venezuela

(n) armchair

buzo 1. Pri. (n) diver 2. Arg., Par.
(n) sweatshirt 3. Col.
(n) turtleneck

buzón postal Col. (n phr) post office
box

¡Bye! Dom.R., Nic. (int) Bye!;
Goodbye!

C

cabalgar Col., Par. (v) ride
horseback
caballeros Chi., Col., Cub., Dom.R.,
Mex., Nic., Venz. (n) men's
bathroom)
caballeroso Mex. (adj) polite
caballete 1. Pri. (n phr) bridge of
nose2. Pri. (n) easel
caballito 1. Cub., Ecu., Pue.R.,
Venz. (n) pony 2. Mex.
(n) shot glass (small) 3. Pan.
(n) dragonfly
caballito de San Pedro Pue.R.
(n phr) horsefly, gadfly
caballito del diablo Cub.
(n phr) dragonfly
caballitos Pri. (n) carousel (with
horses)
caballo Mex. (n) shot glass (big)
cabaña 1. Pri. (n) cabin 2. Arg.
(n) hut 3. Chi. (n) cottage
4. Chi., Nic. (n) bungalow
cabañita Bol. (n) bungalow
cabellera Col. (n) hair
cabello Pri. (n) hair
cabezudo Par. (n) brat
cabina telefónica Pri.
(n phr) telephone booth
cabinera Col. (n) flight attendant
cabito Nic. (n) stump
cable Arg., Cub., Mex. (n) cable
television
cablevisión Mex. (n) cable
television
cabo Dom.R., Nic. (n) stump

cabro Chi. (n) guy
cabros Chi. (n)
guys (dual gender
plural)
cacahuate Mex. (n) peanut
cacahuete Spa. (n) peanut
cacata Dom.R. (n) spider
cacatúa Pri. (n) cockatoo
cacerola 1. Pri. (n) saucepan
2. Arg., Par. (n) pot
cachete 1. Arg. (n) buttock 2. Chi.,
Col., Dom.R., Mex., Nic.,
Pan., Per., Venz.
(n) cheek
cachito 1. Per. (n) croissant 2. Per.
(n) pigtail
cachucha Col., Dom.R. (n) cap
cacto Pri. (n) cactus
cactus Arg., Chi., Col., Dom.R.,
Mex., Pan., Pue.R., Spa.
(n) cactus
cadena 1. Pri. (n) network
(television) 2. Col. (n) range
(mountain) 3. Spa. (n) channel
café 1. Pri. (n) coffee bar 2. Bol.,
Chi., Cos.R., Mex., Nic.
(adj) brown (eyes)
café bar Cos.R. (n phr) coffee bar
cafetera 1. Pri. (n) coffee maker
2. Par. (n) mug, coffee
cafetería Col., Nic., Par., Pue.R.,
Spa. (n) coffee bar
cafiche Chi. (n) pimp
caficho Par. (n) pimp
caída de agua Dom.R.

ABBREVIATIONS: Arg.=Argentina Bol.=Bolivia Chi.=Chile Col.=Colombia Cos.R.=Costa Rica
Cub.=Cuba Dom.R.=Dominican Republic Ecu.=Ecuador ElS.=El Salvador Gua.=Guatemala
Hon.=Honduras Mex.=Mexico Nic.=Nicaragua Pan.=Panama Par.=Paraguay Per.=Peru
Pri.=Primary Term Pue.R.=Puerto Rico Spa.=Spain Uru.=Uruguay Venz.=Venezuela

(n phr) waterfall
caja de cambios Pri.
(n phr) gearbox
caja de velocidades ElS., Gua.,
Mex., Nic. (n phr) gearbox
cajón Arg., Chi., Col., Ecu., Mex.,
Nic., Par., Per., Spa., Uru.
(n) drawer
cajuela Mex. (n) trunk (car)
cake Cub., Pan. (n) cake
calabacín (n) zucchini
calabacita Mex. (n) zucchini
calabaza 1. Pri. (n) pumpkin
2. Col., Cos.R., Cub., Ecu.,
Par., Spa. (n) squash 3. Par.
(n) zucchini
calaca Mex. (n) skeleton
calamar Pri. (n) squid
calar Pri. (v) stall (car)
calarse Spa. (v) stall (car)
calavera Col., Cos.R., Mex.
(n) skull
calcetín Pri. (n) sock
caldera Bol. (n) kettle
caldero Cub. (n) kettle
calesita Arg., Par., Uru.
(n) carousel (with horses)
callado Chi., Col., Nic., Venz.
(adj) quiet
calle adoquinada Mex., Nic.
(n phr) street, cobblestone
calle cerrada Col., Mex.
(n phr) street, dead-end
calle ciega Venz. (n phr) street,
dead-end
calle de adoquín Gua.
(n phr) street,
cobblestone
calle de adoquines Chi., Pue.R.,
Spa., Uru. (n phr) street,
cobblestone
calle de dirección única Spa.
(n phr) street, one-way

calle de guijarro Pri.
(n phr) street, cobblestone
calle de ladrillo Pan.
(n phr) street, cobblestone
calle de paralelepípedos Chi.
(n phr) street, cobblestone
calle de piedras Per.
(n phr) street, cobblestone
calle de un solo sentido Col., Mex., Per.
(n phr) street, one-way
calle de una mano Pri.
(n phr) street, one-way
calle de una sola dirección Ecu.
(n phr) street, one-way
calle de una sola vía ElS., Gua.,
Hon. (n phr) street, one-way
calle de una vía Cos.R., Dom.R.,
Nic., Pan., Pue.R., Venz.
(n phr) street, one-way
calle empedrada Arg., Bol., Col.,
Ecu.,Venz. (n phr) street,
cobblestone
calle sentido único Par.
(n phr) street,one-way
calle sin salida Pri. (n phr) street,
dead-end
callejón Pri. (n) alley
callo Per. (n) wart
calzón Nic. (n) panties
calzón bikini Ecu. (n phr) bikini
briefs
calzoncillos 1. Pri. (n) briefs,
boxer shorts 2. Col. (n) bikini
briefs
calzoncillos boxer Dom.R.
(n phr) boxer shorts
calzoncillo corto Pan.
(n phr) bikini briefs
calzoncillos largos Nic., Pan.
(n phr) boxer shorts
calzones 1. Pri. (n) panties 2. Cub.
(n) boxer shorts 3. Mex., Uru.
(n) briefs

ABBREVIATIONS: Arg.=Argentina Bol.=Bolivia Chi.=Chile Col.=Colombia Cos.R.=Costa Rica
Cub.=Cuba Dom.R.=Dominican Republic Ecu.=Ecuador ElS.=El Salvador Gua.=Guatemala
Hon.=Honduras Mex.=Mexico Nic.=Nicaragua Pan.=Panama Par.=Paraguay Per.=Peru
Pri.=Primary Term Pue.R.=Puerto Rico Spa.=Spain Uru.=Uruguay Venz.=Venezuela

cama 1. Pri. (n) bed, single 2. Gua.,
Mex., Nic. (n phr) bed, double
cama camarote Col., Dom.R.,
Pan. (n phr) bunkbed
cama camera 1. Arg. (n phr) bed,
king-sized; bed, queen-sized
2. Par. (n phr) bed, queen-sized
cama de flores Mex.
(n phr) flower bed
cama de matrimonio Spa.
(n phr) bed, double
cama de soltero Chi. (n phr) bed,
single
cama doble 1. Pri. (n phr) bed,
double 2. Pri. (n phr) bed,
queen-sized
cama dos plazas Par. (n phr) bed,
double
cama extra grande Nic.
(n phr) bed, king-sized
cama grande 1. Pri. (n phr) bed,
king-sized 2. Nic. (n phr) bed,
queen-sized
cama imperial Gua. (n phr) bed,
single
cama individual Mex., Venz.
(n phr) bed, single
cama king Pan., Venz. (n phr) bed,
king-sized
cama king size Col., Dom.R.
(n phr) bed, king-sized
cama king-size Mex. (n phr) bed,
king-sized
cama litera Cub. (n phr) bunkbed
cama matrimonial 1. Gua., Mex.
(n phr) bed, double 2. Pan.
(n phr) bed, queen-sized
cama queen Venz. (n phr) bed,
queen-sized
cama queen size Dom.R.
(n phr) bed, queen-sized
cama queen-size Mex.
(n phr) bed,

queen-sized
cama sencilla Col., Ecu., Pue.R.
(n phr) bed, single
cama tres cuartos Pan.
(n phr) bed, single
camanance 1. Cos.R. (n) cleft
(chin) 2. Cos.R., ElS., Gua.,
Hon., Nic. (n) dimple
camanchaca Chi. (n) fog
cámara Chi., Par., Spa. (n) inner
tube (bicycle tire)
camarero (n) waiter
camarón 1. Pri. (n) shrimp 2. Arg.,
Ecu., Nic., Par., Uru. (n) prawn
camarón de agua dulce Chi.
(n phr) crayfish
camarón gigante Chi.
(n phr) prawn
camarote 1. Chi. (n) berth 2. Chi.
(n) bunkbed
cambiar de cambios Pue.R.
(v phr) shift gear
cambiar de tren Col., Cub.
(v phr) change (train)
cambiar la marcha Spa.
(v phr) shift gear
cambiar la velocidad Pri.
(v phr) shift gear
cambiarse de casa Col., Nic.
(v phr) move
cambio Arg. (n) stick shift
cambio automático Spa.
(n phr) automatic transmission
cambio manual Spa. (n phr) stick
shift
cambios Arg., Chi., Cub., Dom.R.,
Nic., Pan., Pue.R., Uru., Venz.
(n) gears
cambur Venz. (n) banana
caminador Col. (n) treadmill
caminadora Mex., Uru.
(n) treadmill
caminor Par. (n) treadmill

ABBREVIATIONS: Arg.=Argentina Bol.=Bolivia Chi.=Chile Col.=Colombia Cos.R.=Costa Rica
Cub.=Cuba Dom.R.=Dominican Republic Ecu.=Ecuador ElS.=El Salvador Gua.=Guatemala
Hon.=Honduras Mex.=Mexico Nic.=Nicaragua Pan.=Panama Par.=Paraguay Per.=Peru
Pri.=Primary Term Pue.R.=Puerto Rico Spa.=Spain Uru.=Uruguay Venz.=Venezuela

camión 1. Pri. (n) van 2. Mex.
(n) bus
camión de helados Par.
(n phr) ice cream truck
camión del helado Col., Spa.
(n phr) ice cream truck
camionero Mex. (n) bus driver
camioneta 1. Pri. (n) pickup truck
2. Pri. (n) station wagon
3. Cos.R., Mex., Nic., Venz.
(n) van 4. ElS., Gua., Hon.
(n) bus
camioneta pickup Mex., Venz.
(n phr) pickup truck
camisa de dormir Chi., Col.
(n phr) nightgown
camisa de manga corta Pri.
(n phr) shirt, short-sleeved
camisa de manga larga Pri.
(n phr) shirt, long-sleeved
camisa de noche Ecu.
(n phr) nightgown
camisa de trabajo Pri.
(n phr) sweatshirt
camisa de vestir Arg., Dom.R.,
Mex., Nic., Pan., Par., Uru.,
Venz.(n phr) shirt, dressy
camisa formal Pri. (n phr) shirt,
dressy
camiseta 1. Pri. (n) t-shirt 2. Arg.
(n) vest 3. Per. (n) knit shirt
camisón Pri. (n) nightgown
camote Bol., Ecu., Gua., Mex.,
Nic., Pan., Per. (n) sweet
potato
campanilla Bol. (n) bell (bicycle)
camper Mex., Nic. (n) recreational
vehicle
campera Arg. (n) jacket
campesino Col., Par. (n) farmer
campo de golf Pri. (n phr) golf
course
campo santo Chi. (n phr) cemetery

canal 1. Pri. (n) channel 2. Venz.
(n) lane
canas Col. (adj) gray (hair)
canasta Arg., Mex., Nic., Pan.,
Per., Uru. (n) basket
(basketball)
canasto Dom.R., Pue.R. (n) basket
(basketball)
cancha Nic., Par. (n) field (sports)
cancha de golf Arg. (n phr) golf
course
canción 1. Pri. (n) song 2. Pue.R.
(n) hymn
canción de amor Pri. (n phr) love
song
canción de moda Pri. (n phr) hit
(song)
canción romántica Col., Nic.,
Par., Pue.R. (n phr) love song
candado Col. (n) goatee
candidato Nic. (n) contestant
caneca Col. (n) basket (basketball)
cangrejo Pri. (n) crab
cangrejo de río Pri.
(n phr) crayfish
canilla Chi. (n) shin
canino Pri. (n) canine (tooth)
caño de escape Arg., Par.
(n phr) exhaust pipe
canoso Pri. (adj) gray (hair)
cantaloupe Col. (n) cantaloupe
cantalupa Cub. (n) cantaloupe
cantar afinado Par. (v phr) sing
harmony
cantar afinados Pue.R. (v phr)
sing harmony
cantar en armonía Pri.
(v phr) sing harmony
cantero Arg. (n) flower bed
cántico Pri. (n) hymn
cantina Mex., Nic., Pan. (n) bar
cantina de agua Ecu.
(n phr) kettle

cantinero Col., Ecu., ElS., Gua.,
Hon., Mex., Nic., Pan., Par.,
Pue.R. (n) bartender
canto Col. (n) song
capa 1. Pri. (n) cloak; cape 2. Pue.R.
(n) raincoat 3. Par., Pue.R.
(n) parka
capa de agua Cub. (n phr) raincoat
capacitar Pri. (v) train (for job)
caperuza Cub. (n) hood
capote 1. Pri. (n) cape 2. Nic.
(n) parka 3. Pan. (n) raincoat
capote para la lluvia Nic.
(n phr) raincoat
capucha Pri. (n) hood
capuchón Chi. (n) hood
capul Col. (n) bangs (hair)
capullo Spa. (n) bud
car jack Pue.R. (v phr) car jack
(crime)
carabinero Chi. (n) police officer
caracol Pri. (n) snail
carajito/a Dom.R. (n) brat
caraotas Venz. (n) beans
caraotas negras Venz.
(n phr) beans, black
caravana Spa. (n) recreational
vehicle
carcelero Venz. (n) warden (prison)
cardenal Pri. (n) bruise
cardigán Pri. (n) cardigan
cargador de maletas Venz.
(n phr) porter
cargoso Bol. (n) pest (person)
caricatura Mex. (n) cartoon
caricaturas Pan. (n) cartoon
cariño 1. Col. (n) love, lovey
2. Pan.(n) dear, darling, honey
3. Spa. (n) sweetheart
carnet de chofer Chi.
(n phr) driver's license
carnet de conducir Spa.
(n phr) driver's license

carnet de conductor Arg.
(n phr) driver's license
carnosa Mex. (n) succulent (plant)
carpa Pri. (n) tent
carpeta 1. Cub. (n) notebook
2. Spa. (n) folder
carpeta con ganchos Arg.
(n phr) three-ring binder
carpeta de archivo Pri.
(n phr) folder
carpeta de argollas Pri.
(n phr) three-ring binder
carpeta de tres anillos Spa.
(n phr) three-ring binder
carpeta de tres hoyos Dom.R.
(n phr) three-ring binder
carpool Nic. (v) carpool
carrera de obstáculos Cub.,
Dom.R., ElS., Gua., Hon., Nic.,
Venz. (n phr) hurdles race
carreta (n) wagon
carrete de celo Spa. (n phr) tape
dispenser
carrete de cinta Pri. (n phr) tape
dispenser
carretera Nic., Spa. (n) expressway
carril 1. Pri. (n) lane 2. Par.
(n) median
carril del centro Pue.R.
(n phr) median
carrillo Spa. (n) cheek
carrito Dom.R. (n) trolley
carrito chocón Col., Dom.R.
(n phr) bumper car
carrito de helados Col., Nic.
(n phr) ice cream truck
carro Pri. (n) car
carro alegórico Chi. (n) float
(parade)
carrocería Pri. (n) car body
carro chocón Mex., Nic., Per.,
Venz. (n phr) bumper car
carro comedor Venz. (n phr) dining

ABBREVIATIONS: Arg.=Argentina Bol.=Bolivia Chi.=Chile Col.=Colombia Cos.R.=Costa Rica
Cub.=Cuba Dom.R.=Dominican Republic Ecu.=Ecuador ElS.=El Salvador Gua.=Guatemala
Hon.=Honduras Mex.=Mexico Nic.=Nicaragua Pan.=Panama Par.=Paraguay Per.=Peru
Pri.=Primary Term Pue.R.=Puerto Rico Spa.=Spain Uru.=Uruguay Venz.=Venezuela

car (train)
carro de carrera Cub., Dom.R.,
ElS., Gua., Hon., Nic., Pan.,
Pue.R. (n phr) racecar
carro de carreras Col., Per., Venz.
(n phr) racecar
carro de deporte Cub.
(n phr) sportscar
carro de helados Mex. (n phr) ice
cream truck
carro deportivo Pri. (n phr) sports
car
carro loco Pri. (n phr) bumper car
carro particular Chi., Ecu., Nic.
(n phr) car, private
carro privado Pri. (n phr) car,
private
carroza Pri. (n) float (parade)
carrusel Chi., Col., Ecu., ElS.,
Gua., Hon., Pan., Venz.
(n) carousel (with horses)
cartel Arg. (n) road sign; shop sign
cartel de néon Arg. (n phr) neon
sign
cartel lumínico Par. (n phr) neon
sign
cartelera Chi., Col., Cub., Par.
(n) billboard
cartera 1. Pri. (n) wallet 2. Pri.
(n) handbag 3. Bol.
(n) briefcase
cartera de hombre Dom.R.
(n phr) wallet
cartera de maquillaje Pue.R.
(n phr) makeup kit
cartucho de tinta Pri.
(n phr) toner cartridge
cartucho de toner Nic., Par.
(n phr) toner cartridge
cartucho del toner Dom.R.
(n phr) toner cartridge
cartucho tonificador Mex.
(n phr) toner cartridge

casa Arg. (n) cottage
casa adosada Spa.
(n phr) townhouse
casa-botes Dom.R. (n) boathouse
casa campestre ElS., Gua., Hon.
(n phr) bungalow
casa de campo 1. Pri.
(n phr) cottage 2. Venz.
(n phr) bungalow
casa de ciudad Col. (n phr) townhouse
casa de perro Chi., Venz.
(n phr) doghouse
casa de playa ElS., Gua., Hon. (n phr)
bungalow
casa doble Nic. (n phr) duplex
casa dúplex Dom.R., Pue.R.
(n phr) duplex
casa en hilera Pri.
(n phr) townhouse
casa independiente Pri.
(n phr) bungalow
casamiento Nic. (n) wedding
casa pareada Chi. (n phr) duplex
**casa particular en complejos
residenciales** Gua.
(n phr) townhouse
casa particular en la ciudad Chi.
(n phr) townhouse
casa pegada Bol., Uru.
(n phr) townhouse
casa-quinta Arg. (n) cottage
casa rodante Chi., Par.
(n phr) recreational
vehicle
casca Per. (n) jacket
cascada (n) waterfall
cascarrabias Nic., Venz.
(adj) grumpy
caserío Nic. (n) village
caseta de botes Pri.
(n phr) boathouse
casete Arg., Col., Venz. (n) tape
(cassette)

ABBREVIATIONS: Arg.=Argentina Bol.=Bolivia Chi.=Chile Col.=Colombia Cos.R.=Costa Rica
Cub.=Cuba Dom.R.=Dominican Republic Ecu.=Ecuador ElS.=El Salvador Gua.=Guatemala
Hon.=Honduras Mex.=Mexico Nic.=Nicaragua Pan.=Panama Par.=Paraguay Per.=Peru
Pri.=Primary Term Pue.R.=Puerto Rico Spa.=Spain Uru.=Uruguay Venz.=Venezuela

casette Cub., Dom.R.
(n) videocassette
casilla 1. Arg. (n) hut 2. Bol.
(n) post office box
casilla postal Chi. (n phr) post
office box
casis Pri. (n) black currant
casita de campo Col.
(n phr) cottage
casita de herramientas Pue.R.
(n phr) shed
casita de paja Dom.R.
(n phr) hut
casita playera Col.
(n phr) bungalow
cassette Dom.R., Mex., Nic., Par.
(n) tape (cassette)
castaña 1. Pri. (n) chestnut 2. Chi.
(n) cashew
castaña de cajú Arg., Par., Uru.
(n phr) cashew
castaño 1. Pri. (adj) brown (eyes)
2. Arg., Mex., Nic., Par., Spa.
(adj) brown (hair)
cata Chi. (n) cockatoo
catarata Spa. (n) waterfall
catarina Mex. (n) ladybug
catire Venz. (adj) blond (hair)
catire/a Venz. (n) blond (person)
catre 1. Pri. (n) chair, lounging
2. Chi. (n) box spring
3. Dom.R.
(n) cradle, crib
caucho 1. Col. (n) rubber band
2. Venz. (n) tire (bicycle)
3. Venz. (n) tire (car)
caucho de repuesto Venz.
(n phr) spare tire
caucho pinchado Venz.
(n phr) flat tire
caverna Col. (n) cave
cavidad Venz. (n) sinus
cazo Spa. (n) saucepan

CD Arg., Col., Nic., Pan., Spa.
(n) compact disk
CD player Dom.R.
(n phr) compact disk player
CD-player Cos.R., Nic., Par.
(n) compact disk player
cebolla 1. Bol., Par. (n) onion,
vidalia 2. Pan. (n) bun (hair)
cebolla colorada Ecu., Par.
(n phr) onion, red (Bermuda)
cebolla de cambray Mex.
(n phr) onion, pickling
cebolla larga Col. (n phr) scallion
cebolla morada Mex., Nic.
(n phr) onion, red (Bermuda)
cebolla roja Pri. (n phr) onion, red
(Bermuda)
cebolla verde Pri. (n phr) scallion
cebolla vidalia Col., Nic.
(n phr) onion, vidalia
cebolleta Spa. (n) onion, pickling
cebollín 1. Chi., Nic. (n) onion,
pickling 2. ElS., Gua., Hon.,
Nic., Venz. (n) scallion 3. Nic.
(n) shallot
cebollina 1. Col. (n) onion,
pickling 2. Pan. (n) scallion
cebollino 1. Pri. (n) onion,
pickling 2. Mex. (n) scallion;
shallot
cebollit Par. (n) onion, pickling
cebollita 1. Mex. (n) shallot 2. Par.
(n) scallion; shallot
cebollita verde Bol.
(n phr) scallion
cedazo Pri. (n) sieve
celesta Pri. (n) celesta
celeste Col., Nic. (n) celesta
celo Spa. (n) tape
cementerio Pri. (n) cemetery
cena Pri. (n) dinner
centella Col. (n) lightning
centímetro Cub. (n) tape measure

centro de la calle Pri.
(n phr) median
centro de la ciudad Pri.
(n phr) downtown
centro de negocios Dom.R.
(n phr) business district
centro del pueblo Pue.R.
(n phr) downtown
cepillo Arg., Col., Dom.R., Mex.,
Nic., Spa.,Uru. (n) plane
(carpentry)
cercado de arbustos Mex.
(n phr) hedge
cerdo Col., Cub., Dom.R., Nic.,
Per., Pue.R., Spa., Venz.
(n) pig
cereza Par., Pue.R. (n) berry
cereza agria Venz.
(n phr) cranberry
cerilla Pri. (n) matchstick
cerillo Mex., Nic. (n) matchstick
cerquillo Cub., Ecu., Per. (n) bangs
(hair)
cerrado Col. (adj) cloudy
cerro Chi., Nic., Par. (n) hill
cervatillo Dom.R. (n) reindeer
césped Pri. (n) lawn
cesta Pri. (n) basket (basketball)
cesto Bol. (n) basket (basketball)
chabacano Mex. (n) apricot
chaise Pri. (n) chair, lounging
chal Mex. (n) cape
chaleco 1. Pri. (n) vest 2. Arg.
(n) cardigan
chalet Chi. (n) bungalow; cottage
chalina Par. (adj) cute
chalote Pri. (n) shallot
chamaca Mex. (n) girl
chamaco Mex. (n) boy
chamarra 1. Mex., Nic. (n) jacket
2. Nic. (n) cardigan
chamarra tejida Mex.
(n phr) cardigan

champiñón Col., Mex., Par., Spa.
(n) mushroom
champú Pri. (n) shampoo
chamullento Chi. (n) liar
chancho Arg., Bol., Chi., Cos.R.,
Ecu., Nic., Per., Uru. (n) pig
chanclas Spa. (n) rubbers (shoes)
chanclas de hule ElS., Gua., Hon.
(n phr) rubbers (shoes)
chanclas de plástico Mex.
(n phr) rubbers (shoes)
chancletas 1. Cos.R., Nic., Pan.
(n) slippers 2. Cub., Nic.,
Pue.R. (n) sandals
chancletas de goma Cub., Pue.R.
(n phr) rubbers (shoes)
chanclos de goma Pri. (n phr) rubbers
(shoes)
chanclos Pri. (n) clogs
chango Mex. (n) monkey
chaparro 1. Mex. (adj) short
2. Mex., Nic. (adj) short
(person)
chapas Nic. (colloq.) (n) earrings
chapulín Nic. (n) locust
chaqueta 1. Pri. (n) jacket 2. Chi.,
Pue.R. (n) coat 3. Nic.
(n) cardigan
chaqueta de punto Spa.
(n phr) cardigan
charca Pri. (n) pond
charco Arg., Chi., Par., Uru.
(n) pond
charlatán 1. Pri. (n) tattler
2. Arg., Col., Par.
(adj) talkative
chasis 1. Pri. (n) chassis 2. Pan.
(n) car body
chasquillas Chi. (n) bags (under
eyes)
chassis Dom.R., Pue.R. (n) chassis
¡Chao! Chi. (int) Bye!; Goodbye!
¡Chau! Arg., Par. (int) Bye!;

Goodbye!
chauchas 1. Arg., Uru. (n) beans,
broad 2. Arg., Uru. (n) beans,
green
chavalo/a Nic. (n) boy; girl; child;
kid; teenager
chayote Pan. (n) squash
che duo Par. (n) buddy; pal
chef Pri. (n) chef
chele 1. Nic. (adj) blond (hair)
2. Nic. (n) blond (person)
chequeador de boletos Venz.
(n phr) ticket collector
chequeador de tickets Venz.
(n phr) ticket collector
chequear el equipaje Dom.R.,
Nic., Venz. (v phr) check in
(baggage)
chévere Pue.R. (adj) nice
chica Arg., Uru. (n) girl
chícharos Cub., Mex. (n) peas,
green
chicharra Chi., Nic., Pue.R., Venz.
(n) cicada
chiche Mex. (n) breast
chichi Mex. (n) breast
chico Cub., Pue.R. (n) guy
chico/a 1. Pri. (n) kid 2. Arg., Chi.,
Col. (adj) small 3. Arg.
(n) child
chicos Arg., Ecu. (n) guys (dual
gender plural)
chigüín Nic. (n) boy; child; kid
chilacayote Pri. (n) squash
chile Pri. (n) pepper, hot
chile dulce Cos.R. (n phr) pepper,
sweet
chile picante Cos.R.
(n phr) pepper, hot
chilla Pue.R. (n) mistress
chillo Dom.R., Pue.R. (n) snapper
chiltoma Nic. (n) pepper, sweet
chimenea Pri. (n) fireplace

china 1. Dom.R., Pue.R. (n) orange
2. Nic. (n) babysitter
china mandarina Pue.R.
(n phr) mandarine orange
chinche 1. Pri. (n) bug 2. Nic.
(n) tack 3. Col. (n) stud
chincheta Spa. (n) tack
chinchorro Venz. (n) hammock
chineado Cos.R. (adj) spoiled
(child)
chinelas 1. Arg., Nic. (n) slippers
2. Nic. (n) rubbers (shoes)
chinero 1. Pue.R. (n) buffet
2. Nic., Pue.R. (n) display
cabinet
chingo Nic. (adj) short
chinita Chi. (n) ladybug
chino 1. Col. (n) boy 2. Mex.
(adj) curly (hair)
chino/a Col. (n) child
chinpinilla Nic. (n) shin
chiqueado Mex. (adj) spoiled
(child)
chiquillo/a Pue.R. (n) brat
chiquillos Chi. (n) guys (dual gender
plural)
chiquito Pri. (adj) small
chiquito/a Cub. (n) kid
chiriso Nic. (adj) straight (hair)
chiriva Pri. (n) parsnip
chismoso/a Chi., Cub., Gua.
(n) tattler
chistoso Col., Dom.R., Ecu., Nic.,
Pan. (adj) funny
chiva Dom.R., Venz. (n) goatee
chivato Cub., Spa. (n) tattler
chivera Col. (n) goatee
chiviría Gua. (n) parsnip
chivita Dom.R., Ecu. (n) goatee
chivo 1. Cub. (n) goatee 2. Nic.
(n) pimp
chivón Cub. (n) pest (person)
chocar Pri. (v) crash (traffic)

chocha (n) woodcock
choclo 1. Arg. (n) sweet corn
   2. Bol., Chi., Ecu., Per., Uru.
   (n) corn
chocoyo Nic. (n) parakeet
chofer Chi., Nic., Par. (n) bus driver
chofer de colectivo Arg.
   (n phr) bus driver
chofer de guagua Dom.R., Pue.R.
   (n phr) bus driver
chofer de micro Arg. (n phr) bus
   driver
chofer de taxi Chi., Col., Cos.R.
   (n phr) taxi driver
chomba Chi. (n) sweater
chompa 1. Col. (n) jersey 2. Per.
   (n) pullover 3. Per. (n) sweater
chompipe Nic. (n) turkey
chongo Mex. (n) bun (hair)
choque de frente Pri.
   (n phr) head-on collision
choque frente a frente Per.
   (n phr) head-on collision
choque frontal Nic., Spa., Uru.
   (n phr) head-on collision
choro Chi. (n) mussel
choza Pri. (n) cabin; hut
chulito Pue.R. (adj) cute
chulo 1. Dom.R. (adj) nice 2. ElS.,
   Gua., Hon., Mex., Per., Venz.
   (adj) cute 3. Pri. (n) pimp
chuncho Chi. (n) owl
chupaflor Ecu. (n) hummingbird
chupito Spa. (n) shot glass
churro Bol., Col., Par.
   (adj) handsome
¡Ciao! Col. (int) Bye!
ciclón Dom.R. (n) hurricane
cielo, mi Cub. (n phr) dear; darling;
   honey
ciénaga Chi. (n) swamp
cierre Par. (n) fly (pants)
ciervo Arg., Bol., Cos.R., ElS., Gua.,

Hon., Spa., Uru. (n) deer
cifrar Uru., Venz. (v) encrypt
   (computer)
cigarra 1. Pri. (n) cicada 2. Nic.
   (n) locust
cigarrería Col. (n) liquor store
cigarrillo Pri. (n) cigarette
cigarrillo de marihuana Pri.
   (n phr) marijuana cigarette
cigarro Mex., Nic. (n) cigarette
cigarro Pri. (n) cigar
cima Chi., Nic. (n) peak
   (mountain)
cine Nic. (n) movie theater
cine continuado Venz.
   (n phr) double feature
   (movies)
cinta 1. Pri. (n) tape (cassette)
   2. Chi., Col., Cub. (n) film
cinta adhesiva Pri. (n phr) tape
cinta de medir Pan. (n phr) tape
   measure
cinta de vídeo Spa.
   (n phr) videocassette
cinta elástica Pri. (n phr) rubber
   band
cinta métrica Arg., Col., Dom.R.,
   Mex., Nic., Spa. (n phr) tape
   measure
cinta pegante Ecu. (n phr) tape
cinto Par. (n) belt
cintura Pri. (n) waist
cinturón Pri. (n) belt
cipota Nic. (n) girl
cipote Nic. (n) boy; child; kid
ciruela Cos.R., Dom.R.
   (n) nectarine
ciruela de negra Pri.
   (n phr) nectarine
ciruela negra Pan.
   (n phr) nectarine
cítara Nic. (n) sitar comedia
ciudad Pri. (n) city

ABBREVIATIONS: Arg.=Argentina Bol.=Bolivia Chi.=Chile Col.=Colombia Cos.R.=Costa Rica
Cub.=Cuba Dom.R.=Dominican Republic Ecu.=Ecuador ElS.=El Salvador Gua.=Guatemala
Hon.=Honduras Mex.=Mexico Nic.=Nicaragua Pan.=Panama Par.=Paraguay Per.=Peru
Pri.=Primary Term Pue.R.=Puerto Rico Spa.=Spain Uru.=Uruguay Venz.=Venezuela

clarín Pri. (n) bugle
clase económica Dom.R.
   (n phr) second class
clauadista Cub. (n) diver
clavija Pri. (n) dowel
clínica Col. (n) hospital
clip Pri. (n) paperclip
clóset 1. Pri. (n) closet (clothes)
   2. Col., Cos.R., Cub., Mex.,
   Pan., Per. (n) closet (general)
club de golf Pan. (n phr) golf club
cobertizo de lanchas Gua., Nic.
   (n phr) boathouse
cobertizo para las lanchas Col.
   (n phr) boathouse
cobertizo Pri. (n) shed
cobija Pri. (n) blanket
cobrador Nic. (n) ticket collector
cobres Col. (n) brass section
coca Col., Nic. (n) cocaine
cocaína Pri. (n) cocaine
coche 1. Arg., Chi., Mex., Par.,
   Spa., Uru. (n) car 2. ElS., Gua.,
   Hon. (n) pig
coche cama Pri. (n phr) sleeping
   car (train)
coche comedor Pri. (n phr) dining
   car (train)
coche de carrera Pri.
   (n phr) racecar
coche de carreras Spa.
   (n phr) racecar
coche deportivo Spa., Uru.
   (n phr) sports car
coche particular Par., Spa., Uru.
   (n phr) car, private
coche restaurante Spa.
   (n phr) dining car (train)
coche sport Bol. (n phr) sports car
cochino Cos.R., Cub., Mex., Venz.
   (n) pig
cocina Arg., Bol., Chi., Nic., Per.,
   Spa., Uru. (n) stove

cocinar en el horno Spa.
   (v phr) bake
cocinero Col., Par., Spa. (n) chef
cocuyo Cub. (n) firefly
codificar Par., Venz. (v) encrypt
   (computer)
cogote Col., Nic. (n) nape
cojer nota Cub. (v phr) get high
   (drugs)
col 1. Cub., Ecu., Mex., Spa.
   (n) cabbage, green 2. Cub., Spa.
   (n) cabbage, white
cola 1. Arg. (n) ponytail (hair)
   2. Bol., Cos.R. (n) pigtail
   3. Arg., Col., Par., Uru.
   (n) butt
cola de caballo Pri.
   (n phr) ponytail (hair)
coladera 1. Bol., Col. (n) colander
   2. Col., Mex. (n) sieve
colador 1. Pri. (n) colander 2. Chi.,
   Cub., Venz. (n) sieve
colador de papas Nic.
   (n phr) potato masher
col blanca Mex. (n phr) cabbage,
   white
colcha Ecu., Nic. (n) blanket
colchón 1. Pri. (n) mattress 2. Nic.
   (n) box spring
colchón de resortes Pri.
   (n phr) box spring
colectivo Bol., Col. (n) bus
colegio Arg., Col., Gua., Nic.
   (n) school
coles de Bruselas Pri.
   (n phr) Brussels sprouts
coleta 1. Spa. (n) ponytail (hair)
   2. Spa., Uru. (n) pigtail
colgante con cadena Spa.
   (n phr) necklace, pendant
colibrí Pri. (n) hummingbird
colina Pri. (n) hill
colinabo Nic. (n) rutabaga

colisión frente a frente Col.
(n phr) head-on collision
colita 1. Arg. (n) ponytail (hair)
2. Chi., Col., Dom.R., Mex.,
Venz. (n) pigtail
collar Par. (n) necklace, pendant
collar con colgante Nic.
(n phr) necklace, pendant
collar con medallón Pri.
(n phr) necklace, pendant
colleras Chi. (n) cufflinks
colmado Pue.R. (n) grocery
colmillo Cub., Mex., Nic., Par.,
Spa. (n) canine (tooth)
colocarse Pri. (v) get high (drugs)
colonia Mex. (n) suburb
colorete Col. (n) lipstick
columna vertebral Pri.
(n phr) spine
comadrona Col., Dom.R., ElS.,
Gua., Hon., Nic., Spa. (n)
midwife
combinable Cos.R., Ecu., Per., Spa.
(n) station wagon
combinación Pri. (n) petticoat;
slip
comedia Chi., Col., Cub., Dom.R.,
Nic., Spa. (n) sitcom, situation
comedy
comedia de situación Pri.
(n phr) sitcom, situation
comedy
comedor auxiliar ElS., Gua.. Hon.
(n phr) pantry
comején Ecu., ElS., Gua., Hon.,
Nic. (n) termite
comejón Cos.R., Cub., Dom.R., Pan.,
Pue.R. (n) termite
comer hasta hartarse por un
precio fijo Par. (v phr) eat at
an "all you can eat" buffet
comercial 1. Dom.R., Mex., Pan.,
Venz. (n) commercial 2. Nic.

(n) infomercial
comercial informativa Pri.
(n phr) infomercial
comerciante Col. (n) grocer
comida 1. Arg., Col., Per., Pue.R.
(n) dinner 2. Dom.R., Mex.,
Spa. (n) lunch
comida enlatada Col., Cub.,
Dom.R., Nic., Pan.
(n phr) canned food
comida sin límite Par. (n phr) buffet
comida tarde Nic. (n phr) brunch
comisaría Pri. (n) police station
cómoda Arg., Chi., Col., Nic., Per.
(n) dresser
¿Cómo estás? Bol., Nic.
(phr) How's it going?
¿Cómo te (le) va? Pri. (phr) How's
it going?
¿Cómo tú estás? Dom.R.
(phr) How's it going?
compact disk Spa. (n phr) compact
disk
compactera Par. (n) compact disk
player
compadre Chi., Cub. (n) buddy; pal
compañera Nic. (n) wife
compañero/a Pri. (n) buddy; pal
compartir agujas Pri.
(v phr) share needles (drugs)
compartir carros Gua.
(v phr) carpool
compartir coches Pri.
(v phr) carpool
compartir inyectadoras Venz.
(v phr) share needles
compartir jeringas Col., Nic.
(v phr) share needles
compartir viajes en carro Col.
(v phr) carpool
compás de cuatro por cuatro
Nic., Spa. (n phr) four-four,
common time

ABBREVIATIONS: Arg.=Argentina Bol.=Bolivia Chi.=Chile Col.=Colombia Cos.R.=Costa Rica
Cub.=Cuba Dom.R.=Dominican Republic Ecu.=Ecuador ElS.=El Salvador Gua.=Guatemala
Hon.=Honduras Mex.=Mexico Nic.=Nicaragua Pan.=Panama Par.=Paraguay Per.=Peru
Pri.=Primary Term Pue.R.=Puerto Rico Spa.=Spain Uru.=Uruguay Venz.=Venezuela

compás de dos por cuatro Nic.,
Par., Spa. (n phr) two-four
time
compás mayor Pri. (n phr) four-
four, common time
compás menor, compasillo Pri.
(n phr) two-four time
compás Pri. (n) bar (music)
competencia de obstáculos Col.
(n phr) hurdles race
competidor Pri. (n) contestant
compinche Dom.R. (n) buddy, pal
compras Cos.R. (n) grocery
comprometida Mex. (n) fiancée
(female)
comprometido Mex. (n) fiancé
(male)
computador Col. (n) computer
computador personal Bol.
(n phr) PC
computadora Pri. (n) computer
computadora personal Arg., Gua.,
Mex., Nic., Venz. (n phr) PC
concha ElS., Gua., Nic., Par., Spa.
(n) scallop
conchuela Pan. (n) scallop
concubina Mex. (n) mistress
concursante Chi., Nic., Par.
(n) contestant
concurso televisivo Cos.R. (n phr)
game show (television)
condominio Cub., ElS., Gua., Hon.,
Nic., Pue.R., Spa.
(n) condominium
condominios Pri. (n) condominium
conducir 1. Chi., Col., Pan., Spa.
(v) drive (car) 2. Col.
(v) conduct (music)
conducir borracho Spa.
(v phr) drivedrunk
conducir ebrio Spa. (v phr) drive
drunk
conducir en estado de

embriaguez
Arg., Pue.R. (v phr) drive
drunk
conductor Chi., Ecu. (n) ticket
collector
conductor de autobús Pri.
(n phr) bus driver
conductor de libre Venz.
(n phr) taxi driver
conductor de taxi Pri. (n phr) taxi
driver
conejo Pue.R. (n) hare
conejos Mex. (n) biceps
confidente Pri. (n) love seat
confluencia Col. (n) cloverleaf
junction
conga Pri. (n) conga drum
congelador Pri. (n) freezer
congestión Chi. (n) traffic jam
congestionamiento Pri. (n) traffic
jam
conjunto Pri. (n) outfit
conmovedor Col.
(adj) emocionante
consejero Pri. (n) consultant;
counselor
consentido Col., Ecu., Mex., Nic.
(adj) spoiled (child)
conserje Pri. (n) janitor
conserva (de alimentos) Pri.
(n) preserves
conservas 1. Chi., Col., Nic.
(n) preserves 2. Nic.
(n) canned food
construcción Arg., Pue.R. (n) road
works
consultor Chi., Cos.R., Cub.,
Dom.R., Ecu., Nic., Par., Per.,
Venz. (n) consultant
consultorio médico Pri.
(n phr) doctor's office
consumidor de drogas Pri.
(n phr) drug user

consumir drogas Col., ElS., Gua.,
Hon. (v phr) use drugs
contable 1. Dom.R., Spa.
(n) certified public accountant
(CPA) 2. Spa. (n) bookkeeper
contador 1. Pri. (n) bookkeeper
2. Chi., Dom.R., Par.
(n) certified public accountant
(CPA)
contador público Col.
(n phr) certified public
accountant (CPA)
contador público autorizado
Cos.R., Nic., Pan.
(n phr) certified public
accountant (CPA)
contador público certificado Pri.
(n phr) certified public
accountant (CPA)
contaminación Pri. (n) pollution
contendor Col. (n) challenger
(boxing)
contrabajo 1. Col. (n) bass (voice)
2. Nic. (n) contrabassoon
contrabajón Pri.
(n) contrabassoon
contrafagot Mex.
(n) contrabassoon
contralor Dom.R., Nic.
(n) comptroller
contraventanas Mex. (n) shutters
contrincante Pri. (n) challenger
(boxing)
control remoto Pri.
(n phr) remote control
controlador Pri. (n) comptroller
conversador Pan. (adj) talkative
convertible Pri. (n) convertible
cónyuge Col., Nic. (n) wife
copa ancha de boca estrecha Pri.
(n phr) snifter
copa de cognac Chi. (n phr) snifter
copa de la rueda Col.

(n phr) hubcap
copa de trago Pri. (n phr) shot
glass
copiadora Pri. (n) copier
copiador óptico Venz.
(n phr) scanner, optical
copita Col., Nic. (n) shot glass
coquito 1. Dom.R. (n) hazelnut
2. Venz. (n) ladybug
corazón Mex., Nic. (n) sweetheart
corbata de gatito Pan. (n phr) bow
tie
corbata de gato Bol. (n phr) bow
tie
corbata de lacito Dom.R.
(n phr) bow tie
corbata de lazo Uru., Venz.
(n phr) bow tie
corbata de moñito Mex.
(n phr) bow tie
corbata mariposa Pri. (n phr) bow
tie
corbata michi Per. (n phr) bow tie
corbatín Col., Nic. (n) bow tie
corchete Chi. (n) staple
corchetera Chi. (n) stapler
cordillera Chi., Nic. (n) range
(mountain)
cordón Pri. (n) shoelace
corneta 1. Col. (n) bugle 2. Mex.,
Nic., Par., Spa. (n) cornet
corneta francesa Nic.
(n phr) French horn
corneta inglesa Nic.
(n phr) English horn
cornetín 1. Pri. (n) cornet 2. Spa.
(n) bugle
corno francés Pri. (n phr) French
horn
corno inglés Pri. (n phr) English
horn
corpiño Arg., Par. (n) bra, brassiere
correa Col., Dom.R., Pan., Pue.R.

ABBREVIATIONS: Arg.=Argentina Bol.=Bolivia Chi.=Chile Col.=Colombia Cos.R.=Costa Rica
Cub.=Cuba Dom.R.=Dominican Republic Ecu.=Ecuador ElS.=El Salvador Gua.=Guatemala
Hon.=Honduras Mex.=Mexico Nic.=Nicaragua Pan.=Panama Par.=Paraguay Per.=Peru
Pri.=Primary Term Pue.R.=Puerto Rico Spa.=Spain Uru.=Uruguay Venz.=Venezuela

(n) belt
correa del ventilador Pri.
(n phr) fan belt
corredor de bienes raíces Pri.
(n phr) realtor
correo 1. Arg., Cub. (n) post office
2. Par. (n) mail room
correo electrónico Pri.
(n phr) e-mail
correr Cub. (v) sprint
correr a toda velocidad Col.,
Dom.R., Nic., Par.
(v phr) sprint
correr bicicleta Pue.R. (v phr) ride
(bicycle)
cortacésped Spa. (n) lawn mower
cortacéspedes Pri. (n) lawn mower
cortadora Bol. (n) lawn mower
cortadora de grama Pue.R.
(n phr) lawn mower
cortador de césped Per.
(n phr) lawn mower
cortador del pasto Per.
(n phr) lawn mower
cortadores de galletas Pri.
(n phr) cookie cutters
cortagrama ElS., Gua., Hon., Venz.
(n) lawn mower
cortapastas Pri. (n) pastry cutting
wheel
cortapasto Chi. (n) lawn mower
cortaplumas Chi., Spa., Venz.
(n) penknife
cortar Arg., Chi., Dom.R., Mex.,
Nic. (v) break up
(relationship)
cortar con el vicio Col., Nic.
(v phr) quit using drugs
corte Cub., Mex., Pue.R.
(n) courthouse
cortés Pri. (adj) polite
cortinas Col. (n) blinds
corto 1. Chi., Mex., Nic., Pan.,

Pue.R. (adj) short 2. Col.
(adj) small
costa 1. Pri. (n) shoreline 2. Chi.,
Col., Nic., Par., Pue.R.
(n) seashore
costra Pri. (n) scab
costurera Pri. (n) seamstress
costurero Col., Spa. (n) tailor
coto Col. (n) Adam's apple
cotorra 1. Col., Dom.R. (n) parrot
2. Par. (n) parakeet
counter Pue.R. (n) counter
coverall Per. (n) overalls
coyuntura Dom.R., Spa. (n) joint
CPA Dom.R., Pan. (n) certified
public accountant (CPA)
cranberry Pue.R. (n) cranberry
cráneo Pri. (n) skull
crawl Pri. (n) crawl (swimming)
crecer 1. Pri. (v) grow up 2. Cos.R.,
Dom.R., Ecu., Nic., Pan.,
Pue.R. (v) rise (bread)
crecimeinto Dom.R. (n) root
(hair)
crema de protección solar Spa.
(n phr) sunscreen
crema dental Col.
(n phr) toothpaste
cremera Pri. (n) creamer
crespo 1. Col., Nic., Per. (adj) curly
(hair) 2. Nic., Venz. (adj) wavy
(hair)
criada Par. (n) babysitter
criatura Col., Gua., Par. (n) infant
crineja Venz. (n) braid (hair)
crique Nic. (n) stream
cristal trasero Pue.R. (n phr) rear
window
croissant Pri. (n) croissant
cruasant Dom.R. (n) croissant
cruce de peatones Dom.R.
(n phr) crosswalk
cruce peatonal Col., Par.

ABBREVIATIONS: Arg.=Argentina Bol.=Bolivia Chi.=Chile Col.=Colombia Cos.R.=Costa Rica
Cub.=Cuba Dom.R.=Dominican Republic Ecu.=Ecuador ElS.=El Salvador Gua.=Guatemala
Hon.=Honduras Mex.=Mexico Nic.=Nicaragua Pan.=Panama Par.=Paraguay Per.=Peru
Pri.=Primary Term Pue.R.=Puerto Rico Spa.=Spain Uru.=Uruguay Venz.=Venezuela

(n phr) crosswalk
cuaderno 1. Pri. (n) notebook;
pad, writing; pad (paper)
cuaderno amarillo Pri.
(n phr) pad, yellow
cuaderno de notas Col.
(n phr) pad (paper)
cuaderno legal Pri. (n phr) pad,
legal
cuadra Col., Dom.R., Ecu., Nic.,
Pan., Par. (n) city block
cuadrilátero Chi., Par. (n) ring
(boxing)
cuadrilátero de boxeo Col., Nic.,
Pue.R., Uru. (n phr) ring
(boxing)
cuadro Nic.(n) frame (movie)
cuartel Pri. (n) barracks
cuarteto de cuerda Spa.
(n phr) string quartet
cuarteto de cuerdas Pri.
(n phr) string quartet
cuarto Arg., Col., Cub., Dom.R.,
Mex., Pue.R. (n) bedroom
cuarto de baño Bol., Chi., Cos.R.,
Ecu., Nic., Par., Spa., Uru.,
Venz. (n phr) bathroom
cuarto de correos Pri. (n phr) mail
room
cuarto de estar Pri. (n phr) living
room
cuarto del correo Spa.
(n phr) mail room
cuate ElS., Gua., Hon., Mex., Nic.,
Par. (n) buddy, pal
cuatro tracciónes Dom.R.
(n phr) four-wheel drive
cubeta 1. Col., Mex., Spa.
(n) bucket 2. Mex., Nic.,
Pue.R. (n) pail
cubeta de hielo Pue.R. (n phr) ice
bucket
cubículo Col., Dom.R., Gua., Mex.,

Nic., Pan., Pue.R., Venz.
(n) office cubicle
cubierta Spa. (n) tread (tire)
cubierto Cos.R., Cub., Gua.
(adj) cloudy
cubiertos Pri. (n) silverware
cubo 1. Pri. (n) bucket 2. Cub.
(n) pail
cubrecama Nic. (n) sheet, contour
cucaracha Chi. (n) beetle
cucha Arg. (n) doghouse
cuchara de cocaína Pri.
(n phr) cocaine spoon
cuchara de escurrir Col.
(n phr) draining spoon
cucharas de medida Nic.
(n phr) measuring spoons
cuchara para cocaína Spa.
(n phr) cocaine spoon
cuchara para escurrir Pri.
(n phr) draining spoon
cuchara para la cocaína Col.
(n phr) cocaine spoon
cucharas medidoras Dom.R.
(n phr) measuring spoons
cucharas para medir Pri.
(n phr) measuring spoons
cuchi Bol. (n) pig
cuchilla Pue.R. (n) penknife
cuchilla de afeitar Cub., Spa.
(n phr) razor
cuchilla raspadora Col.
(n phr) scraper
cuchillo para manteca Arg.
(n phr) knife, butter
cuchillo para mantequilla Pri.
(n phr) knife, butter
cuclillo Col., Nic., Venz.
(n) cuckoo
cuco Pri. (n) cuckoo
cucú Mex., Par. (n) cuckoo
cucubano Pue.R. (n) firefly
cuculele Par. (n) cuckoo

cuello Chi. (n) neck (guitar)
cuello de pico Pri. (n phr) v-neck
cuello de tortuga Col., Mex.,
    Pue.R. (n phr) turtleneck
cuello en V Arg., Chi., Col., Gua.,
    Mex., Venz. (n phr) v-neck
cuello Jorge Chavez Per.
    (n phr) turtleneck
cuello tortuga Dom.R., Nic., Pan.,
    Venz. (n phr) turtleneck
cuello V Dom.R., Pan., Per.,
    Pue.R. (n phr) v-neck
cuello vuelto Pri.
    (n phr) turtleneck
cuenco Spa. (n) bowl
cuenta kilómetros Chi.
    (n phr) speedometer
cuentakilómetro Cub.
    (n) speedometer
cuerda Col. (n) chord
cuerdas Pri. (n) snare (of drum)
cuernito Mex. (n) croissant
cuerno francés Col.
    (n phr) French horn
cuerno inglés Col. (n phr) English
    horn

cuesta Pue.R. (n) hill
cueva Pri. (n) cave
cuidador de niños Venz.
    (n phr) babysitter
cuidadora de niños Per.
    (n phr) babysitter
cuidar niños Chi., Col., Ecu., Nic.,
    Per., Pue.R., Venz.
    (v phr) babysit
culebra Pri. (n) snake
culo Col., Par., Spa. (n) butt
culto Col. (adj) polite
cumbre Nic. (n) peak
    (mountain)
cuna Pri. (n) cradle, crib
cuneta Col., Nic., Spa. (n) ditch
cura Col., Nic., Pue.R., Spa., Venz.
    (n) priest
curioso Dom.R. (n) snoop
currículo Mex. (n) résumé (work
    history)
currículum (vitae) Pri. (n) résumé
    (work history)
cuté Dom.R. (n) nail polish
cutex Chi. (n) nail polish

D

dado Arg. (adj) outgoing

damas Chi., Col., Cub., Dom.R.,
Mex., Nic., Pue.R., Venz.
(n) women's (bathroom)

damasco Arg., Chi., Uru.
(n) apricot

danés de fruta Nic. (n) Danish

danesa Pan. (n) Danish

dar Arg. (v) show (movie)

dar a luz Pri. (v phr) give birth

dar flor Col. (v phr) bloom

darse un viaje Dom.R. (v phr) get
high (drugs)

dar vuelta a la derecha, izquierda
Mex. (v phr) turn right, left

datos Pri. (n) data

de agudos Pri. (n phr) treble
(stereo)

decaído Nic. (adj) gloomy (person)

de estatura baja Mex. (adj) short
(person)

de horario completo Arg.
(adj phr) full-time (work)

de jornada completa Pri.
(adj phr) full-time (work)

de mal humor 1. Dom.R.
(ad phrj) gloomy (person)
2. Pue.R. (adj phr) grumpy

de medio tiempo Mex., Par.
(adj phr) part-time (work)

de posición adelantada Col., ElS.,
Gua., Hon. (n phr) offside

de tiempo completo Col., Mex.,
Ni   (adj phr) full-time (work)

decorado Col. (n) set (movie)

decorador de pasteles Nic.
(n phr) icing syringe

decorador para pasteleros Venz.
(n phr) icing syringe

dedo chiquito Cub. (n phr) pinkie
finger

dedo corazón Col. (n phr) middle
finger

dedo del corazón Pri.
(n phr) middle finger

dedo del medio Cub., Dom.R.,
Venz. (n phr) middle finger

dedo gordo 1. Pri. (n phr) big toe
2. Arg. (n phr) thumb

dedo gordo del pie Arg., Cub.,
Dom.R., Nic., Spa., Venz.
(n phr) big toe

dedo medio Mex., Nic., Par., Uru.
(n phr) middle finger

dedo meñique Pri. (n phr) pinkie
finger

defensa 1. Pri. (n) back (soccer)
2. Mex. (n) bumper; fender

defensor Spa. (n) back (soccer)

dejar las drogas Pri. (v phr) quit
using drugs

deleitable Col. (adj) divino

deletear Arg. (v) delete

delfín Chi., Ecu., Par. (n) porpoise

delicioso 1. Pri. (adj) delicious
2. Nic. (adj) tasty

delightful Pri. (adj) divino

demora Arg., Col. (n) delay

dentadura Col. (n) teeth

dentifrice Pri. (n phr) toothpaste

departamento Arg., Bol., Chi.,
Mex. (n) apartment

departamento de bomberos Mex.
(n phr) fire station
dependencia Pri. (n) addiction
dependiente Pri. (n) salesperson
dependiente de colmado Dom.R.
(n phr) grocer
dependiente de supermercado
Dom.R.(n phr) grocer
dependiente de tienda Dom.R.
(n phr) grocer
deportista Nic., Pan. (n) athlete
depósito Arg., Col. (n) storage
room
depósito de gasolina Spa.
(n phr) gas tank
deprimido Venz. (adj) gloomy
(person)
depurar Pri. (v) debug (computer)
derecho a la vía Col. (n phr) right
of way
derecho de paso Arg., Cub., Pue.R.
(n phr) right of way
derecho de vía ElS., Gua., Hon.,
Pan. (n phr) right of way
desacelerar Col., Cub., Par.
(v) decelerate
desarmador Mex., Nic., Per.
(n) screw driver
desatornillador Nic.
(n) screwdriver
desayuno Uru. (n) brunch
desayuno-almuerzo Venz.
(n) brunch
descapotable Spa. (n) convertible
descarga Cub. (n) jam session
desembarque Chi. (n) arrival
desinfectar Dom.R. (v) debug
(computer)
desnatador Mex. (n) skimmer
desnatadora Col. (n) skimmer
desocupado Col., Nic. (adj) vacant
desodorante Pri. (n) antiperspirant
despachar Chi. (v) check in

(baggage)
despedida de soltera Pri.
(n phr) bridal shower
despedir Pri. (v) fire
despensa 1. Pri. (n) pantry 2. Chi.
(n) storage room 3. Dom.R.
(n) buffet
desplantador Pri. (n) trowel
desplazar Pri. (v) scroll
(computer)
destacamento policial Dom.R.
(n phr) police station
destapador 1. Pri. (n) bottle
opener 2. Chi. (n) corkscrew
destornillador Pri. (n) screwdriver
desvestirse Pri. (v) undress
desviación Mex. (n) detour
desvío Pri. (n) detour
detective Chi., Cub., Mex., Pan.,
Venz. (n) police detective
detective de la policía ElS., Gua.,
Hon., Nic. (n phr) police detective
detective policíaco Col.
(n phr) police detective
detective policial Dom.R.
(n phr) police detective
día de clase Par., Pue.R.
(n phr) school day
día de clases Dom.R., Nic., Per.
(n phr) school day
día de colegio Col. (n phr) school
day
día de entre semana
(n phr) weekday
día de escuela Mex., Venz.
(n phr) school day
día de fiesta Mex. (n phr) holiday
día de semana Arg., Col., Dom.R.,
Pue.R., Venz. (n phr) weekday
día de trabajo Col., Cub., Per.,
Pue.R. (n phr) work day
día de vacaciones Mex.
(n phr) holiday

día entre semana Cub., Gua., Nic.,
  Spa. (n phr) weekday
día feriado Pri. (n phr) holiday
día festivo Col., Spa.
  (n phr) holiday
día hábil (n phr) work day
día laborable Col., Dom.R., Spa.
  (n phr) work day
día lectivo Pri. (n phr) school day
días de enfermedad Cub.
  (n phr) sick leave
dibujo animado Pri.
  (n phr) cartoon
dibujos animados Col., Spa.
  (n phr)   cartoon
dibujo de llanta Mex.
  (n phr) tread (tire)
dicharachero Col. (adj) talkative
dientes Pri. (n) teeth
difícil Pri. (adj) difficult
dificultoso Col. (adj) difficult
¿Dígame? Pri. (int) Hello?
  (answering telephone)
director ejecutivo Dom.R.
  (n phr) chief executive officer
  (CEO)
director general Cos.R., Mex., Nic.
  (n phr) chief executive officer
director/a de la cárcel (n phr) warden
  (prison)
dirigible Col., Spa. (n) blimp
dirigible no rígido Pri.
  (n phr) blimp
dirigir Pri. (v) conduct (music)
dirreccional Mex. (n) turning light
disco Col. (n) record album
disco compacto Pri.
  (n phr) compact disk
disco duro Pri. (n phr) hard drive
disminuir la velocidad Pri.
  (v phr) decelerate
dispensador de cinta adhesiva
  Venz. (n phr) tape dispenser

dispensador de cinta pegante
  Col. (n phr) tape dispenser
dispensador de durex Mex.
  (n phr) tape dispenser
distribuir Pue.R. (v) deal (drugs)
distrito residencial Pri.
  (n phr) uptown
divertido Pri. (adj) funny
divino Arg. (adj) cute
división Dom.R. (n) office divider
divisor Bol., Ecu., Par. (n) office
  divider
divorciado Pri. (adj) divorced
divorciarse Pri. (v) divorce
dobladillo Cub. (n) cuff (pants)
doblado Dom.R. (n) cuff (pants)
doblaje Dom.R., Pue.R. (n) stunt
doblar Pri. (v) lip synch
doblar a la derecha, izquierda
  Pri. (v phr) turn right, left
doble 1. Dom.R., Mex., Nic.,
  Pue.R., Spa. (n) stuntman
  2. Col. (n) double feature
  (movies)
doble barbilla Dom.R.
  (n phr) double chin
doblecleta Pue.R. (n) bike, tandem
doble función Pri. (n phr) double
  feature (movies)
doble pera Chi. (n phr) double chin
doble presentación Dom.R.
  (n phr) double feature
  (movies)
doble tanda Nic. (n phr) double
  feature (movies)
doble tracción Nic. (n phr) four-
  wheel drive
doblez 1. Col., Spa. (n) cuff
  (pants)
  2. Pan. (n) crease (pants)
docente Nic. (n) teacher
doctor Arg., Col., Chi., Nic.
  (n) doctor

---

doliente Col. (n) patient
dona Col., ElS., Gua., Hon., Mex.,
Pan., Par., Pue.R.
(n) doughnut
Doña Cos.R., Nic., Pan., Par.
(n) Ma'am, Madam
dónut Pri. (n) doughnut
dorado Nic. (n) bluefish
dorarse al sol Col. (v phr) tan
dormitorio Pri. (n) bedroom
dorso Mex., Nic. (n) backstroke
(swimming)
drive Dom. R., Nic., Pue.R.
(n) drive (computer)
drive-in Col., Pue.R. (n) drive-in
drogadicción Pri. (n) drug
addiction; drug habit
drogadicto Pri. (n) drug addict
drogarse Pri. (v) use drugs
drogas blandas Pri. (n phr) soft
drugs
drogas duras Pri. (n phr) hard drugs

drogas fuertes Col., Nic., Par.
(n phr) hard drugs
drogas más suaves Col.
(n phr) soft drugs
drogas suaves Mex., Nic., Par.
(n phr) soft drugs
drogo Nic. (adj) addicted (colloq.)
droguería Col. (n) drug store
dueto Col. (n) duo
dulce Pan. (n) cake
dulcito relleno Dom.R.
(n phr) tart
dúo Pri. (n) duo
dúplex Pri. (n) duplex
duplex Par. (n) townhouse
dúplex horizontal Mex.
(n phr) townhouse
durazno Pri. (n) peach
durazno pelado Chi.
(n phr) nectarine
durex Mex. (n) tape
duro Dom.R. (adj) curly (hair)

E

ebrio Nic. (adj) intoxicated
echar Arg., Col. (v) fire
echar dedo Col. (v phr) hitchhike
ecler Pan. (n) cream puff
edificación Col. (n) building
edificio 1. Pri. (n) building 2. Chi.,
    Col. (n) apartment building
edificio de apartamentos Pri.
    (n phr) apartment building
edificio de departamentos Arg., Bol.,
    Mex. (n phr) apartment building
edificio de los tribunales Col.
    (n phr) courthouse
edificio de pisos Spa.
    (n phr) apartment building
edil Nic. (n) mayor
editor Col., Nic., Par., Pue.R., Spa.,
    Venz. (n) editor
educado Pri. (adj) polite
efectos de sonido Arg., Col., Mex.,
    Nic., Pan., Pue.R., Spa., Venz.
    (n phr) sound effects
efectos sonoros Pri. (n phr) sound
    effects
ejecutiva Col. (n) businesswoman
ejecutivo Col. (n) businessman
ejotes ElS., Gua., Hon., Mex.
    (n) beans, green
el que toca el tambor Col.
    (n phr) drummer
elástico Bol., Chi. (n) rubber band
elenco Chi., Nic., Pan., Par., Pue.R.
    (n) cast (show)
elevador Cub., Mex., Nic., Pan.,
    Pue.R. (n) elevator
elevarse Pue.R. (v) get high (drugs)

eliminar Pri. (v) delete
elote Mex. (n) corn (on the cob)
e-mail Arg., Dom.R., Mex., Pue.R.,
    Spa. (n) e-mail
embarazada Pri. (adj) pregnant
embarcación Col. (n) ship
embarcar Spa., Venz. (v) board
embarcarse Pri. (v) board
embarque Chi. (n) departure
embellecedor Uru. (n) hubcap
emborracharse Pri. (v) become
    intoxicated
embotellamiento Arg., Nic., Par.,
    Per., Uru. (n) traffic jam
embriagado Pri. (adj) intoxicated
embriagarse Chi. (v) become
    intoxicated
embustero 1. Col. (n) cheater
    2. Col., Nic. (n) liar
emisión Cub. (n) broadcast
emisión televisiva Pri.
    (n phr) broadcast
emitir Pri. (v) broadcast
emocionante Col. (adj) exciting
empalme Col. (n) cloverleaf junction
empleado/a temporal Col.,
    Cos.R., Gua., Venz.
    (n phr) temporary worker
empresa Col. (n) factory
empresaria Arg., Chi., Cos.R.,
    Nic., Par. (n) businesswoman
empresario Arg., Chi., Nic., Par.
    (n) businessman
en estado Venz. (adj phr) pregnant
enagüa 1. Chi. (n) petticoat
    2. Chi., Pue.R. (n) slip

enagua Par. (n) petticoat; slip
enaguas Mex., Venz. (n) petticoat
enamorada Ecu., Per. (n) girlfriend
enamorado Ecu., Per.
  (n) boyfriend
enamorado/a Pri. (n) sweetheart
encantador Col. (adj) divino
encapotado Col. (adj) cloudy
encarcelado Col. (n) prisoner
encendedor Pri. (n) lighter
encender 1. Bol., Chi., Cub., Ecu.,
  Gua., Nic., Par., Spa., Uru.
  (v) turn on (television)
  2. Chi., Dom.R., Nic. (v) start
  (car)
encinta Col., Pan., Per.
  (adj) pregnant
encrespado Par. (adj) curly (hair)
encriptar Col., Mex., Spa.
  (v) encrypt (computer)
encuestado/a Arg., Cos.R., Cub.,
  Ecu., ElS., Gua., Hon., Per.,
  Pue.R. (n) interviewee
encuestador/a Arg., Cos.R., Cub.,
  Ecu., ElS., Gua., Hon., Per.,
  Pue.R. (n) interviewer
encurtido Venz. (n) pickle
endibia Arg., Col., Spa. (n) endive
endivia Col., Par. (n) endive
enfermo/a Arg., Bol., Cub., Cos.R.,
  Ecu., Gua., Uru. (n) patient
enfogono Pue.R. (adj) angry
enfurecido Ecu. (adj) angry
engalanarse Par., Pue.R. (v) dress
  up
engrampador Per. (n) stapler
engrapadora Pri. (n) stapler
engrasado Mex. (n) lubrication
engrase Pri. (n) lubrication
engreído Per. (adj) spoiled (child)
enojado Pri. (adj) angry
¿En qué andas/an? Col.
  (int phr) What's up?

enredadera Bol., Col., Cub., Mex.,
  Nic., Pue.R. (n) climbing plant
enrulado Arg., Pan., Par.
  (adj) curly (hair)
ensaladera Pri. (n) bowl, salad
ensayo Chi., Nic. (n) jam session
entero Uru. (n) overalls
entierro Pri. (n) burial
entonar Venz. (v) tune up
entrada 1. Pri. (n) entrance fee
  2. Arg., Dom.R., Ecu., Uru.
  (n) appetizer 3. Col. (n) main
  course
entrada gratis Chi., Cub., Dom.R.,
  ElS., Gua., Hon., Nic., Pan.,
  Pue.R. (n phr) free admission
entrada gratuita Spa. (n phr) free
  admission
entrada lateral Col., Nic.
  (n phr) side entrance
entrada libre Pri. (n phr) free
  admission
entremés Venz. (n) appetizer
entremetido Col. (n) snoop
entrenador Arg., Bol., Chi., Cub.,
  Nic. (n) instructor
  (sports)
entrenador de deportes Venz.
  (n phr) instructor (sports)
entrenar Col., Cub., Dom.R., Ecu.,
  Pan., Venz. (v) train (for job)
entrevistado/a Pri. (n) interviewee
entrevistador/a Pri.
  (n) interviewer
entrometido Dom.R., Gua., Par.
  (n) snoop
entronque en forma de trébol
  Col. (n phr) cloverleaf
  junction
eperlano Pri. (n) smelt
equipaje Pri. (n) baggage
equipo artístico Pri. (n phr) cast
  (show)

ABBREVIATIONS: Arg.=Argentina Bol.=Bolivia Chi.=Chile Col.=Colombia Cos.R.=Costa Rica Cub.=Cuba Dom.R.=Dominican Republic Ecu.=Ecuador ElS.=El Salvador Gua.=Guatemala Hon.=Honduras Mex.=Mexico Nic.=Nicaragua Pan.=Panama Par.=Paraguay Per.=Peru Pri.=Primary Term Pue.R.=Puerto Rico Spa.=Spain Uru.=Uruguay Venz.=Venezuela

equipo de música para CD Arg.
(n phr) compact disk player
equitación Pri. (n) horseback
riding
equivocado (adj) wrong
erróneo Col., Nic. (adj) wrong
escaladora Pri. (n) stair machine
escalera Mex. (n) stair machine
escalera automática Col.
(n phr) escalator
escalera eléctrica Dom.R., Mex.
(n phr) escalator
escalera mecánica Pri.
(n phr) escalator
escalope ElS., Gua., Hon. ElS., Gua.,
Nic.(n) scallop
escáner Chi., Cub., Mex., Nic.,
Pan., Spa. (n) scanner, optical
escaparate Cos.R., Cub., Nic., Per.,
Spa. (n) shop window
escape 1. Mex., Nic. (n) exhaust
pipe 2. Nic. (n) muffler
escarabajo 1. Pri. (n) beetle 2. Par.
(n) ladybug
escardador Uru. (n) reamer
escariador Pri. (n) reamer
escariadora Mex. (n) reamer
escarola Pri. (n) endive
escenario Pri. (n) set (movie)
escorpión Arg., Chi., Col., Cos.R.,
Nic., Pan., Spa., Uru., Venz.
(n) scorpion
escote en V Uru. (n phr) v-neck
escote V Par. (n phr) v-neck
escuela Pri. (n) school
escurridor de verduras Cos.R.,
Dom.R., Mex., Per., Spa., Uru.
(n phr) colander
esfero Col. (n) pen, ball-point
esmalte de uñas Pri. (n phr) nail
polish
espaldal Pue.R. (n) cabecera
espaldar Ecu., Nic. (n) headboard

espantoso 1. Arg., Chi., Col., Nic.
(adj) awful 2. Nic.
(adj) terrifying
espárrago Mex. (n) stud
espátula 1. Mex., Nic., Par.
(n) painter's knife 2. Pan.
(n) turner 3. Nic., Pue.R.
(n) scraper
especialista Spa. (n) stuntman
especialista en acrobacias Venz.
(n phr) stuntman
espejo retrovisor Pri. (n phr) rear-
view mirror
espejo trasero Uru. (n phr) rear-
view mirror
espejuelos 1. Cub., Pue.R. (n) eye
glasses 2. Cub., Venz.
(n) spectacles
espejuelos bifocales Cub., Pue.R.
(n phr) bifocals
esperando Col. (adj) pregnant
espesura Col. (n) foliage
espiga Mex. (n) dowel; stud
espina dorsal Ecu., Gua.
(n phr) spine
espinaso Ecu. (n) spine
espinazo Col. (n) spine
espinilla 1. Pri. (n) shin 2. Chi.,
Col., Cos.R., Dom.R., Nic.,
Spa., Venz. (n) pimple
esplanada Mex. (n) plain
(topography)
esposo/a Col., Cos.R., Cub.,
Dom.R., Mex., Nic. (n) spouse
espray de pelo Cub., Nic.
(n phr) hairspray
esprín Pan. (n) box spring
esprintar Pri. (v) sprint
espuma para el pelo ElS., Gua.,
Hon., Spa. (n phr) hair mousse
espumadera 1. Pri. (n) skimmer
2. Par., Spa. (n) draining spoon
esqueleto Pri. (n) skeleton

esquí acuático (n phr) water skiing
esquí náutico Cos.R., Ecu., ElS.,
Gua., Hon., Per., Venz.
(n phr) water skiing
estación de bomberos Pri.
(n phr) fire station
estación de policía Col., Cub.,
Gua., Nic., Pan., Pue.R.
(n phr) police station
estacionamiento Pri. (n) parking
lot
estacionar Pri. (v) park
estadio Pri. (n) stadium
estafador Col. (n) cheater
estanque Col., ElS., Gua., Hon.,
Mex., Nic., Venz. (n) pond
estante Pan. (n) closet
(clothes)
estar bajo la influencia del
alcohol o de las drogas Spa.
(v phr) become intoxicated
estar de novio Arg. (v phr) date
estar desorientado por desfase
de horarios Dom.R.
(v phr) jet-lag, to have
estarter Pue.R. (n) starter
estilista Mex., Nic., Pan.
(n) hairdresser
estilo braza Pri.
(n phr) breaststroke
(swimming)
estilo crol Gua., Spa. (n phr) crawl
(swimming)
estilo espalda Pri. (n phr) backstroke
(swimming)
estilo libre Chi., Nic. (n phr) crawl
(swimming)
estilo pecho Chi., Col., Cub., Par.,
Pue.R., Venz.
(n phr) breaststroke
(swimming)

estilográfica Uru. (n) pen,
fountain
estrafalario Nic. (adj) odd
estrella Cub., Dom.R., Pan.
(n) ferris wheel
estrellar Col. (v) crash (traffic)
estruendoso Col., Nic.
(adj) resonant
estuche de maquillaje Pri.
(n phr) makeup kit
estudio de abogados Arg.
(n phr) lawyer's office
estudio juridico Ecu., Par.
(n phr) lawyer's office
estudios Chi. (n) set (movie)
estufa 1. Pri. (n) stove 2. Arg.
(n) fireplace
estupendo Col. (adj) amazing
etiqueta 1. Pri. (n) label 2. Mex.
(n) dog tag
etiqueta adhesiva Pri.
(n phr) label, adhesive
excitante Pue.R.
(adj) emocionante
exciting Pri. (adj) emocionante
exequias Col. (n) burial
exhibidor Nic. (n) shop window
exhibir Nic. (v) show (movie)
éxito Col., Cos.R., Nic. (n) hit
(song)
exosto Col. (n) exhaust pipe
explorador óptico Pri.
(n phr) scanner, optical
explorar el Internet Venz.
(v phr) surf the net
exquisito 1. Col. (adj) divino
2. Per. (adj) delicious
extra Arg., Nic. (n) stuntman
extraño Chi., Col., Nic.
(adj) odd
extrovertido Pri. (adj) outgoing

F

fábrica Pri. (n) factory
factoría Dom.R., Pue.R. (n) factory
faja Cos.R., Nic. (n) belt
falda 1. Pri. (n) skirt 2. Bol. (n) dress
   (woman's)
falda corta Col., Pue.R. (n) miniskirt
familiar Pri. (n) family member
farmaceuta Col., Venz. (n) pharmacist
farmacéutico Pri. (n) pharmacist
farmacia Pri. (n) drug store
faro 1. Pri. (n) spoke (bicycle wheel)
   2. Arg. (n) reflector (bicycle)
farol Pri. (n) street lamp
farola Spa. (n) street lamp
faroles delanteros Col.
   (n phr) headlights
faros Pri. (n) headlights
faros de emergencia Ecu.
   (n phr) emergency lights
faros intensos Ecu. (n phr) brights
   (headlights)
fastidioso Mex., Venz. (n) pest
   (person)
fender Pue.R. (n) fender
feria Mex., Nic., Pue.R. (n) fairground
feriado Arg., Nic. (n) holiday
ferry Col., Cos.R., Dom.R., Nic., Spa.,
   Venz. (n) ferry
fichero giratorio Pri. (n phr) rolodex
fichero rolodex Nic. (n phr) rolodex
film Venz. (n) film
filmación Nic., Venz. (n) shooting
   (movie)
filmar Nic., Venz. (v) shoot (movie)
filme Arg., Cos.R., Ecu., Uru., Pan.
   (n) film

filo Dom.R., Pue.R. (n) crease (pants)
fisgón Pri. (n) snoop
flat Pan. (n) flat tire
flautín Col., Mex., Par., Spa.
   (n) piccolo
fleco Col., Mex., Nic. (n) bangs (hair)
flequillo Pri. (n) bangs (hair)
flojo Bol., Chi., Mex., Venz. (adj) lazy
flor de avispa Nic. (n phr) hibiscus
florecer Pri. (v) bloom
florería Cub. (n) florist's shop
florista Pri. (n) florist's shop
floristería Col., Dom.R., Nic., Pan.,
   Pue.R.,Venz. (n) florist's shop
foca marina Dom.R. (n phr) walrus
focos Arg., Cub. (n) headlights
focus delanteros Nic.
   (n phr) headlights
folder Dom.R., Mex., Nic., Pan.,
   Pue.R. (n) folder
folder de argollas Col. (n phr) three-
   ring binder
folder de tres anillos Nic.
   (n phr) three-ring binder
follaje Pri. (n) foliage
fondo 1. Mex., Venz. (n) slip 2. Venz.
   (n) petticoat
fontanero Nic., Spa. (n) plumber
fosanasal Nic. (n) nostril
fosforera Cub. (n) lighter
fósforo Pri. (n) matchstick
fotocopiadora Nic., Par., Spa.
   (n) copier
foyer Pri. (n) lobby
frac Pri. (n) tailcoat
fraccionamiento Mex. (n) suburb

frazada Arg., Bol., Col., Cub., Par.,
Uru. (n) blanket
freezer Arg., Nic., Par., Pue.R.
(n) freezer
frejoles Ecu. (n) beans
fresa Pri. (n) strawberry
fresadora Spa. (n) reamer
frigorífoco Spa. (n) refrigerator
frijoles 1. Pri. (n) beans, black 2. Col.,
Cub., Gua., Hon., Mex., Nic.,
Pan. (n) beans
frijoles blancos Nic. beans, lima
frijoles colorados Cub., Nic.
(n phr) beans, kidney
frijoles de media luna Pri.
(n phr) beans, lima
frijoles de soja Pri.
(n phr) soybeans
frijoles negros Col., Cub., ElS., Gua.,
Hon., Mex., Nic., Pan.
(n phr) beans, black
frijoles rojos Col. (n phr) beans,
kidney
frijolitos verdes Nic. (n phr) beans,
green
frijol nacido Nic., Pan. (n phr) bean
sprouts
frisa Pue.R. (n) blanket

frondosidad Col. (n) foliage
fruta bomba Cub. (n phr) papaya
frutal Arg. (n) fruit tree
frutería Pue.R. (n) fruit stand
frutilla 1. Arg., Par. (n) strawberry
2. Nic. (n) berry, blueberry,
cranberry
fuente de agua (n phr) water fountain
fuente de servir Pri. (n phr) platter
fuera de juego Pri. (n phr) offside
fuera de posición Pue.R.
(n phr) offside
fuerte Chi. (adj) loud (noise)
fulano/a Cos.R., Mex., Pan. (n) guy
fulo Pan. (adj) blond (hair)
fulo/a Pan. (n) blond (person)
función doble Uru. (n phr) double
feature (movies)
funda Pri. (n) pillowcase
funeral Dom.R. (n) wake
funeraria Pri. (n) funeral home
funicular Pri. (n) funicular
furgón Col., Uru. (n) van
furgoneta Spa., Venz. (n) van
furioso Dom.R. (adj) angry
fuslero Bol., Chi. (n) rolling pin
fustán Nic. (n) petticoat; slip
fútbol Pri. (n) soccer

G

gabán 1. Pue.R. (n) jacket (men's)
2. Nic. (n) trench coat
gabardina 1. Col., Spa. (n) raincoat
2. Mex. (n) trench coat 3. Col.
(n) overcoat
gabete Pue.R. (n) shoelace
gabinete Pue.R. (n) pantry
gafas 1. Col. (n) spectacles 2. Col.,
Spa. (n) eyeglasses
gafas bifocales Spa. (n phr) bifocals
gafas de buceo Spa. (n phr) goggles,
swimming
gafas de esquí Spa. (n phr) goggles,
ski
gafas de protección Mex.
(n phr) glasses, safety
gafas de seguridad Spa.
(n phr) glasses, safety
gafas trifocales Spa. (n phr) trifocals
gáfiter [from "gas fitter"] Chi.
(n) plumber
galera Arg. (n) hat, top
galería Dom.R. (n) porch
galleta Pri. (n) cookie; biscuit; cracker
galleta de dulce Per. (n phr) cookie
galleta de soda Nic., Venz.
(n phr) cracker
galleta dulce ElS., Gua., Hon.
(n phr) cookie
galleta saltina Col. (n phr) cracker
galletica 1. Dom.R. (n) cracker 2. Cub.
(n) cookie
galletita 1. Arg. (n) biscuit; cracker
2. Arg., Cos.R., Par., Pue.R.,
Uru. (n) cookie

galletitas saladas Par. (n) cracker
gallina Pan. (n) chicken
gallina sorda ElS., Gua., Hon.
(n phr) woodcock
gallineta Col., ElS., Gua., Hon.
(n) woodcock
gallusa Pan. (n) bangs (hair)
galpón Chi., Par. (n) shed
gamba 1. Pri. (n) prawn 2. Spa.
(n) shrimp
ganadero Chi. (n) farmer
ganchito 1. Arg. (n) staple 2. Arg.,
Uru. (n) paperclip
ganchito de pelo Venz.
(n phr) barrette
gancho de pelo Nic. (n) barrette
gancho para el pelo Dom.R., Pan.,
Per., Spa. (n phr) barrette
ganga Col. (adj) cheap
garaje Pri. (n) garage (repairs); garage
(storage)
garaje para botes Col.
(n phr) boathouse
garañón Chi., Gua., Nic. (n) stallion
garlador Col. (adj) talkative
garrafa Col., Nic., Spa. (n) decanter
garúa Per. (n) drizzle
garzón Chi. (n) waiter
gasfitero Ecu. (n) plumber
gasolina Pri. (n) gasolina (vehicle)
gata Bol., Chi., Nic., Per. (n) jack (car)
gato 1. Pri. (n) jack (car) 2. Cos.R.,
Nic. (adj) green (eyes) 3. Nic.
(adj) blue (eyes)
gaveta Pri. (n) drawer

gavetero 1. Venz. (n) dresser 2. Col.
(n) file cabinet
gears Pri. (n) velocidades
gel fijador Ecu. (n phr) hair gel
gel para el pelo Pri. (n phr) hair gel
gelatina para el pelo Dom.R., ElS.,
Gua., Hon. (n phr) hair gel
gemelos Pri. (n) cufflinks
gemelos de teatro Pri. (n phr) glasses,
opera
gerente Col., Par. (n) office manager
gerente de oficina Cub., Mex., Nic.,
Pue.R., Venz. (n phr) office
manager
gerente deportivo Venz.
(n phr) manager (sports)
gerente ejecutivo Chi. (n phr) chief
executive officer (CEO)
gerente general Col., Cos.R., Nic.
(n phr) chief executive officer
(CEO)
germinados de soja Pri. (n phr) bean
sprouts
gillette Arg., Chi. (n) razor
girar Nic. (v) turn right, left
globo Chi., Col., Nic. (n) hot air
balloon
globo aerostático Pri. (n phr) hot air
balloon
globo de aire caliente Venz.
(n phr) hot air balloon
gofre (n) waffle
goggles Pue.R. (n) goggles, swimming
gogles Mex. (n) goggles, swimming
gogles para esquiar Mex.
(n phr) goggles, ski
goleador Pan. (n) goalie
golero Uru. (n) goalie
golpe Venz. (n) bruise
goma 1. Arg., Cub., Dom.R., Pue.R.
(n) tire (car) 2. Arg., Dom.R.,
Pue.R. (n) tire (bicycle)
goma de auxilio Arg. (n phr) spare tire

goma de repuesta Pue.R.
(n phr) spare tire
goma de repuesto Cub., Dom.R.
(n phr) spare tire
goma elástica Spa., Uru.
(n phr) rubber band
goma pinchada Arg., Dom.R.
(n phr) flat tire
goma ponchada Cub. (n phr) flat tire
goma vacía Pue.R. (n phr) flat tire
gomina para el pelo Spa. (n phr) hair
gel
gomita Arg., Dom.R., Pue.R.
(n) rubber band
gorra Pri. (n) cap
grabado de la llanta Nic. (n phr) tread
(tire)
grabadora de vídeo Col.
(n phr) videocassette recorder
(VCR)
grabar Arg., Nic. (v) store (computer
data)
gracioso 1. Pri. (adj) funny 2. Dom.R.,
Ecu., Pan. (adj) cute
grama 1. Dom.R., ElS., Gua., Hon.,
Nic., Pue.R., Venz. (n) lawn
2. Nic. (n) grass
grampa Par., Per. (n) staple
granada Pri. (n) pomegranate
granadilla Cos.R. (n) pomegranate
grandes almacenes Pri.
(n phr) department store
granjero Par., Per. (n) farmer
grano Pri. (n) pimple
grapa 1. Pri. (n) staple 2. Col.
(n) clamp
grapadora Pue.R., Spa. (n) stapler
grapas de cocaína Mex.
(n phr) cocaine spoon
grapefruit Nic. (n) grapefruit
graves Pri. (n) bass (stereo)
greca Dom.R. (n) coffee maker
grosella 1. Col., Mex., Nic., Par.

(n) black currant 2. Nic., Pue.R.

(n) gooseberry

grosella silvestre Pri.

(n phr) gooseberry

grosero Col. (adj) impolite

gruñón Col., Nic. (adj) grumpy

guacamaya ElS., Gua., Hon., Mex.

(n) macaw

guacamayo Pri. (n) macaw

guachinango Mex. (n) snapper

guadaña Pri. (n) scythe

guagua 1. Chi. (n) baby 2. Cub.,
Dom.R., Pue.R. (n) bus

guagüero Cub. (n) bus driver

guagüita Pue.R. (n) station wagon

guajolote Mex. (n) turkey

guallo Dom.R. (n) grater

guanajo Cub. (n) turkey

guandules Dom.R. (n) beans,
broad

guapa Pri. (adj) pretty

guapo 1. Pri. (adj) handsome 2. Cub.
(adj) cute 3. Col., Dom.R.
(adj) brave

guarda Par. (n) ticket collector

guardabarro 1. Col., Nic., Spa.
(n) fender 2. Nic. (n) bumper

guardafango Cub., Ecu., ElS., Gua.,
Hon., Venz. (n) fender

guardameta Cub. (n) goalie

guardapelo Cub. (n) locket

guardería Arg., Dom.R., Nic., Par.
(n) daycare center

guardapolvo Cub. (n) overalls

guardar Arg., Mex., Nic., Pan.

(v) store (computer data)

guardarropa Chi. (n) closet (general)

guarda-vallas Col. (n) goalie

guarder Venz. (v) store (computer

guardería infantil Pri. (n phr) daycare
center

guardián Col., Pan., Venz.
(n) guardian

guiar Pue.R. (v) drive (car)

guata Chi. (n) abdomen; belly

guayo Pue.R. (n) grater

güero Mex. (adj) blond (hair)

guardián de la cárcel Venz.
(n phr) warden (prison)

guaro Nic. (n) liquor

güero/a Mex. (n) blond (person)

guía 1. Pri. (n) handlebars (bicycle)
2. Dom.R., Pue.R. (n) steering
wheel

guillo Dom.R. (n) bracelet

guiñador Bol. (n) blinker (light)

guindilla Spa. (n) pepper, hot

guindo Nic. (n) cliff

guineo Dom.R., Ecu., Pan., Pue.R.
(n) banana

guiño Arg. (n) blinker (light); turning
light

guión Nic., Par. (n) screenplay

guión cinematográfico Pri. (n phr)
screenplay

guisantes Pue.R., Spa. (n) peas,
green

guitarra oriental Venz. (n phr) sitar

guitarrear Pri. (v) strum

guitarreo Pri. (n) strumming

H

habas 1. Pri. (n) beans, broad 2. Spa.
(n) beans, lima
habas limas Cub. (n phr) beans, lima
habichuelas 1. Pri. (n) beans, green;
beans, kidney 2. Dom.R., Pue. R.
(n) beans
habichuelas de soya Pue.R.
(n phr) bean sprouts
habichuelas negras Pue.R.
(n phr) beans, black
habichuelas rojas Dom.R.
(n phr) beans, kidney
habichuelas verdes Pue.R.
(n phr) beans, green
habitación Pan. (n) bedroom
hábito Col., Nic., Par. (n) habit (drugs)
hablador 1. Pri. (adj) talkative 2. Mex.
(n) tattler
hablantín Nic. (adj) talkative
hacer autostop Pri. (v phr) hitchhike
hacer clic Pri. (v phr) click (computer)
hacer dedo Arg., Chi., Par.
(v phr) hitchhike
hacer de niñero/a Pri. (v phr) babysit
hacer mímica Dom.R., Nic. (v phr) lip
synch
hacer pool Arg. (v phr) carpool
hacer un cambio Arg. (v phr) shift
gear
hacer un transbordo de trenes Venz.
(v phr) change (train)
hacer una conexión Arg.
(v phr) change (train)
hacha Pri. (n) hatchet
hachuela Col. (n) hatchet
hairy Pri. (adj) velloso

halcón Pri. (n) hawk
hall de entrada Arg., Chi.
(n phr) lobby
¿Haló? Pan., Pue.R. (int) Hello?
(answering telephone)
hamaca 1. Pri. (n) hammock 2. Spa.
(n) chair, lounging
handbol Pri. (n) handball
haragán Col., Dom.R., Nic., Uru.
(adj) lazy
harto Col. (adj) boring
¡Hasta la vista! Pue.R. (int phr) See
you later!
¡Hasta luego! Pri. (int phr) See you
later!
¡Hasta mañana! Ecu. (int phr) Good
night!
hebilla Arg., Bol., Col., Cub., Pue.R.
(n) barrette
hechado a perder Mex.
(adj phr) rotten (food)
heladera Arg., Par. (n) refrigerator
heladería Pri. (n) ice cream parlor
heladero Pri. (n) ice cream truck
hematoma Dom.R. (n) bruise
hendidura Pri. (n) cleft (chin)
herbolario Uru. (n) herbalist's shop
hermanastra Chi., Nic., Spa.
(n phr) half sister
hermanastro Chi., Nic., Spa.
(n phr) half brother
hermoso Pri. (adj) beautiful
hibisco Pri. (n) hibiscus
hidroala Pri. (n) hydrofoil boat
hidroavión Chi., Nic., Par.
(n) hydrofoil boat

hidrofoil Mex. (n) hydrofoil boat
hielera Dom.R., Ecu., Gua., Mex.,
     Par., Venz. (n) ice bucket
hierba Nic. (n) marijuana
hierba silvestre Mex. (n phr) weed
himno Bol., Col., Dom.R., Mex., Nic.,
     Par., Pue.R., Spa., Venz.
     (n) hymn
hit Cos.R., Cub., Dom.R. (n) hit
     (song)
hogar Arg. (n) fireplace
hogar de ancianos Pri.
     (n phr) retirement home
hoja Col. (n) table leaf
hoja de vida Col. (n phr) résumé
     (work history)
hojaldra Nic. (n) puff pastry
hojaldre Pri. (n) puff pastry
hojilla de afeitar Venz. (n phr) razor
¿Hola? Arg., Bol., Par., Uru.
     (int) Hello? (answering
     telephone)
holgazán Mex. (adj) lazy
hombre de negocios Pri.
     (n phr) businessman
hombre profesional Pan.
     (n phr) businessman
hombre rana Chi., Par. (n) diver
hombrillo Venz. (n) road shoulder
hongo Pri. (n) mushroom
hora de entrada o salida a los trabajos
     Per. (n phr) rush hour
hora del tapón Pue.R. (n phr) rush
     hour
hora de tráfico Cub., Mex.
     (n phr) rush hour
hora pico Pri. (n phr) rush hour
hora punta Spa. (n phr) rush hour
horario Pri. (n) timetable
horas de oficina Pri. (n phr) office
     hours

horas de trabajo Cub. (n phr) office
     hours
horas hábiles Nic. (n phr) office hours
hornada Pri. (n) batch
hornalla Par. (n) batch
horneada Chi. (n) batch
hornear Pri. (v) bake
horrendo Col. (adj) awful
horrible Pri. (adj) awful
horripilante Col. (adj) terrifying
horroroso Col. (adj) awful
hortaliza Pue.R. (n) orchard
hospital Pri. (n) hospital
hotcake Mex. (n) pancake
hoyito 1. Chi., Dom.R., Mex.
     (n) dimple 2. Dom.R. (n) cleft
     (chin)
hoyo 1. Bol. (n) dimple 2. Chi.,
     Dom.R. (n) pothole 3. Dom.R.
     (n) bump (road)
hoyo de la nariz Dom.R.
     (n phr) nostril
hoyo en uno Pri. (n phr) hole in one
hoyuelo Pri. (n) dimple
hoz 1. Pri. (n) sickle 2. Par. (n) scythe
huachinango Mex. (n) snapper
huaraches de plástico Mex.
     (n phr) rubbers (shoes)
hueco Col., Cos.R., Ecu., Pan.
     (n) pothole
huella del caucho Venz. (n phr) tread
     (tire)
huerta Arg., Spa. (n) vegetable
     garden
huerto Pri. (n) orchard; vegetable
     garden
huincha Chi. (n) tape measure
hule ElS., Gua., Hon., Nic. (n) rubber
     band
humedales Nic. (n) wetlands
huracán Pri. (n) hurricane

I-J-K

iceberg Pri. (n) iceberg
icon Pue.R. (n) icon (computer)
icono Pri. (n) icon (computer)
imagen Pri. (n) frame (movie)
impermeable 1. Pri. (n) raincoat
2. Col., Spa. (n) trench coat
imponente Pri. (adj) tremendous
imprenta Pri. (n) print shop
impresora Pri. (n) printer (computer)
impresionante Pri. (adj) impressive
incentivo Pri. (n) fringe benefit
incómodo Col. (adj) bothersome
incorrecto Nic., Pue.R., Spa.
(adj) wrong
increíble Arg., Chi., Dom.R., Nic.
(adj) amazing
index card Pri. (n phr) ficha
indicador de medir el aceite Venz.
(n phr) dipstick
indicador del nivel de aceite Pri.
(n phr) dipstick
industria Col. (n) factory
inflarse Col. (v) rise (bread)
información Col. (n) data
información de interés Uru.
(n phr) infomercial
informativo breve Col. (n phr) news
brief
infracción Mex. (n) ticket, traffic
infracción por exceso de velocidad
Mex., Nic. (n phr) ticket,
speeding
inhalar Arg., Col., Mex., Nic., Pue.R.
(v) inhale (drugs)
inmobiliario Arg. (n) realtor
insecto Col., Dom.R., Nic., Per.,

Pue.R. (n) bug
insoportable Chi. (n) pest (person)
instructor de deportes Pri.
(n phr) instructor (sports)
instructor deportivo Col.
(n phr) instructor (sports)
instrumentos de metal Spa.
(n phr) bronze section
intendencia Uru. (n) city hall
intendente Par., Uru. (n) mayor
interiores Venz. (n) briefs
interiores bikini Venz. (n) bikini
briefs
intermitente Cub., Spa. (n) turning
light
intermitente Pri. (n) blinker (light)
intérprete Col., Mex. (n) performer
interventor Venz. (n) comptroller
intruso Chi. (n) snoop
inundar Pue.R. (v) stall (car)
invernadero Mex. (n) nursery (plants)
investigador Spa. (n) police
detective
ir a caballo Cub. (v phr) ride
horseback
ir juntos en un carro Venz.
(v phr) carpool
iris Nic., Par., Venz. (n) iris
isla 1. Arg., Col., Par., Venz. (n) traffic
island 2. Venz. (n) median
isla de tráfico Col. (n phr) median
isleta Pri. (n) traffic island
itinerario Col. (n) timetable

jaca Pri. (n) pony
jaiba 1. Chi., Nic. (n) crab 2. Col.,

ABBREVIATIONS: Arg.=Argentina Bol.=Bolivia Chi.=Chile Col.=Colombia Cos.R.=Costa Rica
Cub.=Cuba Dom.R.=Dominican Republic Ecu.=Ecuador ElS.=El Salvador Gua.=Guatemala
Hon.=Honduras Mex.=Mexico Nic.=Nicaragua Pan.=Panama Par.=Paraguay Per.=Peru
Pri.=Primary Term Pue.R.=Puerto Rico Spa.=Spain Uru.=Uruguay Venz.=Venezuela

Dom.R., Nic. (n) crayfish
jalea Mex. (n) hair gel
jameo Pue.R. (n) jam session
jardinera Nic. (n) flower bed
jardín infantil Col. (n phr) daycare
center
jarra 1. Pri. (n) pitcher 2. Arg.
(n) decanter 3. Chi., Pue.R.,
Nic., Spa., Venz. (n) mug
jarra de cerveza Nic., Pue.R., Spa.,
Venz. (n phr) mug, beer
jarra para café Pri. (n phr) mug,
coffee
jarra para cerveza Pri. (n phr) mug,
beer
jarrilla Nic. (n) kettle
jarrita Arg. (n) mug; coffee mug
jarrita de leche Nic. (n phr) creamer
jarrita para café Venz. (n phr) mug,
coffee
jarrita para leche Spa.
(n phr) creamer
jarrito Arg. (n) mug; coffee mug
jarro Pri. (n) mug
jarro de cerveza Mex. (n phr) mug,
beer
jarro para café Mex. (n phr) mug,
coffee
jarrón Chi. (n) pitcher
jazz Dom.R., Spa. (n) jazz music
jeanes Col. (n) jeans
jeans Pri. (n) blue jeans
jefe Pri. (n) boss
jefe de cocina Col., Per. (n) chef
jefe de oficina Pri. (n phr) office
manager
jefe ejecutivo principal Pri.

(n phr) chief executive officer
(CEO)
jeringuilla de decoración Pri. (n phr)
icing syringe
jeringuilla para decorar Col.
(n phr) icing syringe
jersey 1. Pri. (n) jersey 2. Spa.
(n) pullover; sweater; sweatshirt
jet Pri. (n) jet
jibia Chi. (n) squid
jitomate Mex. (n) tomato
joint Dom.R. (n) marijuana cigarette
jornalero Chi., Nic. (n) temporary
worker
jote Chi. (n) vulture
judías verdes Spa. (n phr) beans,
green
juego de maquillaje Col.
(n phr) makeup kit
juego de vídeo Col., Cos.R., Dom.R.,
Mex., Nic., Venz. (n) videogame
juey Pue.R. (n) crayfish
juez 1. Bol., Col., Ecu., Nic., Per.
(n) referee 2. Nic. (n) umpire
(baseball)
juguetón Col. (adj) naughty
juky Par. (adj) cute
jungla Chi., Col., Dom.R., Pue.R.,
Venz. (n) selva
jungle Pri. (n) selva
jurista Col. (n) lawyer
juzgado Nic., Par., Spa. (n) courthouse

kepi Par. (n) cap
keyboard Pue.R. (n) keyboard
(computer)
kiwi Pri. (n) kiwi

L

label Dom.R., Pue.R. (n) label
label adhesiva Dom.R., Pue.R.
(n phr) label, adhesive
labio leporino Chi. (n phr) cleft (chin)
laca para el pelo Pri. (n phr) hairspray
lacio Pri. (adj) straight (hair)
ladilla Cub. (n) pest (person)
laguna Chi., Dom.R., Nic., Venz.
(n) pond
lámina de aluminio Cos.R., ElS.,
Gua., Hon., Pan., Per.
(n phr) aluminum foil
LAN Pri. (n) LAN (local area
network)
lancha Cub. (n) ferry
langostino 1. Arg., Col., Cub., Mex.,
Pan., Spa. (n) prawn 2. Chi.
(n) shrimp
lanzamiento de bala Nic. (n phr) shot
put
lanzamiento de pesa Pue.R.
(n phr) shot put
lanzamiento de peso Pri. (n phr) shot
put
lapa Nic. (n) macaw
lapicera Arg., Chi., Uru. (n) pen
lapicera a fuente Chi. (n phr) pen,
fountain
lapicera de pasta Chi. (n phr) pen,
ball-point
lapicera fuente Arg., Par. (n phr) pen,
fountain
lapicero 1. Nic., Per. (n) pen 2. Per.
(n) pen, ball-point
lapicero de tinta Per. (n phr) pen,
fountain

lapis de libios Nic. (n phr) lipstick
lápiz de labios Spa., Uru.
(n phr) lipstick
lápiz labial Pri. (n phr) lipstick
lata Cos.R. (n) bus
lata de aceite Arg., Cub., Par., Venz.
(n phr) oil can
lata de regar Venz. (n phr) watering
can
latas de conservas Chi. (n phr) canned
food
lateral Mex. (n) offside
laucha Chi. (n) mouse
laundry Pue.R. (n) dry cleaner's
lava vajilla Uru. (n phr) dishwasher
lavadero Arg. (n) laundry
lavadora de platos Col., Cub., Pue.R.
(n phr) dishwasher
lavandería 1. Pri. (n) laundry 2. Col.,
Dom.R., Nic. (n) dry cleaner's
lavaplatos Pri. (n) dishwasher
lavavajilla Arg. (n) dishwasher
lavavajillas Spa. (n) dishwasher
lazo Pue.R. (n) bow tie
lechera Arg. (n) creamer
lechosa Dom.R., Pue.R. (n) papaya
lechoso Venz. (n) papaya
lechuga repollada Dom.R.
(n phr) cabbage, green
lechuza Arg., Col., Cub., Dom.R., Par.
(n) owl
lenguado Pri. (n) flounder
lentes 1. Col. (n) spectacles 2. Col.,
Dom.R., Ecu., Pan., Par., Per.,
Venz. (n) eyeglasses
lentes bifocales Pri. (n phr) bifocals

---

lentes de ópera Venz. (n phr) glasses,
opera
lentes para leer Mex. (n phr) half-
glasses
lentes protectores Venz.
(n phr) glasses, safety
lentes trifocales Venz.
(n phr) trifocals
leotardo Pri. (n) leotard; tights
leotardos Spa. (n) tights
letra de una canción Pri.
(n phr) lyrics
letras de una canción Dom.R.
(n phr) lyrics
letrero comercial Pri. (n phr) shop
sign
letrero de carretera Pri. (n phr) road
sign
letrero de néon Dom.R. (n phr) neon
sign
leudarse Pri. (v) rise (bread)
levantamiento de pesas
(n phr) weight lifting
levantarse Bol., Chi., Col., ElS., Gua.,
Hon., Mex., Spa. (v) rise (bread)
leyendas Cub., Pan., Uru. (n) subtitles
lezana Col. (n) awl
lezna Pri. (n) awl
libélula Pri. (n) dragonfly
libre 1. Pri. (adj) vacant 2. Venz.
(n) taxi
librería Pri. (n) bookstore
libreta 1. Dom.R., Pue.R.
(n) notebook 2. Bol., Cub., Pan.,
Pue.R.,Venz. (n) pad (paper)
3. Col., Cub., Dom.R., Nic.,
Pue.R., Venz. (n) pad, writing
libreta amarilla Bol., Col. Dom.R.,
Nic. (n phr) pad, yellow
libreta de papel amarilla Pue.R.,
Venz. (n phr) pad, yellow
libreta legal Bol. (n phr) pad, legal
libreta tamaño legal Dom.R., Pan.,

Pue.R., Venz. (n phr) pad, legal
libreto Dom.R., ElS., Gua., Hon.
(n) screenplay
licencia de conducir Pri.
(n phr) driver's license
licencia de manejar Cub., Nic., Venz.
(n phr) driver's license
licencia por enfermedad Col.,
Dom.R. (n phr) sick leave
licor 1. Col., Cub., Gua., Mex., Pan.,
Venz. (n) liquor 2. ElS., Pan.
(n) hard liquor
licor de alto contenido alcohólico
Col. (n phr) hard liquor
licor espiritoso Pri. (n phr) hard liquor
licor fuerte Bol., Dom.R., Nic., Venz.
(n phr) hard liquor
licorera Pri. (n) decanter
licorería Bol., Col., Mex., Nic., Par.
(n) liquor store
licuadora Pri. (n) blender
liebre Pri. (n) hare
liero Arg. (adj) naughty
liga Cub., Mex., Pan., Per., Venz.
(n) rubber band
ligas Pri. (n) suspenders
ligero Pri. (adj) light (weight)
ligeros Mex. (n) suspenders
ligón Pue.R. (n) snoop
lima Pri. (n) lime
límite de velocidad Pri. (n phr) speed
limit
limón Cub., Pan. (n) lime
limpiabrisas Col. (n) wipers
(windshield)
limpiador Chi. (n) janitor
limpiaparabrisas (n) wipers
(windshield)
limpia-parabrisas Venz. (n) wipers
(windshield)
limpiar Pue.R., Venz. (v) debug
(computer)
limpiavidrios Dom.R. (n) wipers

(windshield)
linda Arg., Col., Cub., Pue.R.
(adj) pretty
lindo 1. Arg., Ecu., Par., Pue.R., Venz.
(adj) beautiful 2. Cub., ElS.,
Gua., Hon., Per., Venz.
(adj) cute
línea Cub. (n) lane
línea aérea Col., Dom.R., Nic.
(n phr) airline
lipstick Pue.R. (n) lipstick
lipstick Pan. (n) lipstick
liquor store Dom.R., Pue.R.
(n phr) liquor store
lirio Pri. (n) iris
liso Chi., Col., Nic., Spa., Venz.
(adj) straight (hair)
litera 1. Pri. (n) berth; bunkbed
2. Col. (n) sleeping car (train)
litoral Col. (n) shoreline
liviano Arg., Chi., Nic., Par. (adj) light
(weight)
living Arg. (n) living room
llano Col., Dom.R. (n) plain
(topography)
llanta 1. Pri. (n) rim (bicycle wheel);
tire (car) 2. Bol., Col., Cos.R.,
Gua., Mex., Pan., Per. (n) tire
(bicycle)
llanta de refacción Mex. (n phr) spare
tire
llanta de repuesto Bol., Ecu., Gua.,
Nic., Pan., Par. (n phr) spare tire
llanta desinflada Cos.R., Per., Uru.
(n phr) flat tire
llanta pache Gua. (n phr) flat tire
llanta pinchada Bol., Col., Gua.,
Mex. (n phr) flat tire
llanta ponchada Mex., Nic.
(n phr) flat tire
llanta reventada Pri. (n phr) flat tire
llanura Pri. (n) plain (topography)
llave 1. Chi. (n) screwdriver 2. Mex.

(n) valve (trumpet)
llegada Pri. (n) arrival
llevar (v) wear (clothing)
llevar puesto Cub., Dom.R., Par.
(v phr) wear (clothing)
llovizna Pri. (n) drizzle
lluvia tenue Col. (n phr) drizzle
lobby Arg., Dom.R., Mex., Pue.R.
(n) lobby
lóbulo Pri. (n) tip of nose
loby Pan. (n) lobby
loción solar Pri. (n phr) sunscreen
locote Par. (n) pepper, sweet
locuaz Pri. (adj) talkative
lodera Nic. (n) bumper, fender
loma Chi., Cub., Pan. (n) hill
lomo Pri. (n) road shoulder
lomo de toro Chi. (n phr) bump
(road)
loro Pri. (n) parrot
lote Cos.R., Nic. (n) batch
love seat Dom.R., Mex. (n phr) love
seat
loza Chi., Pan. (n) china
LSD Pri. (n) LSD
lubricación Col., Dom.R., Gua., Nic.,
Pan. (n) lubrication
lubrificación Chi. (n) lubrication
luces Arg., Chi., Cub., Pan., Pue.R.
(n) headlights
luces altas Arg., Chi., Dom.R., Mex.,
Nic., Pan., Venz. (n phr) brights
(headlights)
luces de emergencia Pri.
(n phr) emergency lights
luces delanteras Dom.R., Mex., Venz.
(n phr) headlights
luces fuertes Pri. (n phr) brights
(headlights)
luces intermitentes Pue.R.
(n phr) emergency lights
luces largas Cub., Pue.R., Spa.
(n phr) brights (headlights)

ABBREVIATIONS: Arg.=Argentina Bol.=Bolivia Chi.=Chile Col.=Colombia Cos.R.=Costa Rica
Cub.=Cuba Dom.R.=Dominican Republic Ecu.=Ecuador ElS.=El Salvador Gua.=Guatemala
Hon.=Honduras Mex.=Mexico Nic.=Nicaragua Pan.=Panama Par.=Paraguay Per.=Peru
Pri.=Primary Term Pue.R.=Puerto Rico Spa.=Spain Uru.=Uruguay Venz.=Venezuela

luciérnaga Pri. (n) firefly
lugar del Web Venz.
    (n phr) website
lúgubre Pri. (adj) gloomy (person)
luminaria Nic. (n) street lamp
lunar Cub., Ecu., Per., Venz.
    (n) birthmark
lunar de nacimiento Nic.
    (n phr) birthmark
luneta Arg. (n) rear window
luz Arg., Nic. (n) reflector (bicycle)
luz alta Par. (n phr) brights
    (headlights)

luz de cruce Venz. (n) blinker (light)
luz de doblar Dom.R. (n phr) turning
    light
luz del indicador Chi. (n phr) turning
    light
luz direccional (n phr) turning light

luz direccional Pan. (n) blinker (light)
luz intermitente Pri. (n) blinker (light)
luz para doblar Col. (n phr) turning
    light
luz para voltear Per. (n phr) turning
    light

M

macetero Bol. (n) flower bed
machaca Pri. (n) pest (person)
macho 1. Cos.R. (adj) blue (light-
colored eyes) 2. Cos.R. (n) blond
(person with light hair)
machucador de papas Per.
(n phr) potato masher
macizo Pri. (n) flower bed
madurar Col., Par. (v) grow up
mae Cos.R. (n) guy
maestro/a Nic. (n) teacher
maestro de ceremonias Per.
(n phr) host (show)
maestro de educación física Pue.R.
(n phr) instructor (sports)
magdalena Spa. (n) muffin
magulladura ElS., Gua., Hon., Venz.
(n) bruise
mahones Pue.R. (n) blue jeans
maíz Pri. (n) corn
majador de papas Pri. (n phr) potato
masher
maje Nic. (n) guy
majes Nic. (n) guys (dual gender
plural)
mala hierba (n phr) weed
malacostumbrado Col. (adj) spoiled
(child)
malanga Cub. (n) taro
malcriado 1. Arg., Col., Cub., Nic.,
Pan., Pue.R. (adj) spoiled (child)
2. Cub., Nic., Pan. (n) brat
3. Nic. (adj) impolite
maldito Arg. (adj) evil
maleducado 1. Spa. (adj) spoiled
(child) 2. Nic., Spa.

(adj) impolite
maleta 1. Pri. (n) suitcase 2. Par.,
Venz. (n) trunk (car)
maletas Col., Cos.R., Nic., Par.
(n) baggage
maletera 1. Bol. (n) porter 2. Bol.,
Per. (n) trunk (car)
maletero 1. Pri. (n) porter 2. Cub.,
Nic., Pan., Spa. (n) trunk (car)
maletín 1. Pri. (n) attaché case 2. Col.,
Cub., Nic., Par., Per., Pue.R.
(n) briefcase
maleza Arg., Chi., Dom.R., Ecu., Nic.
(n) weed
malhumorado Pri. (adj) grumpy
maligno Venz. (adj) evil
malla 1. Chi., Par. (n) leotard 2. Par.
(n) bathing suit 3. Par. (n) tights
mallas Mex., Nic., Venz. (n) tights
mallas de ejercicio Venz.
(n phr) leotard
malo 1. Arg., Chi., Col., Dom.R., Nic.
(adj) evil 2. Dom.R. (adj) curly
(hair)
malva Par. (n) okra
malvado 1. Pri. (adj) evil 2. Chi.
(adj) naughty
mamá Arg., Col., Nic., Par. (n) mother
mameluco Arg., Dom.R., Pue.R.
(n) overalls
manada Col. (n) flock
manager deportivo Pri.
(n phr) manager (sports)
mancha de nacimiento Mex.
(n phr) birthmark
mancornas Col., Ecu. (n) cufflinks

ABBREVIATIONS: Arg.=Argentina Bol.=Bolivia Chi.=Chile Col.=Colombia Cos.R.=Costa Rica
Cub.=Cuba Dom.R.=Dominican Republic Ecu.=Ecuador ElS.=El Salvador Gua.=Guatemala
Hon.=Honduras Mex.=Mexico Nic.=Nicaragua Pan.=Panama Par.=Paraguay Per.=Peru
Pri.=Primary Term Pue.R.=Puerto Rico Spa.=Spain Uru.=Uruguay Venz.=Venezuela

mancuernas Pan. (n) cufflinks
mancuernillas ElS., Gua., Hon., Mex.,
　Nic. (n) cufflinks
mandarina Pri. (n) mandarine orange
mandíbula Pri. (n) jaw
mando a distancia Spa.
　(n phr) remote control
mandolín Chi. (n) mandolin
mandolina Pri. (n) mandolin
manejar Pri. (v) drive (car)
manejar borracho Pri. (v phr) drive
　drunk
manejar embriagado Col.
　(v phr) drive drunk
manejar en estado de ebriedad Chi.,
　Nic. (v phr) drive drunk
manejar en estado de embriaguez
　Dom.R. (v phr) drive drunk
manejar tomado Cos.R. (v phr) drive
　drunk
mangos Par., Per. (n) handlebar grips
　(bicycle)
maní Pri. (n) peanut
manicure Chi. (n) manicurist
manicurista Dom.R., Ecu., Mex.,
　Nic., Pan., Per., Venz.
　(n) manicurist
manicuro/a Pri. (n) manicurist
manigueta Nic. (n phr) drawer knob
manija Par. (n) mug, beer
manilla Venz. (n) drawer knob
manillar Spa., Uru. (n) handlebars
　(bicycle)
manillas Col. (n) handlebar grips
　(bicycle)
manta Spa. (n) blanket
manta religiosa Pri. (n phr) praying
　mantis
mantenedora Nic. (n) freezer
mantenimiento de calles Venz.
　(n phr) road works
mantilla Pue.R. (n) praying mantis
mantis religiosa Par., Spa.

　(n phr) praying mantis
manto Col. (n) cloak
manubrio 1. Arg., Bol., Chi., Col.,
　Gua., Mex., Nic., Par., Pue.R.,
　Venz. (n) handlebars (bicycle)
　2. Chi., Par. (n) steering wheel
　3. Dom. R. (n) drawer knob
manubrios Ecu. (n) handlebars
　(bicycle)
manzana Pri. (n) city block
manzana de Adán Pri.
　(n phr) Adam's apple
maple Gua., Mex., Nic. (n) maple
　(tree)
máquina de afeitar Col., Nic.
　(n phr) razor
máquina de caminar Dom.R.
　(n phr) treadmill
máquina de correr Pue.R.
　(n phr) treadmill
máquina de cortar yerba Cub.
　(n phr) lawn mower
máquina de cortar pasto Arg.
　(n phr) lawn mower
máquina de hacer ejercicios Dom.R.,
　Par. (n phr) stair machine
máquina escalera Cos.R. (n phr) stair
　machine
máquina para cortar el pasto Col.
　(n phr) lawn mower
marca de nacimiento Pri.
　(n phr) birthmark
marcador Pri. (n) marker
marcha Cos.R. (n) stick shift
marcha atrás Pri. (n phr) reverse
marchas Cos.R. (n) gears
marco Col. (n) frame (movie)
maría palito Pan. (n phr) praying
　mantis
marihuana Pri. (n) marijuana
marimba Cub., Par. (n) xylophone
mariquita Pri. (n) ladybug
marisma 1. Pri. (n) swamp 2. Chi.

(n) wetlands
marmita Pri. (n) kettle
marquesina Dom.R. (n) garage (storage)
marrano Col., ElS., Gua., Hon., Mex., Nic., Pan. (n) pig
marrón 1. Arg., Col., Dom.R., Par., Per., Spa. (adj) brown (eyes) 2. Pue.R. (n) sledgehammer
marrueco Chi. (n) fly (pants)
marsopa Pri. (n) porpoise
masa de mil hojas Chi. (n phr) puff pastry
mascota Dom.R. (n) notebook
masita Arg. (n) cookie
mástil Pri. (n) neck (guitar)
mata 1. Cub. (n) bush; shrub 2. Dom.R. (n) tree
matapiojos Chi. (n) dragonfly
materiales de oficina Cub. (n phr) office supplies
matorral Col., Nic. (n) hedge
matres Pue.R. (n) mattress
matrimonio Nic. (n) wedding
maya Arg. (n) bathing suit
mayor de edad Col. (n) adult
mazo Chi., Dom.R., Mex., Nic., Par. (n) sledgehammer
mecedor Col. (n) chair, rocking
mecedora Pri. (n) chair, rocking
mechudo Nic. (adj) hairy
medallón 1. Chi. (n) necklace, pendant 2. Dom.R., Par. (n) locket
media Col., Cub., Dom.R., Ecu., Pan., Pue.R., Venz. (n) sock
media (tres cuartos) Arg., Uru. (n) sock
media fina Par. (n phr) pantyhose
media luna 1. Pri. (n phr) half-glasses 2. Chi. (n phr) croissant
medialuna Arg., Col., Par. (n) croissant

media naranja Col., Nic. (n phr) spouse
media nylon Par., Per. (n phr) pantyhose
media pantalón 1. Pri. (n phr) pantyhose 2. Col. (n phr) tights
media panty Dom.R. (n phr) pantyhose
mediana Spa. (n) median
medias 1. Spa. (n) tights 2. Nic. (n) pantyhose 3. Par. (n) sock
medias gruesas Chi. (n phr) tights
medias largas Arg. (n phr) pantyhose
medias nylon Pue.R. (n phr) pantyhose
medias panty Venz. (n phr) pantyhose
médico Pri. (n) doctor
medida para bebida Chi. (n phr) shot glass
medio Arg. (n) middle finger
mediofondo Dom.R. (n) petticoat; slip
medios-lentes Venz. (n) half-glasses
medio tiempo Nic. (adj phr) part-time (work)
mejilla Pri. (n) cheek
mejillón Pri. (n) mussel
melocotón Cub., Dom.R., Nic., Par., Per., Pue.R., Spa. (n) peach
melón Col., Nic., Pan., Per., Venz. (n) cantaloupe
melón calameño Chi. (n phr) cantaloupe
melón chino Pri. (n phr) cantaloupe
melón de agua Cub. (n phr) watermelon
memoria de reserva Venz. (n phr) buffer storage
memoria intermedia Col., Nic., Venz. (n phr) buffer storage
memoria intermediaria Pri. (n phr) buffer storage
memoria temporal Col., Venz.

ABBREVIATIONS: Arg.=Argentina Bol.=Bolivia Chi.=Chile Col.=Colombia Cos.R.=Costa Rica Cub.=Cuba Dom.R.=Dominican Republic Ecu.=Ecuador ElS.=El Salvador Gua.=Guatemala Hon.=Honduras Mex.=Mexico Nic.=Nicaragua Pan.=Panama Par.=Paraguay Per.=Peru Pri.=Primary Term Pue.R.=Puerto Rico Spa.=Spain Uru.=Uruguay Venz.=Venezuela

(n phr) buffer storage
meñique Nic. (n) pinkie finger
mentiroso Pri. (n) liar
mentón Arg., Col., Par. (n) chin
menudo Col. (adj) small
mercado Col. (n) grocery
merienda Pri. (n) snack
mermelada Per., Spa. (n) preserves
mesa de buffet Mex. (n phr) buffet
mesa de cocina Pri. (n phr) table,
   kitchen
mesa de luz Arg. (n phr) table, night
mesa de noche Col., ElS., Gua., Hon.,
   Nic., Pue.R., Venz. (n phr) table,
   night
mesa de servicio Col., Nic.
   (n phr) table, serving
mesa de servir Venz. (n phr) table,
   serving
mesada Arg. (n) counter
mesero Chi., Col., Cub., Dom.R.,
   ElS., Gua., Hon., Mex., Nic.,
   Pan., Pue.R. (n) waiter
mesilla de noche Pri. (n phr) table,
   night
mesita de cocina Pan. (n phr) table,
   kitchen
mesita de luz Arg. (n phr) table, night
mesita de noche Bol., Cub., Dom.R.,
   Pan., Par. (n phr) table, night
mesita de servicio Pri. (n phr) table,
   serving
mesita rodante Arg. (n phr) table,
   serving
mesonero Venz. (n) waiter
metales Mex., Nic. (n) brass section
meteorólogo (n phr) weather reporter
meter un cambio Col., Nic.
   (v phr) shift gear
meterse un viaje Venz. (v phr) get
   high (drugs)
metiche Col., Cub., Dom.R., Ecu.,
   Mex., Par. (n) snoop

metido Col., Cub. (n) snoop
metro 1. Pri. (n) tape measure 2. Mex.
   (n) local train
metrópoli Col. (n) city
meza de servir Par. (n phr) table,
   serving
mezclador Cub. (n) mixer
mezquino Mex., Nic. (n) wart
mico Col. (n) monkey
micro 1. Pri. (n) microwave (oven)
   2. Chi., Par. (n) bus
microbus Per. (n) van
microonda Arg., Col., Cub., Par., Uru.
   (n) microwave (oven)
microondas Chi., Mex., Nic., Pue.R.,
   Spa., Venz. (n) microwave
   (oven)
miedoso Bol. (adj) terrifying
miembro de la familia Col.
   (n phr) family member
milhoja Venz. (n) puff pastry
mimado Pri. (adj) spoiled (child)
minifalda Pri. (n) miniskirt
minitrusa Pri. (n) bikini briefs
mirar televisión Col., Nic.
   (v phr) watch television
mirlo Pri. (n) blackbird
mocasines Chi., Col., Cub., Ecu., Nic.,
   Par., Venz. (n) loafers
mocoso Pri. (n) brat
modista Arg., Chi., Col., Nic., Pan.,
   Spa. (n) seamstress
módulo Dom.R., Nic. (n) modular
   office
mofle Pri. (n) muffler
moho Dom.R., Par. (n) moss
molar Col. (n) molar
molde Par. (n) tart
molde de bizcocho Dom.R. (n phr) pie
   pan
molde de galletitas Par. (n phr) cookie
   cutters
molde para bollos Nic. (n phr) muffin

pan
molde para magdalenas Spa.
(n phr) muffin pan
molde para muffin Arg.
(n phr) muffin pan
molde para mufin Mex.
(n phr) muffin pan
molde para pan Par. (n phr) muffin
pan
molde para pancitos Bol.
(n phr) muffin pan
molde para panecillos Pri.
(n phr) muffin pan
molde para pastel Pri. (n phr) pie pan
molde para pastelitos Bol.
(n phr) muffin pan
molde para pay Mex. (n phr) pie pan
molde para pie Chi., Nic. (n phr) pie
pan
molde para quequitos Per.
(n phr) muffin pan
molde para tartas Arg. (n phr) pie
pan
moldecito Pri. (n) tart
moldes Arg. (n) cookie cutters
moldes de galletas Chi., Dom.R.,
Venz. (n phr) cookie cutters
moledor de carne Pan., Pue.R.
(n phr) meat grinder
moledor de papas Chi. (n phr) potato
masher
moledora de carne Arg., Col.,
Dom.R. (n phr) meat grinder
molesto 1. Pri. (adj) bothersome
2. Pue.R. (adj) angry
molestoso Venz. (adj) bothersome
molidora Cub. (n) meat grinder
molino de carne Pri. (n phr) meat
grinder
mollete Gua. (n) muffin
molondrón Dom.R. (n) okra
monedero Pri. (n) coin purse
moñito Arg., Par. (n) bow tie

monitor Pri. (n) monitor (computer)
mono 1. Pri. (n) monkey; overalls
2. Pri. (adj) cute 3. Col.
(adj) blond (hair)
mono/a Col. (n) blond (person)
moño 1. Pri. (n) bun (hair) 2. Chi.
(n) pigtail 3. Pan. (n) braid (hair)
montañera Pri. (n) bike, mountain
montar a caballo Col., Nic., Par.
(v phr) ride horseback
montar bicicleta Nic. (v phr) ride
bicycle
montar cicla Col. (v phr) ride bicycle
montar en bicicleta Pri. (v phr) ride
bicycle
montarse Col. (v) get on (bus)
monte Cos.R., Nic. (n) marijuana
montón Nic. (n) batch
mora Per. (n) blueberry
mora azul Mex. (n phr) blueberry
mora roja Mex. (n phr) cranberry
morado Col., Cub., Dom.R. (n) bruise
moratón Spa. (n) bruise
moreno Pri. (adj) brown (hair)
moreno/a Pri. (n) brunette (person)
morete Cos.R. (n) bruise
moretón Arg., Bol., Chi., Mex., Nic.,
Pan., Par. (n) bruise
morocho Uru. (adj) brown (hair)
morocho/a Arg., Uru. (n) brunette
(person)
morsa (n) walrus
mosa Col. (n) mistress
moscardón Col. (n) horsefly, gadfly
mostrador 1. Pri. (n) counter 2. Col.
(n) buffet
mostrar Venz. (v) show (movie)
mota Cos.R. (n) marijuana
mother board Pan.
(n phr) motherboard
moto Pri. (n) motorcycle, motorbike
motocicleta Pri. (n) motorcycle,
motorbike

motocine Pri. (n) drive-in
motor de arranque Par., Spa.
   (n phr) starter
motora Pue.R. (n) motorcycle,
   motorbike
motosierra Arg., Cos.R., Nic., Par.,
   Spa. (n) chainsaw
mountain bike Dom.R., Par., Pue.R.,
   Spa. (n phr) bike, mountain
mouse para el pelo Mex. (n phr) hair
   mousse
mousse para el pelo Pri. (n phr) hair
   mousse
mover Pan. (v) scroll (computer)
mozo 1. Arg., Bol., Chi., Cos.R.,
   Dom.R., Uru. (n) waiter 2. Spa.
   (n) porter
muchachita Dom.R. (n) girl
muchachito Dom.R. (n) boy
muchachito/a Dom.R. (n) brat
muchacho Pri. (n) guy
muchacho/a Dom.R. (n) kid
muchachos Pri. (n) guys (dual gender
   plural)
mudarse Pri. (v) move
muela Pri. (n) molar
muelle de carga Col., Nic.
   (n phr) loading dock
muffin Arg., Col. (n) muffin
muffler Dom.R. (n) muffler
mufin Mex. (n) muffin
mufler Mex. (n) muffler

mujer de negocios Pri.
   (n phr) businesswoman
multa Pri. (n) ticket, traffic
mujer profesional Pan.
   (n phr) businesswoman
multa por exceso de velocidad Pri.
   (n phr) ticket, speeding
multa por infracción Par.
   (n phr) ticket, speeding
muñequitos Cub., Dom.R., Nic.,
   Pue.R. (n) cartoon
municipalidad Chi., Col., Ecu., ElS.,
   Gua., Hon., Par. (n) city hall
muñón Nic. (n) stump
mus para el pelo Dom.R. (n phr) hair
   mousse
musculosa Arg. (n) vest
música Mex., Pue.R. (n) sound track
música de jazz Col., Nic. (n phr) jazz
   music
música de rock Col., Par. (n phr) rock
   music
música jazz Pri. (n phr) jazz music
musical Dom.R., Nic., Pue.R.
   (n) musical (movie)
música rock Pri. (n phr) rock
   music
músico Mex. (n) performer
mustang Nic. (n) mustang
mustango Pri. (n) mustang
muy agradable ElS., Gua., Hon.
   (adj phr) divino

N

Ña Par. (n) Señora
nabo Par. (n) rutabaga
nabo de suecia Col. (n phr) rutabaga
nabo sueco Pri. (n phr) rutabaga
nafta Arg., Par. (n) gasolina (vehicle)
nalga 1. Pri. (n) buttock 2. Pan.
    (n) butt
nalgas Cub. (n) butt
nana 1. Chi., Col., Mex., Venz.
    (n) nanny 2. Mex. (n) babysitter
ñandú Col., Par. (n) ostrich
naranja Pri. (n) orange
narcomanía Col. (n) drug addiction;
    drug habit
narcómano 1. Col. (adj) addicted
    2. Col. (n) drug addict
narcotraficante Bol., Cos.R., Cub.,
    Nic., Venz. (n) drug dealer
narigón Arg., Bol., Chi., Uru.
    (adj) big-nosed
narina Chi. (n) nostril
narizón Pri. (adj) big-nosed
narizú Dom.R. (adj) big-nosed
navaja 1. Pri. (n) penknife 2. Pan.
    (n) razor
navaja de pintor Pri. (n phr) painter's
    knife
navegar en el Internet Bol., Ecu.
    (v phr) surf the net
navegar la red Arg. (v phr) surf the
    net
navegar por Internet Col., Nic.
    (v phr) surf the net
navegar por la Internet Chi., Gua.
    (v phr) surf the net
navegar por la red Par., Spa., Uru.

(v phr) surf the net
navío Chi. (n) ship
neblina 1. Pri. (n) mist 2. Arg., Col.,
    Cub., Dom.R., Mex., Nic., Per.
    (n) fog
necio Nic., Pue.R. (adj) naughty
necio/a Ecu., Nic. (n) pest (person)
nectarín Mex. (n) nectarine
nectarina Col., Cub., Nic.
    (n) nectarine
nectarine Pue.R., Venz. (n) nectarine
nectarino ElS., Gua., Hon.
    (n) nectarine
negociación Pue.R. (n) drug deal
negocio de drogas Ecu., Venz.
    (n phr) drug deal
nena Arg., Par., Uru. (n) girl
nene 1. Arg., Pue.R., Uru. (n) boy
    2. Nic. (n) infant
nene/a Uru. (n) child
neumático 1. Pri. (n) tire (bicycle)
    2. Cos.R., Nic. (n) inner tube
    (bicycle tire)
neumático desinflado Uru. (n phr) flat
    tire
neumático pinchado Spa. (n phr) flat
    tire
nevera Col., Dom.R., Ecu., Pue.R.,
    Spa., Venz. (n) refrigerator
nevería Mex. (n) ice cream parlor
neverita Dom.R. (n) water fountain
niebla 1. Pri. (n) fog 2. Arg., Pue.R.
    (n) mist
niña Pri. (n) girl
niñera Pri. (n) nanny
niñero/a Pri. (n) babysitter

niñito/a Venz. (n) toddler

niño Pri. (n) boy

niño/a 1. Pri. (n) child; infant 2. Col.,
    Venz. (n) kid 3. Spa. (n) toddler

niño/a chiquito/a Col. (n phr) toddler

niño/a de edad pre-escolar Mex.
    (n phr) toddler

niño/a malcriado/a Col. (n phr) brat

niño/a que empieza a andar ElS.,
    Gua., Hon., Mex., Nic.
    (n phr) toddler

nivel Pri. (n) level

nivelador Chi. (n) level

no profesional Cub. (n phr) amateur

nodriza Chi. (n) babysitter

ñoño Dom.R. (adj) spoiled (child)

noria Pri. (n) ferris wheel

¡Nos vemos! Dom.R., ElS., Gua., Nic.,
    Pan., Par. (int phr) See you later!

¡Nos vemos mas tarde! Par.
    (int phr) See you later!

noticiario Spa. (n) newscast

noticias Mex. (n) newscast

noticiero Arg., Chi., Col., Dom.R.,
Ecu., Mex., Pan., Par.
    (n) newscast

noticiero breve Mex. (n phr) news
    brief

novato Per. (n) amateur

novela Arg., Cub. (n) soap opera

novia Pri. (n) fiancée (female);
    girlfriend

novio Pri. (n) boyfriend; fiancé (male)

nublado Pri. (adj) cloudy

nuboso Cos.R., Cub., Gua.
    (adj) cloudy

nuca Pri. (n) nape

nuez 1. Cub. (n) Adam's apple
    2. Mex., Nic., Par. (n) pecan
    3. Par., Pue.R. (n) nutmeg 4. Nic.,
    Pan., Par. (n) walnut

nuez de Adán Arg. (n phr) Adam's
    apple

nuez de la garganta Spa.
    (n phr) Adam's apple

nuez de la India Pri. (n phr) cashew

nuez del Brasil Col. (n phr) Brazil nut

nursery Pue.R. (n) daycare center

O

obras Pri. (n) road works
obras viales Nic. (n phr) road works
obstáculos Chi. (n) hurdles race
ocultar Pri. (v) encrypt (computer)
offside Arg. (n) offside
oficial de policía Venz. (n phr) police
officer
oficial ejecutivo jefe Venz. (n phr) chief
executivo officer (CEO)
oficina 1. Pri. (n) office suite 2. Bol.
(n) office cubicle
oficina de abogados Col., Pue.R.
(n phr) lawyer's office
oficina de correos Pri. (n phr) post
office
oficina del doctor Pue.R.
(n phr) doctor's office
oficina del médico Pue.R.
(n phr) doctor's office
oficina modular Pri. (n phr) modular
office
oficina postal Col. (n phr) post office
oído Col., Mex., Nic. (n) ear
¿Oigo? Cub. (int) Hello? (answering
telephone)
ojeras Pri. (n) bags (under eyes)
ojiazul Col. (adj) blue (eyes)
ojiverde Col. (adj) green (eyes)
ojo de gato (reflectante en la calle)
Nic. (n phr) stud
ojotas Arg. (n) clogs
ojotas de goma Arg. (n phr) rubbers
(shoes)
okra Mex., Nic. (n) okra

oler Cub., Dom.R. (v) inhale (drugs)
oliva Cos.R. (n) olive
olla 1. Pri. (n) pot 2. Arg., Nic., Pue.R.
(n) saucepan
olla grande Mex. (n phr) kettle
olla para hornear Venz.
(n phr) roasting pan
ombligo Pri. (n) belly button; navel
omelete Pri. (n) omelet
ómnibus Arg., Par., Per., Uru. (n) bus
onces Col. (n) brunch
ondulado 1. Pri. (adj) wavy (hair)
2. Bol., Chi., Col., Venz.
(adj) curly (hair)
ondulines Chi. (n) hair rollers
one way Pan. (n phr) street, one-way
ordenador Spa. (n) computer
ordenador personal (OP) Spa.
(n phr) PC
orificio nasal Venz. (n phr) nostril
orilla Col. (n) shoreline
orilla de la carretera Col., Cos.R.
(n phr) road shoulder
orilla del mar Pri. (n phr) seashore
osamenta Col. (n) skeleton
ostión 1. Chi. (n) scallop 2. Mex.
(n) oyster
ostra Pri. (n) oyster
otomana Pri. (n) ottoman
ottomán Pue.R. (n) ottoman
oveja Pri. (n) sheep
overales Mex. (n) overalls
overol Chi., Col., Pan.
(n) overalls

ABBREVIATIONS: Arg.=Argentina Bol.=Bolivia Chi.=Chile Col.=Colombia Cos.R.=Costa Rica
Cub.=Cuba Dom.R.=Dominican Republic Ecu.=Ecuador ElS.=El Salvador Gua.=Guatemala
Hon.=Honduras Mex.=Mexico Nic.=Nicaragua Pan.=Panama Par.=Paraguay Per.=Peru
Pri.=Primary Term Pue.R.=Puerto Rico Spa.=Spain Uru.=Uruguay Venz.=Venezuela

P

pacana Pri. (n) pecan
paciente Pri. (n) patient
padre Chi., Col., Mex., Nic. (n) priest
padrillo Pri. (n) stallion
padrote Nic. (n) stallion
página del Web Venz. (n phr) website
página principal Arg. (n phr) website
página Web Nic. (n phr) website
pajarería Pri. (n) pet shop
pajarita Cub., Spa. (n) bow tie
pajarito Dom.R. (n) bug
pajón Dom.R. (n) weed
pala Pri. (n) shovel; spade; turner
palacio de justicia Dom.R., Spa.
    (n phr) courthouse
palana Per. (n) shovel
palanca de cambios Pri. (n phr) stick
    shift
palanca de velocidades Mex.
    (n phr) stick shift
palaustre Pue.R. (n) trowel
palé Chi. (n) pallet
palet Mex. (n) pallet
paleta 1. Pri. (n) pallet 2. Chi.
    (n) trowel 3. Venz. (n) turner
palito Nic., Pue.R. (n) bush
palma Pri. (n) palm (tree)
palmera Arg., Col., Mex., Nic.
    (n) palm (tree)
palo de amasar Arg. (n phr) rolling
    pin
palo de golf Pri. (n phr) golf club
palo de luz Dom.R. (n phr) street lamp
paloma Pri. (n) dove
palomo Col. (n) dove
palta Arg., Bol., Chi., Per., Uru.

(n) avocado
palustre Mex. (n) trowel
pan 1. Par. (n) bread, white 2. Pue.R.
    (n) roll
pana Dom.R. (n) buddy, pal
panadería Pri. (n) bakery
pan blanco Arg., Col., Dom.R., Mex.,
    Spa., Venz. (n phr) bread, white
pan blanco de molde Nic.
    (n phr) bread, white
pan blanco rebanado Uru.
    (n phr) bread, white
pan blanco tajado Pri. (n phr) bread,
    white
pan camarón Dom.R.
    (n phr) croissant
pan centeno Chi. (n phr) bread, rye
pan cortado Cos.R. (n phr) bread,
    sliced
pan de caja Mex. (n phr) bread, sliced
pan de centeno Arg., Col., Cub.,
    Dom.R., Ecu., Spa., Venz.
    (n phr) bread, rye
pan de fruta Dom.R. (n phr) chestnut
pan de molde 1. Pri. (n phr) bread,
    sliced 2. Cub. (n phr) bread,
    white
pan de sandwich Dom.R., Par.
    (n phr) bread, sliced
pan dulce Mex. (n phr) Danish
pan en rodajas Venz. (n phr) bread,
    sliced
pan especial Pue.R. (n phr) bread,
    sliced; bread, white
pan flauta Pan., Par. (n phr) baguette
pan francés Bol., Chi., Col., Dom.R.,

Nic., Pan., Venz.
(n phr) baguette
pan lactal Arg. (n phr) bread, sliced
pan negro Pri. (n phr) bread, rye
pan para hamburgeusas Mex., Pan.
(n phr) bun
pan para hot dogs Mex. (n phr) bun
pan pequeño Col. (n phr) bun
pan tajado Col. (n phr) bread, sliced
pan tostado Mex., Pan. (n phr) toast
pancake Cub., Dom.R., Pan., Pue.R.
(n) pancake
pancito 1. Pri. (n) roll 2. Arg., Par.,
Uru. (n) bun 3. Bol., Par.
(n) muffin
pancora Chi. (n) crab
pandereta Chi., Col., Cub., Dom.R.,
Ecu., Nic., Pue.R., Spa.
(n) tambourine
pandero Pri. (n) tambourine
panecillo 1. Pri. (n) bun; muffin
2. Col., Pan. (n) roll 3. Pue.R.
(n) biscuit
panqué Mex. (n) muffin
panqueca Venz. (n) pancake
panqueque Pri. (n) pancake
pantaleta Mex. (n) panties
pantaletas Venz. (n) panties
pantalla Arg., Chi. (n) monitor
(computer)
pantalla solar Arg. (n phr) sunscreen
pantallas Pue.R. (n) earrings
pantallas de clips Pue.R.
(n phr) earrings, clip
pantallas de gancho Pue.R.
(n phr) earrings, pierced
pantalón corto Pue.R. (n phr) shorts
pantalón de mezclilla Mex.
(n phr) blue jeans
pantaloncillos Dom.R. (n) briefs
pantaloncitos cortos Pan.
(n phr) shorts
pantalones corto Par. (n phr) shorts

pantalones cortos Pri. (n phr) shorts
pantalones de peto Mex.
(n phr) overalls
pantalones vaqueros Spa. (n phr) blue
jeans
pantano 1. Pri. (n) wetlands 2. Chi.,
Col., Dom.R., Ecu., Mex., Venz.
(n) swamp
panteón Mex. (n) cemetery
panticitos del bikini Pue.R.
(n phr) bikini briefs
panties Dom.R., Pue.R. (n) panties
pantihose Pan. (n) pantyhose
pantimedia Mex. (n) pantyhose
pantimedias Par., Uru. (n) pantyhose
pantis Cub., Pan. (n) panties
pantry Dom.R., ElS., Gua.. Hon., Nic.
(n) pantry
pantuflas Pri. (n) slippers
panty Spa. (n) pantyhose
pantyhose Dom.R., Nic. (n) pantyhose
panza Arg., Cos.R., Dom.R., Mex.,
Nic., Par., Uru. (n) belly
panzona Nic. (adj) pregnant
papa 1. Pri. (n) potato 2. Nic.
(n) father
papa dulce Chi. (n phr) sweet potato
papada Pri. (n phr) double chin
papás Col., Nic. (n) parents
papas fritas Pri. (n phr) French fries
papaya Pri. (n) papaya
papel aluminio Chi., Col., Nic., Pan.
(n phr) aluminum foil
papel de aluminio Pri.
(n phr) aluminum foil
papitas fritas Dom.R. (n phr) French
fries
papo Pan. (n) hibiscus
parabolica Col., Nic. (n) satellite
television
parabrisas Cub., Nic., Per. (n) wipers
(windshield)
parachoques Pri. (n) bumper

ABBREVIATIONS: Arg.=Argentina Bol.=Bolivia Chi.=Chile Col.=Colombia Cos.R.=Costa Rica
Cub.=Cuba Dom.R.=Dominican Republic Ecu.=Ecuador ElS.=El Salvador Gua.=Guatemala
Hon.=Honduras Mex.=Mexico Nic.=Nicaragua Pan.=Panama Par.=Paraguay Per.=Peru
Pri.=Primary Term Pue.R.=Puerto Rico Spa.=Spain Uru.=Uruguay Venz.=Venezuela

parada Par. (n) bus stop
parada de autobús Pri. (n phr) bus
stop
parada de bus Col., Nic., Cos.R., Pan.
(n phr) bus stop
parada de guagua Cub., Dom.R.,
Pue.R. (n phr) bus stop
parada de lata Cos.R. (n phr) bus stop
parada de libres Venz. (n phr) taxi
stand
parada de omnibus Par.
(n phr) request stop
parada de taxi Pri. (n phr) taxi stand
parada de taxis Venz. (n phr) taxi
stand
parada del colectivo Bol. (n phr) bus
stop
parada del micro Chi. (n phr) bus
stop
parada del ómnibus Arg., Per., Uru.
(n phr) bus stop
parada discrecional Spa.
(n phr) request stop (bus)
parada facultativa Pri. (n phr) request
stop (bus)
parada pedida Venz. (n phr) request
stop (bus)
parada solicitada Mex.
(n phr) request stop (bus)
paragolpes Arg., Par. (n) bumper
paragolpes Arg. (n) fender
parar Arg., Cub., Ecu., Mex., Pan.
(v) stall (car)
pararse Chi., Nic. (v) stall (car)
pare Arg., Chi., Col., Pue.R. stop
(sign)
pareja Nic. (n) wife
pargo Pri. (n) snapper
pariente Arg., Chi., Ecu., Mex., Nic.,
Par., Pue.R., Venz. (n) family
member
parir Col., Cos.R., Dom.R., Nic., Pan.
(v phr) give birth

parka Pri. (n) parka
parking Pue.R., Spa. (n) parking lot
parque 1. Pri. (n) park 2. Pue.R.
(n) stadium
parque de atracciones Pri.
(n phr) fairground
parque de bomberos Bol., Cos.R.,
Ecu., Spa., Uru. (n phr) fire
station
parque de diversiones Dom.R., Ecu.,
Pue.R. (n phr) fairground
parqueadero Col., Pan. (n) parking lot
parquear Bol., Col., Cos.R., Cub.,
Dom.R., ElS., Gua., Hon., Nic.,
Pan. (v) park
parqueo Bol., Cos.R., Cub., Dom.R.
ElS., Gua., Hon., Nic.
(n) parking lot
parrilla del radiador Arg., Col., Par.
(n phr) radiator grill
parte de tiempo Mex. (adj phr) part-
time (work)
parte del tronco Mex. (n phr) stump
partera Pri. (n) midwife
participante Cub., Pue.R.
(n) contestant
partido Dom.R., Mex., Nic., Venz.
(n) part (hair)
partidor Pri. (n) office divider
partidura Chi., Pan. (n) part (hair)
part-time Pue.R. (adj) part-time
(work)
pasadizo subterráneo Col., Par.
(n phr) underpass
pasador 1. Mex., Nic. (n) dowel
2. Mex. (n) stud
pasaje 1. Arg., Cos.R., Cub., Dom.R.,
Nic. (n) ticket 2. Per. (n) alley
pasaje de ida Arg., Cos.R., Dom.R.,
Par. (n phr) one-way ticket
pasaje de ida y vuelta Arg., Cos.R.,
Dom.R., Par. (n phr) round trip
ticket

pasar 1. Pri. (v) pasar (traffic) 2. Arg.,
Dom.R. (v) show (movie)
pasar la marcha Chi. (v phr) shift
gear
pascón Nic. (n) watering can
pase para conducir Col.
(n phr) driver's license
paseo Pue.R. (n) road shoulder
pasillo Col. (n) lobby
pasita Pan. (n) black currant
paso Chi., Mex. (n) right of way
paso a desnivel 1. Mex., Nic.
(n) cloverleaf junction 2. Nic.
(n) underpass
paso de peatones Pri.
(n phr) crosswalk
paso inferior Spa. (n phr) underpass
paso nivel Chi. (n phr) underpass
paso peatonal Nic. (n) crosswalk
paso subterráneo Pri.
(n phr) underpass
pasta Spa. (n) cookie
pasta de dientes Pri.
(n phr) toothpaste
pasta dental Per., Pue.R.
(n phr) toothpaste
pastel 1. Pri. (n) cake 2. Per.
(n) Danish 3. Dom.R., Pan., Per.,
Pue.R. (n) pie
pastel danés Venz. (n phr) Danish
pastel de crema Venz. (n phr) cream
puff
pastel de frutas Spa. (n phr) tart
pastelería Chi., Col. (n) bakery
pastelillo de fruta y nueces Pri.
(n phr) Danish
pastelito 1. Gua., Nic. (n) tart 2. Mex.
(n) muffin
pastinaca Uru. (n) parsnip
pasto 1. Arg., Bol., Col., Mex., Par.,
Per., Pue.R. (n) lawn 2. Chi.,
Col., Mex., Par., Per. (n) grass
pata de gallina Nic. (n phr) stool

patata Cub., Spa. (n) potato
patatas fritas Spa. (n phr) French fries
patinaje en el hielo Col. (n phr) ice
skating
patinaje en hielo Chi., Cub.
(n phr) ice skating
patinaje sobre hielo Pri. (n phr) ice
skating
patrón Col., Par. (n) boss
pava 1. Arg., Uru. (n) kettle 2. Cos.R.,
Nic. (n) bangs (hair)
pavo Pri. (n) turkey
pay Mex. (n) pie
PC Pri. (n) PC
pecana Bol., ElS., Gua., Hon.
(n) pecan
pecho 1. Pri. (n) chest 2. Dom.R., ElS.,
Gua., Hon., Nic., Pan., Spa.
(n) breast 3. Mex., Nic.
(n) breaststroke (swimming)
pechuga Chi. (n) breast
pedal de gasolina Venz. (n phr) gas
pedal
pedal de la gasolina Pue.R.
(n phr) gas pedal
pedir bola Dom.R. (v phr) hitchhike
pedir cola Venz. (v phr) hitchhike
pedir jalón a dedo ElS., Gua., Hon.
(v phr) hitchhike
pedir parada Nic. (v phr) request stop
pedir pon Pue.R. (v phr) hitchhike
pedir ride Cos.R., Nic.
(v phr) hitchhike
peine Pri. (n) comb
peineta Chi. (n) comb
peinilla Col., Ecu., Pan., Pue.R.
(n) comb
pejerrey Chi., Nic., Par. (n) smelt
pelada Col. (n) girl
peladito/a Col. (n) kid
pelador Pri. (n) peeler
pelapapas Mex. (n) peeler
pelearse Cub. (v) break up

(relationship)
pelicastaño Col. (adj) brown (hair)
película Pri. (n) film
película apta para todo público Nic.
(n phr) movie, G-rated or PG-
rated
película apta para todos los públicos
Spa. (n phr) movie, PG-rated
película censura B Venz.
(n phr) movie, PG-rated
película censurada Col., Dom.R.
(n phr) banned film
película de cowboys Arg.
(n phr) movie, western
película de horror Mex., Pue.R.,
Uru., Venz. (n phr) movie,
horror
película de miedo Pri. (n phr) movie,
horror
película de terror Arg., Col., Cos.R.,
Dom.R., Nic., Par., Pue.R.,
Venz. (n phr) movie, horror
película de vaqueros Pri.
(n phr) movie, western
película doble Bol. (n phr) double
feature (movies)
película musical Pri. (n phr) musical
(movie)
película para adolescentes y adultos
clasificación B Mex. (n phr)
movie, PG-rated
película para adultos Pri.
(n phr) movie, X-rated
película para todo público
clasificación A Mex. (n phr)
movie, G-rated
película para todo público Pri.
(n phr) movie, G-rated or PG-
rated
película porno Col. (n phr) movie, X-
rated
película pornográfica Cub., Par.
(n phr) movie, X-rated

película prohibida Pri. (n phr) banned
film
película público general Pue.R.
(n phr) movie, PG-rated
película sólo para adultos Nic.
(n phr) movie, X-rated
película sólo para adultos
clasificación C Mex. (n phr)
movie, X-rated
película X Pue.R. (n phr) movie, X-
rated
pelma Spa. (n) pest (person)
pelmazo Par., Spa. (n) pest (person)
pelo Pri. (n) hair
pelón Par., Uru. (n) nectarine
pelota de fútbol Pri. (n phr) ball
(soccer)
pelota de golf Pri. (n phr) golf ball
pelota de mano Uru. (n phr)handball
peludo Arg., Chi., Col., Nic., Par.,
Pue.R., Spa., Venz. (adj) hairy
peluquería Pri. (n) hairdresser's shop
peluquero Arg., Ecu., Mex., Par., Per.
(n) barber
peluquero/a Pri. (n) hairdresser
pendientes 1. Pri. (n phr) earrings,
drop 2. Spa. (n) earrings
pendiente con cadena Mex.
(n phr) necklace, pendant
pendiente con medalla Dom.R.
(n phr) necklace, pendant
pendientes de clip Spa.
(n phr) earrings, clip
pendientes de tornillo Spa.
(n phr) earrings, pierced
pendientes de tornillo Spa.
(n phr) earrings, screw
pendientes largos Spa.
(n phr) earrings, drop
penoso Cub., Nic., Pan. (adj) shy
pepinillo 1. Dom.R., Mex., Par.,
Pue.R. (n) pickle 2. Pue.R.
(n) cucumber

pepinillo en vinagre Spa.
(n phr) pickle
pepino 1. Pri. (n) cucumber 2. Cub.
(n) pickle
pepino encurtido Pri. (n phr) pickle
pepita de marañón Pan.
(n phr) cashew
pequeñito/a Pri. (n) toddler
pequeño Pri. (adj) short; short
(person); small
pera Arg., Chi. (n) chin
perdiz Nic., Venz. (n) woodcock
perenne Pri. (n) perennial (plant)
perezoso Pri. (adj) lazy
perico Pri. (n) parakeet
perilla 1. Pri. (n) drawer knob 2. Spa.
(n) goatee
periquito Spa. (n) parakeet
permanente Pue.R. (n) perennial
(plant)
permiso de conductor Arg.
(n phr) driver's license
permiso de convalecencia Pri.
(n phr) sick leave
permiso de convalescencia Venz.
(n phr) sick leave
permiso por enfermedad Arg., Bol.,
ElS., Gua., Hon., Par.
(n phr) sick leave
perol Col., Nic. (n) saucepan
perrera Pri. (n) doghouse
persianas 1. Pri. (n) blinds 2. Col.,
Ecu., Gua., Nic., Par. (n) shutters
persona de pelo castaño Spa.
(n phr) brunette (person)
persona que recoge los boletos Mex.
(n phr) ticket collector
personero ejecutivo de más alto rango
Gua. (n phr) chief executive
officer (CEO)
pesado Nic. (n) pest (person)
pescuezo Col., Nic. (n) neck
pesta Dom.R. (n) pest (person)

peste Col., Pan. (n) pest (person)
pet shop Dom.R., Pue.R. (n phr) pet
shop
peticote Pan. (n) petticoat; slip
petiso Arg., Uru. (adj) short (person)
petit pois Nic., Pan. (n phr) peas,
green
peuco Chi. (n) hawk
pez azul Mex. (n phr) bluefish
pez espada Pri. (n phr) swordfish
pezón Pri. (n) nipple
pibe Arg. (n) guy
pica Chi. (n) spade
picadera Dom.R. (n) snack
picador Pue.R. (n) cutting board;
butcher block
picadora de papel Mex.
(n phr) shredder
picaflor Arg., Col., Pan.
(n) hummingbird
picar Chi. (v) sprint
pícaro Col. (n) cheater
pichel Gua., Nic. (n) pitcher
pichón Pue.R. (n) dove
pickup Cos.R., ElS., Gua., Hon., Pan.,
Per. (n) pickup truck
pico 1. Pri. (n) peak (mountain) 2.
Mex., Par. (n) sickle 3. Venz. (n)
hoe; spade
pícolo Pri. (n) piccolo
pidevías Gua., Nic. (n) turning light
pie Bol., Dom.R. (n) pie
pieza Col., Par. (n) bedroom
piezas de repuesto Cub., Spa.
(n phr) spare parts
pijama 1. Col., Spa. (n) pajamas
2. Dom.R. (n) nightgown
pijamas Dom.R., Pue.R. (n) pajamas
pileta Arg., Par. (n) swimming pool
pilin Par. (n) penis
pillo Cub. (adj) naughty
piloto 1. Pri. (n) pilot 2. Arg., Par.
(n) raincoat

pimentera Pri. (n) pepper shaker
pimentero Arg., Col., Gua., Mex.,
    Nic., Per. (n) pepper shaker
pimentón Pan., Per., Venz. (n) pepper,
    sweet
pimentón rojo Col. (n phr) pepper,
    sweet
pimentón verde Col. (n phr) pepper,
    sweet
pimienta Pue.R. (n) pepper shaker
pimientero Venz. (n) pepper shaker
pimiento Par., Spa. (n) pepper, sweet
pimiento morrón Pri. (n phr) pepper,
    sweet
pimiento picante Ecu. (n phr) pepper,
    hot
piña Pri. (n) pine cone; pineapple
piña de pino Nic. (n phr) pine cone
pincel de repostería Pri. (n phr) pastry
    brush
piño Chi. (n) flock
piñón Per. (n) pine cone
pinta Col. (adj) handsome
pintalabios Cub., Dom.R. (n) lipstick
pintauñas Col., Spa. (n) nail polish
pinta uña Par. (n phr) nail polish
pintura de uñas Cub., Nic., Venz.
    (n phr) nail polish
pinzas 1. Pri. (n) pliers 2. Arg., Col.,
    Spa. (n) tongs 3. Col., Mex.
    (n) pincers 4. Mex. (n) clamp
pipa Col. (n) belly
piscina Pri. (n) swimming pool
pisicorre Cub. (n) station wagon
piso 1. Chi. (n) stool 2. Spa.
    (n) apartment
piso de abajo Col. (n phr) ground
    floor
piso de arriba Dom.R., Nic.
    (n phr) upper floor
piso superior Col. (n phr) upper floor
pista Nic. (n) sound track
pista de sonido Venz. (n phr) sound
track
pistache Mex. (n) pistachio
pistacho Pri. (n) pistachio
pistola de pelo Mex. (n phr) hair dryer
pistón Pri. (n) valve (trumpet)
pitillo de marihuana Cub., Pue.R.
    (n phr) marijuana cigarette
pito Chi. (n) marijuana cigarette
piyama Col., Nic. (n) pajamas
piyamas Pri. (n) pajamas
placa base Venz. (n phr) motherboard
placa de identificación Pri.
    (n phr) dog tag
placa madre Pri. (n phr) motherboard
placard Arg. (n) closet (clothes)
plaga Dom.R. (n) pest (person)
plancha Spa. (n) griddle
planicie Mex., Pue.R. (n) plain
    (topography)
plano Pri. (n) plane (carpentry)
planta alta Pri. (n phr) upper floor
planta baja Pri. (n phr) ground floor
planta de semillero Pri.
    (n phr) seedling
planta de vivero Col. (n phr) seedling
planta superior Spa. (n phr) upper
    floor
plantita Mex. (n) seedling
plataforma 1. Col., Cub., Par., Per.
    (n) platform (train) 2. Par., Uru.
    (n) pallet
plataforma de carga Pri.
    (n phr) loading dock
plátano Pri. (n) banana
platería Col. (n) silverware
platija Pri. (n) flounder
platillo principal Mex. (n phr) main
    course
plató Spa. (n) set (movie)
plato Nic. (n) hubcap
plato de sopa Col., Venz.
    (n phr) bowl, soup
plato fuerte Cub. (n phr) main course

ABBREVIATIONS: Arg.=Argentina Bol.=Bolivia Chi.=Chile Col.=Colombia Cos.R.=Costa Rica
Cub.=Cuba Dom.R.=Dominican Republic Ecu.=Ecuador ElS.=El Salvador Gua.=Guatemala
Hon.=Honduras Mex.=Mexico Nic.=Nicaragua Pan.=Panama Par.=Paraguay Per.=Peru
Pri.=Primary Term Pue.R.=Puerto Rico Spa.=Spain Uru.=Uruguay Venz.=Venezuela

plato hondo 1. Pri. (n) bowl 2. Nic.,
Pan. (n phr) bowl, soup
platón 1. Mex. (n) platter 2. Pan.
(n) bowl, mixing
plato para ensalada Col., Pan.
(n phr) bowl, salad
plato para sopa Pan. (n phr) bowl,
soup
plato principal Pri. (n phr) main
course
platos Pri. (n) dishes
plato sopero Cub., Dom.R., Ecu., Nic.
(n phr) bowl, soup
playa de estacionamiento Arg.
(n phr) parking lot
playera Mex., Nic. (n) knit shirt
playera de punto Mex. (n phr) jersey
playo Nic. (n) prostitute
plaza Arg., Par. (n) park
plenas Col. (n) brights (headlights)
pliegue Cub., ElS., Gua., Hon., Nic.
(n) crease (pants)
plomada Par., Uru. (n) level
plomero Pri. (n) plumber
pluma 1. Pri. (n) pen; ball-point pen
2. Spa. (n) fountain pen
pluma de fuente Pri. (n phr) pen,
fountain
pluma estilográfica Spa. (n phr) pen,
fountain
pluma fuente Bol., Mex., Pue.R.,
Venz.(n phr) pen, fountain
plumón Cub., Mex. (n) marker
pneumático Chi., Col. (n) tire (car)
pneumático pinchado Chi. (n phr) flat
tire
población Col. (n) village
pocillito de café Pue.R.
(n phr) demitasse
pocillo 1. Arg. (n) coffee cup;
demitasse 2. ElS., Gua., Hon.,
Nic. (n) mug
pocillo para café ElS., Gua., Hon.,

Nic. (n phr) mug, coffee
podadera Pri. (n) pruning shears
podadora Bol., Ecu., Par., Pue.R.
(n) pruning shears
podadora de césped Nic. (n phr) lawn
mower
podadora de grama Nic. (n phr) lawn
mower
podadora de pasto Mex. (n phr) lawn
mower
podadoras Mex. (n) pruning shears
podrido Pri. (adj) rotten (food)
polera 1. Arg., Par. (n) turtleneck
2. Chi. (n) t-shirt
policía Pri. (n) police officer
policía acostado Col. (n phr) bump
(road)
polilla Chi., Nic. (n) termite
político Pri. (n) politician
pollera 1. Arg., Par., Uru. (n) skirt
2. Cos.R., Uru. (n) dress
(woman's)
pollina Dom.R., Venz. (n) bangs (hair)
pollo Pri. (n) chicken
polo Pri. (n) knit shirt
polo de cuello alto Spa.
(n phr) turtleneck
polola Chi. (n) girlfriend
pololo Chi. (n) boyfriend
pololo/a Chi. (n) sweetheart
polo-shirt Dom.R. (n) t-shirt
poltrona Chi. (n) chair, lounging
polución Col. (n) pollution
pomátomo Pri. (n) bluefish
pomelo Arg., Chi., Par., Spa., Uru.
(n) grapefruit
pomo Col. (n) drawer knob
pompa Mex. (n) buttock
pompis Mex. (n) buttock
poner en marcha Col. (v phr) start
(car)
ponerse Chi., Dom.R., Mex., Nic.
(v) wear (clothing)

ponerse en onda Nic. (v phr) get high
   (drugs)
ponerse high Dom.R. (v phr) get high
   (drugs)
poney Uru. (n) pony
poni Arg., Spa. (n) pony
ponqué Col. (n) cake; pie
pony Col., Dom.R., Mex., Nic., Pan.,
   Pue.R., Venz. (n) pony
por parte de la jornada Pri.
   (adj phr) part-time (work)
porcelana Pri. (n) china
porch Pan. (n) porch
porche Cub., Nic. (n) porch
poro Mex., Per. (n) leek
poro de la nariz Mex. (n phr) nostril
porotos Pri. (n) beans
porotos de soja Par., Uru.
   (n phr) soybeans
porotos negros Arg., Uru.
   (n phr) beans, black
porra Nic. (n) pot; saucepan
porro 1. Pri. (n) leek 2. Arg., Par.
   (n) marijuana cigarette
porrón Arg. (n) mug, beer
porta equipaje Chi. (n phr) trunk (car)
portafolio 1. Bol. (n) briefcase
   2. Mex. (n) attaché case 3. Pan.
   (n) three-ring binder
portafolios 1. Pri. (n) briefcase 2. Arg.
   (n) attaché case
portamonedas Dom.R. (n) coin purse
portañuela Cub., Nic. (n) fly (pants)
portarrollo Mex. (n) tape dispenser
portaseno Par. (n) bra, brassiere
porteador Pue.R. (n) goalie
portero 1. Pri. (n) goalie 2. Col., Cub.
   (n) porter
pórtico Pri. (n) porch
posición adelantada Par.
   (n phr) offside
poste de luz Nic., Pan. (n phr) street
   lamp

postigos Pri. (n) shutters
postilla Cub., Dom.R. (n) scab
poto 1. Chi. (n) buttock 2. Per. (n)
   butt
potrillo 1. Chi., Nic. (n) colt 2. Col.,
   Nic., Venz. (n) foal
potro 1. Pri. (n) colt; foal 2. Arg., Par.
   (n) mustang
pozo 1. Pri. (n) pothole 2. Uru.
   (n) ditch
pradera Pri. (n) prairie
precio de entrada Nic., Pue.R., Venz.
   (n phr) entrance fee
precio de la entrada Col.
   (n phr) entrance fee
precio del billete de avión Spa.
   (n phr) airfare
precio del boleto Venz. (n phr) airfare
precio del pasaje Pri. (n phr) airfare
preciosa Chi. (adj) pretty
precioso Arg. (adj) beautiful
precipicio Cub., Pan., Par. (n) cliff
prefecto Chi. (n) mayor
preferencia Dom.R., Ecu., Nic., Spa.
   (n) right of way
preferencial Par. (n) right of way
pre-jardín Par. (n) daycare center
premolar Cos.R. (n) canine (tooth)
preñada Col. (adj) pregnant
prenda Arg. (n) garment
prenda de vestir ElS., Gua., Hon.,
   Nic., Spa. (n phr) garment
prender 1. Pri. (v) turn on (television)
   2. Chi., Col., Dom.R., Pue.R.
   (v) start (car)
prensa 1. Pri. (n) vise 2. Cos.R.
   (n) clamp
prensapapas Mex. (n) potato masher
presa Cos.R. (n) traffic jam
presentador Pri. (n) host (show)
presentar Col., Nic. (v) show (movie)
preservas Dom.R. (n) preserves
presidente Arg., Par. (n) chief

executive officer (CEO)
presidente municipal Mex.
(n phr) mayor
presilla Cub. (n) staple
presilladora Cub., Par. (n) stapler
preso Pri. (n) inmate; prisoner
prestación complementaria ElS.,
Gua., Hon. (n phr) fringe benefit
prestaciones sociales Nic.
(n phr) fringe benefit
prestarse jeringas Mex. (v phr) share
needles
primer piso Col., Dom.R. (n phr)
ground floor
primer plato Ecu. (n phr) appetizer
primera Arg. (adj) first class
primera clase Pri. (adj phr) first class
primoroso Col. (adj) cute
printer Pue.R. (n) printer (computer)
prioridad de circulación Venz.
(n phr) right of way
prioridad Pri. (n) right of way
prisionero 1. Col. (n) inmate; prisoner
2. Pan. (n) prisoner
procesamiento de palabras
(n phr) word processing
procesamiento de texto Cub., Ecu.
(n phr) word processing
procesamiento de textos Arg., Mex.,
Par. (n phr) word processing
programa Pri. (n) program
**programa comercial para promocionar
algo** Col.
(n phr) infomercial
programa concurso Pri. (n phr) game
show (television)
programa de charlas Col. (n phr) talk
show
programa de concurso Col.
(n phr) game show (television)
programa de concursos Dom.R.,
Gua., Mex., Nic., Venz.
(n phr) game show (television)

programa de entretenimientos Arg.
(n phr) game show (television)
programa de entrevistas Pri.
(n phr) talk show
programa de televisión Arg., Dom.R.,
Venz. (n phr) broadcast
programa doble Mex. (n phr) double
feature (movies)
programa en vivo 1. Arg. (n phr) live
broadcast 2. Nic. (n phr) talk
show
programas Nic., Spa. (n) software
prometida Col., Cos.R., Dom.R., Nic.,
Pan., Par. (n) fiancée (female)
prometido Col., Cos.R., Dom.R., Nic.,
Pan., Par. (n) fiancé (male)
promotor/a Chi. (n) salesperson
pronóstico del tiempo Arg., Nic., Par.
(n phr) weather report
propaganda Arg., Chi., Col., Ecu.,
Pan., Par., Per., Venz.
(n) commercial
propiedad horizontal Uru.
(n phr) apartment building
propulsión total Pri. (n phr) four-
wheel drive
protector Arg. (n) sunscreen
protector de sol Venz.
(n phr) sunscreen
protectores Nic. (n) glasses, safety
protector solar Chi., Cos.R., Nic.,
Par. (n phr) sunscreen
proyectar Pri. (v) show (movie)
prueba anti-doping Pri. (n phr) drug
test
prueba anti-drogas Col., Uru., Venz.
(n phr) drug test
prueba antidrogas Nic. (n phr) drug
test
prueba de drogas Cub., Mex., Pue.R.
(n phr) drug test
prueba para drogas Pan. (n phr) drug
test

ABBREVIATIONS: Arg.=Argentina Bol.=Bolivia Chi.=Chile Col.=Colombia Cos.R.=Costa Rica
Cub.=Cuba Dom.R.=Dominican Republic Ecu.=Ecuador ElS.=El Salvador Gua.=Guatemala
Hon.=Honduras Mex.=Mexico Nic.=Nicaragua Pan.=Panama Par.=Paraguay Per.=Peru
Pri.=Primary Term Pue.R.=Puerto Rico Spa.=Spain Uru.=Uruguay Venz.=Venezuela

puchero Spa. (n) pot
pucho Chi. (n) cigarette
pueblecito Cub. (n) village
pueblito Dom.R., Par. (n) village
pueblo 1. Arg. (n) village 2. Pue.R.
    (n) downtown
puente Dom.R. (n) plantar arch (foot)
puente de la nariz Mex., Nic., Venz.
    (n phr) bridge of nose
puerco Pri. (n) pig
puerro Arg., Col., Dom.R., Ecu., ElS.,
    Gua., Hon., Nic., Spa., Uru.
    (n) leek
puerta de servicio Arg., Par.
    (n phr) side entrance
puerta del costado Cub. (n phr) side
    entrance
puerta del lado Mex. (n phr) side
    entrance
puerta lateral Pri. (n phr) side
    entrance
puerto de carga Par. (n phr) loading
    dock
puesto de diarios Arg.
    (n phr) newsstand
puesto de frutas Pri. (n phr) fruit
    stand
puesto de periódicos Pri.
    (n phr) newsstand
puesto de periódicos y de revistas
    Col.(n phr) newsstand
pugilista Chi. (n) boxer
pulgar Pri. (n) thumb
pulover Arg. (n) sweater
pulóver Pri. (n) pullover
pulpería ElS., Nic. (n) grocery
pulpero Nic. (n) grocer
pulsar Col., Cub. (v) click (computer)
pulsera Pri. (n) bracelet
pulso Cub. (n) bracelet
puños Pri. (n) handlebar grips
    (bicycle)
punta bola Bol. (n phr) pen, ball-point
punta de la nariz Chi., Col., Mex.,
    Nic., Spa., Venz. (n phr) tip of
    nose
punzón Bol., Col., Nic., Spa., Venz.
    (n) awl
pupo 1. Arg., Chi. (n) navel 2. Chi.
    (n) belly button
puro 1. Pri. (n) cigar 2. Cos.R., Nic.
    (n) marijuana cigarette

Q

quebrada Nic. (n) stream
quedar varado Cos.R. (v phr) stall
   (car)
¿Qué ha habido? Ecu.
   (int phr) How's it going?
¿Qué hay? Chi., Col., Par.
   (int phr) What's up?
¿Qué hay de nuevo? Dom.R.
   (int phr) What's up?
quemacocos Mex. (n) sunroof
quemado Arg., Chi., Cub., Dom.R.
   (adj) tan (skin)
quemarse Arg., Chi., Cub., Dom.R.
   (v) tan
¿Qué onda? Nic. (int phr) What's up?
¿Qué pasa? (int phr) What's up?
¿Qué pasó? Nic. (int phr) What's up?
queque Bol., Cos.R., Nic., Per.
   (n) cake
quequisque Nic. (n) taro

quequito Per. (n) muffin
querida Cub., Nic. (n) mistress
querido Spa. (n) sweetheart
querido/a Pri. (n) dear; darling;
   honey
¿Qué tal? Arg., Ecu., Mex., Nic.,
   Pue.R., Uru. (int phr) How's it
   going?
quijada 1. Col., Nic. (n) jaw 2. Per.
   (n) chin
quimbombó Pri. (n) okra
quinta 1. Arg., Nic. (n) cottage 2. Arg.
   (n) vegetable garden
quiosco Nic., Par. (n) newsstand
quisquemel Mex. (n) cape
quitagrapas Spa. (n) staple remover
quitarse la ropa Col., Venz.
   (v phr) undress
¿Quiubo? Pan. (int phr) What's up?
quivi Uru. (n) kiwi

R

rabí Spa. (n) rabbi
rabino Pri. (n) rabbi
rabo de caballo Pue.R.
 (n phr) ponytail (hair)
radio Col., Spa., Venz. (n) spoke
 (bicycle wheel)
raíz Pri. (n) root (hair)
rallador Pri. (n) grater
rallo Col. (n) grater
ranuras Pri. (n) tread (tire)
rápido Pri. (adj) quick
raptar Bol. (v) car jack (crime)
rascador Pri. (n) scraper
rasgar Cos.R. (v) strum
rasgueado Col., Nic., Spa.
 (n) strumming
rasguear Col., Nic., Spa. (v) strum
rasgueo Cos.R., Nic. (n) strumming
raspa Mex. (n) painter's knife; scraper
raspador Par., Venz. (n) scraper
raspadora Chi. (n) scraper
rastrillo 1. Arg., Chi., Col., Cub.,
 Dom.R., Mex., Nic., Pan., Par.
 (n) lawn rake 2. Mex. (n) razor
rasuradora Pri. (n) razor
ratón Pri. (n) mouse
ratones Nic. (n) biceps
raya Pri. (n) crease (pants); part (hair)
rayo Arg., Col., Cub., Gua., Mex.,
 Nic. (n) spoke (bicycle wheel)
rayo Pri. (n) lightning
rebaño Pri. (n) flock
rebasar Dom.R., Mex., Nic. (v) pass
 (traffic)
recámara Mex. (n) bedroom
recepción Arg., Chi., Nic., Par.

 (n) lobby
recinto Pri. (n) office cubicle
recluso 1. Col., Nic. (n) inmate 2. Col.
 (n) prisoner
recogedor de basura Col., Venz.
 (n phr) garbage collector
recolector de basura Nic.
 (n phr) garbage collector
recolector de tiquetes Col.
 (n phr) ticket collector
red de área amplia Cub., Mex., Spa.
 (n phr) WAN (wide area
 network)
red de área ancha Uru. (n phr) WAN
 (wide area network)
red de área extendida Col., Par.
 (n phr) WAN (wide area
 network)
red de área extensa Venz.
 (n phr) WAN (wide area
 network)
red de área local Par., Spa., Venz.
 (n phr) LAN (local area network)
red local LAN Mex. (n phr) LAN
 (local area network)
redactor Pri. (n) editor
redoblante Cos.R., Nic. (n) snare
 drum
reducir la marcha Chi. (v phr) shift
 gear
reducir la velocidad Chi., Dom.R.,
 Pue.R., Spa. (v phr) decelerate
refacciones Mex. (n) spare parts
refajo Dom.R., Pue.R. (n) petticoat
refere Mex. (n) referee
referee Arg. (n) referee

réferi Nic. (n) referee
referí Pan. (n) referee
reflector Pri. (n) reflector (bicycle)
refrí Cos.R. (n) refrigerator
refrigerador 1. Pri. (n) refrigerator
    2. Bol. (n) freezer
refrigeradora Ecu., Nic., Per.
    (n) refrigerator
refrigerio Col., Nic. (n) snack
refugio Chi. (n) cabin
regadera 1. Pri. (n) watering can
    2. Cub., Par. (n) sprinkler
regador Arg. (n) sprinkler
regador de plantas Mex.
    (n phr) watering can
regalón Chi. (adj) spoiled (child)
regilete Mex. (n) sprinkler
registrar el equipaje Pri.
    (v phr) check in (baggage)
registro de conducir Par.
    (n phr) driver's license
reglar Cub. (v) tune up
rejilla del radiador Pri.
    (n phr) radiator grill
relámpago 1. Pri. (n) lightning
    2. Nic. (n) cream puff
relicario Pri. (n) locket
remera Arg. (n) t-shirt
remera de manga corta Arg.
    (n phr) shirt, short-sleeved
remera de manga larga Arg.
    (n phr) shirt, long-sleeved
remolacha Pri. (n) beet
remolque Pri. (n) trailer
removedor de grapas Col.
    (n phr) staple remover
reno Pri. (n) reindeer
rentar Mex., Pue.R. (v) rent (housing)
reo 1. Chi. (n) prisoner 2. Pan.
    (n) inmate
reparto Col., Mex., Nic., Spa., Venz.
    (n) cast (show)
repisa para zapatos Col. (n phr) shoe

rack
repolla Pri. (n) cream puff
repollito Chi. (n) cream puff
repollitos Nic. (n) Brussels sprouts
repollitos de Bruselas Arg., Uru.
    (n phr) Brussels sprouts
repollitos italianos Chi.
    (n phr) Brussels sprouts
repollo 1. Pri. (n) cabbage, white
    2. Col., Nic. (n) cabbage, green
repollo verde Pri. (n phr) cabbage,
    green
reporte Cub. (n) newscast
reporte del estado del tiempo Col.
    (n phr) weather report
reporte del tiempo Venz.
    (n phr) weather report
reporte meteorológico Venz.
    (n phr) weather report
reportero Col., Cos.R., Dom.R., Mex.,
    Nic., Pan., Pue.R., Venz. (n)
    reporter
reportero del tiempo Venz.
    (n phr) weather reporter
reportero meteorológico Venz.
    (n phr) weather reporter
repostería Pue.R. (n) bakery
representante de ventas Cos.R.
    (n phr) door-to-door salesperson
reproductor de CD Spa.
    (n phr) compact disk player
reproductor de compact-disc Cub.
    (n phr) compact disk player
reproductor de discos compactos
    ElS., Gua., Hon., Venz.
    (n phr) compact disk player
repuestas Pue.R. (n) spare parts
repuestos Pri. (n) spare parts
residencial Nic. (n) suburb
resonante Mex. (adj) resonant
resumé Pue.R. (n) résumé (work
    history)
resúmen de noticias Gua., Par.

ABBREVIATIONS: Arg.=Argentina Bol.=Bolivia Chi.=Chile Col.=Colombia Cos.R.=Costa Rica
Cub.=Cuba Dom.R.=Dominican Republic Ecu.=Ecuador ElS.=El Salvador Gua.=Guatemala
Hon.=Honduras Mex.=Mexico Nic.=Nicaragua Pan.=Panama Par.=Paraguay Per.=Peru
Pri.=Primary Term Pue.R.=Puerto Rico Spa.=Spain Uru.=Uruguay Venz.=Venezuela

(n phr) news brief
resúmen de noticias Per., Venz.
(n phr) news brief
resúmen noticioso Cos.R., Nic.
(n phr) news brief
retador Col., Dom.R., Mex., Nic., Par.
(n) challenger (boxing)
retador de boxeo Venz.
(n phr) challenger (boxing)
retiro para ancianos Pan.
(n phr) retirement home
retollar Pue.R. (v) bloom
retoños de soya ElS., Gua., Hon.
(n phr) bean sprouts
retraso Pri. (n) delay
retroceso Venz. (n) reverse
retrovisor Nic. (n) rear-view mirror
reversa Col., Dom.R., Mex., Pan., Par.
(n) reverse
revisar Pri. (v) tune up
revisor Pri. (n) ticket collector
rezadora Nic. (n) praying mantis
riachuelo Col., Dom.R., Pue.R.
(n) stream
rico 1. Arg., Col., Nic., Spa. (adj) tasty
2. Arg., Pue.R. (adj) delicious
3. Nic., Venz. (adj) delightful
rin 1. Mex., Nic. (n) rim (bicycle
wheel) 2. Pan. (n) hubcap
ring de boxeo Pri. (n phr) ring
(boxing)
risco Pue.R. (n) cliff
riversa Pue.R. (n) reverse
rizado Pri. (adj) curly (hair)
róbalo Gua. (n) flounder
robar un carro Venz. (v phr) car jack
(crime)
robar un vehículo con alguien dentro
Spa. (v phr) car jack (crime)
robarse un carro Cub. (v phr) car
jack (crime)
robar con violencia Nic.
(v phr) carjack (crime)

rociador Pri. (n) sprinkler
rock Dom.R., Spa. (n) rock music
roco 1. Nic. (n) adult (colloq.) 2. Nic.
(adj) old
rodaje Pri. (n) shooting (movie)
rodana Mex. (n) washer
rodar Pri. (v) shoot (movie)
rodete para cortar masa Col.
(n phr) pastry cutting wheel
rodillo Pri. (n) rolling pin
rollo Pri. (n) Swiss roll
rollo cinta adhesiva Par. (n phr) tape
dispenser
rollos Nic., Pan., Venz. (n) hair rollers
rollo de tape Dom.R., Nic.
(n phr) tape dispenser
rolodex Pue.R. (n) rolodex
rolos Cub., Pue.R. (n) hair rollers
romper Pri. (v) break up (relationship)
rompeviento Uru. (n) turtleneck
ropa Mex. (n) garment
ropa blanca Cos.R., Bol., Uru.
(n phr) underwear
ropa casual Dom.R. (n phr) casual
clothes
ropa de etiqueta Mex. (n phr) formal
wear
ropa de interior Cub.
(n phr) underwear
ropa de vestir Dom.R. (n phr) formal
wear
ropa formal Pri. (n phr) formal wear
ropa informal Pri. (n phr) casual
clothes
ropa interior Pri. (n phr) underwear
ropero 1. Pri. (n) dresser 2. Bol., Chi.,
Cos.R., Ecu., Nic., Par., Uru. (n)
closet (clothes)
rosca 1. Chi. (n) doughnut 2. Uru.
(n) Swiss roll
rosca de pan Pri. (n phr) bagel
roto de la nariz Pue.R. (n phr) nostril
rotulador Spa. (n) marker

rótulo Cos.R., Nic. (n) billboard
rouge Arg., Bol., Chi. (n) lipstick
rubio Pri. (adj) blond (hair)
rubio/a Pri. (n) blond (person)
rueda 1. Arg., Cub., Spa. (n) tire (car)
2. Cub. (n) tire (bicycle) 3. Venz.
(n) ferris wheel 4. Par., Venz.
(n) rim (bicycle wheel)
rueda de andar Pri. (n phr) treadmill
rueda de auxilio Arg., Par.
(n phr) spare tire
rueda de Chicago Col., Nic., Par.
(n phr) ferris wheel
rueda de la fortuna Mex.
(n phr) ferris wheel
rueda de repuesto Pri. (n phr) spare
tire

rueda gigante Chi. (n phr) ferris
wheel
rueda muscovita Ecu. (n phr) ferris
wheel
rueda para cortar masa Nic.
(n phr) pastry cutting wheel
rueda pinchada Spa. (n phr) flat tire
ruedo doble Venz. (n phr) cuff (pants)
ruidoso 1. Pri. (adj) loud (noise)
2. Nic. (adj) resonant
ruleros Pri. (n) hair rollers
rulos Col., Spa. (n) hair rollers
runcho Pan. (adj) cheap
rush hour Arg. (n phr) rush hour
rutabaga Col. (n) rutabaga
RV Pue.R. (n) recreational
vehicle

S

sábana Nic. (n) blanket
sábana bajera ajustable Spa.
  (n phr) sheet, contour
sábana de cajón Pri. (n phr) sheet,
  contour
sábana de elástico Arg. (n phr) sheet,
  contour
sábana de esquinera Venz.
  (n phr) sheet, contour
sábana de forro Col. (n phr) sheet,
  contour
sábana elástica Par. (n phr) sheet,
  contour
sabandija Pue.R. (n) pest (person)
sabroso Pri. (adj) tasty
saca corchetes Chi. (n phr) staple
  remover
saca corcho Pan., Uru. (n phr) bottle
  opener
sacacorchos Pri. (n) corkscrew
saca grampas Par. (n phr) staple
  remover
sacagrapas Bol., Ecu., ElS., Gua.,
  Hon., Nic.(n) staple remover
saca-grapas Venz. (n) staple remover
saco 1. Pri. (n) coat 2. Bol. (n) jersey;
  pullover 3. Dom.R., Pan.
  (n) jacket
saco de lana Arg. (n phr) cardigan
saco de piel Pri. (n phr) coat, fur
saco de visón Pri. (n phr) coat, mink
sala Pri. (n phr) living room
sala de correos Pri. (n phr) mail room
sala de espera Venz. (n phr) lobby
salario Col., Mex., Nic., Pan., Par.
  (n) salary

salida Pri. (n) departure
salida de baño Nic. (n) bathrobe
salir Chi. (n) starter
salir con Dom.R., Gua., Mex., Nic.,
  Venz. (v phr) date
salón de belleza Dom.R., Mex., Nic.,
  Pan., Pue.R. (n phr) hairdresser's
  shop
salto a lo alto Pue.R. (n phr) high
  jump
salto a lo largo Pue.R. (n phr) broad
  jump
salto alto Chi., Col., ElS., Gua., Hon.,
  Nic., Par. (n phr) high jump
salto ancho Col. (n phr) broad jump
salto con garrocha Pri. (n phr) pole
  vault
salto con pértiga Nic., Pue.R.
  (n phr) pole vault
salto de altura Pri. (n phr) high jump
salto de garrocha Venz. (n phr) pole
  vault
salto de longitud Pri. (n phr) broad
  jump
salto de pértiga Spa. (n phr) pole
  vault
salto en esquíes Venz. (n phr) ski
  jump
salto largo Chi., ElS., Gua., Hon.,
  Nic., Par. (n phr) broad jump
salto triple Pri. (n phr) triple jump
sandalias Pri. (n) sandals
sandalias de plástico Mex.
  (n phr) rubbers (shoes)
sandía (n) watermelon
sanja Cos.R. (n) ditch

sardina Col. (n) girl
sartén eléctrica Col., Pan.
    (n phr) griddle
sartén para asar Pri. (n phr) roasting
    pan
sastre Pri. (n) tailor
saya Cub. (n) skirt
sayuela Cub. (n) petticoat; slip
scanner Arg., Dom.R., Par., Pue.R.
    (n) scanner, optical
scroll Pue.R. (v) scroll (computer)
secador Arg., Par. (n) hair dryer
secador de pelo Chi., Spa., Venz.
    (n phr) hair dryer
secadora Pri. (n) dryer
secadora de pelo Cub., Mex., Nic.
    (n phr) hair dryer
secadora de ropa Pue.R. (n phr) dryer
secadora manual Pri. (n phr) hair
    dryer
secarropas Arg. (n) dryer
sector residencial Pue.R.
    (n phr) residencial area
sedán Pri. (n) sedan
segadora Venz. (n) lawn mower
segueta Pue.R. (n) hacksaw
segunda Arg. (n) second class
segunda clase Pri. (n phr) second class
sello Spa. (n) ring, signet
selva tropical Pri. (n phr) rain forest
semental 1. Arg., Col., Dom.R., Gua.,
    Nic., Par., Spa., Venz.
    (n) stallion 2. Nic. (n) stud
semilla de cajuil Dom.R.
    (n phr) cashew
semilla de marañón Nic.
    (n phr) cashew
semillas de soya Col., Gua.
    (n phr) soybeans
semillero Pri. (n) nursery (plants)
señal de cruce Venz. (n phr) turning
    light
señal de tráfico Dom.R., Spa., Uru.

(n phr) road sign
señal de tránsito Nic., Par., Venz.
    (n phr) road sign
señal del camino Per. (n phr) road
    sign
señalero Par. (n) blinker (light)
señal intermitente Uru.
    (n phr) turning light
señalización en la carretera Chi.
    (n phr) road sign
seno Pri. (n) sinus; breast
seno nasal Mex., Spa. (n phr) sinus
Señora 1. Pri. (n) Ma'am; Madam
    2. Dom.R., Nic., Par. (n) wife
sentirse mal por el vuelo Mex.
    (v phr) jet-lag, to have
sentirse mal por la altura Mex.
    (v phr) jet-lag, to have
separado Col. (adj) divorced
separador Col. (n) median; office
    divider
separarse Col. (v) break up
    (relationship); divorce
sepelio Chi., Col., Mex. (n) burial
sequestrar en auto Pri. (v phr) car
    jack (crime)
serpiente Chi., Cub. (n) snake
serrucho 1. Arg., Cub., Nic., Per.
    (n) saw 2. Cub., Nic., Venz.
    (n) hacksaw 3. Uru. (n) bucksaw
serrucho eléctrico Pri.
    (n phr) chainsaw
sesión de dos películas seguidas Spa.
    (n phr) double feature (movies)
sesión de música improvisado Col.
    (n phr) jam session
seta Spa. (n) mushroom
seto Pri. (n) hedge
shampoo Arg., Nic. (n) shampoo
shorts Arg., Chi., Col., Dom.R.,
    Mex.,Nic., Venz. (n) shorts
show Cub., Dom.R. (n) program
shower Pri. (n) bridal shower

ABBREVIATIONS: Arg.=Argentina Bol.=Bolivia Chi.=Chile Col.=Colombia Cos.R.=Costa Rica
Cub.=Cuba Dom.R.=Dominican Republic Ecu.=Ecuador ElS.=El Salvador Gua.=Guatemala
Hon.=Honduras Mex.=Mexico Nic.=Nicaragua Pan.=Panama Par.=Paraguay Per.=Peru
Pri.=Primary Term Pue.R.=Puerto Rico Spa.=Spain Uru.=Uruguay Venz.=Venezuela

shute Gua. (n) snoop
sierra 1. Pri. (n) range (mountain);
  saw 2. Par. (n) bucksaw
sierra de ballesta Pri. (n phr) bucksaw
sierra de bastidor Spa.
  (n phr) bucksaw
sierra de cadena Mex., Pue.R.
  (n phr) chainsaw
sierra de metal Pri. (n phr) hacksaw
sierra eléctrica Chi., Col., Uru.
  (n phr) chainsaw
sierra para cortar metal Col.
  (n phr) hacksaw
sierra para metal Mex., Spa.
  (n phr) hacksaw
sierra para metales Venz.
  (n phr) hacksaw
silenciador Arg., Col., Ecu., Par.,
  Spa., Uru. (n) muffler
silencioso Pri. (adj) quiet
silla Bol., Col. (n) seat (bicycle)
silla con coderas Mex.
  (n phr) armchair
silla con escalón Venz. (n phr) chair,
  step
silla de brazos Pri. (n phr) armchair
silla de director Pri. (n phr) chair,
  director's
silla de extensión Col. (n phr) chair,
  lounging
silla ejecutiva Mex. (n phr) chair,
  director's
silla hamaca Arg. (n phr) chair,
  rocking
silla plegable Pri. (n phr) chair,
  folding; chair, director's
silla plegadiza Dom.R. (n phr) chair,
  folding
silla reclinable Pue.R. (n phr) chair,
  lounging
sillín Chi., Dom.R., Ecu., Pue.R., Spa.,
  Uru. (n) seat (bicycle)
sillón 1. Arg., Chi., Dom.R., Nic.,

Spa., Uru. (n) armchair 2. Cub.,
  Pue.R. (n) chair, rocking
sillón ejecutivo Mex., Par.
  (n phr) chair, director's
sillón reclinable Mex., Nic.
  (n phr) chair, lounging
silloncito Arg. (n) love seat
símbolo gráfico Cub. (n phr) icon
  (computer)
simpático 1. Pri. (adj) nice 2. Chi.
  (adj) cute; funny 3. Cub.
  (adj) friendly
síndico Dom.R. (n) mayor
sinvergüenza Dom.R., Pue.R.
  (n) tattler
sismo Col. (n) earthquake
sitar Pri. (n) sitar
sitio de la red Gua. (n phr) website
sitio web (n phr) website
ski acuático Chi., Par. (n phr) water
  skiing
smoking 1. Pri. (n) tuxedo 2. Nic.,
  Par., Venz. (n) tailcoat
snack Spa. (n) snack
snikers Pri. (n) sneakers
sobaco Nic., Pan. (n) armpit
sobrefunda Gua. (n) pillowcase
sobretodo Arg. (n) overcoat
sociable Cub., Nic., Par.
  (adj) outgoing
socio Par. (n) buddy; pal
sofá Pue.R., Spa. (n) love seat
sofá para dos personas Col., ElS.,
  Gua., Hon., Nic., Venz.
  (n phr) love seat
software Pri. (n) software
soja Chi., Spa. (n) soybeans
sollarse Col. (v) get high (drugs)
sombrero de copa Pri. (n phr) hat, top
sombrío Col. (adj) gloomy (person)
somier Spa. (n) box spring
somnier Par. (n) box spring
soñoliento Pri. (adj) sleepy

sonoridad Pri. (n) tone
sonoro Pri. (adj) resonant
sopera Par., Pue.R. (n) bowl, soup
soplete Pri. (n) blowtorch
soporte Col. (n) props
soquete Arg., Uru. (n) sock
sorbetería Nic. (n) ice cream parlor
sortija Pan., Pue.R. (n) ring
sortija de diamante Pue.R.
    (n phr) ring, diamond
sortija de graduación Pue.R.
    (n phr) ring, class
sortija de sello Pri. (n phr) ring, signet
sostén Pri. (n) bra; brassiere
soutien Uru. (n) bra; brassiere
soya Cub., Venz. (n) soybeans
spray de pelo Par., Pue.R.
    (n phr) hairspray
spray para el pelo Dom.R., Mex.,
    Pan. (n phr) hairspray
station Dom.R. (n) station wagon
stop Par., Spa. stop (sign)
suave Col., Nic. (adj) soft
subirse Pri. (v) get on (bus)
subsidio por enfermedad Nic.
    (n phr) sick leave
subtítulos Pri. (n) subtitles
suburbio Col., Cub., Dom.R., Gua.
    (n) suburb
suculenta Pri. (n) succulent
    (plant)
sudadera Chi., Col., Dom.R., Mex.,

Nic., Par., Pue.R. (n) sweatshirt
sudadero Gua. (n) sweatshirt
suecos Dom.R., Mex., Par., Pue.R.
    (n) clogs
sueldo Pri. (n) salary
suelo Nic. (n) soil
suéter 1. Pri. (n) sweater 2. Dom.R.,
    Pan. (n) knit shirt 3. Ecu., Mex.,
    Venz. (n) cardigan 4. Nic., Venz.
    (n) jersey 5. Nic., Venz.
    (n) pullover
suéter abierto Col. (n phr) cardigan
suéter cerrado Col., Mex.
    (n phr) pullover
suite de oficinas Venz. (n phr) office
    suite
sujetador Spa. (n) bra; brassiere
sujetapapel Bol., Cos.R., Cub., ElS.,
    Gua., Hon. (n) paperclip
sunroof Pri. (n) sunroof
super Mex. (n) grocery
supercolmado Dom.R. (n) grocery
supermercado Spa., Venz. (n) grocery
surfear en el Internet Dom.R.
    (v phr) surf the net
surfear la Internet Pri. (v phr) surf
    the net
suspensores Chi. (n) suspenders
susurro Col. (n) hum
swampo Nic. (n) swamp
sweater 1. Arg. (n) pullover 2. Chi.
    (n) cardigan

T

tabaco Cub. (n) cigar
tabaco de marihuana Dom.R.
    (n phr) marijuana cigarette
tábano Pri. (n) horsefly, gadfly
taberna Col. (n) bar; wine shop
tabique Chi., Col., Dom.R. (n) bridge
    of nose
tabla Chi. (n) table leaf
tabla de cocina Arg. (n phr) butcher
    block
tabla de cortar Col., Nic.
    (n phr) cutting board
tabla de extensión Nic. (n phr) table
    leaf
tabla de picar Par. (n phr) butcher
    block
tabla para cortar Chi., Col., Cub.,
    Nic. (n phr) butcher block
tabla para cortar Pri. (n phr) cutting
    board
tablero Pri. (n) table leaf
tablón de extensión Mex.
    (n phr) tableleaf
taburete Mex., Par. (n) ottoman
tachuela Pri. (n) stud; tack
tacita Col. (n) demitasse
tacita de café Pri. (n phr) demitasse
taco 1. Pri. (n) heel (shoe) 2. Chi.
    (n) traffic jam
taco alto Pri. (n phr) heel, high (shoe)
taco de golf Col. (n phr) golf club
tacón Col., Cub., ElS., Gua., Hon.,
    Mex., Nic., Pan., Spa., Venz.
    (n) heel (shoe)
tacón alto Col., Cub., ElS., Gua.,
    Hon., Mex., Nic., Pan., Spa.,

Venz. (n phr) heel, high (shoe)
talacho Mex. (n) hoe
taladradora de mano Arg., Ecu., Per.,
    Spa., Uru. (n phr) drill, hand
taladro Chi. (n) drill, hand
taladro de mano Pri. (n phr) drill,
    hand
taladro manual Col., Mex.
    (n phr) drill, hand
talingo Pan. (n) blackbird
talle Col., Nic. (n) waist
taller Col., Nic., Par. (n) garage
    (repairs)
taller mecánico Arg., Par.
    (n phr) garage (repairs)
taller tipográfico Col. (n phr) print
    shop
talleres gráficos Col. (n phr) print
    shop
tambor 1. Pri. (n) drum 2. Col.
    (n) drummer
tambora Cub. (n) hubcap
tambor de conga Venz. (n phr) conga
    drum
tambor de tenor Col. (n phr) tenor
    drum
tambor militar pequeño Col.
    (n phr) snare drum
tamborilear Pri. (v) drum, tap
tamborilero Pri. (n) drummer
tambor tenor Nic. (n phr) tenor
    drum
tamiz Arg., Col., Spa. (n) sieve
tam-tam Pri. (n) tom-tom
tamtan Spa. (n) tom-tom
tanatorio Spa. (n) funeral home

tanda Col. (n) batch
tándem Col., Spa. (n) bike, tandem
tangas 1. Dom.R., Nic. (n) bikini
briefs 2. Col. (n) panties
tanque de gasolina Pri. (n phr) gas
tank
tanque de nafta Arg. (n phr) gas tank
tantán Col. (n) tom-tom
tapa Spa. (n) appetizer
tapabocina Pue.R. (n) hubcap
tapacubo Ecu., Spa. (n) hubcap
tapacubos Pri. (n) hubcap
tapado 1. Arg. (n) coat 2. Chi.
(adj) cloudy
tapado de piel Arg. (n phr) coat, fur
tapado de visón Arg. (n phr) coat,
mink
taparuedas Chi. (n) hubcap
tape Nic., Pue.R. (n) tape
tapón 1. Dom.R., Pue.R. (n) traffic
jam 2. Mex. (n) hubcap
tapudo Nic. (n) tattler
tarifa Arg., Ecu. (n) airfare
tarifa aérea Col. (n phr) airfare
tarifa de vuelo Mex. (n phr) airfare
tarima Mex. (n) pallet
tarjeta Col., Pue.R. (n) index card
tarjeta madre Col., Nic., Spa.
(n phr) motherboard
tarjeta principal Mex.
(n phr) motherboard
taro Pri. (n) taro
tarola Pri. (n) snare drum
tarro de aceite Col. (n phr) oil can
tarta 1. Pri. (n) pie 2. Bol., Chi.,
Pue.R., Uru., Venz. (n) tart
3. Spa. (n) cake
tartaleta 1. Mex. (n) tart 2. Venz.
(n) pie
tarugo Gua. (n) dowel
taxero Nic. (n) taxi driver
taxi Pri. (n) taxi
taxista Arg., Col., Cub., Dom.R.,

Gua., Mex., Nic., Per., Spa.
(n) taxi driver
taza Pri. (n) cup
taza de café Arg., Nic.
(n phr) demitasse
taza de café Arg., Cub. (n phr) mug,
coffee
taza del caucho Venz. (n phr) hubcap
taza de medida Nic. (n phr)
measuring cups
taza para café Pri. (n phr) cup, coffee
tazas medidoras Dom.R.
(n phr) measuring cups
tazas para medir Pri.
(n phr) measuring cups
tazón 1. Pri. (n) bowl, soup 2. Chi.
(n) mug 3. Col., Mex., Par.
(n) bowl
tazón de café Pue.R. (n phr) mug,
coffee
tazón para batir Mex. (n phr) bowl,
mixing
tazón para medir Pri. (n phr) bowl,
mixing
tazón para mezclar ElS., Gua.,
Hon.,Venz. (n phr) bowl, mixing
techo convertible Nic. (n phr) sunroof
techo corredizo Col., Par., Venz.
(n phr) sunroof
techo descapotable Nic., Venz.
(n phr) sunroof
techo solar Chi., Spa. (n phr) sunroof
teclado Pri. (n) keyboard (computer)
técnico Mex. (n) manager (sports)
tedioso Col. (adj.) boring
teenager Dom.R. (n) teenager
teleaudiencia Col. (n) television
viewer
telecable Dom.R. (n) cable television
telecadena Dom.R. (n) network
(television)
telediario Pri. (n) newscast
teleférico Mex., Venz. (n) funicular

teléfono público Mex., Nic.
(n phr) telephone booth
telenoticias Par. (n) newscast
telenoticiero Cos.R., Dom.R.
(n) newscast
telenovela Pri. (n) soap opera
telepromoción Spa. (n) infomercial
televidente Pri. (n) television viewer
televisión Col., Mex., Spa.
(n) television set
televisión por cable Pri. (n phr) cable
television
televisión por satélite Pri.
(n phr) satellite television
television satelital Par.
(n phr) satellite television
televisión vía satélite Spa.
(n phr) satellite television
televisor Pri. (n) television set
telón Bol. (n) screenplay
tema Arg. (n) song
temblor Chi., Mex., Nic.
(n) earthquake
temblor de tierra Dom.R., Pue.R.
(n) earthquake
temible Col. (adj) terrifying
témpano de hielo Chi. (n phr) iceberg
temporal Bol. (n) temporary worker
temporario Uru. (n) temporary
worker
temporero Pri. (n) temporary worker
tenazas Pri. (n) pincers; tongs
tendero Pri. (n) grocer
tenedor Arg. (n) carving fork
tenedor de libros Cub.
(n phr) bookkeeper
tenedor de trinchar Col., ElS., Gua.,
Hon., Spa. (n phr) carving fork
tenedor para servir Pan., Pue.R.
(n phr) carving fork
tenedor para trinchar Nic.
(n phr) carving fork
tener compromiso Col. (v phr) date

tener desfase horario Nic., Spa.
(v phr) jet-lag, to have
tener jet lag Pri. (v phr) jet-lag, to
have
tener puesto Col., Cub. (v phr) wear
(clothing)
tener un/a beba/bebe/bebé/hijo/hija
Arg. (v phr) give birth
tener una cita Pri. (v phr) date
tenis 1. Col., Cos.R., Cub., Dom.R.,
Nic., Par., Pue.R. (n) sneakers
2. Dom.R., Mex. (n) shoes,
tennis
tenis de lona Mex. (n phr) sneakers
teno Pri. (n) tenor drum
tenor Par., Spa. (n) tenor drum
terminar Chi., Ecu., ElS., Gua., Hon.,
Mex., Nic., Venz. (v) break up
(relationship)
termita Pri. (n) termite
ternera Pri. (n) calf
ternero/a Arg., Col., Nic., Spa.
(n) calf
terno 1. Pri. (n) suit, three-piece
2. Bol., Per. (n) suit
terraza Chi. (n) balcony
terraza cubierta Gua. (n phr) porch
terremoto Pri. (n) earthquake
terreno pantanoso 1. Mex.
(n phr) wetlands 2. Uru.
(n phr) swamp
terreno para ferias Col.
(n phr) fairground
terrible 1. Dom.R. (adj) awful 2. Nic.
(adj) terrifying
terrorífico Col. (adj) terrifying
tesoro 1. Chi. (n) love; lovey 2. Col.
(n) dear; darling; honey
teta Arg., Col., Cos.R., Pan., Par., Uru.
(n) breast
tetera Chi., Col., Per., Spa. (n) kettle
tetilla Col. (n) nipple
¡Te veo luego! Col. (int phr) See you

later!

¡Te veo más tarde! Col. (int phr) See you later!

tevi Par. (n) butt

tezna Col. (n) awl

ticket Dom.R., Par., Venz. (n) ticket

ticket de ida y vuelta Nic. (n phr) round trip ticket

tienda 1. Gua., Pan. (n) grocery 2. Cub. (n) department store

tienda botánica Col. (n phr) herbalist's shop

tienda de abarrotes Mex. (n phr) grocery

tienda de animales Pue. R., Spa. (n phr) pet shop

tienda de animales domésticos Mex. (n phr) pet shop

tienda de bebidas alcohólicas Pri. (n phr) liquor store

tienda de botánica Spa. (n phr) herbalist's shop

tienda de campaña Chi., Cos.R., Dom.R., Mex., Nic., Spa., Venz. (n phr) tent

tienda de comestibles Pri. (n phr) grocery

tienda de departamentos Cos.R. (n phr) department store

tienda de libros Pue.R. (n phr) bookstore

tienda de licores Ecu. (n phr) wine shop

tienda de mascotas Dom.R., Nic., Par. (n phr) pet shop

tienda de mascotes ElS., Gua., Hon. (n phr) pet shop

tienda departamental Mex. (n phr) department store

tienda de vinos Dom.R. (n phr) wine shop

tienda naturalista Par. (n phr) habalist's shop

tienda naturista Mex., Nic. (n phr) herbalist's shop

tienda por departamentos Dom.R., ElS., Gua., Hon., Nic., Pue.R., Venz. (n phr) department store

tights Pue.R. (n) tights

tijera podadora Venz. (n phr) pruning shears

tijera de podar Par. (n phr) pruning shears

tijeras de podar Arg., Dom.R., Nic., Spa. (n phr) pruning shears

tijeras para podar Col. (n phr) pruning shears

timba Nic. (n) belly (colloq.)

timbal Pri. (n) timpani

timbre Pri. (n) bell (bicycle)

tímido Pri. (adj) shy

timón 1. Col., Cub., Gua., Pan. (n) steering wheel 2. Cub., Dom.R., Gua., Pan. (n) handlebars (bicycle)

tímpanos Col., Cub. (n) timpani

tinta Pri. (n) toner

tipo Pri. (n) guy

tipo/a pesado/a ElS., Gua., Hon. (n phr) pest (person)

tipos Pri. (n) guys (dual gender plural)

tips informativos Nic. (n phr) news brief

tiquete Col. (n) ticket

tiquete de ida y vuelta Col. (n phr) round trip ticket

tiquete de una sola vía Col. (n phr) one-way ticket

tirante Col. (n) snare (of drum)

tirantes Gua., Nic., Pan., Spa., Venz. (n) suspenders

tirar dedo Per. (v phr) hitchhike

tirar drogas Pue.R. (v phr) sell drugs

titi Par. (n) breast

titulares Dom.R. (n) news brief

tobo Venz. (n) pail

ABBREVIATIONS: Arg.=Argentina Bol.=Bolivia Chi.=Chile Col.=Colombia Cos.R.=Costa Rica Cub.=Cuba Dom.R.=Dominican Republic Ecu.=Ecuador ElS.=El Salvador Gua.=Guatemala Hon.=Honduras Mex.=Mexico Nic.=Nicaragua Pan.=Panama Par.=Paraguay Per.=Peru Pri.=Primary Term Pue.R.=Puerto Rico Spa.=Spain Uru.=Uruguay Venz.=Venezuela

tocadiscos Pri. (n) compact disk player
tocadiscos para discos compactos
   Mex.(n phr) compact disk player
tocador Pue.R., Spa. (n) dresser
tocador de discos compactos Dom.R.
   (n phr) compact disk player
tocar el tambor Col., Spa.
   (v phr) drum, tap
tocarse Mex. (v) get high (drugs)
tocón Pri. (n) stump
tolda Pan. (n) tent
tomate 1. Pri. (n) tomato 2. Chi.
   (n) bun (hair)
tonalidad Col. (n) key (music)
toner Dom.R., Nic., Par. (n) toner
tonificador Mex. (n) toner
tono 1. Pri. (n) key (music) 2. Col.,
   Dom.R., Mex., Nic. (n) tone
tonos agudos Col., Nic., Par.
   (n phr) treble (stereo)
tope Mex. (n) bump (road)
tórax Chi., Col. (n) chest
torcer a la derecha, izquierda Spa.
   (v phr) turn right, left
tonero/a Nic. (n) turner
tornillo Col., Cos.R., Pue.R., Spa.
   (n) bolt
torno Mex., Nic., Uru. (n) vise
toronja Pri. (n) grapefruit
torre de apartamentos Dom.R.
   (n phr) apartment building
torta 1. Arg., Chi., Ecu., Par., Per.,
   Uru.,Venz. (n) cake 2. Chi.,
   Cos.R. (n) pie 3. Col., Nic.
   (n) tart
torta de huevo Nic. (n phr) omelet
tortilla Bol., Col., Cub., Par., Per.,
   Pue.R., Spa., Venz. (n) omelet
tortilla española Dom.R.
   (n phr) omelet
tostada Pri. (n) toast
tostado Col. (adj) tan (skin)
tostador Pri. (n) toaster

tostadora Chi., Col., Cub., Dom.R.,
   Ecu., Pue.R., Spa., Venz.
   (n) toaster
townhouse Dom.R., Nic., Pue.R.
   (n) townhouse
toxicomanía Pri. (n) drug abuse
toxido Pan. (n) tuxedo
traba Chi. (n) barrette
trabajador eventual Mex.
   (n phr) temporary worker
trabajador temporal Nic.
   (n phr) temporary worker
trabajar a distancia Nic.
   (v phr) telecommute
trabajoso Col. (adj) difficult
tracción a las cuatro ruedas Spa.
   (n phr) four-wheel drive
tracción de cuatro ruedas Cub.,
   Venz. (n phr) four-wheel drive
tracción en las cuatro ruedas Arg.,
   Chi., Col., Gua., Mex.
   (n phr) four-wheel drive
traer un alucine Mex. (v phr) get high
   (drugs)
traficante de drogas Pri. (n phr) drug
   dealer
traficar Mex., Venz. (v) deal (drugs)
traficar con Col., ElS., Gua., Hon.,
   Nic. (v phr) deal (drugs)
tráfico 1. Pri. (n) traffic 2. Cub.
   (n) traffic jam
tráfico de drogas Col., Dom.R., Gua.,
   Nic., Spa., Uru. (n phr) drug deal
trago Chi., Nic. (n) alcoholic beverage
trailer Chi., Cos.R., Cub., Dom.R.,
   Nic., Pan. (n) trailer
traje 1. Pri. (n) suit 2. Arg., Col., Pan.
   (n) dress (woman's) 3. Chi.,
   Nic., Par. (n) outfit 4. Mex.
   (n) garment
traje a medida Par. (n phr) suit,
   tailored
traje a la medida Nic., Venz.

(n phr) suit, tailored

traje con traslape Nic. (n phr) suit, double-breasted

traje cruzado Pri. (n phr) suit, double-breasted

traje de mujer Pue.R. (n phr) dress (woman's)

traje de tres piezas Bol., Dom.R., Mex., Nic., Par., Pue.R., Venz. (n phr) suit, three-piece

traje sastre Pri. (n phr) suit, tailored

traje traslapado Gua. (n phr) suit, double-breasted

trampero Par. (n) cheater

trampolín Pri. (n) ski jump

tramposo Pri. (n) cheater

trancón Col. (n) traffic jam

tranque Cub., Pan. (n) traffic jam

tranquilo Dom.R., Nic., Pan. (adj) quiet

transacción de drogas Pri. (n phr) drug deal

transbordador Pri. (n) ferry

transbordar Pri. (v) change (train)

tránsito Chi., Cos.R., Dom.R. (n) traffic

transmisión 1. Chi., Col., Cos.R., ElS., Gua., Hon., Nic. (n) broadcast 2. Pue.R. (n) gearbox

transmisión automática Pri. (n phr) automatic transmission

transmisión directa Mex. (n phr) live broadcast

transmisión en directa Pri. (n phr) live broadcast

transmisión en directo Arg., Bol., Col., ElS., Gua., Hon., Par., Uru. (n phr) live broadcast

transmisión en vivo Cos.R., Cub., Dom.R., Ecu., Mex., Pan., Par., Spa., Venz. (n phr) live broadcast

transmisión en vivo y en directo

Chi., Nic., Per. (n phr) live broadcast

transmitir Col., Cos.R., ElS., Gua., Hon., Nic., Venz. (v) broadcast

tranvía Pri. (n) trolley

trasero Pri. (n) butt

trasladarse Bol. (v) move

traste Arg., Chi., Par. (n) butt

trastiar Col. (v) move

trastos Pan. (n) dishes

travieso Pri. (adj) naughty

trébol Pri. (n) cloverleaf junction

tremendo Arg., Chi., Cub., Mex., Nic., Venz. (adj) tremendous

tren de cercanías Spa. (n phr) local train

tren directo Pri. (n phr) through train

tren expreso Par., Venz. (n phr) through train

tren local Pri. (n phr) local train

trenza Pri. (n) braid (hair); pigtail

trepadora Pri. (n) climbing plant

tribunal de justicia Pri. (n phr) courthouse

trifocales Pri. (n) trifocals

trigueño Cub., Dom.R. (adj) brown (hair)

trigueño/a Col., Cub., Dom.R. (n) brunette (person)

trinche Pri. (n) carving fork

trinchera Pri. (n) trench coat

tripa del caucho Venz. (n phr) inner tube (bicycle tire)

tripear Pue.R. (v) get high (drugs)

triple salto Arg., Col. (n phr) triple jump

triquet Gua. (n) jack (car)

triste Mex., Nic. (adj) gloomy (person)

triturador de papas Par., Uru. (n phr) potato masher

trituradora Pri. (n) shredder

trole Chi. (n) trolley

trolebús Mex. (n) trolley
trompa de pistones Spa.
    (n phr) French horn
trompeta Nic. (n) bugle
truco Col., Mex. (n) stunt
trusa 1. Col. (n) briefs 2. Cub.
    (n) bathing suit
tubo Pri. (n) inner tube (bicycle tire)
tubo bajo Ecu. (n phr) flat tire
tubo de escape Pri. (n phr) exhaust
    pipe

tubos ElS., Gua., Hon., Mex. (n) hair
    rollers
tuco Nic. (n) stump
tumbadora Cub. (n) conga drum
tuna Cub., Pue.R. (n) tuna
túnica Pri. (n) house robe
turismo Par., Spa. (n) sedan
turnarse alternando coches Mex.
    (v phr) carpool
tutor Pri. (n) guardian
tuxedo Cub., Pue.R. (n) tuxedo

ABBREVIATIONS: Arg.=Argentina Bol.=Bolivia Chi.=Chile Col.=Colombia Cos.R.=Costa Rica Cub.=Cuba Dom.R.=Dominican Republic Ecu.=Ecuador ElS.=El Salvador Gua.=Guatemala Hon.=Honduras Mex.=Mexico Nic.=Nicaragua Pan.=Panama Par.=Paraguay Per.=Peru Pri.=Primary Term Pue.R.=Puerto Rico Spa.=Spain Uru.=Uruguay Venz.=Venezuela

U

ultrapasar Chi. (v) pasar (traffic)
umpire Pri. (n) umpire (baseball)
uña quitagrapas Mex. (n phr) staple
remover
uñas Pri. (n) staple remover
uñas saca grapas Dom. R.
(n phr) staple remover
unidad de disco Pri. (n phr) drive
(computer)

urbe Col. (n) city
usar Arg., Bol., Gua., Pan., Venz.
(v) wear (clothing)
usar drogas Col. (v phr) use drugs
usar la red Mex. (v phr) surf the net
usuario de drogas Pue.R. (n phr) drug
user
útiles de oficina Ecu., Par.
(n phr) office supplies

ABBREVIATIONS: Arg.=Argentina Bol.=Bolivia Chi.=Chile Col.=Colombia Cos.R.=Costa Rica
Cub.=Cuba Dom.R.=Dominican Republic Ecu.=Ecuador ElS.=El Salvador Gua.=Guatemala
Hon.=Honduras Mex.=Mexico Nic.=Nicaragua Pan.=Panama Par.=Paraguay Per.=Peru
Pri.=Primary Term Pue.R.=Puerto Rico Spa.=Spain Uru.=Uruguay Venz.=Venezuela

V

vacante Dom.R. (adj) vacant
vacío Mex., Nic., Venz. (adj) vacant
vago Arg., Cub., Dom.R., Nic., Par.
(adj) lazy
vagón Bol., Ecu., Gua., Nic., Spa.
(n) wagon
vagoneta Bol. (n) recreational vehicle;
station wagon
vagón-restaurante Col. (n) dining car
(train)
vainitas Dom.R., Ecu., Per., Venz.
(n) beans, green
vajilla 1. Col., Dom.R., Mex., Nic.
(n) china 2. Pan. (n) dishes
vajilla fina Pan. (n phr) china
valenciana Pri. (n) cuff (pants)
valeroso Col. (adj) brave
valiente Pri. (adj) brave
valija Arg., Nic., Par. (n) suitcase
valijas Par. (n) baggage
valijera Nic. (n) trunk (car)
valla Col., Dom.R., Nic. (n) billboard
vallas Pri. (n) hurdles race
valle Dom.R., Nic. (n) prairie
van Arg., Chi., Cub., Dom.R., Pan.,
Pue.R. (n) van
vaqueros Arg., Cub., Nic., Par., Spa.,
Uru. (n) blue jeans
vaquita de San Antonio Arg.
(n phr) ladybug
vararse Col. (v) stall (car)
varilla de aceite Pue.R.
(n phr) dipstick
varilla para medir el aceite Col., Nic.
(n phr) dipstick
varillo Col. (n) marijuana cigarette

vasija 1. Col., Pan. (n) bowl 2. Pan.
(n) bowl, mixing
vasija para mezclar Col.
(n phr) bowl, mixing
vasito Pue.R. (n) shot glass
vaso 1. Arg., Nic. (n) tumbler 2. Cub.
(n) mug
vaso de trago corto Dom.R.
(n phr) shot glass
vaso para whiskey Pri. (n) tumbler
vaso tequilero Mex. (n phr) shot glass
VCR Chi., Col. (n) videocassette
recorder (VCR)
vecindad Pri. (n) neighborhood
vecindario Bol., Col., Dom.R., Gua.,
Nic., Per., Pue.R., Spa., Venz.
(n) neighborhood
vehículo de recreo Pri.
(n phr) recreational vehicle
vehículo recreacional Venz.
(n phr) recreational vehicle
vela Cos.R., Nic. (n) wake
velación Col. (n) wake
velador Bol., Chi. (n) table, night
velatorio Spa. (n) wake
velero Dom.R., Nic., Par. (n) sailboat
vello 1. Arg. (n) hair 2. Dom.R.
(n) pubic hair
vello del pubis Uru. (n phr) pubic hair
vello pubiano Pri. (n phr) pubic hair
vello púbico Col., Cos.R., ElS., Gua.,
Mex., Nic., Par., Venz. (n phr) pubic
hair
velludo Bol., Dom.R., Ecu., Pan., Uru.
(adj) velloso
velocidad máxima Mex., Pue.R.

(n phr) speed limit
velocímetro Pri. (n) speedometer
velorio (n) wake
veloz Chi., Col. (adj) quick
venado Pri. (n) deer
vendedor/a Chi., Col., Dom.R., Ecu.,
 ElS., Gua., Hon., Mex., Nic.,
 Par., Venz. (n) salesperson
vendedor/a casa por casa Nic.
 (n phr) door-to-door salesperson
vendedor/a a domicilio Pri.
 (n phr) door-to-door salesperson
vendedor/a puerta a puerta Col.
 (n phr) door-to-door salesperson
vender Pri. (v) deal (drugs)
vender drogas Pri. (v phr) sell drugs
venera Pri. (n) scallop
ventana de la nariz Cub.
 (n phr) nostril
ventana trasera Pri. (n phr) rear
 window
ventanilla Pri. (n) nostril
ventanilla trasera Col. (n phr) rear
 window
ver la televisión Spa. (v phr) watch
 television
ver tele (visión) Pri. (v phr) watch
 television
verde Pri. (adj) green (eyes)
vereda Arg., Chi., Cos.R., Ecu., Per.,
 Uru. (n) sidewalk
verga Nic. (n) penis
verruga (n) wart
vestíbulo Cub., ElS., Gua., Hon., Spa.,
 Venz. (n) lobby
vestido 1. Pri. (n) dress (woman's);
 garment (for either gender)
 2. Col., Pan. (n) suit
vestido casero Col. (n phr) house robe
vestido de baño Col., Ecu., Pan.
 (n phr) bathing suit
vestido de tres piezas Pan.
 (n phr) suit, three-piece

vestido hecho a la medida Col.
 (n phr) suit, tailored
vestido sastre Pan. (n phr) suit,
 tailored
vestidura Cub. (n) garment
vestimenta Col. (n) outfit
vestir Chi., Par. (v) wear (clothing)
vestirse Pri. (v) dress (oneself)
vestirse de etiqueta Pri. (v phr) dress
 up
vestirse elegante Chi., Col.
 (v phr) dress up
vestirse formal Dom.R. (v phr) dress
 up
vetarro Nic. (adj) old; (n) adult
 (colloq.)
veterinaria Mex. (n) pet shop
vía rápida Mex. (n phr) expressway
vía única Chi. (n phr) street, one-way
víbora Arg., Bol., Mex., Uru.
 (n) snake
vicio Pri. (n) habit (drugs)
vicio de drogas Cub. (n phr) drug
 habit
vida, mi Cub., Pue.R. (n phr) dear;
 darling; honey
vidajeno/a Pan. (n) snoop
vidalia Pri. (n) onion, vidalia
vídeo Spa. (n) videocassette recorder
 (VCR)
videocasete Pri. (n) videocassette
videocasetera Arg., Mex., Nic.
 (n) videocassette recorder (VCR)
videograbadora Pri. (n) videocassette
 recorder (VCR)
videojuego Pri. (n) videogame
vidriera Arg. (n) shop window
vieira Arg., Venz. (n) scallop
vieja Arg., Col., Par., Nic. (n) mother
viejo/a Nic. (n) adult
vientre Col., Dom.R., Nic.
 (n) abdomen
viga vertical Mex. (n phr) stud

villorrio Col. (n) village
vinatería Mex., Nic., Pue.R. (n) wine
    shop
vinería Uru. (n) wine shop
violoncelo Pri. (n) violoncello
violonchelo Spa. (n) violoncello
virar a la derecha, izquierda Cos.R.
    (v phr) turn right, left
vitrina 1. Pri. (n) display cabinet;
    shop window

2. Col. (n) buffet
víveres Dom.R. (n) grocery
vivero Arg., Col., Dom.R., Nic., Par.
    (n) nursery (plants)
volante Pri. (n) steering wheel
volar Bol., Per. (v) get high (drugs)
volarse Chi. (v) get high (drugs)
voleto Col. (n) ticket
volley Par. (n) volleyball
voz de bajo Nic. (n phr) bass (voice)

ABBREVIATIONS: Arg.=Argentina Bol.=Bolivia Chi.=Chile Col.=Colombia Cos.R.=Costa Rica
Cub.=Cuba Dom.R.=Dominican Republic Ecu.=Ecuador ElS.=El Salvador Gua.=Guatemala
Hon.=Honduras Mex.=Mexico Nic.=Nicaragua Pan.=Panama Par.=Paraguay Per.=Peru
Pri.=Primary Term Pue.R.=Puerto Rico Spa.=Spain Uru.=Uruguay Venz.=Venezuela

W

waffle Col., Mex., Par. (n) waffle
wafle Gua., Nic. (n) waffle
WAN (n) WAN (wide area network)
web-site Dom.R., Pue.R. (n)
website

western Spa. (n) movie, western
wipers Pue.R. (n) wipers (windshield)
word processing Pue.R. (n phr) word
processing

ABBREVIATIONS: Arg.=Argentina Bol.=Bolivia Chi.=Chile Col.=Colombia Cos.R.=Costa Rica
Cub.=Cuba Dom.R.=Dominican Republic Ecu.=Ecuador ElS.=El Salvador Gua.=Guatemala
Hon.=Honduras Mex.=Mexico Nic.=Nicaragua Pan.=Panama Par.=Paraguay Per.=Peru
Pri.=Primary Term Pue.R.=Puerto Rico Spa.=Spain Uru.=Uruguay Venz.=Venezuela

X-Y-Z

xilófono (n) xylophone

yautía Dom.R. (n) taro
yerba 1. Col. (n) marijuana 2. Cub.,
   Dom.R. (n) lawn 3. Pue.R.
   (n) grass
yerba mala Pue.R. (n phr) weed
yugos Cub. (n) cufflinks
yunta Pue.R. (n) sickle
yuntas Pue.R., Venz. (n) cufflinks
yuyo Arg., Par. (n) weed

zancos Chi. (n) clogs
zanja Pri. (n) ditch
zapalillas Cub. (n) slippers
zapallito Bol. (n) squash
zapallito italiano Chi. (n phr) zucchini
zapallo 1. Bol., Chi., Pan. (n) pumpkin
   2. Uru. (n) squash
zapapico Mex. (n) scythe
zapatera Pri. (n) shoe rack
zapatero Col., Par. (n) shoe rack
zapatillas 1. Arg., Chi., Pan. (n) shoes,
   tennis 2. Arg., Chi., Pan., Per.,
   Uru. (n) sneakers 3. Par.
   (n) rubbers (shoes)
zapatillas de casa Spa. (n phr) slippers
zapatillas de deporte Spa.
   (n phr) shoes, tennis
zapatillas de lona Spa.
   (n phr) sneakers
zapatos bajitos Dom.R. (n phr) loafers
zapatos de andar Pri. (n phr) loafers
zapatos de caminar Col.
   (n phr) shoes, hiking
zapatos de casa Mex. (n phr) loafers

zapatos de caucho 1. Col.
   (n phr) rubbers (shoes) 2. Ecu.
   (n phr) sneakers
apatos de charol Pri. (n phr) shoes,
   patent leather
zapatos de cuero Dom.R., Venz.
   (n phr) shoes, patent leather
zapatos de cuero barnizado Arg.,
   Bol., Cos.R., Ecu., Per., Pue.R.
   (n phr) shoes, patent leather
zapatos de goma 1. Chi., Uru.
   (n phr) rubbers (shoes)
   2. Venz. (n phr) shoes, tennis;
   sneakers
zapatos de lona con suela de hule
   ElS., Gua., Hon.
   (n phr) sneakers
zapatos de patente Venz.
   (n phr) shoes, patent leather
zapatos de piel Dom.R.
   (n phr) shoes, patent leather
zapatos de tenis Pri. (n) shoes, tennis
zapatos estilo mocasín ElS., Gua.,
   Hon., Spa. (n phr) loafers
zapatos tenis Col., Nic.
   (n phr) shoes, tennis
zaranda Nic. (n) sieve
zarcillos Venz. (n) earrings; pierced
   earrings
zarcillos de presión Venz.
   (n phr) earrings, clip
zarcillos de tornillo Venz.
   (n phr) earrings, screw
zepelín Cub., Nic., Venz. (n) blimp
ziper Dom.R. (n) fly (pants)
zipper Pue.R. (n) fly (pants)

---

*ABBREVIATIONS: Arg.=Argentina Bol.=Bolivia Chi.=Chile Col.=Colombia Cos.R.=Costa Rica
Cub.=Cuba Dom.R.=Dominican Republic Ecu.=Ecuador ElS.=El Salvador Gua.=Guatemala
Hon.=Honduras Mex.=Mexico Nic.=Nicaragua Pan.=Panama Par.=Paraguay Per.=Peru
Pri.=Primary Term Pue.R.=Puerto Rico Spa.=Spain Uru.=Uruguay Venz.=Venezuela*

zobaco Col., Dom.R. (n) armpit

zona comercial Col., Cub., Mex., Nic., Pue.R. (n phr) business district

zona de negocios Spa. (n phr) business district

zona residencial 1. Pri.

(n phr) residencial area 2. Nic. (n phr) uptown

zorra Pan. (n) fox

zorro Pri. (n) fox

zucchini Nic. (n) zucchini

zuecos Col., Cub., Nic., Spa., Uru. (n) clogs

zumbido Pri. (n) hum

ABBREVIATIONS: Arg.=Argentina Bol.=Bolivia Chi.=Chile Col.=Colombia Cos.R.=Costa Rica Cub.=Cuba Dom.R.=Dominican Republic Ecu.=Ecuador ElS.=El Salvador Gua.=Guatemala Hon.=Honduras Mex.=Mexico Nic.=Nicaragua Pan.=Panama Par.=Paraguay Per.=Peru Pri.=Primary Term Pue.R.=Puerto Rico Spa.=Spain Uru.=Uruguay Venz.=Venezuela

PART III: SUBJECT AREAS

Animals: Birds

blackbird (n) mirlo
  Pan. talingo
chicken (n) pollo
  Pan. gallina
cock (n) gallo
cockatoo (n) cacatúa
  Chi. cata
crow (n) cuervo
cuckoo (n) cuco
  Col., Nic., Venz. cuclillo
  Mex. Cucú
  Par. cucú, cuculele
dove (n) paloma
  Col. palomo
  Pue.R. pichón
duck (n) pato
gander (n) ganso
hawk (n) halcón
  Bol. alcón
  Chi. peuco
hen (n) gallina
heron (n) garza
hummingbird (n) colibrí
  Arg., Col., Pan. picaflor
  Ecu. chupaflor
macaw (n) guacamayo
  ElS., Gua., Mex. guacamaya
  Nic. lapa
nightingale (n) ruiseñor
ostrich (n) avestruz
  Col., Par. ñandú
owl (n) búho
  Arg., Col., Cub., Dom.R., Par.
  lechuza
  Chi. chuncho
parakeet (n) perico
  Nic. chocoyo
  Par. Cotorra
  Spa. periquito
parrot (n) loro
  Col., Dom.R. cotorra
partridge (n) perdiz
peacock (n) pavo real
penguin (n) pingüino
pheasant (n) faisán
pigeon (n) paloma
quail (n) codorniz
robin (n) petirrojo
rooster (n) gallo
seagull (n) gaviota
sparrow (n) gorrión
stork (n) cigüeña
swallow (n) golondrina
swan (n) cisne
turkey (n) pavo
  Cub. guanajo
  Mex. guajolote
  Nic. chompipe
turtledove (n) tórtola
vulture (n) buitre
  Chi. jote
  Cub. aura tiñosa
woodcock (n) chocha
  Col. gallineta
  ElS., Gua. gallina sorda,
  gallineta
  Nic., Venz. perdiz
woodpecker (n) pájaro carpintero

Animals: Insects & Bugs

bee (n) abeja
beetle (n) escarabajo
  Chi. cucaracha
  Dom.R. avejón
bug (n) bicho, chinche
  Col., Nic., Per., Pue.R. insecto
  Dom.R. insecto, pajarito
bumblebee (n) abejorro
  Pue.R. avejita

---

centipede (n) ciempiés
cicada (n) cigarra
   Chi., Nic., Pue.R., Venz.
   chicharra
cockroach (n) cucaracha
cricket (n) grillo
dragonfly (n) libélula
   Chi. matapiojos
   Cub. caballito del diablo
   Pan. caballito
firefly (n) luciérnaga
   Cub. cocuyo
   Pue.R. cucubano
flea (n) pulga
fly (n) mosca
grasshopper (n) saltamontes
hornet (n) avispón
horsefly, gadfly (n) tábano
   Col. moscardón
   Pue.R. caballito de San Pedro
insect (n) insecto
ladybug (n) mariquita
   Arg. vaquita de San Antonio
   Chi. chinita
   Mex. catarina
   Par. escarabajo
   Venz. coquito
louse (n) piojo
moth (n) polilla
praying mantis (n phr) manta religiosa
   Nic. rezadora
   Pan. maría palito
   Par., Spa. mantis religiosa
   Pue.R. mantilla
scorpion (n) alacrán
   Arg., Chi., Col., Cos.R., Nic.,
   Pan., Spa., Uru., Venz.
   escorpión
spider (n) araña
   Dom.R. cacata
termite (n) termita
   Cos.R., Cub., Dom.R., Pan.,
   Pue.R. comejón

   Chi. polilla
   Ecu., ElS., Gua., Hon. comején
   Nic. comején, polilla
wasp (n) avispa
   Pan. abejorro
yellow jacket (n phr) avispa con pintas
   amarillas
   Nic. avispa chaqueta amarilla
   Pan., Par. abispa

Animals: Mammals

bull (n) toro
calf (n) ternera
   Arg., Nic. ternero
   Col., Spa. becerro, ternero
caribou (n) caribú
cat (n) gato
colt (n) potro
   Chi., Nic. potrillo
cow (n) vaca
deer (n) venado
   Arg., Bol., Cos.R., ElS., Gua.,
   Hon., Spa., Uru. ciervo
dolphin (n) delfín
ewe (n) oveja
flock (n) rebaño
   Arg. bandada
   Chi. piño
   Col. manada
foal (n) potro
   Col., Nic. Venz. potrillo
fox (n) zorro
   Pan. zorra
goat (n) cabra (male), chivo (female)
hare (n) liebre
   Pue.R. conejo
horse (n) caballo
mare (n) yegua
mole (n) topo
monkey (n) mono
   Col. mico

ABBREVIATIONS: Arg.=Argentina Bol.=Bolivia Chi.=Chile Col.=Colombia Cos.R.=Costa Rica
Cub.=Cuba Dom.R.=Dominican Republic Ecu.=Ecuador ElS.=El Salvador Gua.=Guatemala
Hon.=Honduras Mex.=Mexico Nic.=Nicaragua Pan.=Panama Par.=Paraguay Per.=Peru
Pri.=Primary Term Pue.R.=Puerto Rico Spa.=Spain Uru.=Uruguay Venz.=Venezuela

Mex. chango
moose (n) anta
Arg., Nic., Par., Spa., Venz. alce
Chi. ante
Col., Mex. alce, ante
mouse (n) ratón
Chi. laucha
mustang (n) mustango
Arg. potro
Nic. mustang
ox (n) buey
pig (n) puerco
Per. cerdo, chancho
Bol. chancho, cuchi
Arg., Chi., Ecu.,.Uru. chancho
Col. cerdo, marrano
Cos.R. chancho, cochino
Cub. cochino
ElS., Gua., Hon. coche,
marrano
Mex. cochino, marrano
Nic. cerdo, chancho, marrano
Pan. marrano
Dom.R., Pue.R., Spa. cerdo
Venz. cerdo, cochino
pony (n) jaca
Col., Dom.R., Mex., Nic., Pan.,
Par. pony
Cub., Ecu. caballito
Pue.R., Venz. caballito, pony
Arg., Spa. poni
Uru. poney
porcupine (n) puerco espín
porpoise (n) marsopa
Chi., Ecu., Par. delfín
rabbit (n) conejo
rat (n) rata
reindeer (n) reno
Dom.R. cervatillo
seal (n) foca
sheep (n) oveja
Mex. borrego
squirrel (n) ardilla

stallion (n) padrillo
Arg., Col., Dom.R., Par., Spa.,
Venz. semental
Chi. garañón
Gua. garañón, semental
Nic. garañón, padrote, semental
walrus (n) morsa
Dom.R. foca marina
wapiti (n) ciervo canadiense
wolf (n) lobo

Animals: Mollusks & Crustaceans

clam (n) almeja
cockle (n) berberecho
crab (n) cangrejo
Chi. jaiba, pancora
Nic., Pan. jaiba
crayfish (n) cangrejo de río
Chi. camarón de agua dulce
Col., Dom.R., Nic. jaiba
Pue.R. juey
lobster (n) langosta
mussel (n) mejillón
Chi. choro
octopus (n) pulpo
oyster (n) ostra
Mex. ostión
prawn (n) gamba
Arg. camarón, langostino
Chi. camarón gigante
Col., Cub., Mex., Pan., Spa.
langostino
Ecu., Nic., Par., Uru. camarón
scallop (n) venera
Arg., Venz. vieira
Chi. ostión
ElS., Gua., Nic. concha,
escalope
Pan. conchuela
Par. Spa. concha

shrimp (n) camarón
    Chi. langostino
    Spa. gamba
snail (n) caracol
    Dom.R., Nic. babosa
squid (n) calamar
    Chi. jibia

Animals: Reptiles, Amphibians & Fish

anchovy (n) anchoa
    Chi. anchoveta
    Cos.R., Dom.R., Pue.R., boquerón
    Per. anchoveta, boquerón
bass (n) róbalo
bluefish (n) pomátomo
    Mex. anjova, pez azul
    Nic. dorado
carp (n) carpa
catfish (n) bagre
    Spa. barbo
cod (n) bacalao
eel (n) anguila
flounder (n) lenguado, platija
    Gua. róbalo
herring (n) arenque
lizard (n) lagartija (small lizard), lagarto (large lizard)
mackerel (n) caballa
perch (n) perca
pike (n) lucio
pompano (n) pámpano
salmon (n) salmón
sardine (n) sardina
smelt (n) eperlano
    Chi. pejerrey
snake (n) culebra
    Arg., Bol., Mex., Uru. víbora
    Chi., Cub. serpiente

snapper (n) pargo
    Dom.R., Pue.R. chillo
    Mex. guachinango, huachinango
sole (n) lenguado
sturgeon (n) esturión
swordfish (n) pez espada
    Chi. albacora
trout (n) trucha
tuna (n) atún
    Cub., Pue.R. tuna

Common Adjectives

amazing (adj) asombroso
    Arg., Chi., Dom.R., Nic. increíble
    Col. estupendo
angry (adj) enojado
    Col., Cub., Venz. bravo
    Dom.R. furioso
    Ecu. enfurecido
    Nic. arrecho
    Pue.R. enfogono, molesto
awful (adj) horrible
    Arg., Chi., Nic. espantoso
    Col. espantoso, horrendo, horroroso
    Dom.R. terrible bad (adj) malo
beautiful (adj) bonito, hermoso
    Arg. lindo, precioso
    Chi., Col., Cos.R., Cub., Dom.R. bello
    Ecu., Par., Pue.R., Venz. lindo
best (adj) el mejor
better (adj) mejor que
big (adj) grande
boring (adj) aburrido
    Col. harto, tedioso
bothersome (adj) molesto
    Col. incómodo
    Venz. molestoso
brave (adj) valiente
    Col. valeroso

Dom.R. guapo
cheap (adj) barato
    Col. asequible, ganga
    Pan. runcho
closed (adj) cerrado
cold (adj) frío
cute (adj) mono
    Arg. divino
    Bol. amoroso
    Chi. simpático
    Col. primoroso
    Cub. guapo, lindo
    Dom.R., Ecu., Pan. gracioso
    Mex. chulo
    ElS., Gua., Hon., Per., Venz.
    chulo, lindo
    Nic. bonito
    Par. chalina, juky
    Pue.R. bonito, chulito
dark (adj) oscuro
delicious (adj) delicioso
    Arg., Pue.R. rico
    Per. exquisito
delightful (adj) divino
    Chi. agradable
    Col. deleitable,
    encantador, exquisito
    ElS., Gua., Hon. muy agradable
    Venz. rico
difficult (adj) difícil
    Col. dificultoso,
early (adj) temprano
easy (adj) fácil, sencillo
empty (adj) vacío
evil (adj) malvado
    Arg. maldito, malo
    Chi., Dom.R., Nic. malo
    Col. maligno, malo
    Venz. maligno
exciting (adj) emocionante
    Col. conmovedor,
    impresionante
    Pue.R. excitante

expensive (adj) caro, costoso
far (adj) lejos
friendly (adj) amistoso
    Col., Mex., Pue.R. amigable
    Cub. simpático
full (adj) lleno
fun (adj) divertido, entretenido
funny (adj) divertido, gracioso
    Chi. simpático
    Col., Dom.R., Ecu., Nic., Pan.
    chistoso
gloomy (person) (adj) lúgubre
    Col. sombrío
    Cub. melancólico
    Dom.R. de mal humor
    Mex. triste
    Nic. decaído, triste
    Venz. deprimido
good (adj) bueno
grumpy (adj) malhumorado
    Chi. andar de malas pulgas
    Col. gruñón, protestón,
    refunfuñón, rezongón
    Nic. cascarrabias, gruñón
    Pue.R. de mal humor
    Venz. cascarrabias
hairy (adj) velloso
    Arg., Chi., Col., Par., Pue.R.,
    Spa., Venz. peludo
    Bol., Dom.R., Ecu., Pan., Uru.
    velludo
    Nic. mechudo, peludo
handsome (adj) guapo
    Arg. buen mozo
    Bol. churro
    Chi., Dom.R. buenmozo
    Col. bien parecido, buenmozo,
    churro, majo
    Venz. bien parecido
heavy (adj) pesado
impolite (adj) descortés,
    mal educado
    Col. grosero

Nic. malcriado,
maleducado
Spa. maleducado
impressive (adj) impresionante
Col. emocionante
intelligent (adj) inteligente
interesting (adj) interesante
late (adj) tarde
lazy (adj) perezoso
Arg., Cub. vago
Bol., Chi., Venz. flojo
Col., Uru. haragán
Dom.R., Nic. haragán, vago
Mex. flojo, holgazán
light (color) (adj) claro
light (weight) (adj) ligero
Arg., Chi., Nic., Par. liviano
loud (noise) (adj) ruidoso
Chi. fuerte
magnificent (adj) magnífico
naughty (adj) travieso
Arg. liero
Chi. malvado
Col. juguetón
Cub. pillo
Dom.R. bellaco
Pue.R. necio
Nic., Pue.R. necio
near (adj) cerca
new (adj) nuevo
nice (adj) simpático
Col., Cub., Nic., Spa. amable
Dom.R. chulo
Pue.R. chévere
Venz. agradable
occupied (adj) ocupado
open (adj) abierto
outgoing (adj) extrovertido
Arg. dado
Cub. Nic., Par. sociable
overwhelming (adj) abrumador
Chi., Col., Nic. agobiante
polite (adj) cortés, educado

Col. atento, culto
Mex. caballeroso
pretty (adj) guapa
Arg., Cub., Pue.R. linda
Chi. bonita, preciosa
Col. bella, bonita, linda
Dom.R., Ecu., ElS., Gua., Nic.,
Pan., Uru. bonita
quick (adj) rápido
Chi., Col. veloz
quiet (adj) silencioso
Chi., Col., Venz. callado
Dom.R., Pan. tranquilo
Nic. callado, tranquilo
right (adj) correcto
rotten (food) (adj) podrido
Mex. hechado a perder
round (adj) redondo
sad (adj) triste
scared (adj) asustado
Col. atemorizado
sexy (adj) sexy
short (adj) pequeño
Arg., Per., Spa. bajo
Chi., Pan., Pue.R. corto
Col., Dom.R. bajito
Mex. bajo, chaparro, corto
Nic. corto, chingo
shy (adj) tímido
Cub., Nic., Pan. penoso
sleepy (adj) soñoliento
Dom.R. asueñado
Mex.., Nic., Par. adormilado
small (adj) chiquito, pequeño
Arg., Chi. chico
Col. chico, corto, menudo
sour (adj) agrio
Col. ácido, amárgo
Nic., Pan. ácido
spoiled (child) (adj) mimado
Arg., Cub., Pan., Pue.R.
malcriado
Chi. regalón

ABBREVIATIONS: Arg.=Argentina Bol.=Bolivia Chi.=Chile Col.=Colombia Cos.R.=Costa Rica
Cub.=Cuba Dom.R.=Dominican Republic Ecu.=Ecuador ElS.=El Salvador Gua.=Guatemala
Hon.=Honduras Mex.=Mexico Nic.=Nicaragua Pan.=Panama Par.=Paraguay Per.=Peru
Pri.=Primary Term Pue.R.=Puerto Rico Spa.=Spain Uru.=Uruguay Venz.=Venezuela

Col. consentido,
malacostumbrado, malcriado
Cos.R. chineado
Dom.R. ñoño
Ecu. consentido
Mex. chiqueado, consentido
Nic. consentido, malcriado
Per. engreído
square (adj) cuadrado
superb (adj) magnífico
sweet (adj) dulce
talkative (adj) hablador, locuaz
Arg., Par. charlatán
Col. charlatán, dicharachero,
garlador
Nic. hablantín
Pan. conversador
tall (adj) alto
tasty (adj) sabroso
Arg., Spa. rico
Col. apetitoso, rico, suculento
Nic. delicioso, rico
terrible (adj) terrible
terrifying (adj) aterrador
Bol. miedoso
Col. aterrorizante, horripilante,
temible, terrorífico
Nic. espantoso, terrible
tremendous (adj) imponente
Arg., Chi., Cub., Mex., Nic,
Venz. tremendo
Col. asombroso
vacant (adj) libre
Col. desocupado
Dom.R. vacante
Mex., Venz. vacío
Nic. desocupado, vacío
warm (adj) tibio
worse (adj) peor que
worst (adj) el peor
wrong (adj) equivocado
Col. erróneo
Nic. erróneo, incorrecto

Pue.R., Spa. incorrecto
young (adj) joven

Drug Culture

addicted (adj) adicto
Col. narcómano
Nic. drogadicto, drogo (colloq.)
addiction (n) dependencia
Col., Cos.R., Dom.R., Mex., Nic.,
Pan., Pue.R. adicción
alcoholic (n) alcohólico
alcoholic beverage (n phr) bebida
alcohólica
Chi., Nic. trago
become intoxicated (v phr)
intoxicarse
Chi. embriagarse
Cub., Mex., Nic. Pan.
emborracharse
Spa. estar bajo la influencia del
alcohol o de las drogas
cocaine (n) cocaína
Col., Nic. coca
cocaine spoon (n phr) cuchara de
cocaína
Col. cuchara para la cocaína
Mex. grapas de cocaína
Spa. cuchara para cocaína
deal (drugs) (v phr) vender
Col., ElS., Gua., Nic. traficar con
Mex., Venz. traficar
Pue.R. distribuir
drug abuse (n phr) toxicomanía
Col., Cub., Dom.R., Par., Pue.R.
abuso de drogas
drug addict (n phr) drogadicto
Col. narcómano
drug addiction (n phr) drogadicción
Col. narcomanía
Pue.R. adicción a las drogas
drug deal (n phr) transacción de

drogas
Col., Dom.R., Gua., Nic., Spa.,
Uru. tráfico de drogas
Ecu., Venz. negocio de drogas
Pue.R. negociación
drug dealer (n phr) traficante de
drogas
Bol., Cos.R., Cub., Venz.
narcotraficante
drug habit (n phr) drogadicción
Col. narcomanía
Cub. vicio de drogas
drug paraphernalia (n phr) parafernalia
de drogas
drug runner (n phr) narcotraficante
drug squad (n phr) brigada anti-drogas
drug test (n phr) prueba anti-doping
Col., Uru., Venz. prueba anti-
drogas
Cub., Mex., Pue.R. prueba de
drogas
Nic. prueba antidrogas
Pan. prueba para drogas
drug user (n phr) consumidor de
drogas
Pue.R. usuario de drogas
drunk (adj) borracho
Col. bebido
drunkard (n) borracho
Col. beodo, borrachín
Dom.R. borrachón
get high (drugs) (v phr) colocarse
Bol., Per. volar
Chi. volarse
Col. entrar en onda, sollarse,
soltarse, volar
Cub. cojer nota
Dom.R. darse un viaje, ponerse
high
Mex. tocarse, traer un alucine
Nic. ponerse en onda
Pue.R. elevarse, tripear
Venz. meterse un viaje

habit (n) vicio
Col., Nic., Par. hábito
hard drugs (n phr) drogas duras
Col. drogas fuertes
Nic., Par. drogas fuertes
hard liquor (n phr) licor espiritoso
Bol., Dom.R., Venz. licor fuerte
Col. licor de alto contenido
alcohólico
ElS., Pan. licor
Mex., Par. bebidas fuertes
Spa. bebida alcohólica fuerte
Uru. bebida alcohólica
heroin (n) heroína
inhale (drugs) (v) aspirar
Arg., Col., Mex., Nic., Pue.R.
inhalar
Cub., Dom.R. oler
inject (drugs) (v phr) inyectar(se)
intoxicated (adj) borracho
Nic. ebrio, borracho
Pan. borracho
Spa. bajo la influencia
liquor (n) bebidas fuertes
Col., Cub., ElS., Gua., Hon.,
Mex., Pan., Venz. licor
Nic. guaro
Par. bebidas alcóholicas
Spa. bebida alcohólica fuerte
LSD (n) LSD
Cos.R., Cub., Nic. ácido
marijuana (n) marihuana
Col. yerba
Cos.R. monte, mota
Nic. Hierba, monte
marijuana cigarette (n phr) cigarrillo
de marihuana
Arg. porro
Chi. pito
Col. varillo
Cos.R. puro
Cub., Pue.R. pitillo de marihuana
Dom.R. joint, tabaco de

ABBREVIATIONS: Arg.=Argentina Bol.=Bolivia Chi.=Chile Col.=Colombia Cos.R.=Costa Rica
Cub.=Cuba Dom.R.=Dominican Republic Ecu.=Ecuador ElS.=El Salvador Gua.=Guatemala
Hon.=Honduras Mex.=Mexico Nic.=Nicaragua Pan.=Panama Par.=Paraguay Per.=Peru
Pri.=Primary Term Pue.R.=Puerto Rico Spa.=Spain Uru.=Uruguay Venz.=Venezuela

marihuana
marijuana pipe (n phr) pipa de
marihuana
quit using drugs (v phr) dejar las
drogas
Col., Nic. cortar con el vicio
sell drugs (v phr) vender drogas
Pue.R. tirar drogas
share needles (v phr) compartir agujas
Col., Nic. compartir jeringas
Mex. prestarse jeringas
Venz. compartir inyectadoras
soft drugs (n phr) drogas blandas
Col. drogas más suaves, drogas
menos fuertes, drogas no tan
dañinas
Mex., Nic., Par. drogas suaves
use drugs (v phr) drogarse
Col. consumir drogas, usar drogas
ElS., Gua. consumir drogas

Food: Breads & Pastries

bagel (n) rosca de pan
Bol., Col., Pue.R. bagel
baguette (n) baguette
Bol., Chi., Col., Dom.R.,
Nic.,Venz. pan francés
Pan. pan flauta, pan francés
Par. pan flauta
Spa. barra de pan
bake (v) hornear
Spa. cocinar en el horno
batch (n) hornada
Chi. horneada
Col. tanda
Cos.R. lote
Nic. lote, montón
Par. hornalla
biscuit (n) bizcocho, galleta
Arg. galletita
Dom.R. bizcochito

Mex. bisquet
Pue.R. panecillo
bread, rye (n phr) pan negro
Arg., Col., Cub., Dom.R.,
Ecu., Spa., Venz. pan de
centeno
Chi. pan centeno
bread, sliced (n phr) pan de molde
Arg. pan lactal
Col. pan tajado
Cos.R. pan cortado
Dom.R., Par. pan de sandwich
Mex. pan de caja
Pue.R. pan especial
Venz. pan en rodajas
bread, white (n phr) pan blanco
tajado
Arg., Col., Dom.R., Mex.,
Spa., Venz. pan blanco
Cub. pan de molde
Nic. pan blanco de molde
Par. pan
Pue.R. pan especial
Uru. pan blanco rebanado
bun (n) panecillo
Arg., Par., Uru. pancito
Bol., Spa. bollo
Col. pan pequeño
Cos.R. bollito
Mex. pan para hamburgeusas,
pan para hot dogs
Nic. bollo de pan
Pan. pan para hamburguesas
cake (n) pastel
Arg., Chi., Ecu., Par., Uru.,
Venz. torta
Bol., Cos.R., Nic. queque
Col. ponqué
Cub. cake
Dom.R., Pue.R. bizcocho
Pan. cake, dulce
Per. queque, torta
Spa. tarta

cookie (n) galleta
Arg. masita
Chi., Col., Mex., Nic.,
Cos.R., Par., Pue.R., Uru.
galletita
Cub. galletica
ElS., Gua., Hon. galleta
dulce
Per. galleta de dulce
Spa. galleta, pasta
cracker (n) galleta
Arg. galletita
Dom.R. galletica
Nic., Venz. galleta de soda
Par. galletita salada
cream puff (n phr) repolla
Bol., ElS., Gua., Hon., Spa. bollo
de crema
Chi. repollito
Nic. relámpago
Pan. ecler
Uru. bomba de crema
Venz. pastel de crema
croissant (n) croissant
Arg., Col., Par. medialuna
Chi. media luna
Dom.R. cruasant, pan camarón
Mex. cuernito
Per. cachito
Danish (n) pastelillo de fruta y nueces
Mex. pan dulce
Nic. danés de frutas
Pan. danesa
Per. pastel
Venz. pastel danés
dough (n) masa
doughnut (n) dónut
Chi. rosca
Col. dona, rosca
Col., ElS., Gua., Hon., Mex.,
Pan., Pue.R. dona
hallah (Jewish) (n) hallah
knead (v) amasar

muffin (n) panecillo
Arg., Col. muffin
Bol., Par. pancito
Gua. mollete
Mex. mufin, panqué, pastelito
Nic. bollo
Per. quequito
Spa. magdalena
pancake (n) panqueque
Cub., Dom.R., Pan., Pue.R.
pancake
Mex. hotcake
Venz. panqueca
pie (n) pastel, tarta
Bol. pie
Chi., Cos.R. torta
Col. ponqué
Dom.R., Nic. pastel, pie
Mex. pay
Pan., Per., Pue.R. pastel
Venz. tartaleta
puff pastry (n phr) hojaldre
Chi. masa de mil hojas
Nic. hojaldra
Venz. milhoja
rise (bread) (v) leudarse
Bol., Chi., ElS., Gua., Hon.,
Mex., Spa. levantarse
Col. inflarse, levantarse
Cos.R., Dom.R., Ecu., Nic.,
Pan., Pue.R. crecer
roll (n) pancito
Col., Pan. panecillo
ElS., Gua., Spa. bollo
Pue.R. pan
soufflé (n) soufflé
Swiss roll (n phr) rollo
Nic., Spa. brazo de gitano
Uru. rosca
Venz. bollo de pan
tart (n) moldecito
Bol., Chi., Pue.R., Uru., Venz.
tarta

Col. torta
Dom.R. dulcito relleno
Gua. pastelito
Mex. tartaleta
Nic. pastelito, torta
Par. molde
Spa. pastel de frutas
toast (n) tostada
Mex., Pan. pan tostado
waffle (n) gofre
Col. barquillo, waffle
Gua., Nic. wafle
Mex., Par. waffle

Food:
Fruits & Vegetables

almond (n) almendra
apple (n) manzana
apricot (n) albaricoque
Arg., Chi., Uru. damasco
Mex. chabacano
artichoke (n) alcachofa
Arg., Uru. alcaucil
asparagus (n) espárrago
avocado (n) aguacate
Arg., Bol., Chi., Per., Uru. palta
banana (n) plátano
Arg., Par., Uru. banana
Col., Cos.R., Nic. banano
Dom.R., Pan., Pue.R. guineo
Ecu. banano, guineo
Venz. cambur
bean sprouts (n phr) germinados de
soja
Arg., Uru. brotes de soja
ElS., Gua. retoños de soya
Nic., Pan. frijol nacido
Par. brotes de soje
Pue.R. habichuelas de soya
beans (n) porotos

Col., Cub., Gua., Mex., Nic.,
Pan. frijoles
Dom.R., Pue. R. habichuelas
Ecu. Frejoles
Spa. alubias
Venz. caraotas
beans, black (n phr) frijoles
Arg., Par., Uru. porotos
negros
Col., Cub., ElS., Gua., Hon.,
Mex., Nic., Pan. frijoles
negros
Pue.R. habichuelas negras
Spa. alubias negras
Venz. caraotas negras
beans, broad (n phr) habas
Arg., Uru. chauchas
Dom.R. guandules
beans, green (n phr) habichuelas
Arg., Uru. chauchas
Dom.R., Ecu., Per., Venz.
vainitas
ElS., Gua., Hon., Mex. ejotes
Nic. frijolitos verdes
Par. arvejas
Pue.R. habichuelas verdes
Spa. judías verdes
beans, kidney (n phr) habichuelas
Col. frijoles rojos
Cub., Nic. frijoles colorados
Dom.R. habichuelas rojas
Spa. alubias rojas
beans, lima (n phr) frijoles de media
luna
Cub. habas limas
Nic. frijoles blancos
Spa. habas
beet (n) remolacha
Bol., Chi., Per. beterraga
Mex. betabel
berry (n) baya
Nic. frutilla

Par., Pue.R. cereza
black currant (n phr) casis
Col., Mex., Nic., Par. grosella
Pan. pasita
blueberry (n) arándano
Mex. mora azul
Nic. frutilla
Per. mora
Brazil nut (n phr) nuez de Brasil
Col. nuez del Brasil
broccoli (n) brócoli
Brussels sprouts (n phr) coles de
Bruselas
Arg., Uru. repollitos de
Bruselas
Chi. repollitos italianos
Nic. repollitos
cabbage, green (n phr) repollo
verde
Cub., Ecu., Mex., Spa. col
Col., Nic. repollo
Dom.R. lechuga repollada
cabbage, white (n phr) repollo
Cub., Spa. col
Mex. col blanca
cantaloupe (n) melón chino
Chi. melón calameño
Col. cantaloupe, melón
Cub. cantalupa
Nic., Pan., Per., Venz.
melón
carrot (n) zanahoria
cashew (n) nuez de la India
Arg., Par., Uru. castaña de
cajú
Chi. castaña
Dom.R. semilla de cajuil
Nic. semilla de marañón
Pan. pepita de marañon
Pue.R. avellana
cauliflower (n) coliflor
chard (n) acelga
cherry (n) cereza

chestnut (n) castaña
Dom.R. pan de fruta
chickpeas (n) garbanzos
coconut (n) coco
corn (n) maíz
Bol., Chi., Ecu., Per., Uru.
choclo (choclo in Arg. is sweet
corn)
Cub. mazorca (on the cob)
Mex. elote (on the cob)
cranberry (n) arándano agrio
Mex. mora roja
Nic. frutilla
Pue.R. cranberry
Venz. cereza agria
cucumber (n) pepino
Pue.R. pepinillo
date (n) dátil
eggplant (n) berenjena
endive (n) escarola
Arg., Col., Spa. endibia
Col. Endivia
Nic. achicoria
fennel (n) hinojo
fig (n) higo
French fries (n phr) papas fritas
Dom.R. papitas fritas
Spa. patatas fritas
garlic (n) ajo
gooseberry (n) grosella silvestre
Nic., Pue.R. grosella
grape (n) uva
grapefruit (n) toronja
Arg., Chi., Par., Spa., Uru.
pomelo
guava (n) guayaba
hazelnut (n) avellana
Dom.R. coquito
horseradish (n) rábano picante
huckleberry (n) mora
kiwi (n) kiwi
Uru. quivi
kohlrabi (n) colinabo

leek (n) porro
    Arg., Col., Dom.R., Ecu., ElS.,
    Gua., Hon., Spa., Uru. puerro
    Mex., Per. poro
lemon (n) limón
lentils (n) lentejas
lettuce (n) lechuga
lime (n) lima
    Cub., Pan. limón
mandarine orange (n phr) mandarina
    Pue.R. china mandarina
melon (n) melón
mushroom (n) hongo
    Col., Mex., Par. champiñón
    Spa. champiñón, seta
nectarine (n) ciruela de negra
    Chi. durazno pelado
    Col., Cub., Nic. nectarina
    Cos.R., Dom.R. ciruela
    ElS., Gua. nectarino
    Mex. nectarín
    Pan. ciruela negra
    Par., Uru. Pelón
    Pue.R., Venz. nectarine
    Spa. briñón
    Uru. pelón
okra (n) quimbombó
    Dom.R. molondrón
    Mex., Nic. okra
    Par. malva
olive (n) aceituna
    Cos.R. oliva
onion (n) cebolla
onion, pickling (n phr) cebollino
    Chi., Nic. cebollín
    Col. cebollina
    Dom.R. escabeche
    Mex. cebolla de cambray
    Par. cebollit
    Spa. cebolleta
onion, red (Bermuda) (n phr) cebolla
    roja
    Ecu., Par. cebolla colorada

    Mex., Nic. cebolla morada
onion, vidalia (n phr) vidalia
    Bol., Par. cebolla
    Col., Nic. cebolla vidalia
orange (n) naranja
    Dom.R., Pue.R. china
papaya (n) papaya
    Cub. fruta bomba
    Dom.R., Pue.R. lechosa
    Venz. lechoso
parsnip (n) chiriva
    Col. chirivia, chirivía
    Gua. chiviría
    Uru. pastinaca
peach (n) durazno
    Cub., Dom.R., Nic., Par., Per.,
    Pue.R., Spa. melocotón
peanut (n) maní
    Mex. cacahuate
    Spa. cacahuete
pear (n) pera
peas, green (n phr) arvejas
    Cub., Mex. chícharos
    Nic., Pan. petit pois
    Per. arvejitas
    Pue.R., Spa. guisantes
pecan (n) pacana
    Bol., ElS., Gua., Hon. pecana
    Mex., Nic. nuez
pepper, hot (n phr) chile
    Bol., Chi., Venz., Par., Per. ají
    Col., Cub., Pan., Pue.R. ají
    picante
    Cos.R., Nic. chile picante
    Ecu. pimiento picante
    Spa. guindilla
pepper, sweet (n phr) pimiento
    morrón
    Col. pimentón rojo, pimentón
    verde
    Cos.R. chile dulce
    Nic. chiltoma
    Pan. ají dulce, pimentón

Par. locote, pimiento
Per., Venz. pimentón
Spa. pimiento
pine nut (n phr) piñón
pineapple (n) piña
Uru. ananá
pistachio (n) pistacho
Mex. pistache
plum (n) ciruela
pomegranate (n) granada
Cos.R. granadilla
potato (n) papa
Cub., Spa. patata
pumpkin (n) calabaza
Bol., Chi., Pan. zapallo
Col., Venz. ahuyama
quince (n) membrillo
radish (n) rábano
rhubarb (n) ruibarbo
rutabaga (n) nabo sueco
Col. nabo de suecia, rutabaga
Nic. colinabo
Par. nabo
scallion (n) cebolla verde
Bol. cebollita verde
Col. cebolla larga
ElS., Gua., Hon., Nic., Venz.
cebollín
Pan. cebollina
Mex. cebollino
Par. cebollita
shallot (n) chalote
Mex. cebollino, cebollita
Nic. cebollín
Par. cebollita
soybeans (n) frijoles de soja
Chi., Spa. soja
Col., Gua. semillas de soya
Cub., Venz. soya
Nic. frijol de soya
Par., Uru. porotos de soja
spinach (n) espinaca
squash (n) chilacayote

Bol. zapallito
Col., Cos.R., Cub., Ecu., Par.,
Spa. calabaza
Dom.R., Venz. Auyama
Nic. ayote
Pan. chayote
Uru. zapallo
strawberry (n) fresa
Arg., Par. frutilla
sweet potato (n phr) batata
Bol., Ecu., Gua., Mex., Nic., Pan.,
Per. camote
Chi. papa dulce
Cub., Uru. boniato
taro (n) taro
Cub. malanga
Dom.R. yautía
Nic. quequisque
tomato (n) tomate
Mex. jitomate
turnip (n) nabo
watercress (n) berro
watermelon (n) sandía
Col., Venz. patilla
Cub. melón de agua
Dom.R. pastilla
yam (n) ñame
zucchini (n) calabacín
Chi. zapallito italiano
Mex. calabacita
Nic. zucchini
Par. calabaza

Food: Kitchen & Meals

aluminum foil (n phr) papel de
aluminio
Chi., Col., Nic., Pan. papel
aluminio
Cos.R., ElS., Gua., Pan., Per. lámina
de aluminio
appetizer (n) aperitivo

Arg., Dom.R., Uru. entrada
Col. antojitos
Cos.R. bocas
Ecu. entrada, primer plato
Nic. bocas, boquitas
Pan. abreboca
Per. bocaditos
Venz. entremés
baster (n) gotero
blender (n) licuadora
Cub., Dom.R., Spa., Venz.
batidora
bottle opener (n phr) destapador
Chi., Cos.R., Nic., Par. abridor
Pan., Uru. abridor, saca
corcho
Pue.R. abridor de botellas
Spa. abrebotellas
bowl (n) plato hondo
Chi. bol
Col. tazón, vasija
Mex., Par. tazón
Pan. vasija
Spa. cuenco
bowl, mixing (n phr) tazón para medir
Arg., Par. bol
Col. vasija para mezclar
ElS., Gua., Venz. tazón para
mezclar
Mex. tazón para batir
Pan. platón, vasija
bowl, salad (n phr) ensaladera
Col., Pan. plato para ensalada
bowl, soup (n phr) tazón
Col., Venz. plato de sopa
Cub., Dom.R., Ecu. plato
sopero
Nic. plato hondo, plato sopero
Pan. plato hondo, plato para
sopa
Par., Pue.R. sopera
bowl, sugar (n phr) azucarera

brunch (n) brunch
Col. onces
Mex., Par. almuerzo
Nic. comida tarde
Uru. desayuno
Venz. desayuno-almuerzo
butcher block (n phr) bloque de
carnicero
Arg. tabla de cocina
Chi., Col., Nic. tabla para
cortar
Par. tabla de picar
Pue.R. picador
can opener (n phr) abrelatas
Chi. abridor de latas
Cos.R. abridor
canned food (n phr) alimentos
enlatados
Chi. latas de conservas
Col., Dom.R., Pan. comida
enlatada
Nic. comida enlatada,
conservas
carving fork (n phr) trinche
Arg. tenedor
Col., ElS., Gua., Hon.,
Spa. tenedor de trinchar
Nic. tenedor para trinchar
Pan., Pue.R. tenedor para
servir
china (n) porcelana
Chi. loza
Col., Dom.R., Mex. Nic., vajilla
Pan. loza, vajilla fina
coffee maker (n phr) cafetera
Dom.R. greca
colander (n) colador
Bol., Col. coladera
Cos.R., Dom.R., Mex., Per.,
Spa., Uru. escurridor de
verduras
condiments (n) condimentos

breakfast (n) desayuno

cookie cutters (n phr) cortadores de
    galletas
    Arg. moldes
    Chi., Dom.R., Par., Venz. moldes
    de galletas
corkscrew (n) sacacorchos
    Chi. destapador
counter (n) mostrador
    Arg. mesada
    Pue.R. counter
creamer (n) cremera
    Arg. Lechera
    Nic. jarrita de leche
    Spa. jarrita para leche
cup, coffee (n phr) taza para café
    Arg. pocillo, taza de café
    Nic. taza de café
cutting board (n phr) tabla para cortar
    Col., Nic. tabla de cortar
    Pue.R. picador
decanter (n) licorera
    Arg. jarra
    Col., Nic., Spa. garrafa
demitasse (n) tacita de café
    Arg. pocillo, taza de café
    Col. tacita
    Pue.R. pocillito de café
dessert (n) postre
dill (n) eneldo
dinner (n) cena
    Arg., Col., Per., Pue.R. comida
dishes (n) platos
    Pan. trastos, vajilla
dishwasher (n) lavaplatos
    Arg. lavavajilla
    Col., Cub., Pue.R. lavadora de
    platos
    Spa. lavavajillas
    Uru. lava vajilla
disposer (n) triturador
draining spoon (n phr) cuchara para
    escurrir
    Col. cuchara de escurrir

Spa. espumadera
dryer (n) secadora
    Arg. secarropas
    Pue.R. secadora de ropa
egg beater (n phr) batidor manual
    Chi., Nic., Pue.R. batidora
    Ecu. batidor de mano
egg timer (n phr) minutero para
    huevos
freezer (n) congelador
    Arg., Par., Pue.R. freezer
    Bol. refrigerador
    Nic. freezer, mantenedora
funnel (n) embudo
garbage disposer (n phr) triturador de
    basura
ginger (n) jengibre
glass (n) vaso
glassware (n) cristalería
goblet (n) copa
goblet, water (n phr) copa para agua
grater (n) rallador
    Col. rallo
    Dom.R. guallo
    Pue.R. guayo
gravy boat (n) salsera
griddle (n) asador eléctrico
    Col., Pan. sartén eléctrica
    Spa. plancha
grill (n) parrilla
ice bucket (n phr) balde de hielo
    Dom.R., Ecu., Gua., Mex.,
    Venz. hielera
    Nic., Pue.R. cubeta de hielo
icing syringe (n phr) jeringuilla de
    decoración
    Col. jeringuilla para decorar
    Nic. decorador de pasteles
    Venz. decorador para pasteleros
juicer (n) exprimidor
kettle (n) marmita
    Arg., Uru. pava
    Bol. caldera

Chi., Col., Per., Spa. tetera
Cub. caldero
Ecu. cantina de agua
Mex. olla grande
Nic. jarrilla
knife (n) cuchillo
knife sharpener (n phr) afilador de
cuchillo
Dom.R. amolador
knife, butter (n phr) cuchillo para
mantequilla
Arg. cuchillo para manteca
knife, electric (n phr) cuchillo eléctrico
knife, kitchen (n phr) cuchillo de
cocina
knife, steak (n phr) cuchillo para carne
ladle (n) cucharón
lunch (n) almuerzo
Dom.R., Mex., Spa. comida
main course (nphr) plato principal
Arg., Chi., Dom.R., Nic., Par.,
Per., Pue.R., Spa., Uru., Venz.
plato principal
Col. entrada
Mex. platillo principal
measuring cups (n phr) tazas para
medir
Dom.R., Nic. tazas medidoras
measuring spoons (n phr) cucharas
para medir
Dom.R. cucharas medidoras
Nic. cucharas de medida
meat grinder (n phr) molino de carne
Arg., Col., Dom.R. moledora de
carne
Cub. molidora
Pan., Pue.R. moledor de carne
microwave (oven) (n) micro
Arg., Col., Cub., Par., Uru.
microonda
Chi., Mex., Nic., Pue.R., Spa.,
Venz. microondas
mixer (n) batidora

Cub. mezclador
muffin pan (n phr) molde para
panecillos
Arg. molde para muffin
Bol. molde para pancitos
Mex. molde para mufin, molde
para pastelitos
Nic. molde para bollos
Par. molde para pan
Per. molde para quequitos
Spa. molde para magdalenas
mug (n) jarro
Arg. jarrita, jarrito
Chi. jarra, tazón
Cub. vaso
ElS., Gua. pocillo
Nic. jarra, pocillo
Pue.R., Spa., Venz. jarra
mug, beer (n phr) jarra para cerveza
Arg. porrón
Mex. jarro de cerveza
Nic., Pue.R., Spa., Venz. jarra de
cerveza
Par. manija
mug, coffee (n phr) jarra para café
Arg. jarrito, jarrita
Cub. taza de café
ElS., Gua., Nic. pocillo para café
Mex. jarro para café
Pue.R. tazón de café
Venz. jarrita para café
nutcracker (n) cascanueces
nutmeg (n) nuez moscada
Par., Pue.R. nuez
omelet (n) omelete
Bol., Col., Cub., Par., Per.,
Pue.R., Spa., Venz. tortilla
Dom.R. tortilla española
Nic. torta de huevo
oregano (n) orégano
oven (n) horno
pan (n) sartén
parsley (n) perejil

pastry brush (n phr) pincel de
  repostería
  Col., Gua., ElS., Nic., Pan.
  brocha de repostería
pastry cutting wheel
  (n phr) cortapastas
  Col. rodete para cortar masa
  Nic. rueda para cortar masa
peeler (n) pelador
  Mex. pelapapas
pepper shaker (n phr) pimentera
  Arg., Col., Gua., Mex., Nic.,
  Per. pimentero
  Pue.R. pimienta
  Venz. pimientero
pickle (n) pepino encurtido
  Cub. pepino
  Dom.R., Mex., Par., Pue.R.
  pepinillo
  Spa. pepinillo en vinagre
  Venz. encurtido
pie pan (n phr) molde para pastel
  Arg. molde para tartas
  Chi. molde para pie
  Dom.R. molde de bizcocho
  Mex. molde para pay
  Nic. model para pastel / pie
pitcher (n) jarra
  Chi. jarrón
  Gua., Nic. pichel
platter (n) fuente de servir
  Col., Nic., Pan., Par. bandeja
  Mex. platón
pot (n) olla
  Arg., Par. cacerola
  Nic. porra
  Spa. puchero
potato masher (n phr) majador de
  papas
  Chi. moledor de papas
  Mex. prensapapas
  Nic. colador de papas
  Par., Uru. triturador de papas

Per. machucador de papas
preserves (n) conserva (de alimentos)
  Chi., Col., Nic. conservas
  Dom.R. preservas
  Per., Spa. mermelada
refrigerator (n) refrigerador
  Arg., Par. heladera
  Col., Dom.R., Pue.R., Venz.
  nevera
  Cos.R. refrí
  Ecu., nevera, refrigeradora
  Nic., Per. refrigeradora
  Spa. frigorífoco, nevera
roasting pan (n phr) sartén para asar
  Col., Nic. bandeja para hornear
  Spa. bandeja para el horno
  Venz. olla para hornear
rolling pin (n phr) rodillo
  Arg. palo de amasar
  Bol., Chi. fuslero
  Per. amasador
rosemary (n) romero
salad (n) ensalada
salt shaker (n phr) salero
saucepan (n) cacerola
  Arg., Pue.R. olla
  Col. perol
  Nic. olla, perol, porra
  Spa. cazo
shot glass (n phr) copa de trago
  Chi. medida para bebida
  Col. copita
  Dom.R. vaso de trago corto
  Mex. caballo (big), caballito
  (small), vaso tequilero
  Nic. copita
  Pue.R. vasito
  Spa. chupito
sieve (n) cedazo
  Arg., Spa. tamiz
  Chi., Cub., Venz. colador
  Col. coladera, tamiz
  Mex. coladera

Nic. zaranda
silverware (n) cubiertos
   Col. platería
skimmer (n) espumadera
   Col. desnatadora
   Mex. desnatador
snack (n) merienda
   Col. bocadillo, refrigerio
   Dom.R. picadera
   Mex. botana
   Spa. snack
snifter (n) copa ancha de boca estrecha
   Chi. copa de cognac
soup tureen (n phr) sopera
spatula (n) espátula
stove (n) estufa
   Arg., Bol., Chi., Nic., Per., Spa.,
   Uru. cocina
teapot (n) tetera
thyme (n) tomillo
toaster (n) tostador
   Chi., Col., Cub., Dom.R., Ecu.,
   Pue.R., Spa., Venz. tostadora
tongs (n) tenazas
   Arg., Col., Spa. pinzas
tumbler (n) vaso para whiskey
   Arg., Nic. vaso
turner (n) pala
   Pan. espátula
   Venz. paleta
vacuum cleaner (n phr) aspiradora
   Cub., Cos.R. aspirador

Hobbies & Recreation: Movies & Television

actor (n) actor
   Col. artista, galán
actress (n) actriz
   Col. artista
animation (n) animación

banned film (n phr) película prohibida
   Col., Dom.R. película censurada
broadcast (v) emitir
   Col., Cos.R., ElS., Gua., Hon.,
   Nic.,Venz. transmitir
broadcast (v) emitir
   Col., Cos.R., ElS., Gua., Hon.,
   Venz. transmitir
cable television (n phr) televisión por
   cable
   Arg., Cub. cable
   Dom.R. telecable
   Mex. cable, cablevisión
cartoon (n) dibujo animado
   Col., Spa. dibujos
   animados
   Cub., Dom.R., Nic., Pue.R.
   muñequitos
   Mex. caricatura
   Pan. caricaturas
cast (show) (n) equipo artístico
   Chi., Pan.. Par., Pue.R. elenco
   Col., Mex., Spa., Venz. reparto
   Nic. reparto, elenco
channel (n) canal
   Spa. cadena
commercial (n) anuncio
   Arg. aviso, propaganda
   Chi., Ecu., Par., Per. propaganda
   Col. anuncio comercial,
   comercial, propaganda
   Dom.R., Mex. comercial
   Pan., Venz. comercial,
   propaganda
double feature (movies) (n phr)
   doble función
   Bol. película doble
   Col. doble
   Dom.R. doble presentación
   Mex. programa doble
   Nic. doble tanda
   Spa. sesión de dos películas

---

seguidas
   Uru. función doble
   Venz. cine continuado
drama (movies) (n) drama
drive-in (n) motocine
   Col., Pue.R. drive-in
   Dom.R. auto-cinema
   Mex. autocinema
   Pan., Per., Venz. autocine
dubbing (n) doblaje
film (n) película
   Arg., Cos.R., Ecu., Uru., Pan.
   filme
   Chi., Col., Cub. cinta
   Venz. film
film, dubbed (n phr) película doblada
film, silent (n phr) película muda
footage (n) metraje
frame (movie) (n phr) imagen
   Col., Nic. cuadro
game show (television) (n phr)
   programa concurso
   Arg. programa de
   entretenimientos
   Col. programa de concurso
   Cos.R. concurso televisivo
   Dom.R., Gua., Mex., Venz.
   programa de concursos
host (show) (n) presentador
   Col. animador
   Dom.R., Mex., Venz. anfitrión/a
   Per. maestro de ceremonias
infomercial (n) comercial informativa
   Col. anuncio informativo,
   programa comercial para
   promocionar algo
   Cos.R. boletín informativo
   Spa. telepromoción
   Uru. información de interés
interview (n) entrevista
interview (v) entrevistar
interviewee (n) entrevistado/a
   Arg., Cos.R., Cub., Ecu., ElS.,

Gua., Hon., Per., Pue.R.
   encuestado/a
interviewer (n) entrevistador/a
   Arg., Cos.R., Cub., Ecu., ElS.,
   Gua., Hon., Per., Pue.R.
   encuestador/a
live broadcast (n phr) transmisión en
   directa
   Arg. programa en vivo,
   transmisión en directo
   Bol., Col., ElS., Gua., Uru.
   transmisión en directo
   Chi., Nic., Per. transmisión en
   vivo y en directo
   Cos.R., Cub., Dom.R., Ecu.,
   Pan., Spa., Venz. transmisión en
   vivo
   Mex. transmisión directa,
   transmisión en vivo
   Par. transmisión en directo,
   transmisión en vivo
movie (n) película
movie, action (n phr) película de
   acción
movie, documentary (n phr) película
   documental
movie, foreign (n phr) película
   extranjera
movie, G-rated (n phr) película para
   todo público
   Mex. película para todo público
   clasificación A
   Nic. apta para todo público
movie, horror (n phr) película de
   miedo
   Arg., Col., Cos.R., Dom.R., Nic.,
   Par.película de terror
   Mex., Uru. película de horror
   Pue.R., Venz. película de horror,
   película de terror
movie, PG-rated (n phr) película
   para todo público
   Mex. película para adolescentes

y adultos clasificación B
Nic. apta para todo público
Pue.R. película público general
Spa. película apta para todos los
públicos
Venz. película censura B
movie, western (n phr) película de
vaqueros
Arg. película de cowboys
Spa. western
movie, X-rated (n phr) película para
adultos
Col. película clasificación X
Cub. película pornográfica
Mex. película sólo para adultos
clasificación C
Nic. película sólo para adultos
Pue.R. película X
musical (movie) (n) película musical
Dom.R., Nic., Pue.R. músical
network (television) (n) cadena
Dom.R. telecadena
news brief (n phr) breves
Chi. breves informativos
Col. informativo breve
Cos.R. resúmen noticioso
Dom.R. titulares
Gua. resúmen de noticias
Mex. noticiero breve
Per., Venz. resúmen de noticias
newscast (n) telediario
Arg., Chi., Col., Ecu., Pan.
noticiero
Cos.R., Nic. telenoticiero
Cub. reporte
Dom.R. noticiero, telenoticiero
Mex. noticias, noticiero
Par. noticiero, telenoticias
Spa. noticiario
premiere (n) estreno
program (n) programa
Cub., Dom.R. show
props (n) accesorios

Col. ayudas de escenario, soporte
Mex. adornos
release (n) estreno
remote control (n phr) control remoto
Spa. mando a distancia
satellite television (n phr) televisión
por satélite
Nic. parabolica
Par. televisión satelital
Spa. televisión vía satélite
screen (television) (n phr) pantalla
screenplay (n) guión cinematográfico
Bol. telón
Bol. telón
Dom.R., ElS., Gua., Hon.
libreto
Nic. guión
Par. guión , libreto
Spa. argumento
script (n) guión
set (movie) (n) escenario
Chi. estudios
Col. decorado
Spa. plató
shoot (movie) (v) rodar
Nic., Venz. filmar
shooting (movie) (n) rodaje
Nic., Venz. filmación
show (movie) (v) proyectar
Arg. dar, pasar
Col. presentar
Dom.R. pasar
Nic. exhibir, presentar
Venz. mostrar
sitcom, situation comedy (n phr)
comedia de situación
Chi., Col., Dom.R., Nic., Spa.
comedia
slow motion (n phr) cámara lenta
soap opera (n phr) telenovela
Arg., Cub. novela
sound effects (n phr) efectos sonoros
Arg., Col., Mex., Nic., Pan.,

Pue.R., Spa., Venz. efectos de
sonido
sound track (n phr) banda sonora
Arg. banda de sonido
Mex., Pue.R. música
Nic. pista
Venz. pista de sonido
stage (n) escenario
stunt (n) acrobática
Col., Mex. truco
Dom.R., Pue.R. doblaje
Nic., Spa., Venz. acrobacia
stuntman (n) acróbata
Arg. extra Arg. extra
Col. aquel que realiza los trucos
Dom.R., Mex., Pue.R. doble
Nic. doble, extra
Spa. doble, especialista
Venz. especialista en acrobacias
subtitles (n) subtítulos
Cub., Pan., Uru. leyendas
talk show (n phr) programa de
entrevistas
Col. programa de charlas
Nic. programa en vivo
television set (n phr) televisor
Col., Mex., Spa. televisión
television viewer (n phr) televidente
Col. teleaudiencia
turn off (television) (v phr) apagar
turn on (television) (v phr) prender
Bol., Chi., Cub., Ecu., Gua.,
Nic., Par., Spa., Uru. encender
videocamera (n) cámara de vídeo
videocassette (n) videocasete
Col. casete para vídeo
Dom.R. casette
Spa. cinta de vídeo
videocassette recorder (VCR) (n phr)
videograbadora
Arg., Mex., Nic. videocasetera
Chi. VCR
Col. grabadora de vídeo, VCR

Spa. vídeo
videogame (n) videojuego
Col., Cos.R., Dom.R., Mex.,
Nic., Venz. juego de vídeo
watch television (v phr) ver tele(visión)
Col., Nic. mirar televisión
Spa. ver la televisión
weather report (n phr) boletín
meteorológico
Arg., Nic., Par. pronóstico del
tiempo
Col. reporte del estado del
tiempo
Venz. reporte del tiempo,
reporte meteorológico
weather reporter (n phr)
meteorólogo
Venz. reportero del tiempo,
reportero meteorológico

Hobbies & Recreation: Music

accordion (n) acordeón
alto (n) contralto
bagpipes (n) gaita
band (music) (n) banda
banjo (n) banjo
Spa. banyo
bar (music) (n) compás
Col. barra (entre compases)
bar rest (n phr) compás de espera
bass (stereo) (n) graves
Col., Nic., Par. bajo
bass (voice) (n) bajo
Col. Contrabajo
Nic. voz de bajo
bass clef (n phr) clave de fa
bass drum (n phr) bombo
bassoon (n) fagot
beat (music) (n) ritmo
bongo drum (n phr) bongó

bow (n) arco
brass section (n phr) bronces
    Col. cobres
    Mex., Nic. metales
    Spa. instrumentos de metal
bugle (n) clarín
    Col. Corneta
    Nic. trompeta
    Spa. cornetín
castanets (n) castañuelas
celesta (n) celesta
    Col. celeste
chord (n) acorde
    Col. cuerda
chorus (people) (n) coro
chorus (refrain) (n) estribillo
clarinet (n) clarinete
classical music (n phr) música clásica
compact disk (n phr) disco compacto
    Arg., Col., Nic., Pan. CD
    Spa. CD, compact disk
compact disk player (n phr) tocadiscos
    Arg. equipo de música para CD
    Col. aparato de CD
    Cos.R., Nic. CD-player
    Cub. reproductor de compact-disc
    Dom.R. CD player, tocador de discos compactos
    ElS., Gua., Venz. reproductor de discos compactos
    Mex. tocadiscos para discos compactos
    Par. CD-player, compactera
    Spa. reproductor de CD
concert (n) concierto
conduct (music) (v) dirigir
    Col. conducir
conductor (n) director de orquesta
conga drum (n phr) conga
    Cub. tumbadora
    Venz. tambor de conga

contrabassoon (n) contrabajón
    Mex. Contrafagot, Nic. contrabajo
cornet (n) cornetín
    Cub., Nic., Par., Mex., Spa. corneta
cymbals (n) platillos
double bass (n phr) contrabajo
double reed (n phr) doble caña
drum (n) tambor
    Dom.R., Nic. batería
drum major (n phr) tambor mayor
drum, tap (v) tamborilear
    Col., Spa. tocar el tambor
drummer (n) tamborilero
    Col. el que toca el tambor, tambor
    Dom.R. baterista
    Nic. baterista, batero (fam.), bataca (fam.)
duo (n) dúo
    Col. dueto
electric guitar (n phr) guitarra eléctrica
English horn (n phr) corno inglés
    Col. cuerno inglés
    Nic. corneta inglesa
flute (n) flauta
flutist (n) flautista
four-four, common time (n phr) compás mayor
    Nic., Spa. compás de cuatro por cuatro
French horn (n phr) corno francés
    Col. cuerno francés
    Nic. corneta francesa
    Spa. trompa de pistones
fret (on guitar) (n) traste
gong (n) gong
group (music) (n) grupo musical
guitar (n) guitarra
guitar player (n phr) guitarrista
harmonica (n) armónica
harp (n) arpa
harpsichord (n) clavicordio
hit (song) (n) canción de moda

ABBREVIATIONS: Arg.=Argentina Bol.=Bolivia Chi.=Chile Col.=Colombia Cos.R.=Costa Rica
Cub.=Cuba Dom.R.=Dominican Republic Ecu.=Ecuador ElS.=El Salvador Gua.=Guatemala
Hon.=Honduras Mex.=Mexico Nic.=Nicaragua Pan.=Panama Par.=Paraguay Per.=Peru
Pri.=Primary Term Pue.R.=Puerto Rico Spa.=Spain Uru.=Uruguay Venz.=Venezuela

Col. éxito
Cos.R., Nic. éxito, hit
Cub., Dom.R. hit
hum (n) zumbido
   Col. susurro
hum (v) tararear
hymn (n) cántico
   Bol., Col., Dom.R., Mex., Nic.,
   Spa., Venz. himno
   Pue.R. canción, himno
jam session (n phr) sesión de músicos
   de jazz o rock que tocan por
   placer propio
   Chi., Nic. ensayo
   Col. sesión de música
   improvisado
   Cub. descarga
   Pue.R. jameo
   Spa. jam session
jazz music (n phr) música jazz
   Col., Nic. música de jazz
   Dom.R., Spa. jazz
kettledrum (n) timbal
key (music) (n) tono
   Col. tonalidad
key (n) tecla
keyboard (n) teclado
lip synch (v phr) doblar
   Dom.R., Nic. hacer mímica
love song (n phr) canción de amor
   Col., Pue.R. canción romántica
lyre (n) lira
lyrics (n) letra de una canción
   Dom.R. letras de una canción
major chord (n phr) acorde mayor
mandolin (n) mandolina
   Chi. mandolín
maraca (n) maraca
metronome (n) metrónomo
minor chord (n phr) acorde menor
mouthpiece (n) boquilla
music stand (n phr) atril
neck (guitar) (n) mástil

Chi. cuello
Nic. brazo
oboe (n) oboe
octave (n) octava
orchestra (n) orquesta
organ (n) órgano
panpipe (n) zampoña
percussion (n) percusión
percussionist (n) percusionista
performer (n) artista
   Col. intérprete
   Mex. intérprete, músico
   Nic. actor, actriz
piano (n) piano
piccolo (n) pícolo
   Col., Mex., Par., Spa. flautín
pipe organ (n) órgano de tubos
play (instrument) (v) tocar
quartet (n) cuarteto
quintet (n) quinteto
record (music) (v) grabar
record album (n phr) álbum
   Col. disco
record player (n phr) tocadiscos
recorder (instrument) (n) flauta dulce
reed (n) caña
resonant (adj) sonoro
   Col. estruendoso
   Mex. resonante
   Nic. estruendoso, ruidoso
rhythm (n) ritmo
rock music (n phr) música rock
   Col., Par. música de rock
   Dom.R., Spa. rock
saxophone (n) saxofón
sextet (n) sexteto
sing (v) cantar
sing harmony (v phr) cantar en
   armonía
   Pue.R. cantar afinados
   Par. cantar afinado
   Pue.R. cantar afinados
single reed (n phr) caña simple

ABBREVIATIONS: Arg.=Argentina Bol.=Bolivia Chi.=Chile Col.=Colombia Cos.R.=Costa Rica
Cub.=Cuba Dom.R.=Dominican Republic Ecu.=Ecuador ElS.=El Salvador Gua.=Guatemala
Hon.=Honduras Mex.=Mexico Nic.=Nicaragua Pan.=Panama Par.=Paraguay Per.=Peru
Pri.=Primary Term Pue.R.=Puerto Rico Spa.=Spain Uru.=Uruguay Venz.=Venezuela

sitar (n) sitar
　　Nic. cítara
　　Venz. guitarra oriental
snare (of drum) (n) cuerdas
　　Nic. bordón　Col. bordón, tirante
snare drum (n phr) tarola
　　Col. tambor militar pequeño
　　Cos.R. , Nic. redoblante
song (n) canción
　　Arg. tema
　　Col. canto
songbook (n) cancionero
soprano (n) soprano
string (n) cuerda
string (v) encordar
string quartet (n phr) cuarteto de
　　cuerdas
　　Spa. cuarteto de cuerda
strum (v) guitarrear
　　Col., Nic., rasgar, rasguear
　　Cos.R. rasgar
　　Spa. rasguear
strumming (n) guitarreo
　　Col., Spa. rasgueado
　　Cos.R. rasgueo
　　Nic. rasgueado, rasgueo
symphony orchestra (n phr) orquesta
　　sinfónica
synthesizer (n) sintetizador
tambour (n) tamborín
tambourine (n) pandero
　　Chi., Col., Cub., Dom.R., Ecu.,
　　Nic., Pue.R., Spa. pandereta
tape (cassette) (n) cinta
　　Arg., Col., Venz. casete
　　Dom.R., Mex., Nic., Par.
　　cassette
tenor (n) tenor
tenor drum (n phr) teno
　　Col. tambor de tenor
　　Nic. tambor tenor
　　Par., Spa. tenor
timpani (n) timbal

　　Col., Cub. tímpanos
tom-tom (n) tam-tam
　　Col. tantán
　　Spa. tamtan
tone (n) sonoridad
　　Col., Dom.R., Mex., Nic. tono
treble (stereo) (n) de agudos
　　Col., Nic., Par. tonos agudos
　　Spa. agudos
treble clef (n phr) clave de sol
triangle (n) triángulo
trio (n) trío
trombone (n) trombón
trumpet (n) trompeta
trumpeter (n) trompetista
tuba (n) tuba
tuning fork (n phr) diapasón
tuning hammer (n phr) afinador
two-four time (n phr) compás menor,
　　compasillo
　　Nic., Par., Spa. compás de dos por
　　cuatro
upright piano (n phr) piano vertical
valve (trumpet) (n) pistón
　　Mex. llave
viola (n) viola
violin (n) violín
violoncello (n) violoncelo
　　Spa. violonchelo
voice (n) voz
xylophone (n) xilófono
　　Cub., Par. marimba
zither (n) cítara

Hobbies & Recreation: Sports

aerobics (n) aerobismo
　　Col., Mex. aerobics
　　Dom.R., ElS., Gua., Nic. Pan.,
　　Pue.R., Uru. aeróbicos
　　Spa. aerobic
amateur (n) amateur
　　Col., Mex., Nic., Venz. aficionado

Chi. amador
Cub. no profesional
Per. novato
athlete (n) atleta
Nic., Pan. deportista
back (soccer) (n) defensa
Spa. defensor
backstroke (swimming) (n) estilo
espalda
Cub. al revés
Mex. dorso
ball (soccer) (n) pelota de fútbol
Col. balón
Pue.R. bola de balompié
Spa. Balón
basket (basketball) (n) cesta
Arg., Mex., Nic., Pan., Per.,
Uru. canasta
Bol. cesto
Col. caneca
Dom.R., Pue.R. canasto
basketball (n) baloncesto
Arg., Per., Uru. basketbol
Mex., Pan., Par. basketball
Nic. basket
boat race (n phr) regata
boxer (n) boxeador
Chi. pugilista
breaststroke (swimming) (n) estilo
braza
Arg. brazada
Chi., Col., Cub., Par., Pue.R.,
Venz. estilo pecho
Dom.R. brazado de pecho
ElS., Gua. brazada de pecho
Mex., Nic. pecho
broad jump (n phr) salto de longitud
Chi., ElS., Gua., Nic., Par. salto
largo
Col. salto ancho
Pue.R. salto a lo largo
butterfly (swimming) (n) estilo
mariposa

canoe (n) canoa
challenger (boxing)
(n) contrincante
Col. contendor, retador
Dom.R., Mex., Nic., Par.
retador
Uru. aspirante
Venz. retador de boxeo
compete (v) competir
contestant (n) competidor
Chi., Par. concursante
Cub., Pue.R. participante
Nic. Candidato, concursante
court (tennis) (n) cancha
crawl (swimming) (n) crawl
Chi., Nic. estilo libre
Gua., Spa. estilo crol
Pue.R., Uru. brazada
discus throwing (n phr) lanzamiento
de disco
diver (n) buceador, buzo
Chi. hombre rana
Cub. clauadista
diving (n) bucear, buceo
forward (soccer) (n) delantero
freestyle (swimming) (n) estilo libre
goalie (n) portero
Arg., Chi., Par., Per. arquero
Col. guarda-vallas
Cub. guardameta
Pan. goleador
Pue.R. porteador
Uru. golero
golf ball (n phr) pelota de golf
Col., Mex., Pue.R. bola de golf
golf club (n phr) palo de golf
Col. taco de golf
Pan. club de golf
golf course (n phr) campo de golf
Arg. cancha de golf
gymnastics (n) gimnasia
handball (n) handbol
ElS., Gua. balonmano

ABBREVIATIONS: Arg.=Argentina Bol.=Bolivia Chi.=Chile Col.=Colombia Cos.R.=Costa Rica
Cub.=Cuba Dom.R.=Dominican Republic Ecu.=Ecuador ElS.=El Salvador Gua.=Guatemala
Hon.=Honduras Mex.=Mexico Nic.=Nicaragua Pan.=Panama Par.=Paraguay Per.=Peru
Pri.=Primary Term Pue.R.=Puerto Rico Spa.=Spain Uru.=Uruguay Venz.=Venezuela

Uru. pelota de mano
high jump (n phr) salto de altura
  Chi., Col., ElS., Gua., Hon. salto
  alto
  Pue.R. salto a lo alto
hole (golf) (n) hoyo
hole in one (n phr) hoyo en uno
  Pue.R. bola en uno
horizontal bar (n phr) barra fija
  Col., Nic., Pan., Par., Pue.R.,
  Venz. barra horizontal
horseback riding (n phr) equitación
  Col., Par. montar a caballo,
  cabalgar
  Cub. ir a caballo
hurdles race (n phr) vallas
  Chi. obstáculos
  Col. competencia de obstáculos
  Cub., Dom.R., ElS., Gua.,
  Hon., Venz. carrera de obstáculos
ice hockey (n phr) hockey sobre hielo
ice skating (n phr) patinaje sobre hielo
  Chi., Cub. patinaje en hielo
  Col. patinaje en el hielo
instructor (sports) (n) instructor de
  deportes
  Arg., Bol., Chi., Cub., Nic.
  entrenador
  Col. instructor deportivo
  Pue.R. maestro de educación
  física
  Venz. entrenador de deportes
javelin throwing (n phr) lanzamiento
  de jabalina
jump (n) salto
kayak (n) kayac
manager (sports) (n) manager
  deportivo
  Col., Pan. administrador
  deportivo
  Mex. técnico
  Mex., Par. técnico
  Venz. administrador deportivo,

gerente deportivo
marathon (n) maratón
motorcycle, motorbike (n)
  motocicleta, moto
  Pue.R. motora
offside (n) fuera de juego
  Arg. offside
  Col., ElS., Gua., Hon. de
  posición adelantada
  Mex. lateral
  Par. posición adelantada
  Pue.R. fuera de posición
parallel bars (n phr) barras paralelas
player (n) jugador
pole vault (n phr) salto con garrocha
  Nic., Pue.R. salto con pértiga
  Spa. salto de pértiga
  Venz. salto de garrocha
racetrack (horse) (n) hipódromo
racetrack (runners or cars) (n) pista
record (sports) (n) récord deportivo
referee (n) árbitro
  Arg. referee
  Bol., Col., Ecu., Per. juez
  Mex. refere
  Nic. juez, réferi
  Pan. referí
relay (swimming) (n) relevo
ring (boxing) (n) ring de boxeo
  Chi., Par. cuadrilátero
  Col., Nic., Pue.R., Uru. cuadrilátero
  de boxeo
rowing (n) remo
runner (n) corredor
shot put (n phr) lanzamiento de peso
  Nic. la nzamiento de bala
  Par., Pue.R. lanzamiento de pesa
ski jump (n phr) trampolín
  Venz. salto en esquíes
skiing (n) esquí
soccer (n) fútbol
  Pue.R. balompié
sprint (v) esprintar

Chi. picar
Col., Dom.R., Par. correr a toda
velocidad
Cub. correr
Nic. balacearse, correr a toda
velocidad
stair machine (n phr) escaladora
Cos.R. máquina escalera
Dom.R. máquina de hacer
ejercicios
Mex. escalera
stationary bicycle (n phr) bicicleta
estacionaria
Mex. bicicleta fija
Pan. bicicleta estable
Par. bicicleta
Spa. bicicleta estática
swimming (n) natación
swimming pool (n phr) piscina
Arg., Par. pileta
Mex. alberca
team (n) equipo
tennis (n) tenis
track (n) pista
trainer (sports) (n) entrenador
treadmill (n) rueda de andar
Col. caminador
Cos.R., Nic. banda sin fin
Dom.R. máquina de caminar
Mex., Uru. caminadora
Par. caminor
Pue.R. máquina de correr
triple jump (n phr) salto triple
Arg., Col. triple salto
umpire (baseball) (n) umpire
Cub., Ecu., Uru., Venz. árbitro
Mex. ampayer
Nic. árbitro, juez
water skiing (n phr) esquí acuático
Chi., Par. ski acuático
Cos.R., Ecu., ElS., Gua., Per.,
Venz. esquí náutico
weight lifting (n phr) levantamiento

de pesas
Chi. alterofilismo
yacht (n) yate
yoga (n) yoga

Hobbies & Recreation: Workbench

anvil (n) yunque
awl (n) lezna
Bol., Nic., Spa., Venz. punzón
Col. lezana, punzón, tezna
Mex. berbiquí
ax (n) hacha
blowtorch (n) soplete
Pan., Pue.R. antorcha
brush (n) brocha, cepillo
bucket (n) balde
Col., Mex., Spa. cubeta
Cub. cubo
bucksaw (n) sierra de ballesta
Nic., Uru. serrucho
Par. sierra
Spa. sierra de bastidor
chainsaw (n) serrucho eléctrico
Arg., Cos.R., Nic., Par.,
Spa. motosierra
Chi., Col., Uru. sierra
eléctrica
Mex., Pue.R. sierra eléctrica
clamp (n) abrazadera
Chi., Par., Uru., Venz.,
Col. grapa
Cos.R. prensa
Mex. Pinzas
Nic., brida
dowel (n) clavija
Gua. tarugo
Mex. espiga, pasador
Nic. pasador
drill bit (n phr) broca

ABBREVIATIONS: Arg.=Argentina Bol.=Bolivia Chi.=Chile Col.=Colombia Cos.R.=Costa Rica
Cub.=Cuba Dom.R.=Dominican Republic Ecu.=Ecuador ElS.=El Salvador Gua.=Guatemala
Hon.=Honduras Mex.=Mexico Nic.=Nicaragua Pan.=Panama Par.=Paraguay Per.=Peru
Pri.=Primary Term Pue.R.=Puerto Rico Spa.=Spain Uru.=Uruguay Venz.=Venezuela

Pue.R., Venz. barrena
drill, hand (n phr) taladro de mano
Arg., Ecu., Per., Spa., Uru.
taladradora de mano
Chi. taladro
Col., Mex. taladro manual
easel (n) caballete
Chi., Col., Spa. atril
file (n) lima
hacksaw (n) sierra de metal
Col. sierra para cortar metal
Cub., Nic. serrucho
Mex., Spa. sierra para metal
Pue.R. segueta
Venz. serrucho, sierra para metales
hatchet (n) hacha
Col. hachuela
hoe (n) azada
Bol. azador
Col., Pan. asadón
Dom.R., Gua., Nic. azadón
Mex. talacho
Venz. azadón, pico
hose, garden (n phr) manguera
ladder (n) escalera
lawn mower (n phr) cortacéspedes
Arg. máquina de cortar pasto
Bol. cortadora
Chi. cortapasto
Col. máquina para cortar el
pasto
Cub. máquina de cortar
hierba
ElS., Gua., Hon. cortagrama
Mex. podadora de pasto
Nic. podadora de césped /
grama
Par. cortacésped, corta-
pasto
Per. cortador de césped,
cortador del pasto
Pue.R. cortadora de grama
Spa. cortacésped

Venz. cortagrama, segadora
lawn rake (n phr) barredora
Arg., Chi., Col., Cub.,
Dom.R., Mex., Nic., Pan.,
Par. rastrillo
level (n) nivel
Chi. nivelador
Par., Uru. plomada
nut (n) tuerca
oil can (n phr) aceitera
Arg., Cub., Nic., Venz. lata de
aceite
Col. tarro de aceite
pail (n) balde
Cub. cubo
Mex., Pue.R. cubeta
Venz. balde, tobo
paintbrush (n) brocha de pintar, pincel
painter's knife (n phr) navaja de pintor
Mex. espátula, raspa
Nic., Par. espátula
pallet (n) paleta
Chi. palé
Mex. palet, tarima
Par., Uru. plataforma
penknife (n) navaja
Chi., Spa., Venz. cortaplumas
Pue.R. cuchilla
pincers (n) tenazas
Col., Mex. pinzas
plane (carpentry) (n) plano
Arg., Col., Dom.R., Mex., Nic.,
Spa., Uru. cepillo
pliers (n) pinzas
Chi., Cos.R., Dom.R., Nic., Per.,
Pue.R., Venz. alicate
Col., Pan., Spa. alicates
Mex. alicatas
pruning shears (n phr) podadera
Arg., Dom.R., Nic., Spa. tijeras
de podar
Bol., Ecu., Pue.R. podadora
Col. tijeras para podar

Mex. podadoras
Par. podadora, tijera de podar
Venz. tijera podadora
rake (n) rastrillo
reamer (n) escariador
   Mex. escariadora
   Pue.R. arado
   Par., Pue.R. arado
   Spa. fresadora
   Uru. escardador
rivet (n) remache
ruler (n) regla
saw (n) sierra
   Arg., Cub., Nic., Per. serrucho
scraper (n) rascador
   Chi. raspadora
   Col. cuchilla raspadora
   Mex. raspa
   Nic., Pue.R. espátula
   Par., Venz. raspador
screwdriver (n) destornillador
   Chi. llave
   Mex., Per. desarmador
   Nic. desarmador, desatornillador
scythe (n) guadaña
   Mex. zapapico
   Par. hoz
shovel (n) pala
   Per. palana
sickle (n) hoz
   Mex. pico
   Pue.R. yunta
sledgehammer (n) almádena
   Chi., Dom.R., Mex., Nic., Par.
   mazo
   Pue.R. marrón
spade (n) pala
   Chi. pica
   Venz. pico
spatula (n) espátula
sprinkler (n) rociador
   Arg. regador
   Cub., Par. regadera

Mex. regilete
Nic., Spa. aspersor
stepladder (n) escalera de mano
stud (n) tachuela
   Col. chinche
   Mex. espárrago, espiga, pasador,
   viga vertical
   Nic. ojo de gato (reflectante en
   la calle), semental
tack (n) tachuela
   Nic. chinche
   Spa. chincheta
tape measure (n phr) metro
   Arg., Col., Dom.R., Mex., Nic.,
   Spa. cinta métrica
   Chi. huincha
   Cub. centímetro
   Pan. cinta de medir
toolbox (n) caja de herramientas
trowel (n) desplantador
   Chi., Nic. paleta
   Mex. palustre
   Par., Venz. aplanadora
   Pue.R. palaustre
vise (n) prensa
   Mex., Nic., Uru. torno
washer (n) arandela
   Mex. rodana
watering can (n phr) regadera
   Mex. regador de plantas
   Nic. pascón
   Venz. lata de regar
wheelbarrow (n) carretilla
wrench (n) llave inglesa

Nature: Vegetation & Landscape

acorn (n) bellota
annual (plant) (n) planta anual
bark (tree) (n) corteza

basin (n) cuenca
beach (n) playa
birch (tree) (n) abedul
bird of paradise (flower) (n) ave del
   Paraíso
bloom (v) florecer
   Col. dar flor
   Pue.R. retollar
branch (n) rama
bud (n) brote
   Col. botón
   Nic. cogollo
   Spa. capullo
bush (n) arbusto
   Cub. mata
   Nic. palito
   Pue.R. arbolito, palito
cactus (n) cacto
   Arg., Chi., Col., Dom.R.,
   Mex., Nic., Pan., Par.,
   Pue.R., Spa. cactus
canyon (n) cañón
cape (n) cabo
carnation (n) clavel
cave (n) cueva
   Col. caverna
cedar (tree) (n) cedro
cliff (n) acantilado
   Cub., Pan. Par. precipicio
   Cos.R. barranco
   Mex. Barranca
   Nic. guindo
   Pue.R. risco
climbing plant (n phr) trepadora
   Bol., Col., Cub., Mex., Pue.R.
   enredadera
clover (n) trébol
daisy (n) margarita
desert (n) desierto
earthquake (n) terremoto
   Chi., Mex. temblor
   Col. remezón, sacudida, sismo,
   temblor de tierra

   Dom.R., Pue.R. temblor de tierra
elm (tree) (n) olmo
fern (n) helecho
flower (n) flor
flower bed (n phr) macizo
   Arg. cantero
   Bol. macetero
   Gua. arriate de flores
   Mex. cama de flores
   Nic. jardinera
foliage (n) follaje
   Col. espesura, frondosidad
forest (n) bosque
fruit tree (n phr) árbol frutal
   Arg. frutal
   Pue.R. árbol de frutas
gardenia (n) gardenia
grass (n) hierba
   Chi. césped, pasto
   Col. pasto, yerba
   Mex., Per. pasto
   Nic. grama
   Pue.R. yerba
hedge (n) seto
   Col. matorral
   Mex. cercado de arbustos
hibiscus (n) hibisco
   Nic. flor de avispa
   Pan. papo
hill (n) colina
   Chi. cerro, loma
   Cub., Pan. loma
   Nic., Par. cerro
   Pue.R. cuesta
iceberg (n) iceberg
   Chi. témpano de hielo
iris (n) lirio
   Nic., Par., Venz. iris
island (n) isla
ivy (n) hiedra
jasmine (n) jazmín
jungle (n) selva
   Chi., Col., Dom.R., Pue.R., Venz.

---

jungla
lagoon (n) laguna
lake (n) lago
landscape (n) paisaje
lawn (n) césped
   Arg., Bol., Mex., Per. pasto
   Col. pasto
   Cub., Dom.R. yerba
   Dom.R., ElS., Gua., Hon., Venz.
   grama
   Nic., Venz. Grama
   Pue.R. grama, pasto
leaf (n) hoja
lily (n) lirio
maple (tree) (n) arce
   Gua., Mex., Nic. maple
moss (n) musgo
   Dom.R, Par. moho
mountain (n) montaña
oak (tree) (n) roble
oasis (n) oasis
ocean (n) océano
orchard (n) huerto
   Pue.R. hortaliza
palm (tree) (n) palma
   Arg., Col., Mex., Nic. palmera
peak (mountain) (n) pico
   Chi. cima
   Nic. cima, cumbre
perennial (plant) (n) perenne
   Pue.R. permanente
pine (tree) (n) pino
pine cone (n phr) piña
   Nic. piña de pino
   Per. piñón
plain (topography) (n) llanura
   Col., Dom.R. llano
   Mex. esplanada, planicie
   Pue.R. planicie
plateau (n) meseta
pond (n) charca
   Arg., Par., Uru. charco
   Chi. charco, laguna

Col., ElS., Gua., Hon., Mex.
estanque
   Dom.R. laguna
   Nic., Venz. estanque, laguna
prairie (n) pradera
   Dom.R., Nic. valle
rain forest (n phr) selva tropical
   Col., Nic. bosque tropical
rainbow (n) arco iris
range (mountain) (n) sierra
   Chi., Nic. cordillera
   Col. cadena
reef (n) arrecife
river (n) río
riverbank (n) orilla del río
rose (n) rosa
rosebush (n) rosal
sand (n) arena
sand dune (n phr) duna de arena
sandbar (n) barra de arena
   Mex., Par. banco de arena
sea (n) mar
seashore (n) orilla del mar
   Chi., Col., Pue.R. costa
seaweed (n) alga
seed (n) semilla
seedling (n) planta de semillero
   Chi. brote
   Col. planta de vivero
   Cos.R., Nic., Par. almácigo
   Mex. plantita
shoreline (n) costa
   Col. litoral, orilla
shrub (n) arbusto
   Cub. mata
soil (n) tierra
   Nic. suelo
   Pue.R. terreno
stem (n) tallo
stream (n) arroyo
   Col. arroyuelo, riachuelo
   Dom.R., Pue.R. riachuelo
   Nic. crique, quebrada

stump (n) tocón
    Dom.R. cabo
    Mex. parte del tronco
    Nic. cabo, cabito, muñón, tuco
succulent (plant) (n) suculenta
    Mex. carnosa
swamp (n) marisma
    Chi. ciénaga, pantano
    Col., Dom.R., Ecu., Mex., Par.,
    Venz. pantano
    Nic. swampo
    Uru. terreno pantanoso
thicket (n) matorral
thistle (n) cardo
thorn (n) espina
tree (n) árbol
    Dom.R. mata
trunk (n) tronco
tulip (n) tulipán
valley (n) valle
vegetable garden (n phr) huerto
    Arg. huerta, quinta
    Spa. huerta
vine (n) vid
violet (plant) (n) violeta
volcano (n) volcán
waterfall (n) cascada
    Dom.R. caída de agua
    Spa. catarata
weed (n) mala hierba
    Arg. maleza, yuyo
    Chi., Ecu., Nic. maleza
    Dom.R. maleza, pajón
    Mex. hierba silvestre
    Par. yuyo
    Pue.R. yerba mala
wetlands (n) pantano
    Chi. marisma
    Mex. terreno pantanoso
    Nic. humedales
wooded (land) (adj) boscoso

Nature: Weather

cloud (n) nube
cloudy (adj) nublado
    Chi. tapado
    Col. cerrado, encapotado
    Cos.R., Cub., Gua. cubierto,
    nuboso
drizzle (n) llovizna
    Col. lluvia tenue
    Nic. brisa
    Per. garúa
fog (n) niebla
    Arg., Cub., Dom.R., Mex., Nic.,
    Per. neblina
    Chi. camanchaca
    Col. bruma, neblina
freezing rain (n phr) lluvia helada
frost (n) escarcha
hail (n) granizo
humid (n) húmedo
hurricane (n) huracán
    Dom.R. ciclón
lightning (n) rayo, relámpago
    Col. centella
mist (n) neblina
    Arg., Pue.R. niebla
    Col. bruma
    Pan. bajareque
rain (n) lluvia
sandstorm (n) tormenta de arena
sleet (n) aguanieve
snow (n) nieve
storm (n) tormenta
    Col. aguacero, borrasca
thunder (n) trueno
tornado (n) tornado
wind (n) viento

Personal Life: Clothing & Accessories

bangle (n) brazalete tubular
bathing suit (n phr) traje de baño
   Arg. maya
   Col., Ecu., Pan. vestido de baño
   Cub. Trusa
   Par. malla
   Spa. bañador
bathrobe (n) bata de baño
   Bol. batón
   Nic. salida de baño
   Par. bata
   Spa. albornoz
belt (n) cinturón
   Col., Dom.R., Pan., Pue.R. correa
   Cos.R., Nic. faja
   Par. cinto
bifocals (n) lentes bifocales
   Arg. anteojos bifocales
   Nic. bifocales
   Pue.R. espejuelos bifocales
   Spa. gafas bifocales
bikini (n) bikini
bikini briefs (n phr) minitrusa
   Arg. bombacha
   Bol., Chi. bikini
   Col. calzoncillos
   Dom.R., Nic. tangas
   Ecu. calzón bikini
   Pan. calzoncillo corto
   Par. bikini, bombacha
   Pue.R. panticitos del bikini
   Spa. braguita de bikini
   Venz. interiores bikini
blouse (n) blusa
blue jeans (n phr) jeans
   Arg., Cub., Nic., Par., Uru. vaqueros
   Col. blue jeans, jeanes
   Mex. pantalón de mezclilla
   Pue.R. mahones
   Spa. pantalones vaqueros, vaqueros
   Venz. blue jeans
boots (n) botas
bow tie (n phr) corbata mariposa
   Arg., Par. moñito
   Bol. corbata de gato
   Col., Nic. corbatín
   Cub., Spa. pajarita
   Dom.R. corbata de lacito
   Mex. corbata de moñito
   Pan. corbata de gatito
   Per. corbata michi
   Pue.R. lazo
   Uru., Venz. corbata de lazo
boxer shorts (n phr) calzoncillos
   Cub. calzones
   Dom.R. calzoncillos boxer
   Nic., Pan. calzoncillos largos
bra, brassiere (n) sostén
   Arg. corpiño
   Col. brassiere
   Cub. ajustador
   Dom.R., Nic., Pan. brasier
   Mex. brasiere
   Par. corpiño, portaseno
   Spa. sujetador
   Uru. soutien
bracelet (n) pulsera
   Cub. pulso
   Dom.R. guillo
bracelet, charm (n phr) pulsera de dijes
briefs (n) calzoncillos
   Col. trusa
   Dom.R. pantaloncillos
   Mex., Uru. calzones
   Venz. interiores
buckle (n) hebilla
buttonhole (n) ojal
cap (n) gorra

ABBREVIATIONS: Arg.=Argentina Bol.=Bolivia Chi.=Chile Col.=Colombia Cos.R.=Costa Rica Cub.=Cuba Dom.R.=Dominican Republic Ecu.=Ecuador ElS.=El Salvador Gua.=Guatemala Hon.=Honduras Mex.=Mexico Nic.=Nicaragua Pan.=Panama Par.=Paraguay Per.=Peru Pri.=Primary Term Pue.R.=Puerto Rico Spa.=Spain Uru.=Uruguay Venz.=Venezuela

Col., Dom.R. cachucha
Par. kepi
cape (n) capa, capote
   Mex. chal, quisquemel
cardigan (n) cardigán
   Arg. chaleco, saco de lana
   Chi. sweater
   Col. suéter abierto
   Ecu., Venz. suéter
   Mex. chamarra tejida,
   suéter
   Nic. chamarra, chaqueta
   Spa. chaqueta de punto
casual clothes (n phr) ropa informal
   Dom.R. ropa casual
cloak (n) capa
   Col. manto
clogs (n) chanclos
   Arg. ojotas
   Chi. zancos
   Col., Cub., Nic., Spa., Uru.
   zuecos
   Dom.R., Mex., Pue.R. suecos
clothes (n) ropa
clothing articles (n phr) prendas de
   vestir
coat (n) saco
   Arg. tapado
   Chi., Pue.R. chaqueta
   Col., Cub., Mex., Nic., Pan.,
   Spa., Venz. abrigo
coat, fur (n phr) saco de piel
   Arg. tapado de piel
   Chi., Col., Dom.R., Mex., Nic.,
   Pan., Pue.R., Spa., Venz. abrigo
   de piel
   Cub. abrigo de pieles
coat, mink (n phr) saco de visón
   Arg. tapado de visón
   Col., Mex., Pan., Pue.R. abrigo
   de mink
   Cub., Dom.R., Nic., Spa., Venz.
   abrigo de visón

collar (n) cuello
crease (pants) (n) raya
   Col. arruga, pliego
   Cub., ElS., Gua., Hon. pliegue
   Dom.R., Pue.R. filo
   Pan. doblez
cuff (pants) (n) valenciana
   Arg. botamanga
   Bol. botapié
   Col., Spa. doblez
   Cub. dobladillo
   Dom.R. doblado
   Nic. bastilla
   Venz. ruedo doble
cuff (shirt) (n) puño
cufflinks (n) gemelos
   Chi. colleras
   Col., Ecu. mancornas
   Cub. yugos
   ElS., Gua., Hon., Mex.
   mancuernillas
   Pan. mancuernas
   Pue.R., Venz. yuntas
dog tag (n phr) placa de identificación
   Mex. etiqueta
dress (oneself) (v) vestirse
   Col. ponerse la ropa
dress (woman's) (n) vestido
   Arg., Col., Pan. traje
   Bol. falda
   Cos.R., Uru. pollera
   Pue.R. traje de mujer
dress up (v phr) vestirse de etiqueta
   Arg., Nic. arreglarse
   Chi., Col. vestirse elegante
   Dom.R. arreglarse, vestirse formal
   Par. arreglarse, engalanarse
   Pue.R. engalanarse
earmuffs (n) orejeras
earrings (n) aretes
   Arg., Par. aros
   Nic. chapas (colloq)
   Pue.R. pantallas

Spa. pendientes
Venz. zarcillos
earrings, clip (n phr) aretes de presión
  Arg. aros de presión
  Nic. aretes de prensar
  Pue.R. pantallas de clips
  Spa. pendientes de clip
  Venz. zarcillos de presión
earrings, drop (n phr) pendientes
  Arg. aros colgantes
  Spa. pendientes largos
earrings, pierced (n phr) aretes de espiga
  Arg. aros de agujero
  Dom.R. aretes de hoyito
  Nic. aretes de meter
  Pue.R. pantallas de gancho
  Spa. pendientes de tornillo
  Venz. zarcillos
earrings, screw (n phr) aretes de tornillo
  Arg. aros de tornillo
  Spa. pendientes de tornillo
  Venz. zarcillos de tornillo
eyeglasses (n) anteojos
  Col. gafas, lentes
  Cub., Pue.R. espejuelos
  Dom.R., Ecu., Pan., Per., Venz. lentes
  Spa. gafas
fly (pants) (n) bragueta
  Chi. marrueco
  Cub., Nic. portañuela
  Dom.R. ziper
  Par. cierre
  Pue.R. zipper
formal wear (n phr) ropa formal
  Dom.R. ropa de vestir
  Mex. ropa de etiqueta
garment (n) vestido
  Arg. prenda
  Cub., ElS., Gua., Nic., Spa. prenda de vestir

  Mex. ropa, traje
girdle (n) faja
glasses, opera (n phr) gemelos de teatro
  Col. binoculares, binóculos
  Cub. anteojos de teatro
  Nic. binoculares
  Venz. lentes de ópera
glasses, safety (n phr) anteojos de camino
  Chi. anteojos de seguridad
  Mex. gafas de protección
  Nic. protectores
  Pue.R. anteojos de protección
  Spa. gafas de seguridad
  Venz. lentes protectores
glove (n) guante
goggles, ski (n phr) anteojos para esquiar
  Arg. antiparras
  Mex. gogles para esquiar
  Spa. gafas de esquí
goggles, swimming (n phr) anteojos para nadar
  Arg. antiparras
  Mex. gogles
  Pue.R. goggles
  Spa. gafas de buceo
half-glasses (n) media luna
  Mex. lentes para leer
  Venz. medios-lentes
hat (n) sombrero
hat, straw (n phr) sombrero de paja
hat, top (n phr) sombrero de copa
  Arg. galera
heel (shoe) (n) taco
  Col., Cub., ElS., Gua., Hon., Mex., Pan., Spa., Venz. tacón
heel, high (shoe) (n phr) taco alto
  Col., Cub., ElS., Gua., Hon., Mex., Nic., Pan., Spa., Venz. tacón alto
hood (n) capucha
  Chi. capuchón
  Cub. caperuza

house robe (n phr) túnica
   Col. vestido casero
   Cub., Dom.R., Spa., Venz. bata
   de casa
   Nic., Par. bata
   Pan. bata de estar en casa
jacket (n) chaqueta
   Arg. campera
   Dom.R., Pan. saco
   Mex., Nic. chamarra
   Per. casca
   Pue.R. blazer (women), gabán
   (men)
jersey (n) jersey
   Bol. saco
   Col. chompa
   Mex. playera de punto
   Nic., Venz. suéter
knit shirt (n phr) polo
   Dom.R., Pan. suéter
   Mex. playera
   Per. camiseta
lapel (n) solapa
leotard (n) leotardo
   Chi. malla
   Venz. mallas de ejercicio
lining (coat) (n) forro
loafers (n) zapatos de andar
   Chi., Col., Cub., Ecu., Nic., Par.,
   Venz. mocasines
   Dom.R. zapatos bajitos
   ElS., Gua., Spa. zapatos estilo
   mocasín
   Mex. zapatos de casa
locket (n) relicario
   Cub. guardapelo
   Dom.R., Par. medallón
long johns (n phr) calzoncillos
   largos
miniskirt (n) minifalda
   Col., Pue.R. falda corta
necklace (n) collar
necklace, choker (n phr) gargantilla

necklace, pendant (n phr) collar con
   medallón
   Chi. medallón
   Dom.R. pendiente con medalla
   Mex. pendiente con cadena
   Nic. collar con colgante
   Par. collar
   Spa. colgante con cadena
necktie (n) corbata
nightgown (n) camisón
   Chi., Col. camisa de dormir
   Cub., Pue.R. bata de dormir
   Ecu. camisa de noche
   Dom.R. pijama
   Nic. bata
outfit (n) conjunto
   Chi., Nic., Par. traje
   Col. vestimenta
overalls (n) mono
   Arg., Dom.R., Pue.R. mameluco
   Chi., Col., Pan. overol
   Cub. guardapolvo
   Mex. overales, pantalones de peto
   Per. coverall
   Uru. entero
overcoat (n) abrigo
   Arg. sobretodo
   Col. Garbardina
pajamas (n) piyamas
   Col. pijama, piyama
   Dom.R., Pue.R. pijamas
   Nic. Piyama
   Spa. pijama
panties (n) calzones
   Arg., Par., Uru. bombachas
   Col. tangas
   Cub., Pan. blúmer, pantis
   Dom.R., Pue.R. panties
   Mex. pantaleta
   Nic. blúmer, calzón
   Spa. bragas
   Venz. pantaletas
pantyhose (n) media pantalón

ABBREVIATIONS: Arg.=Argentina   Bol.=Bolivia   Chi.=Chile   Col.=Colombia   Cos.R.=Costa Rica
Cub.=Cuba   Dom.R.=Dominican Republic   Ecu.=Ecuador   ElS.=El Salvador   Gua.=Guatemala
Hon.=Honduras   Mex.=Mexico   Nic.=Nicaragua   Pan.=Panama   Par.=Paraguay   Per.=Peru
Pri.=Primary Term   Pue.R.=Puerto Rico   Spa.=Spain   Uru.=Uruguay   Venz.=Venezuela

Arg. medias largas
Dom.R. media panty,
pantyhose
Mex. pantimedia
Nic. medias, pantyhose
Pan. pantihose
Per. media nylon
Pue.R. medias nylon
Spa. panty
Par. media fina, media nylon,
pantimedias
Uru. pantimedias
Venz. medias panty
parka (n) parka
Pue.R. capa
petticoat (n) combinación
Chi. enagüa
Cub. sayuela
Dom.R. mediofondo, refajo
Mex. enaguas
Nic. fustán
Pan. peticote
Par. enagua
Pue.R. refajo
Venz. enaguas, fondo
pince nez (n) quevedos
pocket (n) bolsillo
pocket, back (n phr) bolsillo trasero
Dom.R. bolsillo de atrás
pocket, breast (n phr) bolsillo superior
Dom.R., Nic. bolsillo de la camisa
pullover (n) pulóver
Arg. sweater
Bol. saco
Col., Mex. suéter cerrado
Nic. suéter
Per. chompa
Spa. jersey
Venz. suéter
raincoat (n) impermeable
Arg., Par. piloto
Col., Spa. gabardina
Cub. capa de agua

Nic. capote para la lluvia
Pan. capote
Pue.R. capa
ring (n) anillo
Pan., Pue.R. sortija
ring, class (n phr) anillo de graduación
Pue.R. sortija de graduación
ring, diamond (n phr) anillo de
diamante
Pue.R. sortija de diamante
Spa. anillo de diamantes
ring, engagement (n phr) anillo de
compromiso
ring, signet (n phr) sortija de sello
Col. anillo de sello
Spa. sello
ring, solitaire (n phr) solitario
ring, wedding (n phr) anillo de
matrimonio
Arg., Par. alianza, anillo de
casamiento
Nic. anillo de casamiento/boda
Per., Pue.R. aro de matrimonio
robe (n) bata
rubbers (shoes) (n) chanclos de goma
Arg. ojotas de goma
Chi., Uru. zapatos de goma
Col. zapatos de caucho
Cub., Pue.R. chancletas de
goma
ElS., Gua., Hon. chanclas de
hule
Mex. chanclas de plástico,
huaraches de plástico, sandalias
de plástico
Nic. chinelas
Par. zapatillas
Spa. chanclas
sandals (n) sandalias
Cub., Nic. chancletas
scarf (n) bufanda
shirt (n) camisa
shirt, dressy (n phr) camisa formal

Arg., Dom.R., Mex., Nic., Pan.,
Par., Uru., Venz. camisa de vestir
shirt, long-sleeved (n phr) camisa de
manga larga
Arg. remera de manga larga
shirt, short-sleeved (n phr) camisa de
manga corta
Arg. remera de manga corta Arg.
remera de manga corta
shoe rack (n phr) zapatera
Col. repisa para zapatos,
zapatero
Par. zapatero
shoelace (n) cordón
Mex. agujeta
Pue.R. gabete
shoes, hiking (n phr) botas
Chi. bototos
Col. zapatos de caminar
Mex. botas de alpinismo
Spa. botas de monte
shoes, patent leather (n phr) zapatos
de charol
Arg., Bol., Cos.R., Ecu., Per.,
Pue.R. zapatos de cuero
barnizado
Dom.R. zapatos de cuero,
zapatos de piel
Venz. zapatos de cuero, zapatos
de patente
shoes, tennis (n phr) zapatos de tenis
Arg., Chi., Pan. zapatillas
Col., Nic. zapatos tenis Col. zapatos
tenis
Dom.R., Mex. tenis
Spa. zapatillas de deporte
Venz. zapatos de goma
shorts (n) pantalones cortos
Arg., Chi., Col., Dom.R., Mex.,
Nic., Venz. shorts
Cub. bermudas
Pan. pantaloncitos cortos
Par. bermudas, pantalones corto

Pue.R. pantalón corto
skirt (n) falda
Arg. , Par., Uru. pollera
Cub. saya
slip (n) combinación
Chi., Pue.R. enagüa
Cub. sayuela
Dom.R. mediofondo
Nic. fustán
Pan. peticote
Par. enagua
Mex., Venz. fondo
slippers (n) pantuflas
Arg. chinelas
Col. babuchas
Cos.R., Cub., Pan. Chancletas
Nic. chinelas, chancletas
Spa. zapatillas de casa
sneakers (n) snikers
Arg., Chi., Pan., Per., Uru.
zapatillas
Col., Cos.R., Dom.R., Nic., Par.,
Pue.R. tenis
Ecu. zapatos de caucho
ElS., Gua., Hon. zapatos de
lona con suela de hule
Mex. tenis de lona
Spa. zapatillas de lona
Venz. zapatos de goma
sock (n) calcetín
Arg., Uru. media (tres cuartos),
soquete
Col., Cub., Dom.R., Ecu., Pan.,
Pue.R., Venz. media
sole (shoe) (n) suela
spectacles (n) anteojos
Col. gafas, lentes
Cub., Venz. espejuelos
suit (n) traje
Bol., Per. terno
Col., Pan. vestido
suit, double-breasted (n phr) traje
cruzado

Gua. traje traslapado
Nic. traje con traslape
suit, tailored (n phr) traje sastre
Col. vestido hecho a la medida
Pan. vestido sastre
Par. traje a medida
Nic., Venz. traje a la medida
suit, three-piece (n phr) terno
Bol., Dom.R., Mex., Nic., Par.,
Pue.R., Venz. traje de tres piezas
Pan. vestido de tres piezas
suspenders (n) ligas
Chi. suspensores
Dom.R. breteles
Gua., Nic., Pan., Spa., Venz.
tirantes
Mex. ligeros
sweater (n) suéter
Arg. pulover
Chi. chomba
Per. chompa
Spa. jersey
sweatshirt (n) camisa de trabajo
Arg. buzo
Chi., Col., Mex., Nic., Pue.R.
sudadera
Dom.R. abrigo, sudadera
Gua. sudadero
Par. buzo, sudadera
Spa. jersey
tailcoat (n) frac
Nic., Par., Venz. smoking
tights (n) leotardo
Chi. medias gruesas
Col. media pantalón
Mex., Nic., Venz. mallas
Par. malla
Pue.R. tights
Spa. leotardos, medias
trench coat (n phr) trinchera
Col., Spa. impermeable
Mex. gabardina
Nic. gabán

trifocals (n) trifocales
Spa. gafas trifocales
Venz. lentes trifocales
t-shirt (n) camiseta
Arg. remera
Chi. polera
Dom.R. polo-shirt
turban (n) turbante
turtleneck (n) cuello vuelto
Arg., Par. polera
Chi. beatle
Col. buzo, cuello de tortuga
Dom.R., Nic., Pan., Venz. cuello
tortuga
Mex., Pue.R. cuello de tortuga
Per. cuello Jorge Chavez
Spa. polo de cuello alto
Uru. rompeviento
tuxedo (n) smoking
Cub., Pue.R. tuxedo
Pan. toxido
underpants (n) calzoncillos
underwear (n) ropa interior
Cos.R., Bol., Uru. ropa blanca
Cub. ropa de interior
undress (v) desvestirse
Col., Venz. quitarse la ropa
vest (n) chaleco
Arg. camiseta, musculosa
vest (sweater) (n) chaleco
v-neck (n) cuello de pico
Arg., Chi., Col., Gua., Mex.,
Venz. cuello en V
Dom.R., Pan., Per., Pue.R.
cuello V
Par. escote V
Uru. escote en V
wear (clothing) (v) llevar
Arg., Bol., Gua., Pan., Venz.
usar
Chi. ponerse, vestir
Col. tener puesto
Cub. llevar puesto, tener puesto

Dom.R. llevar puesto, ponerse
Mex., Nic. ponerse
Par. llevar puesto, vestir

Personal Life: Greetings & Forms of Address

brat (n) mocoso
Col. niño/a malcriado/a
Cub., Pan. malcriado
Dom.R. carajito/a,
muchachito/a
Nic. malcriado
Par. cabezudo
Pue.R. chiquillo/a
Bye! (int) ¡Adiós!
Arg. ¡Chau!
Chi. ¡Chao!
Col. ¡Ciao!, ¡Hasta luego!
Dom.R. ¡Bye!
cheater (n) tramposo
Col. embustero, estafador, pícaro
Par. trampero
dear, darling, honey (n) querido/a
Arg., Chi., ElS., Gua., Hon., Nic.
mi amor
Col. mi amor, amorcito, tesoro
Cub. mi amor, mi cielo, mi vida
Pan. cariño
Pue.R. mi amor, mi vida
Good afternoon! (int phr) ¡Buenas
tardes!
Good evening! (int phr) ¡Buenas
tardes!
Col., Ecu. ¡Buenas noches!
Good morning! (int phr) ¡Buenos
días!
Arg. ¡Buen día!
Good night! (int phr) ¡Buenas noches!
Ecu. ¡Hasta mañana!
Goodbye! (int) ¡Adiós!
Arg. ¡Chau!
Chi. ¡Chao!

Col. ¡Hasta luego!, ¡Hasta pronto!
Dom.R. ¡Bye!
Hello! (int) ¡Hola!
Hello? (answering telephone) (int)
¿Dígame?
Arg., Bol., Par. ¿Hola?
Cub. ¿Oigo?
Col., Cos.R., Dom.R., Ecu.,
ElS., Gua., Hon., Nic., Per., Venz.
¿Aló?
Mex. ¿Bueno?
Pan., Pue.R. ¿Haló?
Uru. ¿Aló?, ¿Hola?
Hi! (int) ¡Hola!
How's it going? (phr) ¿Cómo te (le) va?
Arg., Mex., Pue.R., Uru. ¿Qué
tal?
Bol. ¿Cómo estás?
Dom.R. ¿Cómo tú estás?
Ecu. ¿Qué ha habido?, ¿Qué tal?
Nic. ¿Qué tal? ¿Cómo
estás?
liar (n) mentiroso
Chi. chamullento
Col. Nic. embustero
love, lovey (n) amor
Chi. tesoro
Col. amorcito, cariño
Cos.R., Nic. amorcito
Ma'am, Madam (n) Señora
Cos.R., Pan. Doña
Nic. Doña, Doñita
Par. Doña, Ña
Miss (n) Señorita
Mr. (n) Señor
Mrs. (n) Señora
pest (person) (n) machaca
Bol. cargoso
Chi. insoportable
Col., Pan. peste
Cub. chivón, ladilla
Dom.R. pesta, plaga
Ecu. necio/a

ABBREVIATIONS: Arg.=Argentina   Bol.=Bolivia   Chi.=Chile   Col.=Colombia   Cos.R.=Costa Rica
Cub.=Cuba   Dom.R.=Dominican Republic   Ecu.=Ecuador   ElS.=El Salvador   Gua.=Guatemala
Hon.=Honduras   Mex.=Mexico   Nic.=Nicaragua   Pan.=Panama   Par.=Paraguay   Per.=Peru
Pri.=Primary Term   Pue.R.=Puerto Rico   Spa.=Spain   Uru.=Uruguay   Venz.=Venezuela

ElS., Gua. tipo/a pesado/a
Mex., Venz. fastidioso
Nic. necio, pesado
Par. pesado, pelmazo
Pue.R. sabandija
Spa. pelma, pelmazo
See you later! (int phr) ¡Hasta luego!
   Col. ¡Te veo luego!, ¡Te veo más
   tarde!, ¡Hasta pronto!
   Dom.R., ElS., Gua., Pan. ¡Nos
   vemos!
   Par. ¡Nos vemos!, ¡Nos vemos mas
   tarde!
   Pue.R. ¡Hasta la vista!
Sir (n) Señor
snoop (n) fisgón
   Chi. intruso
   Col. entremetido, metiche,
   metido
   Cub. metiche, metido
   Dom.R. curioso, entrometido,
    metiche
   Ecu., Mex. metiche
   Gua. entrometido, shute
   Pan. vidajeno/a
   Par. entrometido, metiche
   Pue.R. ligón
   Venz. averiguador
sweetheart (n) enamorado/a
   Chi. pololo/a
   Mex. corazón
   Nic. amor, corazón
   Spa. cariño, querido
tattler (n) charlatán
   Chi., Cub., Gua. chismoso/a
   Dom.R., Pue.R. sinvergüenza
   Mex. hablador
   Nic. tapudo
   Spa. chivato
What's up? (int phr) ¿Qué pasa?
   Chi., Par. ¿Qué hay?
   Col. ¿En qué andas/an?, ¿Qué

Dom.R. ¿Qué hay de nuevo?
Nic. ¿Qué onda? ¿Qué pasó?
Pan. ¿Quiubo?

Personal Life: The Human Body

abdomen (n) abdomen
   Chi. guata
   Col., Dom.R., Nic. vientre
   Par. barriga, panza
   Per., Ur. barriga
Adam's apple (n phr) manzana de
   Adán
   Arg. nuez de Adán
   Col. coto
   Cub. nuez
   Nic. manzana
   Spa. nuez de la garganta
ankle (n) tobillo
anus (n) ano
aorta (n) aorta
appendix (n) apéndice
arm (n) brazo
armpit (n) axila
   Col., Dom.R. zobaco
   Nic., Pan. sobaco
artery (n) arteria
back (n) espalda
bags (under eyes) (n) ojeras
   Chi. chasquillas
   Dom.R. bolsas
bangs (hair) (n) flequillo
   Col. capul, fleco
   Cos.R., Nic. pava
   Cub., Ecu., Per. cerquillo
   Dom.R., Venz. pollina
   Mex. fleco
   Pan. gallusa
beard (n) barba
belly (n) barriga

Arg., Cos.R., Dom.R., Mex.,
Par., Uru. panza
Chi. guata
Col. pipa
Nic. panza, timba (colloq)
Venz. estómago
belly button (n phr) ombligo
Chi. pupo
biceps (n) biceps
Mex. conejos
Mex. conejos
Nic. ratones
big toe (n phr) dedo gordo
Arg., Dom.R., Nic., Par., Spa.,
Venz. dedo gordo del pie
big-nosed (adj) narizón
Arg., Bol., Chi., Par., Uru.
narigón
Dom.R. narizú
birthmark (n) marca de nacimiento
Cub., Ecu., Per., Venz. lunar
Dom.R., Spa. antojo
Mex. mancha de nacimiento
Nic. lunar de nacimiento
blond (hair) (adj) rubio
Col. mono
Mex. güero
Nic. chele
Pan. fulo
Venz. catire
blond (person) (n) rubio/a
Col. mono/a
Cos.R. macho (person with
light hair)
Mex. güero/a
Nic. chele
Pan. fulo/a
Venz. catire/a
blue (eyes) (adj) azul
Col. ojiazul
Cos.R. macho (person with
light-colored eyes)

Nic. gato (ojos claros), ojos
azules
bone (n) hueso
braid (hair) (n) trenza
Pan. moño
Venz. crineja
brain (n) cerebro
breast (n) seno
Arg., Col., Cos.R., Uru. teta
Chi. pechuga
Dom.R., ElS., Gua., Nic., Spa.
pecho
Mex. busto, chiche, chichi
Pan. pecho, teta
Par. teta, titi
bridge of nose (n phr) caballete
Chi., Col., Dom.R. tabique
Mex., Nic., Venz. puente de la
nariz
Par. puente nasal, tabique
brown (eyes) (adj) castaño
Arg., Col., Dom.R., Par., Per.,
Spa. marrón
Bol., Chi., Cos.R., Mex., Nic.
café
brown (hair) (adj) moreno
Arg., Mex., Nic., Par., Spa.
castaño
Col. pelicastaño
Dom.R. trigueño
Uru. morocho
bruise (n) cardenal
Arg., Bol., Chi., Mex., Nic.,
Pan., Par. moretón
Col., Cub. morado
Cos.R. morete
Dom.R. chichón, hematoma,
morado
ElS., Gua., Hon. magulladura
Spa. moratón
Venz. golpe, magulladura
brunette (person) (n) moreno/a
Arg., Uru. morocho/a

blister
(n) ampolla

ABBREVIATIONS: Arg.=Argentina Bol.=Bolivia Chi.=Chile Col.=Colombia Cos.R.=Costa Rica Cub.=Cuba Dom.R.=Dominican Republic Ecu.=Ecuador ElS.=El Salvador Gua.=Guatemala Hon.=Honduras Mex.=Mexico Nic.=Nicaragua Pan.=Panama Par.=Paraguay Per.=Peru Pri.=Primary Term Pue.R.=Puerto Rico Spa.=Spain Uru.=Uruguay Venz.=Venezuela

Col., Dom.R. trigueño/a
Spa. persona de pelo castaño
bun (hair) (n) moño
Chi. tomate
Mex. chongo
Pan. cebolla
butt (n) trasero
Arg. cola, traste
Chi. traste
Col. cola, culo
Cub. nalgas
Mex. asentaderas
Pan. nalga
Par. cola, culo, tevi, traste
Per. poto
buttock (n) nalga
Arg. cachete
Chi. poto
Mex. pompa, pompas
calf (leg) (n) pantorrilla
callus (n) callo
canine (tooth) (n) canino
Cos.R. premolar
Cub., Mex., Nic., Par., Spa.
colmillo
cartilage (n) cartílago
cheek (n) mejilla
Chi., Col., Dom.R., Mex., Nic.,
Pan., Per., Venz. cachete
Spa. carrillo
chest (n) pecho
Chi., Col. tórax
chin (n) barbilla
Arg. mentón, pera
Chi. pera
Col. mentón
Mex. barba
Per. quijada
cleft (chin) (n) hendidura
Chi. labio leporino
Cos.R. camanance
Dom.R. hoyito
Mex. Nic. barba partida

Per. barbida partida
Venz. barbilla hendida
collarbone (n) clavícula
colon (n) colon
cornea (n) córnea
curly (hair) (adj) rizado
Arg., Pan. enrulado
Bol., Chi., Venz. ondulado
Col. crespo, ondulado
Dom.R. duro, malo
Mex. chino Mex. chino
Per. Crespo
Nic., Per. crespo
Par. encrespado, enrulado
Per. crespo
diaphragm (n) diafragma
dimple (n) hoyuelo
Bol. hoyo
Chi., Dom.R., Mex. hoyito
Cos.R., ElS., Gua., Hon.
camanance
double chin (n phr) papada
Chi. doble pera
Dom.R. doble barbilla
duct (n) conducto
ear (n) oreja
Col., Mex., Nic. oído
ear drum (n phr) tímpano
elbow (n) codo
epiglottis (n) epiglotis
esophagus (n) esófago
eye (n) ojo
eyeball (n) globo ocular
eyebrow (n) ceja
eyelash (n) pestaña
eyelid (n) párpado
face (n) cara, rostro
finger (n) dedo
fingernail (n) uña
follicle (n) folículo
foot (n) pie
forearm (n) antebrazo
forehead (n) frente

ABBREVIATIONS: Arg.=Argentina Bol.=Bolivia Chi.=Chile Col.=Colombia Cos.R.=Costa Rica
Cub.=Cuba Dom.R.=Dominican Republic Ecu.=Ecuador ElS.=El Salvador Gua.=Guatemala
Hon.=Honduras Mex.=Mexico Nic.=Nicaragua Pan.=Panama Par.=Paraguay Per.=Peru
Pri.=Primary Term Pue.R.=Puerto Rico Spa.=Spain Uru.=Uruguay Venz.=Venezuela

freckle (n) peca
gallbladder (n) vesícula biliar
gland (n) glándula
goatee (n) barbas de chivo
    Col. chivera
    Cub. chivo
    Dom.R. chiva, chivita
    Ecu. chivita
    Spa. perilla
    Venz. chiva
gray (hair) (adj) canoso
    Col. cano
    Spa. blanco
green (eyes) (adj) verde
    Col. ojiverde
    Cos.R., Nic. gato
groin (n) ingle
gum (n) encía
hair (n) cabello, pelo
    Arg. vello
    Col. cabellera
hand (n) mano
head (n) cabeza
heart (n) corazón
heel (n) talón
hip (n) cadera
incisor (n) incisivo
index finger (n phr) dedo índice
intestine (n) intestino
iris (n) iris
jaw (n) mandíbula
    Col., Nic. quijada
joint (n) articulación
    Dom.R., Spa. coyuntura
kidney (n) riñón
knee (n) rodilla
knee cap (n phr) rótula
larynx (n) laringe
leg (n) pierna
lens (eye) (n) cristalino
lip (n) labio
liver (n) hígado
lobe (ear) (n) lóbulo

lung (n) pulmón
middle finger (n phr) dedo del
    corazón
    Arg. medio
    Col. dedo corazón
    Cub., Dom.R., Venz. dedo del
    medio
    Mex., Nic., Par., Uru. dedo medio
molar (n) muela
    Col. molar
mole (skin) (n) lunar
mouth (n) boca
muscle (n) músculo
mustache (n) bigote
nape (n) nuca
    Col., Nic. cogote
navel (n) ombligo
    Arg., Chi. pupo
neck (n) cuello
nerve (n) nervio
nipple (n) pezón
    Col. tetilla
nose (n) nariz
nostril (n) ventanilla
    Chi. narina
    Cub. ventana de la nariz
    Dom.R. hoyo de la nariz
    Mex. poro de la nariz
    Pue.R. roto de la nariz
    Venz. orificio nasal
    Nic. bata
palate (n) paladar
palm (hand) (n) palma de la mano
pancreas (n) páncreas
part (hair) (n) raya
    Chi., Pan. partidura
    Dom.R., Mex., Nic., Venz.
partido
pelvis (n) pelvis
pharynx (n) faringe
pigtail (n) trenza
    Bol., Cos.R. cola
    Chi. colita, moño

Col., Dom.R., Mex., Venz. colita
Per. cachito
Spa., Uru. coleta
pimple (n) grano
Chi., Cos.R., Dom.R., Spa.
espinilla
Col., Nic., Venz. barro, espinilla
Mex. barro
Par., Per. barrito
pinkie finger (n phr) dedo meñique
Cub. dedo chiquito
Nic. meñique
plantar arch (foot) (n phr) arco plantar
Arg., Mex., Nic., Par., Venz. arco
del pie
Col. arco de la planta del pie
Dom.R. puente
ponytail (hair) (n) cola de caballo
Arg. cola, colita
Pue.R. rabo de caballo
Spa. coleta
pore (n) poro
pubic hair (n phr) vello pubiano
Col., Cos.R., ElS., Gua., Mex.,
Nic., Par., Venz. vello púbico
Cub. pendejo
Dom.R. vello
Uru. vello del pubis
pubis (n) pubis
pupil (n) pupila
rectum (n) recto
red (hair) (adj) pelirrojo
redhead (n) pelirrojo/a
retina (n) retina
rib (n) costilla
ring finger (n phr) dedo anular
root (hair) (n) raíz
Dom.R. crecimeinto
scab (n) costra
Cub., Dom.R. postilla
scalp (n) cuero cabelludo
scar (n) cicatriz
shin (n) espinilla

Chi. canilla
short (person) (adj) pequeño
Arg., Uru. bajito, petiso
Col. bajito, bajo
Dom.R. bajito
Mex. de estatura baja, chaparro
Venz. bajo
shoulder (n) hombro
shoulder blade (n phr) omóplato
sideburn (n) patilla
sinus (n) seno
Mex., Spa. seno nasal
Venz. cavidad
skeleton (n) esqueleto
Col. osamenta
Mex. calaca
skin (n) piel
skull (n) cráneo
Col., Cos.R., Mex. calavera
sole (foot) (n) planta del pie
spine (n) columna vertebral
Col. espinazo
Ecu. espina dorsal, espinaso
Gua. espina dorsal
spleen (n) bazo
stomach (n) estómago
straight (hair) (adj) lacio
Chi., Col., Spa., Venz. liso
Dom.R. bueno
Nic. liso, chiriso
tall (adj) alto
tan (v) broncearse
Arg., Chi., Cub., Dom.R.
quemarse
Col. dorarse al sol
tan (skin) (adj) bronceado
Arg., Chi., Cub., Dom.R.
quemado
Col. tostado
taste bud (n phr) papila gustativa
teeth (n) dientes
Col. dentadura
temple (n) sien

tendon (n) tendón
thigh (n) muslo
thorax (n) tórax
throat (n) garganta
thumb (n) pulgar
  Arg. dedo gordo
tip of nose (n phr) lóbulo
  Chi., Col., Mex., Nic., Spa.,
  Venz. punta de la nariz
tissue (n) tejido
toe (n) dedo del pie
toenail (n) uña del pie
tongue (n) lengua
tonsil (n) amígdala
  Mex. angina
trachea (n) tráquea
triceps (n) tríceps
trunk (n) tronco
urinary bladder (n phr) vejiga
vein (n) vena
vocal cord (n phr) cuerda vocal
waist (n) cintura
  Col. cinto, talle
wart (n) verruga
  Mex. mezquino
  Per. callo
wavy (hair) (adj) ondulado
  Nic., Venz. crespo
wrist (n) muñeca

Personal Life: Personal Articles

antiperspirant (n) desodorante
  Gua., Mex., Pue.R.
  antiperspirante
ashtray (n) cenicero
attaché case (n) maletín
  Arg. portafolios
  Mex. portafolio
backpack (n) mochila
barrette (n) broche para el pelo

  Arg., Bol., Col., Pue.R. hebilla
  Chi. traba
  Dom.R., Pan., Per., Spa.
  gancho para el pelo
  Nic. gancho de pelo
  Venz. ganchito de pelo
briefcase (n) portafolios
  Bol. cartera, portafolio
  Col., Cub., Nic., Par., Per.,
  Pue.R. maletín
cigar (n) cigarro, puro
  Cub. tabaco
cigarette (n) cigarrillo
  Chi. pucho
  Mex. Nic., cigarro
coin purse (n phr) monedero
  Dom.R. portamonedas
comb (n) peine
  Chi. peineta
  Col., Ecu., Pan., Pue.R. peinilla
cream (for skin) (n) crema
curling iron (n phr) tenazas
dental floss (n phr) hilo dental
deodorant (n) desodorante
eyeliner (n) delineador
eyeshadow (n) sombra de ojos
hair dryer (n phr) secadora manual
  Arg., Par. secador
  Chi., Spa., Venz. secador de pelo
  Cub., Nic. secadora de pelo
  Dom.R., Pue.R. blower
  Mex. pistola de pelo, secadora de
  pelo
hair gel (n phr) gel para el pelo
  Dom.R., ElS., Gua. gelatina para
  el pelo
  Ecu. gel fijador
  Mex. jalea
  Spa. gomina para el pelo
hair mousse (n phr) mousse para el
  pelo
  Dom.R. mus para el pelo
  ElS., Gua., Spa. espuma para el

pelo
  Mex. mouse para el pelo
hair rollers (n phr) ruleros
  Chi. ondulines
  Col., Spa. rulos
  Cub., Pue.R. rolos
  ElS., Gua., Mex. tubos
  Nic. rollos, tubos
  Pan., Venz. rollos
hairbrush (n) cepillo de pelo
hairspray (n) laca para el pelo
  Cub., Nic. espray de pelo
  Dom.R., Mex., Pan. spray para el
  pelo
  Par., Pue.R. spray de pelo
handbag (n) cartera
  Col., Cos.R., Gua., Mex., Pan.
  bolsa de mano
  Dom.R. bolso
  Spa., Venz. bolso de mano
keychain (n) llavero
lighter (n) encendedor
  Cub. fosforera
lipstick (n) lápiz labial
  Arg., Bol., Chi. rouge
  Col. colorete
  Cub., Dom.R. pintalabios
  Mex. bilé
  Nic. lápiz de libios
  Pan. lipstick
  Pue.R. lipstic
  Spa., Uru. lápiz de labios
makeup kit (n phr) estuche de
  maquillaje
  Col. juego de maquillaje
  Pue.R. cartera de maquillaje
mascara (n) rímel
matchstick (n) cerilla, fósforo
  Mex., Nic. cerillo
nail clippers (n phr) cortauñas
nail polish (n phr) esmalte de uñas

Chi. cutex
  Col., Spa. pintauñas
  Cub., Nic., Venz. pintura de uñas
  Dom.R. cuté
  Par. pinta uña
pipe (n) pipa
pocket watch (n phr) reloj de bolsillo
razor (n) rasuradora
  Arg., Chi. gillette
  Col., Nic. máquina de afeitar
  Cub., Spa. cuchilla de afeitar
  Dom.R., Pue.R. afeitadora
  Mex. rastrillo Mex. rastrillo
  Pan. navaja
  Venz. hojilla de afeitar
shampoo (n) champú
  Arg., Nic. shampoo
shaving brush (n phr) brocha de
  afeitar
shaving cream (n) crema de afeitar
soap (n) jabón
sunscreen (n) loción solar
  Arg. pantalla solar, protector
  Chi., Cos.R., Nic. protector
  solar
  Dom.R. bloqueador solar
  Mex., Per. bronceador
  Par. bronceador, protector solar
  Spa. crema de protección solar
  Venz. protector de sol
toothbrush (n) cepillo de dientes
toothpaste (n) dentífrico, pasta de
  dientes
  Col. crema dental
  Per., Pue.R. pasta dental
tweezers (n) pinzas
umbrella (n) paraguas, sombrilla
walking stick (n phr) bastón
wallet (n) billetera, cartera
  Dom.R. cartera de hombre
watch (n) reloj

ABBREVIATIONS: Arg.=Argentina Bol.=Bolivia Chi.=Chile Col.=Colombia Cos.R.=Costa Rica
Cub.=Cuba Dom.R.=Dominican Republic Ecu.=Ecuador ElS.=El Salvador Gua.=Guatemala
Hon.=Honduras Mex.=Mexico Nic.=Nicaragua Pan.=Panama Par.=Paraguay Per.=Peru
Pri.=Primary Term Pue.R.=Puerto Rico Spa.=Spain Uru.=Uruguay Venz.=Venezuela

Personal Life: Relationships

adopt (a child) (v) adoptar
adult (n) adulto
   Col. mayor de edad
   Nic. roco (colloq), vetarro (colloq), viejo
aunt (n) tía
baby (n) bebé
   Arg., Uru. beba, bebe
   Chi. guagua
babysit (v) hacer de niñero/a
   Arg., Uru. cuidar a un/a beba/bebe/chico/chica/nene/nena
   Chi., Col., Ecu., Nic., Per., Pue.R., Venz. cuidar niños
   Mex. cuidar a un bebé/niño/a
babysitter (n) guardián
   Arg. babysitter, niñera
   Bol., Col., Dom.R., Ecu., Gua., Pan., Spa., Uru. niñero/a
   Chi. niñera, nodriza
   Mex. nana, niñero/a
   Nic. niñera, china
   Par. niñero/a, criada
   Per. cuidadora de niños
   Venz. cuidador de niños, niñero/a
boy (n) niño
   Arg., Par., Pue.R., Uru. nene
   Col. chino
   Dom.R. muchachito
   Mex. chamaco
   Nic. chavalo, chigüín, cipote
boyfriend (n) novio
   Chi. pololo
   Col. pretendiente
   Ecu., Per. enamorado
break up (relationship)
   (v phr) romper
   Arg., Dom.R. cortar

   Chi., Mex., Nic. cortar, terminar
   Col. separarse
   Cub. pelearse
   Ecu., ElS., Gua., Hon., Venz. terminar
bridal shower (n phr) despedida de soltera
   Col. shower
bride (n) novia
brother (n) hermano
brother-in-law (n) cuñado
burial (n) entierro
   Chi., Mex. sepelio
   Col. exequias, sepelio
child (n) niño/a
   Arg. chico/a
   Col. chino/a
   Nic. chavalo/a, chigüín, cipote
christen (v) bautizar
christening (n) bautizo
   Arg., Col. bautismo
cousin (female) (n) prima
cousin (male) (n) primo
date (v) tener una cita
   Arg. estar de novio
   Col. tener compromiso
   Dom.R., Gua., Mex., Venz. salir con
daughter (n) hija
daughter-in-law (n) nuera
divorce (v) divorciarse
   Col. apartarse
divorced (adj) divorciado
   Col. separado
family (n) familia
family member (n phr) familiar
   Arg., Chi., Ecu., Mex., Pue.R., Venz. pariente
   Col. miembro de la familia
father (n) padre
   Arg., Col. papá
   Mex. papá, papi

Nic. papa
father-in-law (n) suegro
fiancé (male) (n) novio
   Col., Cos.R., Dom.R., Pan.
   prometido
   Mex. comprometido
fiancée (female) (n) novia
   Col., Cos.R., Dom.R., Pan.
   prometida
   Mex. comprometida
first cousin (n phr) primo hermano/
   prima hermana
friend (female) (n) amiga
friend (male) (n) amigo
girl (n) niña
   Arg., Uru. chica, nena
   Dom.R. muchachita
   Mex. chamaca
   Nic. chavala, cipota
   Par. nena
girlfriend (n) novia
   Chi. polola
   Ecu., Per. enamorada
give birth (v phr) dar a luz
   Arg. tener un/a beba/bebe/bebé/
   hijo/hija
   Col. alumbrar, parir
   Cos.R., Dom.R., Pan. parir
goddaughter (n) ahijada
godfather (n) padrino
godmother (n) madrina
godson (n) ahijado
granddaughter (n) nieta
grandfather (n) abuelo
grandmother (n) abuela
grandson (n) nieto
great aunt (n phr) tía abuela
great uncle (n phr) tío abuelo
great-granddaughter (n) bisnieta
great-grandfather (n) bisabuelo
great-grandmother (n) bisabuela
great-grandson (n) bisnieto
great-great-granddaughter (n)

tataranieta
great-great-grandfather (n) tatarabuelo
great-great-grandmother (n)
   tatarabuela
great-great-grandson (n) tataranieto
groom (n) novio
grow up (v phr) crecer
   Col., Par. madurar
guardian (n) tutor
   Col., Pan., Venz. guardián
guy (n) muchacho, tipo
   Arg. pibe
   Chi. cabro
   Cos.R. mae, fulano/a
   Cub., Pue.R. chico
   Mex., Pan. fulano/a
   Nic. maje
guys (dual gender plural) (n)
   muchachos, tipos
   Arg., Ecu. chicos
   Chi. cabros, chiquillos
   Nic. majes
infant (n) niño/a
   Arg., Uru. chico/a, nene/a
   Col., Gua., Par. criatura
   Cub., Mex., Spa. bebé
   Nic. bebé, nene
kid (n) chico/a
   Cub. chiquito/a
   Col., Venz. niño/a, peladito/a
   Dom.R. muchacho/a
lover (n) amante
married (n) casado
mistress (n) amante
   Col. Mosa
   Cub., Spa. querida
   Mex. concubina
   Pue.R. chilla
mother (n) madre
   Arg. mamá, vieja
   Col., Par. mamá
   Nic. mama, vieja
mother-in-law (n) suegra

nanny (n) niñera
   Chi., Col., Mex., Venz. nana
nephew (n) sobrino
niece (n) sobrina
parents (n) padres
   Arg., Uru. viejos
   Col., Nic. papás
pregnant (adj) embarazada
   Col. encinta, esperando,
   preñada
   Nic. panzona
   Pan., Per. encinta
   Venz. en estado
relative (n) pariente
second cousin (n phr) primo/a
   segundo/a
sister (n) hermana
sister-in-law (n) cuñada
son (n) hijo
son-in-law (n) yerno
stepbrother (n) hermanastro
stepdaughter (n) hijastra
stepfather (n) padrastro
stepmother (n) madrastra
stepsister (n) hermanastra
stepson (n) hijastro
teenager (n) adolescente
   Dom.R. teenager
   Nic. chavalo
toddler (n) pequeñito/a
   Arg. beba, bebe, bebé
   Col. niño/a chiquito/a
   ElS., Gua., Hon., Nic. niño/a
   que empieza a andar
   Mex. niño/a de edad pre-escolar,
   niño/a que empieza a andar
   Spa. niño/a
   Venz. niñito/a
uncle (n) tío
wake (n) velorio
   Col. velación
   Cos.R., Nic. vela
   Dom.R. funeral

   Spa. velatorio
widow (n) viuda
widower (n) viudo
young (adj) joven

Shelter & Daily Life: Furnishings

armchair (n) silla de brazos
   Arg., Chi., Nic., Spa., Uru.
   sillón
   Dom.R. butaca, sillón
   Mex. silla con coderas
   Pue.R. butaca
bed (n) cama
bed, double (n phr) cama doble
   Gua., Mex., Nic. cama
   matrimonial
   Par. cama dos plazas
   Spa. cama de matrimonio
bed, king-sized (n phr) cama
   grande
   Arg. cama camera
   Col., Dom.R. cama king size
   Mex. cama king-size
   Nic. cama extra grande
   Pan., Par., Venz. cama king
bed, queen-sized (n phr) cama
   doble
   Arg., Par. cama camera
   Dom.R. cama queen size
   Mex. cama queen-size
   Nic. cama grande
   Pan. cama matrimonial
   Venz. cama queen
bed, single (n phr) cama
   Chi. cama de soltero
   Col., Ecu., Nic., Pue.R. cama
   sencilla
   Gua. cama imperial
   Mex., Venz. cama individual

Pan. cama tres cuartos
Par. cama soltero
bench (n) banco
Arg., Nic. banca
Spa. banqueta
berth (n) litera
Chi., Nic. camarote
blanket (n) cobija
Arg., Bol., Col., Cub., Par.,
Uru. frazada
Ecu. colcha
Nic. colcha, sábana
Pue.R. frisa
Spa. manta
blinds (n) persianas
Col. cortinas
box spring (n phr) colchón de
resortes
Chi. catre
Dom.R., Mex., Venz. box
spring
Nic. colchón
Pan. esprín
Par. somnier
Spa. somier
buffet (n) aparador
Col. mostrador, vitrina
Dom.R. despensa
Gua. bufetera
Mex. mesa de buffet
Par. comida sin límite, comer
hasta hartarse por un precio
fijo
Pue.R. chinero
bunkbed (n) litera
Chi., Nic. camarote
Col., Dom.R., Pan. cama
camarote
chair (n) silla
chair, director's (n phr) silla de
director, silla plegable
Mex. silla ejecutiva, sillón
ejecutivo

Par. sillón ejecutivo
chair, folding (n phr) silla
plegable
Dom.R. silla plegadiza
chair, lounging (n phr) catre,
chaise
Chi. asiento, poltrona
Col. silla de extensión
Mex., Nic. sillón reclinable
Pue.R. silla reclinable
Spa. hamaca
chair, rocking (n phr) mecedora
Arg. silla hamaca
Col. mecedor
Cub., Pue.R. sillón
chair, step (n phr) banco-
escalera
Nic. banco
Venz. silla con escalón
closet (clothes) (n) clóset
Arg. placard
Bol., Chi., Cos.R., Ecu., Uru.
ropero
Pan. estante
Spa. armario
closet (general) (n) armario
Chi. guardarropa
Col., Cos.R., Cub., Mex., Nic.,
Pan., Per. Closet
Par. ropero
cradle, crib (n) cuna
Dom.R. catre
curtains (n) cortinas
desk (n) escritorio
display cabinet (n phr) vitrina
Arg. aparador
Pue.R. chinero
Nic. aparador, chinero
drawer (n) gaveta
Arg., Chi., Col., Ecu., Mex., Per.,
Spa., Uru. cajón
drawer knob (n phr) perilla Col.
pomo

Dom. R. manubrio
Nic. manigueta
Pan. agarrador
Venz. manilla
dresser (n) ropero
  Arg., Chi., Col., Cub., Nic., Per.
  cómoda
  Venz. gavetero
  Pue.R., Spa. tocador
footboard (n) pie de la cama
hammock (n) hamaca
  Venz. chinchorro
headboard (n) cabecera
  Ecu., Nic. espaldar
  Pue.R. espaldal
love seat (n phr) confidente
  Arg. silloncito
  Col., ElS., Gua., Nic., Venz.
  sofá para dos personas
  Dom.R., Mex. love seat
  Pue.R., Spa. sofá
mattress (n) colchón
  Pue.R. matres
ottoman (n) otomana
  Mex., Par. taburete
  Nic. Divan
  Pan. banquillo
  Pue.R. banquillo, ottomán
pillow (n) almohada
pillowcase (n) funda
  Gua. sobrefunda
sheet, bed (n phr) sábana
sheet, contour (n phr) sábana de cajón
  Arg. sábana de elástico
  Col. sábana de forro
  Nic. cubrecama
  Par. sábana elástica
  Spa. sábana bajera ajustable
  Venz. sábana de esquinera
shutters (n) postigos
  Col., Ecu., Gua., Nic., Par.
  persianas
  Mex. contraventanas

sofa (n) sofá
stool (n) banco
  Chi. piso
  Dom.R. banqueta, banquito
  Nic. banquito, pata de gallina
table (n) mesa
table leaf (n phr) tablero
  Chi. tabla
  Col. hoja Col. hoja, lámina
  Nic. tabla de extensión
  Mex. tablón de extensión
table leg (n phr) pata
table, drop-leaf (n phr) mesa plegable
table, kitchen (n phr) mesa de cocina
  Pan. mesita de cocina
table, night (n phr) mesilla de noche
  Arg. mesa de luz, mesita de luz
  Bol. mesita de noche, velador
  Chi. velador
  Col., ElS., Gua., Hon., Nic.,
  Pue.R., Venz. mesa de noche
  Dom.R., Pan., Par. mesita de
  noche
table, ping pong (n phr) mesa de
  ping pong
table, pool (n phr) mesa de billar
table, round (n phr) mesa redonda
table, serving (n phr) mesita de
  servicio
  Arg. mesita rodante
  Col., Nic. mesa de servicio
  Par. meza de servir
  Venz. mesa de servir

Shelter & Daily Living: Housing

apartment (n) apartamento
  Arg., Bol., Chi., Mex.
  departamento
  Spa. piso

apartment building (n phr) edificio de
    apartamentos
    Arg., Bol., Mex. edificio de
    departamentos
    Chi., Col. edificio
    Dom.R. torre de apartamentos
    Spa. edificio de pisos
    Uru. propiedad horizontal
balcony (n) balcón
    Chi. terraza
    Col. balconcillo
barracks (n) cuartel
    Pan. barracas
    Pue.R. barraca
bathroom (n) cuarto de baño
    Bol., Chi., Cos.R., Ecu., Nic.,
    Par., Spa., Uru., Venz. baño
bedroom (n) dormitorio
    Arg., Cub., Pue.R. cuarto
    Col. cuarto, pieza
    Dom.R. aposento, cuarto
    Mex. cuarto, recámara
    Nic. aposento
    Pan. habitación
    Par. pieza
boathouse (n) caseta de botes
    Col. cobertizo para las
    lanchas, garaje para botes
    Dom.R. casa-botes
    Gua., Nic. cobertizo de lanchas
bungalow (n) casa independiente
    Arg., Par., Uru. bungalow
    Bol. cabañita
    Chi. cabaña, chalet
    Col. bungaló
    Dom.R. bungaloo
    ElS., Gua., Hon. casa
    campestre, casa de playa
    Mex. búngalo
    Nic. cabaña
    Pan. bungalu
    Spa. bungaló
    Venz. casa de campo

cabin (n) cabaña, choza
    Chi. refugio
church (n) iglesia
condominium (n) condominios
    Cub., ElS., Gua., Nic., Pue.R.,
    Spa. condominio
cottage (n) casa de campo
    Arg. casa, casa-quinta, quinta
    Chi. cabaña, chalet
    Col. casita de campo
    Nic. quinta
courtyard (n) patio
dining room (n phr) comedor
doghouse (n) perrera
    Arg. cucha
    Chi., Venz. casa de perro
duplex (n) dúplex
    Chi. casa pareada
    Dom.R., Pue.R. casa duplex
    Nic. casa doble
fireplace (n) chimenea
    Arg. estufa, hogar
garage (storage) (n) garaje
    Dom.R. marquesina
ground floor (n phr) planta baja
    Col. piso de abajo, primer piso
    Dom.R. primer piso
hallway (n) pasillo, corredor
hangar (n) hangar
hut (n) choza
    Arg. albergue, cabaña, casilla
    Dom.R. casita de paja
kitchen (n) cocina
living room (n phr) cuarto de estar,
    sala
    Arg. living
main entrance (n phr) entrada
principal mansion (n) mansión
move (v) mudarse
    Bol. trasladarse
    Col. cambiarse de casa, trastiar
    Nic. cambiarse de casa
pantry (n) despensa

Bol., Col., Mex. alacena
Dom.R., Nic. pantry
ElS., Gua., Hon. comedor
auxiliar, pantry
Pue.R. gabinete
porch (n) pórtico
Cub., Nic. porche
Dom.R. galería
Gua. terraza cubierta
Pan. porch
rent (housing) (v) alquilar
Chi., Col. arrendar
Mex., Pue.R. rentar
shed (n) cobertizo
Chi. galpón
Nic. bajareque
Par. galpón
Pue.R. casita de herramientas
side entrance (n phr) puerta lateral
Arg., Par. puerta de servicio
Col., Nic. entrada lateral
Cub. puerta del costado
study (n) estudio
tent (n) carpa
Chi., Cos.R., Dom.R., Mex.,
Nic., Spa., Venz. tienda de
campaña
Pan. tolda
townhouse (n) casa en hilera
Bol., Uru. casa pegada
Col. casa de ciudad, casa
particular en la ciudad
Dom.R., Nic., Pue.R.
townhouse
Gua. casa particular en
complejos residenciales
Mex. dúplex horizontal
Par. duplex
Spa. casa adosada
upper floor (n phr) planta alta
Col. piso superior
Dom.R., Nic. piso de arriba
Spa. planta superior
villa (n) villa

Shelter & Daily Living: Town & City

bakery (n) panadería
Chi., Col. pastelería
Pue.R. repostería
bank (n) banco
bar (n) bar
Col. taberna
Mex., Pan. cantina
billboard (n) anuncio panorámico
Chi., Cub., Par. cartelera
Col. cartelera, valla
Cos.R. rótulo
Dom.R. valla
Mex. anuncio
Nic. valla, rótulo
Pue.R. billboard
bookstore (n) librería
Pue.R. tienda de libros
building (n) edificio
Col. edificación
business district (n phr) barrio
comercial
Col., Cub., Mex., Nic.,
Pue.R. zona comercial
Dom.R. centro de
negocios
Spa. zona de negocios
cathedral (n) catedral
cemetery (n) cementerio
Chi., Col. campo santo
Mex. panteón
city (n) ciudad
Col. metrópoli, urbe
city hall (n phr) ayuntamiento
Bol., Nic., Pue.R. alcaldía
Chi., Col., ElS., Gua., Hon.
municipalidad
Ecu. alcaldía, municipalidad
Uru. intendencia
clinic (n) clínica

coffee bar (n phr) café
  Col., Nic., Pue.R., Spa. cafetería
  Cos.R. café bar
coffee plantation (n phr) cafetal
courthouse (n) tribunal de justicia
  Col. edificio de los tribunales
  Cub., Mex., Pue.R. corte
  Dom.R. palacio de justicia
  Spa. juzgado, palacio de justicia
  Nic. juzgado
  Par. juzgado, tribunal
daycare center (n phr) guardería
  infantil
  Arg., Dom.R. guardería
  Col. jardín infantil
  Par. guardería, pre-jardín
  Pue.R. nursery
department store (n phr) grandes
  almacenes
  Cub. tienda
  Col. almacén grande
  Cos.R. tienda de departamentos
  Dom.R., ElS., Gua., Hon., Nic.,
  Pue.R., Venz. tienda por
  departamentos
  Mex. tienda departamental
  Pan. almacén
docks (n) muelle
doctor's office (n phr) consultorio
  médico
  Pue.R. oficina del médico, oficina
  del doctor
downtown (n) centro de la ciudad
  Pue.R. centro del pueblo,
  pueblo
drug store (n phr) farmacia
  Col. botica, droguería
  Ecu., Per. botica
dump (n) basurero
entrance fee (n phr) entrada
  Col. precio de la entrada
  Nic., Pue.R., Venz. precio de

factory (n) fábrica
  Col. empresa, industria
  Dom.R., Pue.R. factoría
fairground (n) parque de atracciones
  Col. terreno para ferias, terreno
  para circos
  Dom.R., Ecu. parque de
  diversiones
  Mex. feria
  Pue.R. feria, parque de
  diversiones
fire station (n phr) estación de
  bomberos
  Bol., Cos.R., Ecu., Spa., Uru.
  parque de bomberos
  Mex. departamento de bomberos
florist's shop (n phr) florista
  Col., Dom.R., Nic., Pan., Pue.R.,
  Venz. floristería
  Cub., Par. florería
fountain (n) fuente
free admission (n phr) entrada libre
  Chi., Cub., Dom.R., ElS., Gua.,
  Pan., Pue.R. entrada gratis
  Spa. entrada gratuita
fruit stand (n phr) puesto de frutas
  Pue.R. frutería
funeral home (n phr) funeraria
  Spa. tanatorio
grocery (n) tienda de comestibles
  Arg., Par., Uru. almacén
  Col. mercado
  Cos.R. compras
  Cub., Per. bodega
  Dom.R. bodega, supercolmado,
  víveres
  ElS. Nic. pulpería
  Gua. tienda
  Mex. super, tienda de abarrotes
  Pan. abarrotería, tienda
  Pue.R. colmado
  Spa. supermercado
  Venz. abastos, supermercado

hairdresser's shop (n phr) peluquería
Dom.R., Mex., NIc., Pan. salón
de belleza
Pue.R. beauty parlor, salón de
belleza
harbor (n) puerto
herbalist's shop (n) botánica
Col. tienda botánica
Mex., Nic. tienda naturista
Par. tienda naturalista
Spa. tienda de botánica
Uru. herbolario
hospital (n) hospital
Col. clínica
hotel (n) hotel
ice cream parlor (n phr) heladería
Mex. nevería
Nic. sorbetería
laundry (n) lavandería
Arg. lavadero
lawyer's office (n phr) bufete de
abogados
Arg. estudio de abogados
Col., Pue.R. oficina de abogados
Ecu., Par. estudio juridico
library (n) biblioteca
liquor store (n phr) tienda de bebidas
alcohólicas
Bol., Mex., Nic. licorería
Col. Cigarreria
Dom.R., Pue.R. liquor store
Pan. bodega
Par. bodega, licorería
market (n) mercado
mosque (n) mezquita
museum (n) museo
neighborhood (n) vecindad
Arg., Ecu., Pan., Par., Uru. barrio
Bol., Gua., Pue.R., Venz.
vecindario
Col., Dom.R., Nic., Per., Spa.
barrio, vecindario
neon sign (n phr) anuncio de neón

Arg. cartel de néon
Col. aviso con luz de neón
Dom.R. letrero de néon
Par. cartel lumínico
newsstand (n) puesto de periódicos
Arg. puesto de diarios
Col. puesto de periódicos y de
revistas
Nic., Par. quiosco
nursery (plants) (n) semillero
Arg., Col., Dom.R., Nic. vivero
Mex. invernadero
park (n) parque
Arg. plaza
pet shop (n phr) pajarería
Col. almacén de mascotas
Dom.R. pet shop, tienda de
mascotas
ElS., Gua. tienda de mascotes
Mex. tienda de animales
domésticos, veterinaria
Nic., Par. tienda de mascotas
Pue.R. pet shop, tienda de
animales
Spa. tienda de animales
police station (n phr) comisaría
Col., Cub., Gua., Nic., Pan.,
Pue.R. estación de policía
Dom.R. destacamento policial
pollution (n) contaminación
Col. polución
post office (n phr) oficina de correos
Arg., Cub. correo
Col. oficina postal
Nic. bedel
print shop (n phr) imprenta
Col. taller tipográfico, talleres
gráficos
residencial area (n phr) zona
residencial
Arg., Par. barrio residencial
Col. área residencial
Pue.R. área residencial, sector

---

residencial
restaurant (n) restaurante
retirement home (n phr) hogar de ancianos
   Arg., Nic. asilo de ancianos
   Col. ancianato
   Mex., Par. asilo
   Pan. retiro para ancianos
school (n) escuela
   Arg., Col., Gua., Nic. colegio
shop sign (n phr) letrero comercial
   Arg. cartel
   Col. anuncio de almacén
shop window (n phr) vitrina
   Arg. vidriera
   Cos.R., Cub., Per., Spa. escaparate
   Mex. aparador
shopping center (n phr) centro comercial
skyscraper (n) rascacielos
square (city) (n) plaza
stadium (n) estadio
   Pue.R. parque
street lamp (n phr) farol
   Dom.R. palo de luz
   Nic. luminaria, poste de luz
   Pan. poste de luz
   Spa. farola
suburb (n) barrio
   Col. barrio en las afueras, suburbio
   Dom.R., Gua. suburbio
   Mex. colonia, fraccionamiento
   Nic. residencial
supermarket (n) supermercado
synagogue (n) sinagoga
telephone booth (n phr) cabina telefónica
   Mex., Nic. teléfono público
theater (n) teatro
university (n) universidad
uptown (n) distrito residencial
   Dom.R. área residencial

   Nic. zona residencial
   Par. barrio residencial
village (n) aldea
   Arg. pueblo
   Col. población
   Cub. pueblecito
   Dom.R. pueblito
   Nic. caserío
vote (v) votar
wine shop (n phr) bodega
   Col. taberna
   Dom.R. tienda de vinos
   Ecu. tienda de licores
   Mex., Pue.R. vinatería
   Uru. vinería
zoo (n) zoológico

Transportation: Bicycle

bell (bicycle) (n) timbre
   Arg., Chi., Dom.R., Uru. bocina
   Bol. campanilla
bicycle (n) bicicleta
bike, hybrid (n phr) bicicleta híbrida
bike, mountain (n phr) montañera
   Arg. bicicleta todo terreno
   Chi., Col., Venz. bicicleta de montaña
   Dom.R., Par., Pue.R. mountain bike
   ElS., Gua. bicicleta montañesa
   Mex. bicicleta de campotraviesa
   Spa. bicicleta de montaña, mountain bike
bike, road (n phr) bicicleta de camino
   Arg., Nic., Par., Uru. bicicleta
   Col. bicicleta para carretera
   Dom.R. bicicleta de carrera Mex. bicicleta turismo
   Spa. bicicleta de carreras
bike, tandem (n phr) bicicleta para

dos personas
Col. bicicleta de dos personas,
bicicleta doble, tándem
Mex. bicicleta doble
Pue.R. doblecleta
Spa. tándem
chain (bicycle) (n) cadena
flat tire (n phr) llanta reventada
Arg., Dom.R. goma pinchada
Bol. llanta pinchada
Chi. pneumático pinchado
Col. llanta desinflada, llanta
pinchada
Cos.R., Per. llanta desinflada
Cub. goma ponchada
Ecu. tubo bajo
Gua. llanta pache, llanta
pinchada
Mex. llanta pinchada, llanta
ponchada
Nic. llanta ponchada
Pan. flat
Pue.R. goma vacía
Spa. neumático pinchado, rueda
pinchada
Uru. llanta desinflada, neumático
desinflado
Venz. caucho pinchado
handlebar grips (bicycle) (n phr)
puños
Col. manillas
Gua., Nic., Venz. agarraderas del
manubrio
Par., Per. mangos
handlebars (bicycle) (n) guía
Arg., Bol., Chi., Col., Mex.,
Pue.R., Venz. manubrio
Cub., Dom.R., Pan. timón
Ecu. manubrios
Gua. manubrio, timón
Spa., Uru. manillar
inner tube (bicycle tire) (n phr) tubo
Chi., Par., Spa. cámara

Cos.R. neumático
Venz. tripa del caucho
pedal (n) pedal
pedal (v) pedalear
reflector (bicycle) (n) reflector
Arg. faro, luz
Nic. luz
ride (bicycle) (v phr) montar en
bicicleta
Arg., Chi., Cos.R., Mex. andar
en bicicleta
Pue.R. correr bicicleta
rim (bicycle wheel) (n) llanta
Chi., Col., Cos.R. aro
Mex., Nic. rin
Par., Venz. rueda
seat (bicycle) (n) asiento
Bol., Col. silla
Chi., Dom.R., Ecu., Pue.R.,
Spa., Uru. sillín
spoke (bicycle wheel) (n) faro
Arg., Cub., Gua., Mex., Nic.
rayo
Col. radio, rayo
Spa., Venz. radio
tire (bicycle) (n) neumático
Arg., Dom.R., Pue.R. goma
Bol., Col., Cos.R., Gua., Mex.,
Pan., Per. llanta
Cub. rueda
Venz. caucho

Transportation:
Car & Traffic

automatic transmission (n phr)
transmisión automática
Spa. cambio automático
back seat (n phr) asiento trasero
battery (n) batería
bend (in road) (n) curva

blinker (light) (n) intermitente, luz
intermitente
Arg. guiño
Bol. guiñador
Pan. luz direccional
Par. señalero
Venz. luz de cruce
brake (n) freno
brake (v) frenar
brights (headlights) (n) luces
fuertes
Arg., Chi., Dom.R., Mex.,
Nic., Pan., Venz. luces altas
Col. plenas
Cub., Pue.R., Spa. luces largas
Ecu. faros intensos
Par. luz alta
bump (road) (n) bache
Chi. lomo de toro
Col. policia acostado
Dom.R. hoyo
Mex. tope
bumper (n) parachoques
Arg., Par. paragolpes
Col., Dom.R., Pan., Pue.R.
bumper
Mex. defensa
Nic. bumper, guardabarro,
lodera
car (n) carro
Arg., Chi., Par. auto,
coche
Col. auto
Mex. auto, automóvil,
coche
Spa. automóvil, coche
Uru. coche
car body (n phr) carrocería
Pan. chasis
car jack (crime) (v phr)
secuestrar un auto
Bol. raptar
Col. asaltar, atracar

Cub. robarse un carro
Mex. asaltar con violencia
Nic. robar con violencia
Pue.R. car jack
Spa. robar un vehículo
con alguien dentro
Uru. atracar un coche
Venz. robar un carro
car, private (n phr) carro
privado
Arg. auto particular
Chi., Ecu., Nic. carro
particular
Par., Spa., Uru. coche
particular
chassis (n) chasis
Dom.R., Nic., Pue.R. chassis
Ecu., Pan., Per. bastidor
city block (n phr) manzana
Dom.R., Ecu., Nic., Pan. cuadra
Pue.R. bloque
cloverleaf junction (n phr) trébol
Col. confluencia, empalme,
entronque en forma de trébol
Mex. paso a desnivel
convertible (n) convertible
Spa. descapotable
crash (vehicle) (v) chocar
Col. estrellar
crosswalk (n) paso de peatones
Col., Par. cruce peatonal
Cub. acera
Dom.R. cruce de peatones
Nic. paso peatonal
curve (in road) (n) curva
decelerate (v) disminuir la velocidad
Chi., Dom.R., Pue.R., Spa.
reducir la velocidad
Col., Cub., Par. desacelerar
detour (n) desvío
Mex. desviación
dipstick (n) indicador del nivel de

ABBREVIATIONS: Arg.=Argentina Bol.=Bolivia Chi.=Chile Col.=Colombia Cos.R.=Costa Rica
Cub.=Cuba Dom.R.=Dominican Republic Ecu.=Ecuador ElS.=El Salvador Gua.=Guatemala
Hon.=Honduras Mex.=Mexico Nic.=Nicaragua Pan.=Panama Par.=Paraguay Per.=Peru
Pri.=Primary Term Pue.R.=Puerto Rico Spa.=Spain Uru.=Uruguay Venz.=Venezuela

Col., Nic. varilla para medir el
aceite
Pue.R. varilla de aceite
Venz. indicador de medir el aceite
ditch (n) zanja
Col., Spa. cuneta
Cos.R. sanja
Uru. pozo
drive (car) (v) manejar
Chi., Col., Pan., Spa. conducir
Pue.R. guiar
driver's seat (n phr) asiento del
conductor
Chi., Nic. asiento del chofer,
asiento del piloto
Cub. asiento del chofer
drive drunk (v phr) manejar borracho
Arg., Pue.R. conducir en estado
de embriaguez
Chi. manejar en estado de
ebriedad
Col. manejar embriagado
Cos.R. manejar tomado
Dom.R. manejar en estado de
embriaguez
Spa. conducir borracho,
conducir ebrio
emergency lights (n phr) luces de
emergencia
Arg. balizas
Ecu. faros de emergencia
Pue.R. luces intermitentes
engine (n) motor
exhaust pipe (n phr) tubo de escape
Arg. caño de escape
Col. exosto
Mex. escape
expressway (n) autopista
Mex. vía rápida
Spa. carretera
Nic., Spa. carretera
fan belt (n phr) correa del ventilador
Mex. banda del ventilador

fender (n) ala
Arg., Par. paragolpes
Col. guardabarro, guardafango
Cub., Ecu., ElS., Gua., Venz.
guardafango
Mex. defensa
Nic. guardabarro, lodera
Pue.R. fender
Spa. guardabarro
flat tire (n phr) llanta reventada
Arg., Dom.R. goma pinchada
Bol. llanta pinchada
Chi. pneumático pinchado
Col. llanta desinflada, llanta
pinchada
Cos.R., Per. llanta desinflada
Cub. goma ponchada
Ecu. tubo bajo
ElS., Gua. llanta pache, llanta
pinchada
Mex. llanta pinchada, llanta
ponchada
Pan. flat
Pue.R. goma vacía
Spa. neumático pinchado, rueda
pinchada
Venz. caucho pinchado
Uru. llanta desinflada, neumático
desinflado
four-wheel drive (n phr) propulsión
total
Arg., Chi., Col., Gua., Mex.
tracción en las cuatro ruedas
Cub., Venz. tracción de cuatro
ruedas
Dom.R. cuatro tracciónes
Nic. doble tracción
Par., Pue.R. 4x4
Spa. tracción a las cuatro ruedas
garage (repairs) (n) garaje
Arg. taller mecánico
Col., Nic. taller
Par. taller, taller mecánico

gas (vehicle) (n) gasolina
    Arg., Par. nafta
gas pedal (n phr) acelerador
    Pue.R. pedal de la gasolina
    Venz. pedal de gasolina
gas tank (n phr) tanque de gasolina
    Arg. tanque de nafta
    Spa. depósito de gasolina
gearbox (n) caja de cambios
    ElS., Gua., Mex., Nic. caja de
    velocidades
    Pue.R. transmisión
gears (n) velocidades
    Arg., Chi., Cub., Dom.R., Pan.,
    Pue.R., Uru., Venz. cambios
    Cos.R. marchas
headlights (n) faros
    Arg., Cub. focos, luces
    Chi., Pan., Pue.R. luces
    Col. faroles delanteros
    Dom.R., Mex., Venz. luces
    delanteras
    Nic. focos delanteros
head-on collision (n phr) choque de
    frente
    Col. colisión frente a frente
    Per. choque frente a frente
    Nic., Spa., Uru. choque frontal
hubcap (n) tapacubos
    Chi. taparuedas
    Col. copa de la rueda
    Cub. tambora
    Ecu., Spa. tabacubo
    Mex. tapón
    Nic. plato
    Pan. rin
    Pue.R. tapabocina
    Uru. embellecedor
    Venz. taza del caucho
ice cream truck (n phr) heladero
    Col. camión del helado, carrito
    de helados
    Mex. carro de helados

    Nic. carrito de helados
    Par. camión de helados
    Spa. camión del helado
jack (car) (n) gato
    Bol., Chi., Nic., Per. gata
    Gua. triquet
lane (n) carril
    Cub. línea
    Venz. canal
limousine (n) limosina
lubrication (n) engrase
    Chi. lubrificación
    Col., Dom.R., Gua., Nic., Pan.
    lubricación
    Mex. engrasado
median (n) centro de la calle
    Col. isla de tráfico, separador
    Nic. boulevard
    Par. carril
    Pue.R. carril del centro
    Spa. mediana
    Venz. isla
muffler (n) mofle
    Arg., Col., Ecu., Par., Spa., Uru.
    silenciador
    Dom.R. muffler
    Mex. muffler
    Nic. escape
    Venz. amortiguador
park (v) estacionar
    Bol., Col., Cos.R., Cub.,
    Dom.R., ElS., Gua., Hon., Nic.,
    Pan. parquear
    Spa. aparcar
parking lot (n phr) estacionamiento
    Arg. playa de estacionamiento
    Bol., Cos.R., Cub., Dom.R.
    ElS., Gua., Hon., Nic. parqueo
    Col., Pan. parqueadero
    Pue.R. parking
    Spa. parking, aparcamiento
pass (traffic) (v) pasar

Cos.R. adelantarse
Dom.R., Mex. rebasar
Nic. adelantar, aventajar,
  rebasar
Spa. adelantar
pedestrian (n) peatón
pickup truck (n phr) camioneta
  Cos.R., ElS., Gua., Hon., Pan.,
  Per. pickup
  Mex., Venz. camioneta pickup
pothole (n) pozo
  Arg., Cub., Gua., Mex., Nic.,
  Spa. bache
  Chi., Dom.R. hoyo
  Col., Cos.R., Ecu., Pan. hueco
racecar (n) coche de carrera
  Arg., Chi. auto de carrera
  Cub., ElS., Gua., Hon., Nic.,
  Pan., Pue.R. carro de carrera
  Col., Per., Venz. carro de carreras
  Dom.R. auto de carrera, carro de
  carrera
  Spa. coche de carreras
radar (traffic) (n) radar
radiator (n) radiador
radiator grill (n phr) rejilla del
  radiador
  Arg., Col., Par. parrilla del
  radiador
rear window (n phr) ventana trasera
  Arg. luneta
  Col. ventanilla trasera
  Pue.R. cristal trasero
rear-view mirror (n phr) espejo
  retrovisor
  Nic. Retrovisor
  Uru. espejo trasero
recreational vehicle (n phr) vehículo
  de recreo
  Bol. vagoneta
  Chi., Par. casa rodante
  Mex. camper
  Pue.R. RV

Spa. caravana
Venz. vehículo recreacional
reverse (n) marcha atrás
  Col., Dom.R., Mex., Pan., Par.
  reversa
  Nic., Venz. retroceso
  Pue.R. riversa
right of way (n phr) prioridad
  Arg., Cub., Pue.R. derecho de
  paso
  Chi., Mex. paso
  Col. derecho a la vía
  Dom.R., Ecu., Spa. preferencia
  ElS., Gua., Pan. derecho de vía
  Nic. preferencia, servidumbre
  Par. preferencial
  Venz. prioridad de circulación
road (n) calle, carretera
road shoulder (n phr) lomo
  Arg., Par. banquina
  Col., Cos.R. orilla de la carretera
  ElS., Gua., Nic. borde de la
  carretera
  Pue.R. paseo
  Spa., Uru. arcén
  Venz. hombrillo
road sign (n phr) letrero de carretera
  Arg. cartel
  Chi. señalización en la carretera
  Col. aviso vial
  Dom.R., Spa., Uru. señal de
  tráfico
  Nic., Par., Venz. señal de tránsito
  Per. señal del camino
road works (n phr) obras
  Arg., Pue.R. construcción
  Col. arreglos en la vía
  Nic. obras viales
  Venz. mantenimiento de calles
road, country (n phr) camino rural
rush hour (n phr) hora pico
  Arg. rush hour
  Cub., Mex. hora de tráfico

Per. hora de entrada o salida a los
trabajos
Pue.R. hora del tapón
Spa. hora punta
sedan (n) sedán
Spa. turismo
shift gear (v phr) cambiar la velocidad
Arg. hacer un cambio
Chi. pasar la marcha, reducir la
marcha
Col., Nic. meter un cambio
Pue.R. cambiar de cambios
Spa. cambiar la marcha
side mirror (n) espejo lateral
sidewalk (n) acera
Arg., Chi., Cos.R., Ecu., Per.,
Uru. vereda
Col., Nic. andén
Mex. banqueta
spare parts (n phr) repuestos
Cub., Spa. piezas de repuesto
Mex. refacciones
Pue.R. repuestas
spare tire (n phr) rueda de repuesto
Arg. goma de auxilio, rueda de
auxilio
Bol., Ecu., Gua., Nic., Pan.
llanta de repuesto
Dom.R. goma de repuesto
Mex. llanta de refacción
Par. llanta de repuesto, rueda de
auxilio
Pue.R. goma de repuesta
Venz. caucho de repuesto
spark plug (n phr) bujía
speed limit (n phr) límite de velocidad
Mex., Pue.R. velocidad máxima
speedometer (n) velocímetro
Chi. cuenta kilómetros
Cub. cuentakilómetro
sports car (n phr) carro deportivo
Arg., Chi., Par. auto deportivo
Bol. coche sport

Cub. carro de deporte
Spa., Uru. coche deportivo
stall (car) (v) calar
Arg., Cub., Ecu., Mex., Pan.
parar
Chi. pararse
Col. vararse
Cos.R. quedar varado
Pue.R. inundar
Nic. ahogarse, pararse
Par. ahogarse
Spa. calarse
Venz. apagarse el carro
start (car) (v) arrancar
Chi., Dom.R. encender,
prender
Col. poner en marcha, prender
Nic. encender
Pue.R. prender
starter (n) arranque
Chi. salir
Cos.R., Mex. arrancador
Par., Spa. motor de arranque
Pue.R. estarter
station wagon (n phr) camioneta
Cos.R., Ecu., Per., Spa.
combinable
Bol. vagoneta
Cub. pisicorre
Dom.R. station, van
Pue.R. guagüita
steering wheel (n phr) volante
Chi., Par. manubrio
Col., Cub., Gua., Nic., Pan.
timón
Dom.R., Pue.R. guía
stick shift (n phr) palanca de cambios
Arg. cambio
Cos.R. marcha
Mex. palanca de velocidades
Spa. cambio manual
stop (sign) (int) alto
Arg., Chi., Col., Pue.R. pare

Par., Spa. stop
street (n) calle
street, cobblestone (n phr) calle de
guijarro
Arg., Bol., Col., Ecu., Venz. calle
empedrada
Chi. calle de adoquines, calle de
paralelepípedos
Gua. calle de adoquín
Mex. calle adoquinada
Pan. calle de ladrillo
Per. calle de piedras
Pue.R., Spa., Uru. calle de
adoquines
street, dead-end (n phr) calle sin salida
Col., Mex. calle cerrada
Dom.R. cul de sac
Venz. calle ciega
street, one-way (n phr) calle de una
mano
Chi. vía única
Col., Mex., Per. calle de un solo
sentido
Cos.R., Dom.R., Nic., Pue.R.,
Venz. calle de una vía
Ecu. calle de una sola dirección
ElS., Gua., Hon. calle de una
sola vía
Pan. calle de una vía, one way
Par. calle sentido único
Spa. calle de dirección única
sunroof (n) sunroof
Chi., Spa. techo solar
Col., Par. techo corredizo
Mex. quemacocos
Nic. techo convertible , techo
descapotable
Venz. techo corredizo, techo
descapotable
ticket, speeding (n phr) multa por
exceso de velocidad
Mex., Nic. infracción por exceso
de velocidad

Pan. boleta por velocidad
Par. multa por infracción
ticket, traffic (n phr) multa
Mex. infracción
Pan. boleta
tire (car) (n) llanta
Arg., Cub. goma, rueda
Chi., Col. pneumático
Dom.R., Pue.R. goma
Spa. rueda
Venz. caucho
traffic (n) tráfico
Chi., Cos.R., Dom.R. tránsito
traffic island (n phr) isleta
Arg., Col., Par., Venz. isla
Nic. bahía peatonal
traffic jam (n phr)
congestionamiento
Arg., Nic., Par., Per., Uru.
embotellamiento
Chi. atascamiento, congestión,
taco
Col. trancón
Cos.R. atasco, presa
Cub. tráfico, tranque
Dom.R., Pue.R. tapón
Pan. tranque
Spa. atasco
traffic light (n phr) semáforo
trailer (n) remolque
Chi., Cos.R., Dom.R., Nic.,
Pan. trailer
tread (tire) (n) ranuras
Mex. dibujo de llanta
Nic. grabado de la llanta
Spa. cubierta
Venz. huella del caucho
truck (n) camión
trunk (car) (n) baúl
Bol., Per. maletera
Chi. porta equipaje
Cub., Pan., Spa. maletero
Mex. cajuela

Nic. maletero, valijera
Par., Venz. maleta
tune up (v phr) revisar
   Cub. reglar
   Dom.R. arreglar
   Gua., Mex., Nic. afinar
   Venz. entonar
turn right, left (v phr) doblar a la
   derecha, izquierda
   Cos.R. virar a la derecha,
   izquierda
   Mex. dar vuelta a la derecha,
   izquierda
   Nic. girar
   Spa. torcer a la derecha,
   izquierda
turning light (n phr) luz direccional
   Arg. guiño
   Chi. luz del indicador
   Col. luz para doblar
   Cub., Spa. intermitente
   Dom.R. luz de doblar
   Gua., Nic. pidevías
   Mex. dirrecional
   Per. luz para voltear
   Uru. señal intermitente
   Venz. señal de cruce
underpass (n) paso subterráneo
   Chi. paso nivel
   Col., Par. pasadizo subterráneo
   Nic. paso a desnivel
   Spa. paso inferior
valve (n) válvula
van (n) camión
   Arg., Chi., Cub., Dom.R., Pue.R.
   van
   Col., Uru. furgón
   Cos.R., Mex. camioneta
   Ecu. buseta
   Pan. busito, van
   Per. microbus
   Spa. furgoneta
   Venz. camioneta, furgoneta

windshield (n) parabrisas
wipers (windshield) (n)
   limpiaparabrisas
   Col. limpiabrisas
   Dom.R. limpiavidrios
   Nic., Per. parabrisas
   Pue.R. wipers
   Venz. limpia-parabrisas

Transportation: Public Transport

airfare (n) precio del pasaje
   Arg., Ecu. tarifa
   Col. tarifa aérea
   Mex. tarifa de vuelo
   Spa. precio del billete de avión
   Venz. precio del boleto
airline (n) aerolínea
   Col., Dom.R., Nic. línea aérea
airplane (n) avión
   Col. aeronave
airport (n) aeropuerto
arrival (n) llegada
   Chi. desembarque
baggage (n) equipaje
   Col., Cos.R., Nic. maletas
   Par. maletas, valijas
blimp (n) dirigible no rígido
   Col., Spa. dirigible
   Cub., Nic., Venz. zepelín
board (v) embarcarse
   Chi., Col., Dom.R., Mex., Par.
   abordar
   Spa., Venz. embarcar
boat (n) barco
   Cub., Nic.,Venz. bote
bumper car (n phr) carro loco
   Arg., Par. autito chocador
   Col., Dom.R. carrito chocón
   Mex., Nic., Per., Venz. carro

chocón
Spa. auto de choque
bus (n) autobús
Arg. bus, ómnibus
Bol. colectivo
Chi. micro
Col. bus, buseta, colectivo
Cos.R. bus, lata
Cub., Dom.R., Pue.R. guagua
ElS., Gua. camioneta
Mex. camión
Nic., Pan. bus
Par. micro, ómnibus
Per., Uru. ómnibus
bus driver (n phr) conductor de
autobús
Arg. chofer de colectivo,
chofer de micro
Chi., Par. chofer
Col. busetero
Cub. guagüero
Dom.R., Pue.R. chofer de
guagua
Mex. camionero
Nic. busero, chofer,
conductor
Pan. busero
bus stop (n phr) parada de
autobús
Arg., Per., Uru. parada del
ómnibus
Bol. parada del colectivo
Chi. parada del micro
Col., Nic., Pan. parada de
bus
Cos.R. parada de bus,
parada de lata
Cub., Dom.R., Pue.R.
parada de guagua
Par. parada
business trip (n phr) viaje de negocios
carousel (with horses)
(n) caballitos

Arg., Par., Uru. calesita
Chi., Col., Ecu., ElS., Gua.,
Hon., Pan., Venz. carrusel
carpool (v) compartir coches
Arg. hacer pool
Col. compartir viajes en
carro
Gua. compartir carros
Mex. turnarse alternando
coches
Nic. carpool
Venz. ir juntos en un carro
change (train) (v) transbordar
Arg. hacer una conexión
Col., Cub. cambiar de tren
Venz. hacer un transbordo
de trenes
check in (baggage) (v phr) registrar el
equipaje
Chi. despachar
Dom.R., Nic., Venz. chequear el
equipaje
commute (v) viajar a diario al trabajo
delay (n) retraso
Arg., Col. demora
Chi. atraso
departure (n) salida
Chi. embarque
dining car (train) (n phr) coche
comedor
Col. vagón-restaurante
Spa. coche restaurante
Venz. carro comedor
driver's license (n phr) licencia de
conducir
Arg. carnet de conductor,
permiso de conductor
Chi. carnet de chofer
Col. pase para conducir
Nic. licencia de manejar
Cub., Venz. licencia de manejar
Par. registro de conducir
Spa. carnet de conducir

ABBREVIATIONS: Arg.=Argentina Bol.=Bolivia Chi.=Chile Col.=Colombia Cos.R.=Costa Rica
Cub.=Cuba Dom.R.=Dominican Republic Ecu.=Ecuador ElS.=El Salvador Gua.=Guatemala
Hon.=Honduras Mex.=Mexico Nic.=Nicaragua Pan.=Panama Par.=Paraguay Per.=Peru
Pri.=Primary Term Pue.R.=Puerto Rico Spa.=Spain Uru.=Uruguay Venz.=Venezuela

elevator (n) ascensor
  Cub., Mex., Nic., Pan., Pue.R.
  elevador
escalator (n) escalera mecánica
  Col. escalera automática
  Dom.R., Mex. escalera eléctrica
fare (n) precio, tarifa
ferris wheel (n phr) noria
  Chi. rueda gigante
  Col., Par. rueda de Chicago,
  rueda giratoria gigante
  Cub., Dom.R., Pan. estrella
  Ecu. rueda muscovita
  Mex. rueda de la fortuna
  Nic. chicagua, rueda de
  Chicago
  Venz. rueda
ferry (n) transbordador
  Col., Cos.R., Dom.R., Spa.,
  Venz. ferry
  Cub. lancha
first class (adj phr) primera clase
  Arg. primera
flight (n) vuelo
float (parade) (n) carroza
  Chi. carro alegórico
flotilla (n) flotilla
funicular (n) funicular
  Mex., Venz. teleférico
get off (bus) (v phr) bajarse
  Bol., Cos.R., Dom.R., Per., Uru.
  apearse
get on (bus) (v phr) subirse
  Col. montarse
helicopter (n) helicóptero
hitchhike (v) hacer autostop
  Arg., Chi. hacer dedo
  Col. echar dedo
  Cos.R. pedir ride
  Dom.R. pedir bola
  ElS., Gua., Hon. pedir jalón a
  dedo
  Per. tirar dedo

Pue.R. pedir pon
  Venz. pedir cola
hot air balloon (n phr) globo
  aerostático
  Chi., Col., Nic. globo
  Venz. globo de aire caliente
hydrofoil boat (n phr) hidroala
  Chi., Nic. hidroavión
  Col. aereodeslizador
  Mex. hidrofoil
jet (n) jet
  Chi. avión a chorro
jet-lag, to have (v phr) tener jet lag
  Dom.R. estar desorientado por
  desfase de horarios
  Mex. sentirse mal por la altura,
  sentirse mal por el vuelo
  Nic., Spa. tener desfase horario
landing (n) aterrizaje
local train (n phr) tren local
  Mex. metro
  Spa. tren de cercanías
ocean liner (n phr) transatlántico
one-way ticket (n phr) billete sencillo
  Arg. boleto de ida, pasaje de ida
  Bol. billete de ida, billete de una
  sola vía
  Chi., Mex., Nic., Pan., Venz.
  boleto de ida
  Col. tiquete de una sola vía
  Cos.R., Dom.R., Par. pasaje de
  ida
  Ecu., Spa. billete de ida
  Per. boleto en un solo sentido
platform (train) (n) andén
  Col., Cub., Par., Per. plataforma
porter (n) maletero
  Bol. maletera
  Col., Cub. portero
  Spa. mozo
  Venz. cargador de maletas
request stop (bus) (n phr) parada
  facultativa

Col. solicitud para hacer detener
el bus
Mex. parada solicitada
Nic. pedir parada
Par. parada de omnibus
Spa. parada discrecional
Venz. parada pedida
rocket (n) cohete
roller coaster (n phr) montaña rusa
round trip ticket (n phr) billete de ida
y vuelta
Arg. boleto de ida y vuelta,
pasaje de ida y vuelta
Chi., Pan., Per., Venz. boleto de
ida y vuelta
Col. tiquete de ida y vuelta
Cos.R., Dom.R., Par. pasaje de
ida y vuelta
Mex. boleto de ida y vuelta,
boleto de viaje Redondo
Nic. boleto de ida y vuelta,
ticket de idea y vuelta
sail (v) navegar
sailboat (n) barco de vela
Col. bote de vela
Dom.R., Nic. velero
Par. barcode vela, velero
second class (n phr) segunda clase
Arg. segunda
Dom.R. clase económica
ship (n) buque
Arg., Cos.R., Nic., Pan., Uru.,
Venz. barco
Chi. barco, navío
Col. barco, embarcación
sleeping car (train) (n phr) coche cama
Col. litera
space shuttle (n phr) transbordador
espacial
submarine (n) submarino

suitcase (n) maleta
Arg., Nic., Par. valija
takeoff (n) despegue
taxi (n) taxi
Venz. libre
taxi stand (n phr) parada de taxi
Venz. parada de libres, parada de
taxis
through train (n phr) tren directo
Par., Venz. tren expreso
ticket (n) billete
Arg., Cub. boleto, pasaje
Chi., Mex., Pan., Per., Pue.R.
boleto
Col. tiquete, voleto
Cos.R. pasaje
Dom.R., Nic. pasaje, ticket
Par., Venz. boleto, ticket
ticket collector (n phr) revisor
Chi., Ecu. conductor
Col. recolector de tiquetes
Mex. persona que recoge los
boletos
Nic. cobrador
Par. guarda
Per. boletero
Venz. chequeador de boletos,
chequeador de tickets
timetable (n) horario
Col. itinerario
train station (n phr) estación de tren
travel (n) viajar
trolley (n) tranvía
Chi. trole
Dom.R. carrito
Mex. trolebús
wagon (n) carreta
Bol., Ecu., Gua., Nic., Spa.
vagón

Workplace: Computer

buffer storage (n phr) memoria
   intermediaria
   Col. memoria intermedia,
   memoria temporal
   Mex. búfer
   Nic. búfer, memoria
   intermedia
   Pue.R. buffer storage
   Venz. memoria de reserva,
   memoria intermedia, memoria
click (computer) (v) hacer clic
   Col., Cub. pulsar
   Pue.R. apretar
computer (n) computadora
   Col. computador
   Spa. ordenador
data (n) datos
   Col. información
debug (computer) (v) depurar
   Dom.R. desinfectar
   Pue.R., Venz. limpiar
delete (v) borrar, eliminar
   Arg. deletear
directory (computer) (n) directorio
DOS (disc operating system) (n phr)
   DOS (sistema operativo de disco)
drive (computer) (n) unidad de disco
   Dom. R., Nic., Pue.R. drive
e-mail (n) correo electrónico
   Arg., Dom.R., Mex., Pue.R., Spa.
   e-mail
encrypt (computer) (v) ocultar
   Col., Mex., Spa. encriptar
   Uru. cifrar
   Venz. cifrar, codificar
file (computer) (n) archivo
hard drive (n phr) disco duro
   Pue.R. hard drive
hardware (n) hardware
icon (computer) (n) icono

Cub. símbolo gráfico
   Pue.R. icon
keyboard (computer) (n) teclado
   Pue.R. keyboard
LAN (local area network) (n phr) LAN
   Mex. red local LAN
   Par., Spa., Venz. red de área local
monitor (computer) (n) monitor
   Arg., Chi. pantalla
motherboard (n) placa madre
   Col., Nic., Spa. tarjeta madre
   Mex. tarjeta principal
   Pan. mother board
   Venz. placa base
network (computer) (n) red
PC (n) PC
   Arg., Gua., Mex., Nic., Venz.
   computadora personal
   Bol. computador personal
   Spa. ordenador personal
printer (computer) (n) impresora
   Pue.R. printer
scanner, optical (n phr) explorador
   óptico
   Arg., Dom.R., Par., Pue.R.
   scanner
   Chi., Cub., Mex., Nic., Pan.,
   Spa. escáner
   Venz. copiador óptico
scroll (computer) (v) desplazar
   Pan. mover
   Pue.R. scroll
software (n) software
   Nic., Spa. programas
store (computer data) (v) almacenar
   Arg., Nic. grabar, guardar
   Dom.R. archivar
   Mex., Pan. guardar
   Venz. guarder
subdirectory (computer)
   (n) subdirectorio
surf the net (v phr) surfear la Internet
   Arg. navegar la red

Bol., Ecu. navegar en el Internet
Chi., Gua. navegar por la
Internet
Col. navegar por Internet
Dom.R. surfear en el Internet
Mex. accesar a la red, buscar en
la red, usar la red
Nic. navegar por Internet
Par., Spa., Uru. navegar por la
red
Venz. explorar el Internet
virus (computer) (n) virus
WAN (wide area network) (n phr)
WAN
Col. red de área extendida
Cub., Mex., Spa. red de área
amplia
Uru. red de área ancha
Venz. red de área extensa
website (n) sitio web
Arg. página principal
Dom.R., Pue.R. web-site
Gua. sitio de la red
Nic. página Web
Venz. lugar del Web, página del
Web
word processing (n phr)
procesamiento de palabras
Arg., Mex., Par. procesamiento
de textos
Cub., Ecu. procesamiento de
texto
Pue.R. word processing

Workplace:
Occupations

architect (n) arquitecto
artist (n) artista
attorney (n) abogado
baker (n) panadero
barber (n) barbero

Arg., Ecu., Mex., Par., Per.
peluquero
bartender (n) barman
Col., Ecu., ElS., Gua., Hon.,
Mex., Pan., Par., Pue.R. cantinero
Dom.R. bartender
Nic. bartender, cantinero
bookkeeper (n) contador
Cub. tenedor de libros
Spa. contable
boss (n) jefe
Col. patrón
bus driver (n phr) conductor de
autobús
Arg. chofer de colectivo, chofer
de micro
Chi. chofer
Col. chofer de bus
Cub. guagüero
Dom.R., Pue.R. chofer de guagua
Mex. camionero
Pan. busero
businessman (n) hombre de
negocios
Arg., Chi., Nic., Par.
empresario
Col. ejecutivo
Pan. hombre profesional
businesswoman (n) mujer de
negocios
Arg., Chi., Cos.R., Nic.,
Par. empresaria
Col. ejecutiva
Pan. mujer profesional
butcher (n) carnicero
carpenter (n) carpintero
cashier (n) cajero/a
certified public accountant (CPA) (n
phr) contador público certificado
Chi. contador
Cos.R. contador público
autorizado
Dom.R. contable, contador, CPA

---

*ABBREVIATIONS: Arg.=Argentina Bol.=Bolivia Chi.=Chile Col.=Colombia Cos.R.=Costa Rica
Cub.=Cuba Dom.R.=Dominican Republic Ecu.=Ecuador ElS.=El Salvador Gua.=Guatemala
Hon.=Honduras Mex.=Mexico Nic.=Nicaragua Pan.=Panama Par.=Paraguay Per.=Peru
Pri.=Primary Term Pue.R.=Puerto Rico Spa.=Spain Uru.=Uruguay Venz.=Venezuela*

Pan. contador público autorizado, CPA
Spa. contable
chef (n) chef
  Col. cocinero, jefe de cocina
  Par., Spa. cocinero
  Per. jefe de cocina
chief executive officer (CEO) (n phr) jefe ejecutivo principal
  Arg., Par., presidente
  Chi. gerente ejecutivo
  Col. gerente general
  Cos.R. director general, gerente general
  Dom.R. director ejecutivo
  Gua. personero ejecutivo de más alto rango
  Mex. director general
  Venz. oficial ejecutivo jefe
coal miner (n phr) minero del carbón
comptroller (n) controlador
  Cos.R. auditor
  Dom.R. contralor
  Venz. interventor
consultant (n) consejero
  Arg., Col., Mex., Pan., Spa. asesor
  Chi., Cos.R., Cub., Dom.R., Ecu., Nic., Par., Per. consultor
  Venz. asesor, consultor
counselor (n) consejero
  Ecu., Mex., Nic., Spa. asesor
craftsperson (n) artesano
dentist (n) dentista
doctor (n) médico
  Arg., Col., Chi. doctor
door-to-door salesperson (n phr) vendedor a domicilio
  Col. vendedor puerta a puerta
  Cos.R. representante de ventas
  Nic. vendedor casa por casa
dry cleaner (n phr) tintorero
editor (n) redactor
  Col., Nic., Par., Pue.R., Spa.,

Venz. editor
electrician (n) electricista
executive (n) ejecutivo
farmer (n) agricultor
  Chi. ganadero
  Col. campesino
  Par. campesino, granjero
  Per. granjero
fire (v) despedir
  Arg. echar
  Col. destituir, echar
  Cub., Dom.R botar
firefighter (n) bombero
flight attendant (n phr) auxiliar de vuelo, azafata
  Col. cabinera
  Cub., Nic., Pan., Venz. aeromozo/a
florist (n) florista
fringe benefit (n phr) incentivo
  Col. beneficio adicional, beneficio suplementario
  Cos.R. beneficio laborable
  ElS., Gua. prestación complementaria
  Nic. prestaciones sociales
full-time (work) (adj) de jornada completa
  Arg. de horario completo
  Col., Mex., Nic. de tiempo completo
  Cub., Dom.R., Venz. a tiempo completo
garbage collector (n phr) basurero
  Col., Venz. recogedor de basura
  Nic. recolector de basura
gardener (n) jardinero
grocer (n) tendero
  Arg., Par., Uru. almacenero
  Col. comerciante
  Cub. bodeguero
  Dom.R. dependiente de colmado/supermercado/tienda

Ecu., Mex. abarrotero
Nic. pulpero
hairdresser (n) peluquero/a
Col. barbero
Mex., Nic., Pan. estilist
healer (n) curandero
hire (v) contratar, emplear
holiday (n) día feriado
Arg. feriado
Col., Spa. día festivo
Mex. día de fiesta, día de
vacaciones
inmate (n) preso
Col. prisionero, recluso
Nic. recluso
Pan. reo
interpreter (n) intérprete
interview (n) entrevista
janitor (n) conserje
Chi. limpiador
Cub. barrendero
judge (n) juez
jury (n) jurado
lawyer (n) abogado
Col. jurista
librarian (n) bibliotecario/a
Dom.R. bibliotecólogo
mail carrier (n phr) cartero
manicurist (n) manicuro/a
Chi. manicure
Dom.R., Ecu., Mex., Nic., Pan.,
Per., Venz. manicurista
mayor (n) alcalde/sa
Chi. prefecto
Dom.R. síndico
Mex. presidente municipal
Nic. edil
Par., Uru. intendente
midwife (n) partera
Col., Dom.R., ElS., Gua., Hon.,
Nic., Spa. comadrona
musician (n) músico
nurse (n) enfermero/a

office manager (n phr) jefe de oficina
Col. administrador, gerente
Cub., Mex., Nic.,Pue.R., Venz.
gerente de oficina
part-time (work) (adj) por parte de la
jornada
Mex. de medio tiempo, parte de
tiempo
Nic. medio tiempo
Par. de medio tiempo
Per., Spa. a tiempo parcial
Pue.R. part-time
patient (n) paciente
Arg., Bol., Cub., Cos.R., Ecu.,
Gua., Uru. enfermo/a
Col. doliente
pharmacist (n) farmacéutico
Col. boticario, farmaceuta
Venz. farmaceuta
pilot (n) piloto
Col. aviador
pimp (n) chulo
Chi. cafiche
ElS., Gua., Hon. alcahuete
Nic. chivo
Par. caficho
plumber (n) plomero
Chi. gáfiter [from "gas fitter"]
Ecu. gasfitero
Spa. fontanero
police detective (n) agente
Chi., Cub., Mex., Pan., Venz.
detective
Col. agente de policía, detective
policíaco
Dom.R. detective policial
ElS., Gua., Hon., Nic. detective
de la policía
Spa. investigador
police officer (n phr) policía
Chi. carabinero
Col., Spa. agente de policía
Dom.R. agente policial

---

*ABBREVIATIONS: Arg.=Argentina Bol.=Bolivia Chi.=Chile Col.=Colombia Cos.R.=Costa Rica
Cub.=Cuba Dom.R.=Dominican Republic Ecu.=Ecuador ElS.=El Salvador Gua.=Guatemala
Hon.=Honduras Mex.=Mexico Nic.=Nicaragua Pan.=Panama Par.=Paraguay Per.=Peru
Pri.=Primary Term Pue.R.=Puerto Rico Spa.=Spain Uru.=Uruguay Venz.=Venezuela*

Venz. oficial de policía
prisoner (n) preso
  Chi. reo
  Col. encarcelado, prisionero, recluso
  Nic. Recluso
  Pan. prisionero
private detective (n phr) detective privado
psychiatrist (n) psiquiatra
psychotherapist (n) psicoterapeuta
publisher (n) editor/a
rabbi (n) rabino
  Spa. rabí
realtor (n) corredor de bienes raíces
  Arg. inmobiliario
  Col. corredor de bienes de finca raíz
  Nic. agente
receptionist (n) recepcionista
salary (n) sueldo
  Col., Mex., Nic., Pan., Par. salario
salesperson (n) dependiente
  Chi. promotor/a, vendedor/a
  Col., Dom.R., Ecu., ElS., Gua., Hon., Mex., Nic., Par., Venz. vendedor/a
school day (n phr) día lectivo
  Col. día de colegio
  Dom.R., Nic., Per. día de clases
  Mex., Venz. día de escuela
  Par., Pue.R. día de clase
scientist (n) científico
seamstress (n) costurera
secretary (n) secretario/a
sick leave (n phr) permiso de convalecencia
  Arg., Bol., ElS., Gua., Hon., Par. permiso por enfermedad
  Col., Dom.R. licencia por enfermedad
  Cub. días de enfermedad
  Nic. subsidio por enfermedad

Venz. permiso de convalescencia
superviser (n) supervisor
tailor (n) sastre
  Col. costurero, modisto
  Spa. costurero
taxi driver (n phr) conductor de taxi
  Arg., Cub., Dom.R., Gua., Mex., Per., Spa. taxista
  Chi., Cos.R. chofer de taxi
  Col. chofer de taxi, taxista
  Nic. taxista, taxero
  Venz. conductor de libre
technician (n) técnico
teller (bank) (n) cajero/a
temporary worker (n phr) temporero
  Bol. temporal
  Chi., Par. jornalero
  Col., Cos.R., Gua., Venz. empleado/a temporal
  Mex. trabajador eventual
  Nic. jornalero, trabajador temporal
  Uru. temporario
train (for job) (v) capacitar
  Col., Cub., Dom.R., Ecu., Pan., Venz. entrenar
translator (n) traductor/a
travel agent (n phr) agente de viajes
veterinarian (n) veterinario
waiter (n) camarero
  Arg., Bol., Cos.R., Dom.R., Uru. mozo
  Chi. garzón, mesero, mozo
  Col., Cub., Dom.R., ElS., Gua., Mex., Nic., Pan., Pue.R. mesero
  Venz. mesonero
warden (prison) (n) director/a de la cárcel
  Nic. alcaide
  Venz. carcelero, guardián de la cárcel
weekday (n) día de entre semana
  Arg., Col., Dom.R., Pue.R.,

ABBREVIATIONS: Arg.=Argentina Bol.=Bolivia Chi.=Chile Col.=Colombia Cos.R.=Costa Rica Cub.=Cuba Dom.R.=Dominican Republic Ecu.=Ecuador ElS.=El Salvador Gua.=Guatemala Hon.=Honduras Mex.=Mexico Nic.=Nicaragua Pan.=Panama Par.=Paraguay Per.=Peru Pri.=Primary Term Pue.R.=Puerto Rico Spa.=Spain Uru.=Uruguay Venz.=Venezuela

Venz. día de semana
Gua., Nic., Spa. día entre
semana
work day (n phr) día hábil
Col. día laborable, día de trabajo
Cub., Per., Pue.R. día de trabajo
Dom.R., Spa. día laborable

Workplace: Office

air conditioning (n phr) aire
acondicionado
Cos.R. airecondicionado
coffee maker (n phr) cafetera
Dom.R. greca
copier (n) copiadora
Spa. fotocopiadora
desk (n) escritorio
envelope (n) sobre
fax machine (n phr) màquina de fax
file (v) archivar
file cabinet (n phr) archivo
Chi. archivador
Mex. archivero
folder (n) carpeta de archivo
Bol. archivador
Dom.R., Mex., Nic., Pan., Pue.R.
folder
Spa. archivadora, carpeta
heating (n) calefacción
index card (n phr) ficha
Col., Pue.R. tarjeta
label (n) etiqueta
Dom.R., Pue.R. label
label, adhesive (n phr) etiqueta
adhesiva
Dom.R., Pue.R. label adhesiva
loading dock (n phr) plataforma de
carga
Col., Nic. muelle de carga
Par. puerto de carga
lobby (n) foyer

Arg. hall de entrada, lobby,
recepción
Chi. hall de entrada, recepción
Col. pasillo
Cub., ElS., Gua., Spa. vestíbulo
Dom.R., Mex., Pue.R. lobby
Nic., Par. recepción
Pan. loby
Venz. sala de espera, vestíbulo
mail room (n phr) cuarto de correos,
sala de correos
Par. correo
Spa. cuarto del correo
marker (n) marcador
Cub., Mex. plumón
Spa. rotulador
modular office (n phr) oficina
modular
Dom.R., Nic. módulo
notebook (n) cuaderno
Cub. carpeta
Dom.R. libreta, mascota
Pue.R. libreta
office building (n phr) edificio de
oficinas
office cubicle (n phr) recinto
Bol. oficina
Col., Dom.R., Gua., Mex., Nic.,
Pan., Pue.R., Venz. cubículo
office divider (n phr) partidor
Bol., Ecu. divisor
Col.separador
Dom.R. división
Mex. biombo separador
office hours (n phr) horas de oficina
Cub. horas de trabajo
Nic. horas hábiles
office suite (n phr) oficina
Venz. suite de oficinas
office supplies (n phr) artículos de
oficina
Cub. materiales de oficina
Ecu., Par. útiles de oficina

pad (paper) (n) cuaderno
  Arg., Chi. bloc
  Bol. libreta legal
  Col. bloc, cuaderno de notas
  Dom.R., Pan., Pue.R., Venz.
  libreta tamaño legal
  Mex. bloc tamaño oficio
  Nic. bloc legal
  Par., Spa. bloc tamaño legal
pad, legal (n phr) cuaderno legal
  Arg., Chi. bloc
  Bol. libreta legal
  Dom.R., Pan., Pue.R., Venz.
  libreta tamaño legal
  Mex. bloc tamaño oficio
  Nic. bloc legal
  Par., Spa. bloc tamaño legal
pad, writing (n phr) cuaderno
  Arg., Chi. bloc
  Col., Dom.R., Pue.R., Venz.
  libreta
  Mex., Par. bloc tamaño carta
  Nic. bloc, libreta
  Spa. bloc de notas
pad, yellow (n phr) cuaderno amarillo
  Arg., Chi. bloc
  Bol., Col. Dom.R. libreta
  amarilla
  Mex., Spa. bloc Amarillo
  Nic. bloc /libreta amarilla
  Pue.R., Venz. libreta de papel
  amarilla
paperclip (n) clip
  Arg., Uru. ganchito
  Bol., Cos.R., Cub., ElS., Gua.,
  Hon. sujetapapel
  Col. clip
pen (n) pluma
  Arg., Chi., Uru. lapicera
  Nic., Per. lapicero
  Spa. bolígrafo
pen, ball-point (n phr) bolígrafo,
  pluma

Bol. punta bola
Chi. lapicera de pasta
Col. esfero
Per. lapicero
pen, fountain (n phr) pluma de fuente
  Arg., Par. lapicera fuente
  Bol., Mex., Pue.R., Venz. pluma
  fuente
  Chi. lapicera a fuente
  Per. lapicero de tinta
  Spa. pluma, pluma estilográfica
  Uru. estilográfica
post office box (n phr) apartado postal
  Bol. casilla
  Chi. casilla postal
  Col. buzón postal
  Spa. apartado de correos
résumé (work history) (n) currículum
  (vitae)
  Col. hoja de vida
  Mex. currículo
  Pue.R. resumé
rolodex (n) fichero giratorio
  Nic. fichero rolodex
  Pue.R. rolodex
rubber band (n phr) cinta elástica
  Arg., Dom.R., Pue.R. gomita
  Bol., Chi. elástico
  Col. caucho
  Cub., Mex., Pan., Per., Venz.
  liga
  ElS., Gua., Hon., Nic. hule
  Spa., Uru. goma elástica
shredder (n) trituradora
  Mex. picadora de papel
staple (n) grapa
  Arg. ganchito
  Chi. corchete
  Cub. presilla
  Par., Per. grampa
staple remover (n phr) uñas
  Bol., Ecu., ElS., Gua., Hon.,
  Nic. sacagrapas

Chi. saca corchetes
Col. removedor de grapas
Dom. R. uñas saca grapas
Mex. uña quitagrapas
Par. saca grampas
Spa. quitagrapas
Venz. saca-grapas
stapler (n) engrapadora
   Arg. abrochadora
   Chi. corchetera
   Cub. presilladora
   Per. engrampador
   Pue.R., Spa. grapadora
storage room (n phr) almacenaje
   Arg., Col. depósito
   Bol., Dom.R., Pue.R., Spa.
   almacén
   Chi. despensa
   Cos.R., Ecu., Gua., Nic. bodega
   Mex. almacén, bodega
swivel chair (n phr) silla giratoria
tape (n) cinta adhesiva
   Ecu. cinta pegante
   Mex. durex
   Nic., Pue.R. tape
   Spa. celo
tape dispenser (n phr) carrete de cinta
   Col. dispensador de cinta
   pegante

Dom.R., Nic. rollo de tape
Mex. dispensador de durex,
portarrollo
Par. rollo cinta adhesiva
Spa. carrete de celo
Venz. dispensador de cinta
adhesiva
three-ring binder (n phr) carpeta de
argollas
   Arg. carpeta con ganchos
   Chi. archivador
   Col. folder de argollas
   Dom.R. carpeta de tres hoyos
   Nic. folder de tres anillos
   Pan. portafolio
   Spa. carpeta de tres anillos
toner (n) tinta
   Dom. R., Nic., Par. toner
   Mex. tonificador
toner cartridge (n phr) cartucho de
tinta
   Dom.R. cartucho del toner
   Dom.R. cartucho del toner
   Mex. cartucho tonificador
   Nic., Par. cartucho de toner
   Mex. cartucho tonificador
water fountain (n phr) fuente de agua
   Arg., Chi., Mex., Venz. bebedero
   Dom.R. neverita

Order Form

Fax orders (Send this form): (301) 725-0333.
Telephone orders: Call 1(800) 296-1961 [in Maryland: (301)725-3906]
E-mail orders: schreiberpublishing@comcast.net   or
books@schreiberpublishing.com
Mail orders to:
Schreiber Publishing, Post Office Box 4193, Rockville MD 20849 USA

Please send the following books, programs, and/or a free catalog. I understand that I may return any of them for a full refund, for any reason, no questions asked:

❑ **The Translator's Handbook** 7th Revised Edition - $25.95
❑ **Spanish Business Dictionary** - Multicultural Spanish - $24.95
❑ **German Business Dictionary** - $24.95
❑ **French (France and Canada) Business Dictionary** - $24.95
❑ **Chinese Business Dictionary** - $24.95
❑ **Japanese Business Dictionary** - $24.95
❑ **Russian Business Dictionary** - $24.95
❑ **Global Business Dictionary (English, French, German, Russian, Japanese, Chinese)** - $33.95
❑ **Spanish Chemical and Pharamceutical Glossary** - $29.95
❑ **The Translator's Self-Training Program** (circle the language/s of your choice): Spanish   French   German   Japanese   Chinese   Italian   Portuguese   Russian   Arabic   Hebrew - $69.00
❑ **The Translator's Self-Training Program Spanish Medical** - $69.00
❑ **The Translator's Self-Training Program Spanish Legal** - $69.00
❑ **The Translator's Self-Training Program - German Patents** - $69.00
❑ **The Translator's Self-Training Program - Japanese Patents** - $69.00
❑ **Multicultural Spanish Dictionary** - How Spanish Differs from Country to Country - $24.95
❑ **21st Century American English Compendium** - The "Odds and Ends" of American English Usage - $24.95

Name: _____

Address: _____

City: _____   State: _____   Zip: _____

Telephone: _____ E-mail: _____
Sales tax: Please add 5% sales tax in Maryland
Shipping (est.): $4 for the first book and $2 for each additional book
International: $9 for the first book, and $5 for each additional book
Payment: ❑ Check ❑ Credit card: ❑ Visa ❑ MasterCard

Card number: _____

Name on card: _____   Exp. Date: ___/___